CHINA FINANCIAL POLICY REPORT

中国金融政策报告

2013

主　编　吴晓灵
副主编　何海峰

中国金融出版社

责任编辑：张　超　单翠霞　王慧荣
责任校对：张志文
责任印制：丁淮宾

图书在版编目（CIP）数据

中国金融政策报告.2013（Zhongguo Jinrong Zhengce Baogao.2013）/吴晓灵主编.
—北京：中国金融出版社，2013.9
　ISBN 978 - 7 - 5049 - 7129 - 6

Ⅰ.①中…　Ⅱ.①吴…　Ⅲ.①金融政策—研究报告—中国—2013　Ⅳ.①F832.0

中国版本图书馆 CIP 数据核字（2013）第 216877 号

出版
发行　中国金融出版社

社址　北京市丰台区益泽路 2 号
市场开发部　（010）63266347，63805472，63439533（传真）
网上书店　http://www.chinafph.com　（010）63286832，63365686（传真）
读者服务部　（010）66070833，62568380
邮编　100071
经销　新华书店
印刷　保利达印务有限公司
尺寸　185 毫米×260 毫米
印张　18.75
字数　369 千
版次　2013 年 9 月第 1 版
印次　2013 年 9 月第 1 次印刷
定价　50.00 元
ISBN 978 - 7 - 5049 - 7129 - 6/F.6689
如出现印装错误本社负责调换　联系电话（010）63263947
编辑部邮箱：jiaocaiyibu@126.com

编 委 会

The Editorial Board

前　言

　　《中国金融政策报告》是中欧陆家嘴国际金融研究院与中国社会科学院金融政策研究中心联合组织编写的年度研究报告，旨在对过去一年国际国内经济背景下中国金融政策的出台与执行情况进行总结和分析。

　　首先需要说明的是，我们非常荣幸和高兴地聘请了两位外国著名学者加入报告顾问团队，他们是哈佛大学经济系理查德·库珀（Richard N. Cooper）教授和哈佛大学法学院哈尔·斯科特（Hal S. Scott）教授。库珀教授长期关注和研究中国经济，他曾在世界银行、联合国、美国联邦政府、美国国家情报委员会等机构担任重要职务。斯科特教授长期关注中国金融的发展与改革，并致力于推动中国与美国金融监管领域的交流——他所开创的中美高级金融论坛已召开了8届。正如本报告的宗旨所系，库珀教授和斯科特教授出任国际顾问，可以使我们更加准确、全面地介绍和传递中国金融的发展变化。我们在这里非常感谢他们对《中国金融政策报告（2013）》的建议。

　　《中国金融政策报告（2013）》基本延续了《中国金融政策报告（2012）》的框架结构，它包括两大模块即主题报告和动态报告。具体地看，《中国金融政策报告（2013）》包括以下内容：

　　第一部分是两篇专题文章——《放权券商，发展中国柜台市场》和《构建大国开放经济的中国金融政策框架》。多层次资本市场建设是推动中国直接金融发展、改善金融结构的重要内容，《放权券商，发展中国柜台市场》不但提出了三项具体可行的政策建议，更界定和廓清了监管当局与金融机构的职责范围。《构建大国开放经济的中国金融政策框架》着眼于中长期中国金融发展，探讨了中国金融政策框架的意义、原则、内部与外部行动。

　　第二部分是年度报告的主题报告"发展中的中国多层次资本市场——问题与对策"。我们认为，中国多层次资本市场应当建立在一个宽大、坚实的"塔基"——场外市场之上，并且形成合理的"金字塔"结构。这一主题报告包括

"中国的资本市场结构"、"中国场外市场发展滞后的原因"、"对中国资本市场监管的反思"和"中国发展多层次资本市场的展望与建议"四个内容。

第一部分和第二部分构成了《中国金融政策报告 (2013)》的上篇即主题报告模块，而《中国金融政策报告 (2013)》的下篇即另一模块"2012年度中国金融政策动态"则由第三、第四和第五部分构成。

第三部分是2012年的"宏观金融政策"。这一部分将对2012年的货币政策、汇率与国际收支相关政策进行回顾、分析，并适度进行政策评价与展望。

第四部分是2012年的"主要金融市场发展政策"。这一部分全面回顾和分析了2012年内"银行业市场发展政策"、"股票市场发展政策"、"保险业市场发展政策"、"债券市场发展政策"、"货币市场发展政策"、"财富管理市场发展政策"、"金融衍生品市场发展政策"、"商品期货市场发展政策"和"外汇市场与黄金市场发展政策"，同时也进行了相应的政策评价与展望。

第五部分是2012年的"金融监管政策"。这一部分对2012年"中国人民银行主要监管政策"、"中国银监会主要监管政策"、"中国证监会主要监管政策"和"中国保监会主要监管政策"进行了回顾和分析，也相应给出了政策的评价与展望。

通过对《中国金融政策报告 (2013)》的编写，我们从2012年初第四次全国金融工作会议召开和2012年9月《金融业发展和改革"十二五"规划》发布等重大事件中深切地感受到，面临中国经济发展方式转变的迫切需要，中国金融必须与实体经济紧密联系在一起——国际金融危机更加突出了这一点；而中国金融对国际金融的影响与贡献开始引起世界的越来越多的注意。我们依然坚信，向国内外读者持续介绍中国金融政策变化是富有价值和意义的。

本报告作为集体研究的结果，作者主要由中欧陆家嘴国际金融研究院、中国社会科学院金融政策研究中心以及其他金融界人士构成，最后由吴晓灵、何海峰对报告全文进行了修改和定稿。先后参加各部分撰稿的执笔人是：吴晓灵、何海峰、吴建刚、于卫国、李雪静、王鑫、王敏、刘学庆、荣艺华、王琪、储幼阳、甘正在、朱小川。刘胜军参与了主题报告选题和结构设计。何海峰和王鑫对报告中文部分进行了校对和统编。何海峰、吴建刚、于卫国、王鑫和朱小川对报告英文部分进行了校对和统编。王鑫对报告的格式进行了编辑加工。

我们一如既往地期盼着各种批评和建议。

中欧陆家嘴国际金融研究院常务副院长
暨中国社会科学院金融政策研究中心主任
何海峰（代序）
2013 年 7 月 31 日

Preface

China Financial Policy Report is an annual research report prepared jointly by the CEIBS Lujiazui Institute of International Finance and the Institute of Financial Policy of Chinese Academy of Social Sciences, designed to summarize and analyze the promulgation and implementation of Chinese financial policies under the international and domestic economic backgrounds in the past year.

First of all, it should be noted that, we are very honored and pleased to have two foreign renowned scholars join in our advisory team: Professor Richard N. Cooper from the Department of Economics of Harvard University, and Professor Hal S. Scott from the Law School of Harvard University. Professor Cooper has been engaged in research on Chinese economy for a long time, and used to hold important positions in such institutions as the World Bank, the United Nations, US Federal Government and National Intelligence Council. Professor Scott shows long-term concern to the development and reform of Chinese finance, and devotes himself to promoting communication of financial regulation between China and USA-the China-U. S. Symposium launched by him has been held for eight sessions. Just as the purpose of this report, by serving as international advisers, Professor Cooper and Professor Scott could help us introduce and convey the development and changes of Chinese finance more accurately and comprehensively. Hereby, we would like to express sincere thanks for their suggestions on *China Financial Policy Report* (2013).

China Financial Policy Report (2013) basically continues the framework of *China Financial Policy Report* (2012), mainly consisting of two parts: theme reports and annual trend reports. Specifically, *China Financial Policy Report* (2013) includes the following content.

It comes first is two column articles – *Loosening Regulation over Securities Traders for Development of Chinese OTC Market* and *Building China's Financial Policy Framework based on an Open and Major Economy*. To develop the multi-level capital market is an important component of promoting Chinese direct financing and improving the financial structure; *Loosening Regulation over Securities Traders for Development of Chinese OTC Market* has not only put forward three concrete and feasible suggestions for policy but also defined the scope of duties of regulatory authorities and financial institutions. *Building China's Financial Policy Framework based on an Open and Major Economy* focuses on the long-term development of Chinese finance, and discussed the significance, principles and internal & external actions of Chinese financial policy framework.

The third chapter of the first part is the theme report "Chinese Multi-Level Capital Market in Development: Problems and Countermeasures". We think that, Chinese multi-level capital market should be built upon a broad and solid "foundation" – OTC market, and form a reasonable "pyramid" structure. This keynote report consists of four aspects: "Chinese Capital Market Structure", "Causes for Lagging Development of Chinese OTC Market", "Reflections on Chinese Capital Market Supervision", and "Outlook and Recommendations for Chinese Multi-Level Capital Market Development".

The second part includes the fourth chapter, the fifth chapter and the sixth chapter, it is so called "China Financial Policy Trends".

The fourth chapter is the "Macro Financial Policy" in 2012, which reviews and analyzes the monetary policy, exchange rate and relevant policies of the balance of international payments in 2012, and performs an appropriate evaluation and outlook on these policies.

The fifth chapter is the "Highlights of Financial Market Development Policy" in 2012, which comprehensively reviews and analyzes the "Banking Market Development Policy", "Stock Market Development Policy", "Insurance Market Development Policy", "Bond Market Development Policy", "Monetary Market Development Policy", "Wealth Management Market Development Policy", "Financial Derivatives Market Development Policy", "Commodity Futures Market Development Policy" and "Foreign Exchange Market and Gold Market Development Policy" in 2012, and meanwhile, performs an appropriate evaluation and outlook on these policies.

The sixth chapter is the "Financial Regulatory Policy" in 2012, which will review and analyze the "Main Regulatory Policy of the People's Bank of China", "Regulatory Policy of the China Banking Regulatory Commission", "Main Regulatory Policy of the China Securities Regulatory Commission" and "Regulatory Policy of the China Insurance Regulatory Commission", and will perform an appropriate evaluation and outlook on these policies.

Through preparation of the *China Financial Policy Report* (2013), we have a deep feeling from such major events as the opening of the 4th national financial work conference in early 2012 and the release of *the "12th Five-Year" Plan for Development and Reform of the Financial Industry* in September 2012 that, facing the urgent need for transformation of China's economic development mode, Chinese finance must be closely linked with the real economy-which has been highlighted by the international financial crisis; The effect and contribution of China's finance to the international finance has begun to draw increasing attention from the world. We still firmly believe that, it is of great value and significance to continuously introduce changes in China's financial policies to readers both at home and abroad.

As a result of the collective research, this report is mainly authored by the CEIBS Lujiazui Institute of International Finance, the Institute of Financial Policy of Chinese Academy of Social Sciences, and other financial professionals; revised and finalized by Wu Xiaoling and He Haifeng. Participants in preparing this report include: Wu Xiaoling, He Haifeng, Wu Jiangang, Yu Weiguo, Li Xuejing, Wang Xin, Wang Min, Liu Xueqing, Rong Yihua, Wang Qi, Chu Youyang, Gan Zhengzai and Zhu Xiaochuan. Liu Shengjun took part in the topic and structure design of the theme report. He Haifeng and Wang Xin collated and organized the Chinese version of this report. He Haifeng, Wu Jiangang, Yu Weiguo, Wang Xin and Zhu Xiaochuan collated and organized the English version of this report. Wang Xin was responsible for editing the format of this report.

Your comments and suggestions are always welcome!

He, Haifeng
Executive Deputy Director of CEIBS Lujiazui Institute of International Finance &
Director of Institute of Financial Policy of Chinese Academy of Social Sciences
July 31 of 2013

目　　录

English Version

Part One   Column Articles and Thematic Report

Part Two   China's Financial Policies in 2012

上 篇

专题文章与主题
报告

专题文章一

放权券商，发展中国柜台市场①

吴晓灵

资本市场的改革目标应该是建立无缝对接的多层次资本市场。现在我们应该放权券商，发展中国的柜台市场，改变中国资本市场"倒金字塔"的格局，构建资本市场发展的"塔基"。

第一，对证监会认可的创新券商，可以在营业部设立询价交易的柜台市场。具备下面条件的企业就可以让它们到合格的创新券商的柜台上做柜台交易。

（1）企业要有经注册会计师审计的财务报表，并定期向券商报告；

（2）交易的股份或其他交易标的要在指定系统登记、托管。

（3）建立合格投资人制度，规范交易主体。

第二，券商柜台的交易结果，要实时报送证券业协会或证监会指定的信息系统。像美国的多层次资本市场一样，建立报价的公告牌，对券商做市的股票在信息系统中报价公告，对非做市的股票仅在信息系统内报备，但不公告，只让监管部门了解当前交易的情况和价格。授权证券业协会对信息披露质量进行监管。证监会应该有权对信息不真实的企业和对信息披露监督不力的券商实行最严厉的惩罚。中国现在有这么多的上市公司作假，最大的问题就在于它们的作假成本和违规成本太低了。所以要想建立一个有序的资本市场，要想有真实的信息披露，对投资者负责，就应该有对信息披露不真实行为的最严厉的惩治制度。让每一个违规者头上都悬着一把"宝剑"，对资本市场的秩序维护是非常有好处的。

第三，可以在券商柜台交易的基础上建立券商内部撮合交易平台或区域性场内市场。区域市场交易的股票可以制定低于主板和创业板的条件，现在地方政府都希望成立区域性的交易场所。美国除了我们知道的纽交所和纳斯达克市场以外，还拥有众多地方的场内交易市场。中国在 1994 年之前其实也有过地方的金融交易中心，只不过当时发

---

① 本文节选自吴晓灵院长在 2013 年 1 月的一个主题演讲，原演讲题目为"发展中国多层次资本市场"。文字已经本人审阅。

展得不够规范。而我们现在可以在总结以前教训的基础上，成立区域性的交易所，但是区域性交易所上市的条件，应该包括股东权益或者公司有形资产净值、税前盈利、社会公众拥有的公司股票的股数、拥有一百股以上股票的投资者的人数、股票的市值、每股的买价、做市商的个数和公司的治理要求，与主板市场相比数量可以不一样，但是这些条件和标准的实质性的内涵，应该是一样的。

为了保证在区域市场交易的股票的质量，我们应该要求三个以上的做市商，如果有三个券商敢为一只股票双边报价，就证明这只股票的投资价值是可以的。最低限度应该在区域性的股票市场当中制定这样的标准，而区域性的市场应该由当地证监局对它进行监管，证监会应该加强对公开上市的全国性市场的监管和统一的市场规则的制定。

最近，证监会公布了非上市公司的监管指引，为场外市场的发展建立了制度基础。上市公众公司的监管指引第 1 号——信息披露，第 2 号——股份转让申请文件，第 3 号——非上市公众公司章程必备条款。2 号令股份转让申请文件，它提到的是要将申请文件提交到证监会，由证监会来决定它能否转让。我认为对现在证监会监管的 200 份以上的非上市公众企业暂时提出这样的要求是可以的。但是从发展的方向来说，应该把股份交易的申请交给券商，让券商作为资本市场中位于筹资者行为和公司的信息披露的第一线的操作者，第一责任人。而证监会应该把它的主要精力放在对规则的制定和对券商行为的规范上。如果哪个券商不尊重自己的市场主体地位，作出违法违规的行为的话，那么就应该受到最严厉的处罚，甚至于取消它在这方面的资格。如果我们不把券商作为市场组织者的主体，而总是让监管当局在市场当中承担过多的责任，我想市场是发展不起来的。金融机构就是市场中介，它的基本职能就是连接投资者和筹资者，如果金融中介不发挥连接作用，那么金融业是难以发展的。

专题文章二

构建大国开放经济的中国金融政策框架

何海峰

自 1978 年以来，中国经济保持了高速增长，取得了令人瞩目的成绩——2012 年中国 GDP 总量位居美国之后排名世界第二，而国际贸易总量则超过美国排名世界第一。这是中国适应全球化国际大背景、不断扩大和深化改革开放的结果。根据国内国际不同机构的预测，在未来 10—20 年内，中国有可能成为全球最大经济体。与经济发展相伴随，中国金融改革与发展也取得了很大成绩——例如，中国金融机构与金融市场的一些总量指标已经成为世界前几名。但是，中国能否成为一个真正的发达经济体，作为现代经济核心的金融则是最关键的必要条件之一，甚至很可能是充分条件之一。

从中长期来看，中国金融改革与发展一个迫切需要重视的问题是——如何构建与大国和开放经济相适应的金融政策框架。这一问题的重要意义至少来自三个方面：国际金融环境的更加复杂、国内金融发展的更多挑战以及金融理论与实践的更深研究。首先，本轮国际金融危机的冲击巨大、影响深远。一方面，一直作为世界榜样的美国金融发展模式面临失败之虞在积极寻求变革；同时，由于经济和金融发展目标的差异，发达国家与发展中国家的货币金融政策国际协调将会越来越难——短期共识不能保证中长期目标和行为的一致性。就中国来说，面对现行国际金融组织、秩序、机制和标准的基本选择只能是参与，差异仅在于积极与否，而积极地参与，不但意味着有机会影响这些体制的安排与设定，同时也必然要求承担更多责任。其次，中国金融发展面临"深水区"的众多挑战。例如，中国经济发展方式转变和结构调整需要什么样的金融支持和如何支持？又如，金融业自身包括的各类金融机构经营方式、公司治理和风险管理还存在哪些问题？最后，传统的金融理论研究与金融实践经验一直无法为中国金融转型与发展提供令人信服的解释，没有回答中国金融政策应具有什么样的新兴大国思维。

建立和完善面向未来的、大国开放特征的金融政策框架，首当其冲的问题是其立足点或者原则是什么。笔者认为，首先，要坚守金融的最基本职能，即融通资金与资本、完成经济中储蓄向投资的转化。国际金融危机再次证明，尽管是高端服务业，金融仍需始终以服务实体经济为首要任务，既不能自娱自乐，也不能低效缺位。对于中国来说，这两种倾向都存在，但后者由来更久。例如，与美国相比，中国总储蓄率和居民储蓄率高出很多，而金融体系和金融机制却无法将其高效转化为资本。其结果是，美国可以维持低储蓄率而中国则不行。理论上看，高储蓄仅仅是经济增长的必要条件，但是，储蓄—投资转化机制却至关重要。有研究表明，美国的储蓄转化效率显著高于日本和德国等其他发达国家。当前，中国面临转变发展方式、提升内需之痛，金融政策决定了金融体系与金融市场进而决定其储蓄—投资转化效率，有鉴于此，以市场化为基础的直接金融应得到更快发展。其次，中国金融政策还要坚持"内外联动"的原则。正是认识到了全球化的大趋势，中国在2001年加入世贸组织时承诺了远高于当年日本和韩国所签署的金融开放条件。在金融国际化和开放日益加快趋势之下，中国金融的内部改革与发展已无法拖延；同时，这些工作也是中国金融国际化目标的实现基础。

从中国内部来看，笔者认为，成为金融大国并不断开放的首要前提是加快实现利率市场化。众所周知，通过市场机制配置资源是中国经济和金融改革的导向，而利率则是金融市场上不同期限资金的价格。受管制的利率既无法反映真实的资金供求，也无法实现金融资源的有效合理配置。一般认为，只有实现了存贷款利率市场化，才真正达到了利率市场化。从利率市场化国际经验来看，多数国家息差将不断收窄，而当前主要发达国家的利率体系均建立在市场化决定基础之上。就中国来说，利率市场化不但可以实现资金的更好配置，还可以为汇率形成机制以及外汇管理体制奠定基础——因为，汇率基本可以看做不同经济体内部利率的比价，人民币汇率问题在很大程度上可以归结为中国与美国等少数主要经济体利率机制的差异。当然，至少在短期内，利率市场化会对中国银行体系造成一定冲击。[①] 其次，放宽金融行业的市场准入。2010年5月，国务院发布了《国务院关于鼓励和引导民间投资健康发展的若干意见》，明确提出，允许民间资金进入金融领域，允许民间资金发起设立各类小型金融机构。就企业数量分布来说，一国经济中为数众多的是小型企业，这一点中外皆同。实践证明，小型企业的金融服务主要来自当地的小型金融机构——它们更加专注，因而也更加高效。[②] 既然中国金融对外开放已成必然，更需放宽民间资本的金融业准入，以开办更多当地小型金融机构，引入和扩大市场竞争，解决小型企业融资困难。长期来看，这将促进中国金融形成合理的层级结构。最后，鼓励金融产品创新。利率市场化和行业准入放宽的一个自然结果将是市场竞争扩大，而金融机构间最主要的竞争形式就是产品创新。如果说美欧金融创新过度的话，中国金融产品创新则是相当不足——其原因与"分业经营、分业监管"体制不无关系，尽管这一体制的本意在于促进金融发展、维护金融稳定。鼓励金融产品创新，不但

---

① 2013年7月20日，中国放开了金融机构贷款利率管制，迈出了利率市场化重要一步；但是，最重要的是存款利率的市场化。

② 根据美国联邦存款保险公司（FDIC）数据，截至2010年底，在全部经营存贷业务的6 790家金融机构中，6 526家属于社区类金融机构（community institution）。

可以促进中国信贷市场、货币和资本市场的有效竞争，对于衍生品市场的建设与发展也大有裨益，甚至对于上海国际金融中心形成也有直接帮助。①

就外部来看，既然国际化是金融大国的应有之义，中国至少需要在三个方面取得重要进展。第一，人民币国际化。② 一国货币被国际广泛接受和使用包括三个阶段：贸易、投资和储备，即在世界范围内实现了货币的交易媒介、计价单位、价值贮藏功能。美国乃至英国的经验无法简单照搬，因为历史条件已大不相同，也不会简单重演；但我们仍可以看到，军事、科技和经济是货币国际化的决定因素，其中经济最为重要。开放经济大国的货币最后极有可能成为国际货币，这似乎不是一个问题，问题是中国该怎么办。因为，尽管都拥有优秀的中央银行，曾经英镑下的资本输出和当前美元下的资本输入是其作为国际货币的不同特征。如果中国经济能够稳定增长，那么人民币国际化似乎可以简化为一个技术层面的政策问题，即国际化的人民币金融产品及对应的金融市场——由此也再次说明，鼓励中国金融产品创新的政策极具战略意义。第二，国际合作。在可预计的相当长时期内，我们都只能是国际金融体系的接受者而不是主导者，理性和现实的选择是谦虚学习与积极参与。从亚洲、太平洋到全球范围内，与国际金融组织、不同金融机构、主要经济体等加强合作，并逐步发挥更大作用。第三，改革和完善金融监管。面对本轮金融危机，中国无法独善其身。一个成功金融大国的金融政策目标，除了能够促进金融创新、维护金融市场有效运行和支持实体经济发展以外，更多指向了能够保证金融稳定。为了实现这一目标，强调宏观金融管理的审慎政策已经确立，中央银行的职能及权威得以强化——这是对系统性风险管理挑战的应对，而开放的中国应更加重视外部冲击对金融稳定的影响。

在未来10—20年内，中国能否成为金融大国可能并不完全取决于自身意愿。需要说明的是，中国已经意识到了应该构建服务于这一目标的金融政策框架——因为，这在《金融业发展和改革"十二五"规划》中被提出来了。但是，如何构建大国、开放经济条件下的中国金融政策框架，相信值得我们思考和解决的问题，一定比本文所讨论的内容要丰富。

---

① 实际上，"十二五"期间上海国际金融中心建设规划对上海的近期目标定位于人民币金融产品的全球定价、交易和创新中心。

② 中国官方文件正式出现"人民币国际化"是在2008年7月，它是当时中国人民银行设立汇率司的一项职能中的关键词。

主题报告：发展中的中国多层次资本市场

——问题与对策

　　中国多层次资本市场的建设起点是 2003 年。我们知道，中国的改革开放至少存在三个重要时间节点：一是 1978 年，中国共产党第十一届三中全会确定要"建设现代化国家"，改革开放由此展开；二是 1993 年，中国共产党第十四届三中全会通过了《中共中央关于建立社会主义市场经济体制若干问题的决定》，中国市场经济建设由此正式拉开序幕；三是 2003 年，中国共产党第十六届三中全会通过了《中共中央关于完善社会主义市场经济体制若干问题的决定》（以下简称《决定》），它旨在完善中国的市场经济体制。《决定》提出要"建立多层次资本市场体系，完善资本市场结构，丰富资本市场产品。规范和发展主板市场，推进风险投资和创业板市场建设"。随后，2004 年 5 月，中小板正式在深交所上市；2009 年 10 月，创业板正式开板。10 年来，中国多层次资本市场建设取得了一定成绩，但与美国等发达市场经济相比，中国的主板、中小板、创业板在制度上还有许多不足。例如，美国既有以纽交所为核心的主板市场，也有以纳斯达克为核心的二板市场，还有遍布各地区的全国性和区域性市场及场外交易市场；而且，针对不同公司的多层次市场之间存在合理的转板机制，充分满足了不同类别、不同规模和不同阶段公司的融资需求。相比之下，中国多层次资本市场仍然存在不少差距，诸多问题需要加快解决，从而可以为中国金融体系完善和实体经济发展提供可持续的支持。

一、中国资本市场的结构

（一）多层次资本市场概述

　　一般地，资本市场是指证券发行和交易的市场，主要包括股票市场和债券市场。资本市场与经济中其他市场非常相似——市场买卖双方高效达成交易，从而实现交易的共赢（消费者剩余和生产者剩余）。资本市场为证券交易提供了流动性，这正是资本市场的主要价值。因此，大部分企业应该愿意进入这个市场来交易产权（包括债权和股权）。所谓资本市场的"多层次"在于，不同金融产品由于风险特征等交易属性不同，为了交易更加有效，需要在不同的细分市场上交易，形成了不同交易标的、交易规则和监管规则，同时也形成了不同风险层次的金融资产管理渠道。从企业角度看，作为经济体中数量最多的中小企业，总是在经历连续不断的成立和消失过程，只有少数企业有机会成长为大企业。一般而言，企业越小，融资需求就越小，投资者数量少，对证券流动性要求太高，对企业信息透明度要求也较低；随着企业规模的扩大，其融资需要也不断增长，投资者数量增加，对证券的流动性和企业信息透明度的要求也在增加。客观上看，企业成长的实践经验告诉我们，需要成立不同层次的资本市场以适应不同阶段的企业融资需要。因此，债权市场风险相对小、风险来源少、个体差异小，而股权市场风险来源多、个体差异大，所以从理论上讲，对资本市场的层次性要求更高，这也是"多层次资本市场体系"主要是指"多层次股票市场"的原因（阙紫康，2007）。在实践方面，成熟市场经济国家资本市场的多层次发展也多是针对股票市场而言。

就股票市场而言，多层次资本市场的结构主要涉及以下内容：股票市场由哪些层次组成、各层次的区别、各层次的规模和各层次相互关系，以及不同层次市场的监管、中介和交易规则有何不同。从多层次资本市场的区分标准来看，实质性差别主要是上市条件、监管要求（特别是信息披露要求）和交易规则。这里需要强调的是，转板机制也是多层次资本市场的重要内容。一般来说，企业都希望进入流动性强的资本市场进行交易，但由于这些市场监管要求高、信息披露成本大，所以大部分企业不愿意进入或达不到要求进入的监管要求。对它们来说，可以先在场外市场层次比较低的市场上市，待条件成熟后再升级到层次较高的市场。这就需要建立不同层次市场之间的沟通机制或转板机制。

什么样的资本市场结构才是一个合理结构？就资本市场不同层次而言，合理的结构应该是层次越低市场的上市条件越低、监管要求越低、流动性越差、企业数量越多，层次越高市场的上市条件越高、监管要求越高、流动性越好、企业数量也越少，这种资本市场的结构可以称为"金字塔结构"。金字塔结构的资本市场刚好与经济中的企业结构相匹配，也与企业成长的历程相吻合，可以认为是一个比较正常和合理的资本市场层次结构。与此相反，"倒金字塔结构"的资本市场很可能就是不合理的资本市场结构。当然，资本市场层次的多少也取决于具体经济体的经济结构和产业结构，资本市场的层次过多或过少都会对效率产生负面影响。

（二）中国资本市场的倒金字塔结构

1. 发展历程及现状

与大多数市场经济体相同，中国资本市场也分为场内市场和场外市场。从1990年中国相继成立上海证券交易所和深圳证券交易所——场内市场算起，经过23年的曲折发展，目前基本建成一个由主板、中小板、创业板及场外市场构成的多层次资本市场体系，规模也不断扩大。截至2013年5月20日，中国境内上市公司达到2 469家，总市值达28.3万亿元。股市到2009年底，超越日本成为列美国之后的全球第二大市值市场。

准确地说，场内市场的发展是从1990年12月1日上海证券交易所试营业开始的。1991年4月，深圳证券交易所获中国人民银行正式批准成立。1991年10月31日，中国南方玻璃股份有限公司与深圳市物业发展（集团）股份有限公司向社会公众招股，这是中国股份制企业首次发行 B 股。2000 年，深交所开始探索筹建创业板，并于 2004 年 5 月先行设立中小企业板。2005 年 4 月 29 日，中国证监会启动了股票分置改革，解决了历史遗留的问题。在人民币资本项下未实现完全自由兑换的情况下，中国于 2002 年 12 月实施允许经批准的境外机构投资者投资于中国证券市场的 QFII 制度，引进了海外资本。沪深 300 股指期货合约自 2010 年 4 月 16 日起正式上市交易，标志中国股票市场的交易工具走向完善。表 1 - 1 是截至 2013 年 5 月 20 日各场内市场的股票数量、总市值、平均市值和标准差的情况。

表 1 - 1 中国场内市场规模 单位：亿元

	股票数量	总市值	平均市值	标准差
创业板	355	11 873	33	34
中小企业板	701	34 911	50	72
主板	1 413	235 953	167	805
上海证券交易所	944	197 634	209	978
深圳证券交易所	469	38 319	82	135
总计	2 469	282 736	115	614

资料来源：课题组整理。

中国场外市场由银行间债券市场、代办股份转让系统和债券柜台交易市场组成。1997 年 6 月，银行间债券市场正式启动。经过 10 多年迅速发展，银行间债券市场已成为我国债券市场的主体部分——债券交易主要是在银行间债券市场进行，只有少部分在交易所进行。债券柜台交易市场交易是指商业银行通过营业网点（含电子银行系统）与投资人继续债券买卖，并办理相关托管与结算等业务的行为。根据每天全国银行间债券市场交易的行情，商业银行在营业网点柜台挂出国债买入和卖出价格，以保证个人和企业投资者及时买卖国债。商业银行的资金和债券余缺则通过银行间债券市场买卖加以平衡。

最早可以追溯到 1992 年和 1993 年，代办股份转让系统分别由证券交易所研究设计联合办公室和中国证券交易系统有限公司分别开办的 STAQ（全国证券交易自动报价系统）和 NET（全国电子交易系统）开始发展，这两个市场主要进行法人股的交易。2001年，中国证券业协会设立了代办股份转让系统，承担从上海、深圳交易所退市公司的流通转让。在地方政府的支持下，各地还成立了 200 多家区域性的产权交易所，这些产权交易机构，遍布各省和主要城市。为了避免产权交易所的重复低层次建设，各地产权交易所进行区域合作以建立区域性市场。例如，1997 年，成立了长江流域产权交易共同市场；2002 年，成立了北方产权交易共同市场；2007 年 6 月，泛珠三角区域 9 省区也共同签署了《泛珠三角区域产权交易机构合作框架协议》，开始联手构建跨省区的区域产权交易共同市场体系。

2006 年 1 月，中关村高科技园区非上市股份制企业开始进入代办股份系统挂牌交易。该系统的功能得到拓展——为原 STAQ、NET 系统挂牌公司和沪、深证券交易所的退市公司以及中关村科技园区非上市股份有限公司代办股份转让，这部分代办股份的公司被称为"三板"市场。2012 年 8 月，非上市股份公司股份转让试点扩大，除北京中关村外，上海张江、天津滨海、武汉东湖等国家级高新区也纳入了股份转让试点园区的范围，截至 2012 年底，挂牌的园区企业已达 200 家。目前，中关村科技园区非上市股份有限公司因为高科技企业故被称为"新三板"市场。2013 年 1 月 16 日，作为国务院批准的全国性证券交易场所的全国中小企业股份转让系统正式揭牌运营。这是全国场外市场建设的标志性事件，意味着中国场外市场进入蓬勃发展阶段；同时，它也表明"金字塔"式多层次资本市场架构正在形成。目前，全国股转系统运行仍沿用原中关村代办试点的技术系统，随着系统及制度的完善，纳入交易的试点也将扩大，有可能先是全国的国家级高新园区，而后再扩至全国符合条件的中小企业。

2. 中国多层次资本市场的特点

第一，层次性不足。中国场内市场虽然分为主板、中小板和创业板，但三者只是上市条件指标上有所不同，在监管要求（特别是披露要求）、上市及退市规则、交易规则上大同小易，很难构成真正的"多层次"资本市场。中国场外市场分为银行间债券市场、全国性场外市场、区域性场外交易市场和银行柜台市场。就股票交易而言，中国尚不存在真正意义上的场外市场。在现有全国范围内的非上市公司股权交易机构中，代办股权转让系统、上海联合产权交易所浦东张江分所、滨海新区天津产权交易中心股权托管交易市场等，虽然都在努力打造与主板、二板对接的三板市场，但其"网上联系、网下结算"的制度达不到系统内全自动交易，融资功能基本处于缺位状态。银行间债券市场作为债券场外市场，投资者结构比较单一，流动性较小，大部分企业很难通过这个市场进行债券融资。

这里，可以就层次性不足问题与美国进行比较。美国证券交易市场主要由三部分构成（徐洪才，2009）：一是主板市场，它包括两家国家级的证券交易所［纽约证券交易所（NYSE）和美国证交所（AMEX）］和多家区域性证券交易所（芝加哥证交所、波士顿证交所、辛辛那提证交所、太平洋证交所、费城证交所等）。纽约证交所就市值而言是全球最大的，截至 2013 年 3 月，上市公司总数约 1 867 家，总市值达到 16.6 万亿美元，2008 年的日平均交易量达到 1 530 亿美元。二是美国纳斯达克市场（美国全国证券商协会下辖的自动报价市场，NASDAQ），它是一个为分散在各地、流动性不足并且不能在 NYSE 或 AMEX 上市股票提供交易的市场。NASDAQ 细分为全球精选市场、全国市场和小型市场三个层次。由于它大幅提高了柜台市场的效率、流动性和公平性，已发展成为美国主要的证券交易市场之一。三是电子告示板市场和粉单市场构成的美国场外市场。由于不同层次之间的交易规则、监管规则、上市条件不同，大部分企业都可以找到适合自己交易的市场，极大地提高了企业融资的效率。

第二，倒金字塔结构。作为中国股权场外市场的产权交易中心主要针对局部的产业园区设立，其交易网没能相互打通，结算系统没能统一，交易效率低下，只有少量企业在这些市场上市，大部分企业寻求到交易所上市，这就形成"千军万马过独木桥"的局面。以2004年美国股票市场为例，NASDAQ挂牌公司3 229家，而历史更悠久的纽交所挂牌公司数只有2 293家，美国证券交易所只有575家。NASDAQ为纽交所培育和输送了大量优秀的公司。而中国由于缺乏较低层次市场对优秀公司的培育和发现，申请上市的企业质量参差不齐而且很难把控，虽然采用实质审批的办法，但也难以防备企业的做假和欺诈。中国证监会对企业上市的审批相当谨慎。对于一家企业来说，从准备上市到上市成功通常要3～5年。我国共有大中小型企业1 800多万家，上市公司的数量只占整体企业数量的约0.077%，即不到总企业数的万分之一；在没有上市的企业中，99.6%是中小型企业，绝大多数都面临着融资困境。

第三，债券市场的场外市场发展滞后。由于债券发行可以节税和为企业带来财务杠杆作用，债券市场应该是比股权市场更好的融资方式。中国企业债券市场一直发展滞后，虽然过去一年中信用债市场出现了一个爆发式的增长，但融资企业的数量很少——基本是大型央企和大型地方国有企业在融资，大量的中小企业融资仍然比较困难。这种情况与中国场外市场的发展滞后密切有关。美国中小企业的发展融资离不开NASDAQ市场，而全美95%的债券也都在这个最大的场外市场中进行交易，使其债券融资占据全部直接融资市场的半壁江山。而且，美国债券市场是以公司债为主的市场，其他类似的债券，即使是市政债、国债或资产担保债的未清算余额都没有公司债大。另外，在中国由于交易所上市要求比较高，大型国有企业成为上市的主体，而这些企业更倾向于股权融资方式，这导致债券市场发展一直比较滞后。

第四，缺乏不同市场的不同交易制度，特别是经纪人制度缺失。王国刚（2006）认为，经纪人制度是一个多层次性和灵活性的基本制度；对于不同的市场应该有不同的交易制度，中国单一的交易所市场使经纪人机制几乎完全缺失。对于场外市场，由于缺乏流动性，做市商等经纪人发挥着提供流动性的作用，其做市效果直接影响证券流动性。而我国由于银行间债券市场投资主体单一，债券品种及期限结构少，债券只数少，缺乏承销商、公开市场交易商与做市商的联动机制等原因做市效果不好；至于场外股权市场，更没有做市商制度。

第五，缺乏不同市场之间的退市和转板制度。退市和转板制度可以使市场具有淘汰和进退机制，建立不同层次的资本市场之间的良性循环关系。在美国，严格的退市和转板制度通过优胜劣汰的方式确保了NASDAQ市场企业的质量。除了纳斯达克全球精选市场、全球市场、资本市场外，低一级的OTCBB（场外交易市场）与纳斯达克也保持相通。NASDAQ内部各层次可自由转板，转板方式分为主动申请和强制转板。

（三）倒金字塔结构的弊端

中国资本市场最主要的特征是倒金字塔结构，前文已经指出这一结构的不合理性。它造成的弊端可以从两个方面显现出来：实体经济的融资困难与结构失衡和交易所市场的异化。

从资本市场对实体经济的影响来说，它会造成投资与融资匹配出现问题，还造成资金价格的扭曲，引起整个经济的失衡。在中国多层次资本市场中，较低层次市场的缺失造成了资金需求方和供给方没办法实现匹配：一方面，它造成大量达不到交易所交易要求的公司很难从股市融资；另一方面，由于大量资金找不到投资渠道，导致资金价格扭曲。我们可以看到，闲置资金大多存入银行，成为银行低成本资金的来源；与此同时，大量企业要高成本借贷。银行利润增长迅速，间接融资一直处于主导地位，而直接融资市场发展受到限制。由于中国的银行以国有为主，这些国有银行会在不同程度上受到政府影响而将资金用于政府投资项目：这将刺激经济规模扩大，而经济增长质量却难以提高；随着投资收益的下降，但融资渠道没有改变，这会导致经济逐渐走向失衡。

从倒金字塔结构对现有市场的影响来看，会造成市场的供求扭曲和寻租行为。场外市场由于规模很小而且缺乏退市与转板制度，这对交易所市场产生了很大负面影响：首先，缺乏价格发现机制，倒逼大量公司到交易所上市以及证监会进行实质性审批；同时，大量想上市的公司采用各种手段以便上市，产生了大量的寻租空间。由于审批时间长，上市成本高，很多优秀的企业选择了放弃在交易所上市，而差的公司却想要冒险一试。其结果是，由于大量投资找不到投资渠道，造成很长一段时间内中国股票市场的高发行价、高盈率和高认购比率的奇特情景，很多上市公司上市目的的扭曲，股市成了圈钱的工具。

总之，多层次资本市场将是中国资本市场发展的出路，而完善场外市场将逐步改变现在的倒金字塔结构，这是中国资本市场各种问题得以解决的基础。下一部分将具体分析造成中国场外市场发展滞后的原因。

二、中国场外市场发展滞后的原因

（一）全国性场外市场发展历程

1. STAQ 和 NET 市场

"法人股"这一概念出现于 1990 年前后。1992 年 5 月 15 日，原国家体改委颁布《股份制有限公司规范意见》，当时的股份制企业只能向法人和拥有主人公地位的内部职工进行定向募集。1994 年 7 月 1 日，《公司法》正式生效，宣布停止批设股份募集公司时，全国共有 6 000 多家股份定向募集公司。当时的基本背景是：由于上市公司多从国企改制而来，为维护企业的国有性质，在改制中设立了国家股和法人股；同时，又出于对个人股与公有股在一个市场流通会危及公有制主体地位的担忧，限定公有股权不能在二级市场流通；对于能够在二级市场流通的股份，被分为个人股和外资股。由于股权不能转让和交易，法人机构的投资出现难收回和无处变现的困难。针对这种情况，专家学者建议建立法人股流通市场。

1992 年 7 月 1 日，法人股内部流通试点开始试运行，全国证券交易自动报价系统——STAQ 是指定的法人股流通市场。1993 年 4 月 28 日，NET 法人股市场正式开通。到 1993 年底，STAQ 系统有上市公司 10 家，NET 系统有上市公司 7 家，会员公司近 500 家，开户的机构投资者约 32 000 人，累计交易金额达 220 亿元。至此，STAQ 与 NET 法人股市场诞生了，STAQ 与 NET 系统也被称为"两网"系统。

在试点初期，机构投资者对法人股市场知之甚少，参与程度十分有限。NET 市场开通后，人们开始对其发展前景表示乐观。其后，STAQ 市场和 NET 市场均出现大涨。从 1992 年 4 月中旬至月底的半个月，STAQ 市场的开户股东已由 1 400 多家猛增到近 2 400 家（到 5 月底突破 6 000 家）。人们开始看到法人股市场的巨大潜力和投资机会，众多个人股民已通过不同方式开设账户，涌入法人股市场。由于事实上的"限定法人间转让"难以实现，不少营业部干脆"网开一面"，"法人股"概念在不少地方早已形同虚设——原本面向法人投资者的市场，流通股份 90% 被自然人所持有。

由于监管力度不足和其他方面的原因，STAQ 和 NET 上市交易的企业只有 17 家。1993 年 5 月 20 日，STAQ 和 NET 分别接到中国证监会"暂缓审批新的法人股挂牌流通"的指示。1993 年 6 月 21 日，中国证监会正式发布了"暂停新股审批上市"的公告。

1997 年，NET 更名为"中央国债登记结算有限责任公司"，其职能也随之更改，主营业务中取消了"股票交易"这一内容，并向证监会提出申请将在 NET 上市的几只法人股交易管理转到深沪交易所。1998 年 4 月，国家整顿场外非法交易市场的行动开始，国务院有关文件对做好善后工作提出 6 条解决措施：一是公司买回自己的股票；二是让其他企业回购；三是通过吸收合并的方式解决；四是将公司的股票转为债券；五是通过推荐在 A 股市场上市；六是原有股东继续持股。1999 年 9 月 9 日与 10 日，STAQ 和 NET 分别以"国庆彩排交通管制"与"设备检修"为由发布"暂停交易"的公告，至今未恢复交易。

2. 老三板市场

STAQ 和 NET 被关闭、主板公司退市，引发了股民群体性上访事件，威胁到资本市场的稳定和发展，急需建立完善的退市机制。为了解决主板退市公司的股份转让和两网系统的历史遗留问题，2001 年 6 月，中国证券业协会发布《证券公司代办股份转让服务业务试点办法》，指定申银万国等 6 家证券公司代办原 STAQ 和 NET 系统挂牌公司的股份转让业务；2001 年 7 月 16 日，由申银万国证券公司代办的杭州大自然第一家正式进入代办股份转让系统，这标志着三板市场的正式诞生。2001 年底，PT 水仙成为第一家登陆代办股份转让系统的主板退市公司，紧接着其他退市公司和两网公司相继挂牌。

三板市场开业初期就非常火暴——股票天天涨停，于是中国证监会感觉压力很大，不断发布警示公告，三板市场炒作之风持续二十多天被迅速刹住。由于市场缺乏流动性，三板市场仅仅出现短暂繁荣。后来我们可以看到，大量 ST 公司即使在主板暂停交易也不愿到三板挂牌；而三板市场公司转到主板上市难度很大，多年来一直处于资本市场的边缘，备受冷落。为此，中国证监会推出了平移机制，三板公司达到上市条件可以直接到交易所恢复上市而不需经过证监会审核，但必须与券商签三板上市协议，退市公司的股东名册要交给主办券商——三板市场的退市机制开始正常运转。

2004 年，三板市场迅速扩容增速，三板市场退市公司和"两网"公司后来发展到 57 家，三板市场基本上成为主板退市公司的收容站，这里垃圾股成堆。

3. 新三板和北京证券交易所

为支持"科教兴国"战略和解决高科技企业融资问题，2006 年 1 月 23 日，证监会与北京中关村科技园区管委会开通了中关村科技园区非上市公司代办股份转让系统，俗称"新三板"——先后共有 77 家中关村科技园区高新技术企业进入新三板。2009 年 8 月 11 日，久其软件成为新三板第一家通过 IPO 登陆深圳中小板市场的公司。

新三板的诞生一定程度上促进了场外市场的发展。但是，由于其制度的设计原因，始终存在流通性不强、融资能力弱、参与人数少、关注度小等问题。

2012 年 8 月，国务院批准扩大非上市股份公司：按照总体规划分步推进、稳步推进的原则，首批扩大试点除中关村科技园区外，新增上海张江高新产业开发区、武汉东湖新技术产业开发区和天津滨海高新区。2012 年 9 月，作为场外交易市场未来交易平台的全国中小企业股份转让系统有限责任公司在北京注册成立。2013 年 1 月 16 日，中国证券业协会全国中小企业股份转让系统正式挂牌。作为全国性场外市场交易市场的运营管理机构，业界人士称之为"北京证券交易所"。

统计显示，截至 2013 年 1 月 14 日，已有 248 家中关村企业参与中关村代办股份报价转让试点，其中已挂牌的中关村企业达到 182 家。如果加上在上海张江、天津滨海和武汉东湖挂牌的 25 家企业，目前已有超过 200 家企业在"新三板"挂牌。

(二) 地方性场外市场发展历程

1. 天津股权交易所

2008 年 3 月国务院批准在天津滨海新区设立全国性非上市公众公司股权交易市场（简称天交所）。当年 9 月，天交所注册营业时提出的定位是全国性场外交易市场、纳斯达克中国版。值得肯定的是，与中关村的代办股权转让系统仍采取协商配对成交方式对比，天交所在制度设计上率先引入了做市商制度。根据天交所的规定，凡具有独立法人资格的投资机构、合伙企业以及具有投资资格的独立经济组织，均可向天交所申报注册成为做市商。同时，天交所"拆细股权、连续交易"等制度，也初步具备了场外交易市场的典型特征。但是，由于天交所不在证监会的监管范围之内，券商难以参与。而没有券商参与，做市商队伍就难以壮大，市场规模也就做不大。由于天津市成立天交所是直接向国务院申报并得到了批准，这一过程中国证监会没有参与。因此，天交所与中国证监会的新三板建设以及天交所挂牌企业在新三板上市，面临一些问题。

2. 河南技术产权交易所

2010 年 5 月，中国工信部选定了河南、北京、上海、重庆、广东的五家产权交易机构开展区域性中小企业产权交易市场试点。其中，河南试点方案借用了沪深交易所的整套模式。2010 年 11 月 12 日，这个名为"国家区域性（河南）中小企业产权交易市场"火暴开盘。开盘当日，全天成交金额近 1.5 亿元，挂牌的 41 家企业股价涨幅大多超过100%，有的甚至翻了 10 倍。然而，6 个交易日后，河南省工信厅便公告"暂停市场交易及相关活动"。截至关闭前，开户人数达到了 2.2 万人。中国证监会认为河南技术产权交易所以产权交易之名、行证券交易之实，违反了《证券法》、《公司法》等法规，向国务院递交了报告。除天津、郑州外，重庆、上海、长春等地也纷纷试图发展当地的场外交易市场。这里需要说明的是，我国《公司法》第一百三十九条规定"股东转让其股份，应当在依法设立的证券交易场所进行或者按照国务院规定的其他方式进行"，所以，如果严格按照《公司法》衡量，很多地方 OTC 可能会面临合法性问题。

（三）中国场外市场发展滞后的原因

1. 法律法规不健全

中国场外市场发展伊始，既没有立法部门和相关监管机构预先设立的相应法律法规，也没有企业自发形成的市场规则。STAQ 和 NET 市场建立时，《公司法》、《证券法》均未出台，甚至连证监会都未成立，这使得法人股市场从一出生就种下了不良的种子。例如，河南技术产权交易所以产权交易之名、行证券交易之实，违反了《证券法》、《公司法》等法规，以致被关闭。

2. 证券发行的审批制和条块分割的监管体制

场外市场应该是较低的准入标准和严格的监管和信息披露，而我国场外市场却在实行审批制，不但效率低，而且还将大量企业排斥在外。由于历史原因，天交所不在证监会的监管范围之内，使得券商难以参与天交所交易活动。我们知道，没有券商参与，做市商队伍就难以壮大，市场规模也就做不大，在天交所挂牌的企业要到新三板上市，也存在困难。

3. 政策定位不清

场外市场的发展应定位于多层次资本市场建设，而当初设计老三板却是为了维护资本市场稳定，为退市公司和两网公司的股份转让寻找出路，解决退市机制的完善问题。

4. 缺乏完善的机制设计

目前场外市场缺乏完善的机制设计，这体现为挂牌标准、交易机制、转板机制等严重缺失。

在挂牌标准方面，与境外市场对比，我国新三板挂牌标准较为严格，需要由主办券商推荐，并需满足 5 个具体条件：第一，存续满 2 年；第二，主营业务突出，具有持续盈利能力；第三，公司治理结构健全，运作规范；第四，股份发行和转让合法合规；第五，取得北京市人民政府出具的非上市公司股份报价转让试点资格确认函。

表 2-1　　　　　　　　　各国（地区）场外市场挂牌标准比较

市场分类		挂牌要求
美国	OTCBB	向 SEC 注册，提交所要求的信息披露文件；一家以上推荐商
	粉单市场	提交 211 表格；至少一家做市商愿意报价
日本	JASDAQ（S）	净资产 2 亿日元以上；税前净利润 1 亿日元以上；流通股 10 万股以上；股东人数 300 人以上；流通市值 5 亿日元以上（上市日）
	JASDAQ（G）	净资产为正值
	绿单市场	具有成长潜力；至少一家证券推荐商
中国台湾	兴柜市场	公开发行公司；至少两家证券商推荐挂牌
	盘商市场	无任何要求

资料来源：白冰、逯云娇：《中国场外市场发展研究——基于国内外场外交易市场的比较分析》，载《经济问题探索》，2012（4）；各国证券业协会；广发证券博士后工作站。

在交易机制方面，我国新三板交易采用了传统的协议转让方式，使得交易成功性低、配对时间长、流动性差。而发达国家场外市场多采用传统做市制度或混合交易制度，做市商的参与激活了市场流动性，缩短了交易时间，提高了市场效率。

表 2-2　　　　　　　　各国（地区）场内与场外交易市场交易制度对比

	市场分类	交易制度
美国	NYSE	竞价交易
	NASDAQ	混合交易
	OTCBB、Pink Sheets	传统做市商
日本	东京证券交易所、大阪证券交易所	竞价交易
	Mothers（TSE）	竞价交易
	Hercules（QSE）	竞价交易
	JASDAQ	混合交易
	Green Sheet	传统做市商
中国台湾	中国台湾证券交易所	竞价交易
	上柜市场	竞价交易
	兴柜市场	竞争做市商

资料来源：白冰、逯云娇：《中国场外市场发展研究——基于国内外场外交易市场的比较分析》，载《经济问题探索》，2012（4）；广发证券博士后工作站。

在转板机制方面，根据目前规则，老三板和新三板转到中小板和创业板上市，与新股上市几乎没有差别，都要经过审批程序。而主板的退市机制也形同虚设，上市资格成为稀缺的壳资源。没有转板和退市机制，使得市场优胜劣汰的资源配置功能不能有效发挥，主板 IPO 的巨大利益使得场外市场的吸引力大大降低。

三、对中国资本市场监管的反思

（一）我国证券市场信息披露的现状

证券市场是充满信息的市场，信息披露在证券市场中占有重要地位。信息披露不但可以使投资者了解证券的真实情况，决定是否进行投资；也可以作为重要的监管制度，有效地保护证券市场的公平性、真实性，更好地保护投资者的权益。目前，我国证券市场形成了主板、中小板、创业板、新三板、场外市场的多层次、立体化的证券发行与交易体系，也形成了上证所、深交所、北交所、区域股权交易中心多足鼎立的格局。但是，在制度建设方面，与证券的发行和交易制度比较完备相比，信息披露制度的建设大多由证监会和交易所在借鉴国外立法的基础上建立起来，比较缺乏实践性，在发展中仍存在一些问题需要反思。

1. 信息披露的内容

我国证券市场成立之初，其监管机构主要是国务院证券委员会及其执行机构（中国证监会）[1]。1993 年 4 月 22 日，国务院证券委员会发布了《股票发行与交易管理暂行条例》，其第六章专门针对上市公司的信息披露进行规定，并要求上市公司及时披露对股票市场价格产生较大影响而投资人尚未得知的重大事件；1993 年 6 月 10 日，中国证监会颁布了《公开发行股票公司信息披露实施细则》[2]，规定了上市公司信息披露的内容和标准，并对持续信息披露做了更为细致的要求。此外，中国证监会对上市公司中期报告、年度报告的内容与格式以及其他要求均进行了规范。

一般来说，证券市场信息披露主要包括证券发行信息披露、持续信息披露以及重大事件临时报告。具体地看，证券发行信息披露是指公司在首次公开发行股份或者公开发行新股时需要向监管部门提交的申请材料以及向投资者公开的相关信息；持续信息披露是指上市公司应当按照法律法规的要求披露上市公司的经营状况、财务状况、控股股东、大股东以及高管人员的变动情况等信息，以使证券市场投资者了解相关情况，及时调整投资策略，保护投资人的合法权益；重大事件临时报告是指上市公司按照有关法律法规要求，在发生重大事项时需向投资者和社会公众披露的信息。

2. 信息披露的法律体系

目前，我国资本市场信息披露的法律体系主要包括三个层次。

第一层次是关于信息披露的重要法律，其主要是《证券法》和《公司法》。其中，《证券法》第三章证券交易中规定证券上市的信息披露以及证券上市后的持续信息公开（包括临时报告制度），也规定了信息披露瑕疵的归责原则。《公司法》第五章以及第七

---

① 1998 年 4 月，国务院证券委员会与中国证监会合并，由中国证监会行使国务院证券委员会的职责。

② 2007 年 1 月 30 日，证监会颁布施行了《上市公司信息披露管理办法》后，《公开发行股票公司信息披露实施细则》则相应废止。

章分别规定了股份公司股份发行以及公司债券发行的相关程序，并要求将相关发行文件进行公告。

第二层次是关于信息披露的行政法规，主要依照《企业债券管理条例》①、《股票发行与交易管理暂行条例》、《国务院关于股份有限公司境内上市外资股的规定》，分别对公司债券发行交易、股份公开发行与股票上市交易、我国境内上市的外国股份有限公司发行与交易的信息披露制度进行了相应的规定。

第三层次是部门规章，包括《公开发行证券的公司信息披露内容与格式准则》、《公开发行证券的公司信息披露编报规则》、《公开发行证券的公司信息披露解释性公告》、《证券公司年度报告内容与格式准则》、《证券期货监督管理信息公开办法（试行）》、《上市公司收购管理办法》、《上市公司信息披露管理办法》等。此外，还包括沪深两大交易所制定的交易规则中对信息披露的有关规定。

3. 信息披露的监管体系

目前，我国资本市场信息披露的监管主体主要是证监会和交易所两个层次。

根据我国《证券法》以及有关信息披露管理的有关规定，证监会既有起草证券期货市场有关法规的权限，也有依法对证券期货违法违规行为进行调查、处罚的权限。证监会发布的《上市公司信息披露管理办法》规定，信息披露义务人未在规定期限内履行信息披露义务，或者所披露的信息有虚假记载、误导性陈述或者重大遗漏以及信息披露义务人未在规定期限内报送有关报告，或者报送的报告有虚假记载、误导性陈述或者重大遗漏等情形，应按《证券法》第一百九十三条的规定进行处罚。此外，证监会2011年第11号令还公布了《信息披露违法行为行政责任认定规则》，详细规定了信息披露违法行为、信息披露义务人信息披露违法的责任认定，信息披露违法行为责任人员及其责任的认定细则。

同时，证券交易所作为证券交易的自律性机构，在制定相关信息披露规则的同时，也负有信息披露管理的职责。例如，上海证券交易所发布了《上海证券交易所公司债券上市规则》和《上海证券交易所证券发行业务指引》，对违法信息披露规则的上市公司，给予通报批评、公开谴责的处罚，情节严重的上报证监会查处。但值得一提的是，证券交易所作为自律性监管的一种，并不享有行政性权力，对证券市场信息披露有瑕疵的上市公司不具有处罚权或其他执法权。除此之外，一些行业协会也承担一定的信息披露管理义务。如中国注册会计师协会对会计师或会计师事务所提供虚假信息等违法行为也会进行一定的处罚。

（二）我国证券市场审核制度的变革

我国证券发行审核制度经历了由行政审批制、核准通道制、保荐人制度三个过程。

---

① 《企业债券管理条例》于1993年8月2日发布施行，2011年1月8日对第26条、第27条进行了修改。

在证券市场建立之初，主要实行行政审批制；1998 年出台《证券法》后，实行核准通道制；2004 年初，正式启动了保荐人制度。

1. 行政审批制

行政审批制（即额度审批制），证券发行完全由行政机关进行审批。审批程序主要分为三个阶段：一是证监会进行额度分配，由证券主管部门根据国家经济发展总体布局和产业政策，确定每年总发行规模。并将总额度分配给各省市及各部委，再由其将额度分配给其所属企业。二是地方政府或各部委进行预选。当发行额度或发行企业家数确定后，由地方政府或各部委根据企业的申请，初步确定若干企业作为预选企业，由证监会进行审核。三是证监会批准发行。分为初审和复审两个阶段，初审由证监会发行部相关工作人员对各省市及各部委推荐的发行人进行初步审查；复审则由证监会的证券发行审核委员会进行。

2. 核准通道制

1998 年 12 月出台《证券法》后，证券发行开始实施核准通道制。一方面取消了发行额度，实行"成熟一个推荐一个"的原则，另一方面在申请发行时间上也要求企业先改制后发行，挂牌运行一年后才能申请发行股票。同时，也将政府审批改为券商推荐，发行人的申请经省级政府或国务院有关部门批准后，由主承销商推荐并向证监会申报，由证监会进行核准。

3. 保荐人制度

2004 年初，我国开始启用保荐人制度：公司公开发行证券及证券上市时，必须由具有保荐机构资格的保荐人推荐。《证券法》第十一条规定："发行人申请公开发行股票、可转换为股票的公司债券，依法采取承销方式的，或者公开发行法律、行政法规规定实行保荐制度的其他证券的，应当聘请具有保荐资格的机构担任保荐人。保荐人应当遵守业务规则和行业规范，诚实守信，勤勉尽责，对发行人的申请文件和信息披露资料进行审慎核查，督导发行人规范运作。"《证券法》第四十九条规定："申请股票、可转换为股票的公司债券或者法律、行政法规规定实行保荐制度的其他证券上市交易，应当聘请具有保荐资格的机构担任保荐人。"保荐人制度比核准通道制进步的地方之一就在于保荐人对其所推荐的公司上市后的一段期间内负有持续督导义务，并对公司在督导期间的不规范行为承担责任。

（三）对中国证券上市审核制度的反思

1. 关于信息披露制度

目前，我国证券市场信息披露制度正处于不断建设和完善的阶段。从法律法规本身来看，所涉及的市场范围和标准已比较齐备，但完整性、真实性、及时性等方面仍存在不足。

在完整性方面，许多上市公司并没有对关联交易中发行人成为股份有限公司之前的演变过程，以及关联交易中所涉及的重大事项进行完全披露，这对市场的透明度以及交易价格、方式的公正性带来不利影响。此外，上市公司所履行的社会责任的情况也未在招股说明书中予以体现，在一定程度上也反映了信息披露的不完整。

在真实性方面，由于投资者和上市公司之间信息的不对称，上市公司为获取高额利益所进行的内幕交易、虚假陈述和严重误导等利用信息披露进行欺诈的行为虽有法律或法规明文禁止，但在实际运作中，这些欺诈行为仍时有发生①。

在及时性方面，很多上市公司在年报、中报或季报中存在隐瞒重大事项、不及时披露信息的情况，往往也影响了投资者的理性判断和投资决策的调整。在真实性和及时性方面，除了信息不对称本身带来这些问题外，中介机构在利益驱动下违反职业道德也起到推波助澜的作用。

特别需要指出的是，随着 2012 年 6 月 15 日证监会《非上市公众公司监督管理办法（征求意见稿）》的出台，一方面为建设全国统一的场外市场扫清了障碍，但同时场外市场信息披露问题也逐渐成为多方关注的焦点。理论上，场外市场监管重点应该是挂牌企业的信息披露，但现阶段我国场外市场尚未出台统一的信息披露政策——北交所的股份转让系统（新三板）、区域股权交易市场都存在不同的制度规则。因此，在制度设计方面，应根据不同层次的场外市场，设计多层次、有差别的信息披露规则，并采取强制性信息披露与资源性信息披露制度相结合。尤其是市场建设初期，为满足中小企业融资需求，可适当降低信息披露标准，并寻求挂牌企业与投资者之间、不同投资者之间、挂牌公司之间信息披露的均衡，从而将可能降低场外市场总体的信息披露成本。

2. 关于"保荐人制度"

回顾我国证券发行"审核制"的变迁历程，我们可以发现：第一，在证券市场发展初期，由于企业上市被定位为稀缺资源，因此"行政审批制"有其特定历史意义。但由于实际操作中缺乏科学性、专业性，"暗箱操作"时有发生等弊端也使其很快被"核准通道制"取代。第二，留有计划经济"烙印"的核准通道制在运行中也出现了诸多问题，例如，券商在向证监会推荐上市企业时，仍有通道的数量及推荐企业的数量限制，在一定程度上不利于同业竞争；且券商的主要责任是上市推荐，并没有担保责任；职责权限也仅限于公司上市之前，而上市后的职责则终止，这很容易使券商为成功推荐企业进行信息造假且法律风险相对很低。最后出现的是"保荐人制度"，在目前我国证券市场"新兴"＋"转轨"的大背景下，伴随着创业板、新三板、场外市场体系的逐步建立，它也面临着由完全集中统一监管向集中监管与自律管理协调发展的"注册制"转变，需要我们进行反思。

事实上，我国保荐人制度在实际运作过程中存在的诸多问题需要解决。首先，保荐

---

① 我国最高人民法院于 2003 年 1 月公布了《关于审理证券市场因虚假陈述引发的民事赔偿案件的若干规定》。

人和保荐代表人职责边界不清。实践中,保荐人常常干预保荐代表人的正常保荐工作,影响保荐代表人的独立性,但却不承担实际保荐责任。其次,保荐人和发行人职责边界不清。通常保荐人的信息来源由发行人掌控,但发行人和保荐人之间信息不对称问题依然存在。最后,保荐人与其他中介机构的职责边界不清。证券发行上市是发行人、券商、律师、审计机构、评估机构等共同作用的结果。保荐人作为推荐人,并不能替代其他中介机构履行诚信义务。因此,当发生违规行为时,很难厘清二者的责任边界。

为解决我国证券市场审核制度存在的问题,在监管渠道上的拓宽,尤其是充分发挥财经媒体和市场参与者对上市公司的监督作用,效果可能更重要、更直接。从国外实践来看,美国"安然事件"就是最好的佐证。因此,证券市场的监管应是董事会、财经媒体、市场参与者、证监会和法院五位一体的综合,缺一不可。

四、中国发展多层次资本市场的展望与建议

(一) 目标与展望

近年来,为推进我国资本市场的发展,一个相互补充、相互促进的多层次资本市场体系也正在逐步建立。2003 年 10 月,中国共产党的十六届三中全会审议通过了《中共中央关于完善社会主义市场经济体制若干问题的决定》,明确表示要"积极推进资本市场的改革开放和稳定发展,扩大直接融资。建立多层次资本市场体系,完善资本市场结构,丰富资本市场产品。规范和发展主板市场,推进风险投资和创业板市场建设。"这个决定的内容是关于多层次资本市场体系建设的政策方面的首次清晰明确的阐述。2004 年 1 月 31 日,《国务院关于推进资本市场改革开放和稳定发展的若干意见》(俗称"国九条") 正式颁布,作为指导资本市场发展的纲领性文件,"国九条"明确提出要"逐步建立满足不同类型企业融资需求的多层次资本市场体系"。并将其细化为"继续规范和发展主板市场,逐步改善主板市场上市公司结构。分步推进创业板市场建设,完善风险投资机制,拓展中小企业融资渠道。积极探索和完善统一监管下的股份转让制度"。2005 年的"十一五"规划纲要 (2006—2010) 再次明确提出了要"建立多层次资本市场体系,完善市场功能,拓宽资金入市渠道,提高直接融资比重"等重点要求。2012 年中国共产党的"十八大报告"再一次明确要求要"深化金融体制改革,健全促进宏观经济稳定、支持实体经济发展的现代金融体系,加快发展多层次资本市场"。

由此可见,我国多层次资本市场的建设目标是包括主板市场、创业板市场以及场外交易市场在内的分工明确、层次丰富、完整协调、互动衔接的多元化、高度开放的资本市场体系。

纵观世界各国发展历程和现状,多层次的资本市场体系并不是各个国家都具备的普遍现象,多层次资本市场通常会出现在那些幅员辽阔、经济发展不平衡的世界大国,而且大多伴随着大国的崛起而逐渐演变而成。美国的崛起与其多层次资本市场的成功快速

发展息息相关，完善、高效的资本市场体系成为推进高新技术企业创新和发展的原动力，是提高企业自主创新能力的基础和保障，也是促进创业投资发展最有效的手段和工具。美国的多层次资本市场体系建设经验，在全球范围内都是被各国所广泛借鉴的对象。而中国同美国一样，地域广阔，区域经济发展不平衡，同时拥有充裕的企业资源和多样化的投资者群体。因此，从发展前景来看，虽然目前中国资本市场的水平与美国不可同日而语，但从决定资本市场发展的实体经济层面的基本因素看，中国也许是全球范围内唯一一个可以发展成类似于美国那样的体系庞大的资本市场的国家。

所以，在可预见的未来，我国的多层次资本市场体系将步入加快发展和加速市场化与国际化的历史新时期，并会在我国经济崛起的过程中扮演着重要的角色，当然这需要我们在政策和制度上进行一系列的改革和完善。

（二）最新进展

从本报告前文可以知道，目前我国已经初步建立起了主板市场（上交所和深交所）、创业板市场以及各类场外交易市场，包括"新三板"和由区域性股权交易所和产权交易所所构成的场外交易市场等。而各类多层次资本市场发展所需制度和规则也在不断制定与完善之中，例如，2012 年新股发行制度和退市制度的改革就成为了多层次资本市场制度建设中的重要一环。

2012 年 3 月，中国证监会就新股发行体制改革方案征求意见。4 月 28 日，证监会正式颁布《关于进一步深化新股发行体制改革的指导意见》，重申新股发行体制改革将坚持市场化方向，以充分、完整、准确的信息披露为中心改进发行审核，并提出六点针对性意见。5 月 18 日，证监会对《证券发行与承销管理办法》进行了相应修改。5 月 23 日，证监会发行监管部、创业板发行监管部下发了《关于新股发行定价相关问题的通知》，对新股发行定价的相关事项进行了明确。6 月 28 日，沪、深交易所分别发布《关于完善上海证券交易所上市公司退市制度的方案》、《关于改进和完善深圳证券交易所主板、中小企业板上市公司退市制度的方案》，并根据方案修订相应的《股票上市规则》。

新股发行中的各种弊端一直是我国资本市场的痼疾，本次新股发行制度改革中首次提出了"老股转让"改革，即所谓存量发行，颇受市场关注。而退市制度则是资本市场一项基础性制度，只有实施有效的退市机制，才能真正促进证券市场中资源的合理有效配置，推动结构调整和产业升级，促进多层次资本市场的建设。在 2013 年的全国证券期货监管工作会议上，时任证监会主席郭树清指出，要"进一步深化发行和退市制度改革。落实以信息披露为中心的审核理念，修订完善首次公开发行股票管理办法等规则制度。继续完善新股定价机制，推动市场相关各方归位尽责，强化对中介机构的监管。开展对首发在审公司财务专项检查工作，推动中介机构切实履职尽责。坚决打击粉饰业绩、包装上市、虚假披露等行为，依法严惩虚假记载、误导性陈述和重大遗漏以及帮助发行人过度包装、合谋造假等违法违规行为。积极稳妥落实新的退市制度改革措施，不断完善相关配套制度规则和市场化机制，实现退市的常态化"。

（三）相关政策建议

基于我们的观察与分析，这里对中国多层次资本市场建设和完善提出对应建议，主要包括三个层面：市场发展、监管制度和法制完善。

1. 在市场发展层面上：减少行政干预、提升市场效率

从国际经验来看，政府对于场外市场一般不进行直接的行政干预，而是通过制定规则或采取其他非直接的手段来进行管理，如果对于场外市场施加过多的行政干预，不仅会带来市场交易成本的提升和监管资源的浪费，而且会使广大中小企业增加融资成本、降低效率。而且，场外市场主要是面对具有一定风险投资偏好和风险承受能力的成熟投资者，亦不需要行政监管给予其过高的保护。多年来，我们对于场外市场的管理多是采取"一刀切"的行政干预做法，出了问题即清理整顿，甚至关门停业，这种做法既破坏了市场发展的自然规律，也抑制了市场创新的动力和资源配置的有效性。因此，我国场外市场的发展重点应在于培育和完善市场机制，提升市场资源配置效率，尊重市场主体的意思自治，构建市场化的管理机制。

在这个大思路下，当前我们有两方面制度需要完善。

其一，证券发行监管的趋势是注册制。虽然核准制有助于防止劣质证券的发行，有利于新兴市场的健康发展，但随着我国证券市场的深入发展，发行监管转向注册制，由市场而不是政府决定新股发行的呼声越来越高。当前，我国区域性的股权交易中心如上海股权交易中心等在发行监管上已经实现了注册制的改革，但对于新三板而言，其挂牌和融资的审核形式上仍然是中国证监会的一项行政许可，仍需证监会出具批文。可见，我国目前的证券发行监管机制仍以核准制为主，中国证监会拥有实质上的审核权。事实上，当前我国场外市场与主板市场之间对接不畅的内在原因就在于发行监管制度方面的障碍和矛盾，这也就是转板机制当前应如何完善的核心问题。

其二，关于"转板机制"。如前所述，我国的企业首次公开发行股票仍需证监会进行实质审核，而在新三板挂牌企业为非公众公司，其要实现转板则必须先经过发审委审核成为公众公司，才能进入主板市场或创业板市场。由此可见，目前我国多层次资本市场的转板制度仍存在着较大的局限和不足，缺乏真正有效便利的转板制度安排。针对目前的情况，首先我们应该进一步加强当前的退市制度改革，提高退市制度的完备性和可操作性，健全"程序性退市"的各项机制，关键是要在制度完善的基础上加大执行力度。在中国，之前就是由于缺乏程序性自动退市，使得退市操作中有较大的机构博弈空间，由此产生的壳资源溢价使上市公司的股价很难低于净值，因而很难产生因资产价值高于市值所驱动的主动退市，这就造成了中国证券市场的低淘汰率和高新增率。其次，我们要加快真正转板制度的设计步伐，在实现发行监管由核准制向注册制转变的大背景下，一方面要建立全国性场外市场与区域性场外市场之间的转板机制，另一方面要建立

场外市场与场内市场之间的交易机制。

2. 在监管制度层面上：完善监管制度，注重风险防范

第一，要建立集中与自律相结合的监管模式。我国的场外交易市场长期以来未被纳入国家监管体系，在监管架构上也较为混乱，当前主板市场、创业板市场和新三板市场由中国证监会监管，而各地产权交易所和股权交易中心大多由地方政府支持组建，依附于各地的金融办或国资委，尚未被纳入证监会的监管范围之中。因此，为了确保多层次资本市场体系的有效运行，必须建立起一个高效率、低成本的市场监管体系，并遵循中国证监会的集中监管与行业组织和场外交易所自律监管相结合的原则。

第二，要完善做市商制度。在具有竞争性和强制性的双向公开报价制度之下，做市商可以凭借信息、资金、人才等优势，以及对上市公司价值、市场走势的评估和判断，为公司股票买卖提供双向报价并进行买卖。2013年1月18日，中国证监会公布了《全国中小企业股份转让系统有限责任公司管理暂行办法》，明确新三板市场将引进做市商制度，这在交易机制上是一个重大的突破。做市商制度的建立在提升市场流动性，有效实现价格发现，充分调动券商的积极性和稳定市场等方面都具有重要意义。

第三，要加强信息披露。信息披露是证券市场监管的有效手段，也是最经济的监管方式。场外市场与主板市场在功能定位和市场运作方面有所不同，那么在信息披露制度方面也应有所区别，应简化信息披露格式，降低信息披露成本，如对于场外市场中的挂牌公司可规定其只需披露年报和半年报，但披露的重点应在于公司的财务状况和管理层的业绩分析预期，同时要更加强调信息披露的准确性和真实性，防止内幕交易和公司欺诈行为的发生。需要补充的是，应当明确挂牌公司以及主办券商、律师事务所、会计师事务所等为挂牌转让等相关业务提供服务的证券服务机构和人员的法律责任。

第四，要建立一个高效、统一的清算结算系统。目前，我国资本市场中各板块市场的清算结算制度和系统均不统一。上交所和深交所与中登公司进行结算，新三板市场也是与中登公司进行结算，但其他的场外交易市场如上海股权托管交易中心、天津股权交易所等均是由自己建立的专门的登记托管清算系统来完成结算任务的。当前，"集中清算（即统一结算清算）"是国际市场发展的趋势，次贷危机引发场外信用掉期违约后，美国等海外市场都在向"场外交易场内结算"的方向走，让场内清算所对场外交易进行统一结算。美国OTC市场与期货市场的结合点主要在统一清算环节。[1] 我们理应顺应国际潮流，整合现有的结算平台资源，加快建立我国场外交易市场统一结算机构和结算制度体系的步伐，切实做到控制风险、节约成本、提升效率。

3. 在法制完善层面上：完善法律体系，加大制裁力度

首先是要完善法律制度体系。法律体系在投资者保护方面是至关重要的，法律体系

---

① 巢新蕊：《交易所整顿收尾　商品场外市场将统一结算清算》，载《经济观察报》，2013 - 01 - 11。

的差异是投资者保护水平差异的最重要因素。在当前的改革中，一方面，我们要通过对《证券法》的修订，明确场外交易市场的法律地位，用一般性的条款对场外交易市场和场外交易行为作出总则性的规定，使其名正言顺，有法可依；另一方面，我们要进一步完善《证券法》中关于虚假陈述、内幕交易和操纵市场等行为的民事责任立法，观察《证券法》的条文，行政责任与刑事责任占据了主导地位，而对于投资者损害赔偿的民事责任制度则规定得过于原则化，缺乏可操作性。最高法院仅在 2003 年出台了《关于审理证券市场因虚假陈述引发的民事赔偿案件的若干规定》，但在内幕交易和操纵市场的民事赔偿方面却缺乏明确的司法解释。因此，我们需要不断完善资本市场的民事责任立法，赋予投资者相应的民事诉权，在受理与管辖、诉讼方式、归责原则、损失认定等方面作出具体的、具有可操作性的法律规定或司法解释。

其次在司法上应加强法律制裁力度。第一，需要完善我国当前的代表人诉讼制度的缺陷，明确诉讼代表人选定的具体程序和方法，吸收美国集团诉讼制度的优势，采取"明示退出、默示加入"的规则，把法院公告期内未选择自动退出集团诉讼的人自动视为集团诉讼的成员，即诉讼判决对那些没有进行权利登记的人仍为有效；第二，建议取消当前证券市场民事赔偿纠纷案件的诉讼前置程序，维护投资者应有的诉讼权利，减少其诉讼难度，保护投资者的基本权益；第三，实行证券诉讼原告举证责任倒置制度，强化上市公司和控股股东以及券商和其他证券服务机构的举证责任，使其在实施侵权行为时，考虑其行为的危害性和法律责任的严重性，这也是维护资本市场投资者根本权益，维护市场秩序的体现和需要。

参考文献

［1］阙紫康：《多层次资本市场发展的理论与经验》，上海，上海交通大学出版社，2007。

［2］徐洪才：《中国多层次资本市场体系与监管研究》，北京，经济管理出版社，2009。

［3］王国刚主编：《建立多层次资本市场体系研究》，北京，人民出版社，2006。

［4］中国三板市场发展历程，http：//wenku. baidu. com/view/a976f74333687e21af45a938. html。

［5］白冰、逯云娇：《中国场外市场发展研究——基于国内外场外交易市场的比较分析》，载《经济问题探索》，2012（4）。

［6］李凤雨：《我国证券市场信息披露的现状、问题与对策》，载《金融发展研究》，2012（10）。

［7］我国证券发行审核制度变革回顾［OL］，中顾法律网，http：//www. 9ask. cn/。

［8］浅议证券发行保荐人制度［OL］，中顾法律网，http：//www. 9ask. cn/。

［9］胡海峰：《多层次资本市场：从自发演进到政府制度设计》，北京，北京师范大学出版社，2010。

［10］顾功耘主编：《场外交易市场法律制度构建》，北京，北京大学出版社，2011。

下　篇

2012年度中国金融政策动态

宏观金融政策

一、货币政策

（一）2012年主要货币政策一览

2012 年，中国人民银行继续实施稳健的货币政策，着力增强政策的灵活性、针对性和前瞻性，根据经济形势变化，适时适度加大预调微调力度。全年制定和颁布的主要货币政策如表 5 – 1 所示。

表 5 – 1　　　　　　　　　　2012 年中国人民银行相关货币政策操作汇总表

时间	政策
2 月 18 日	中国人民银行决定从 2012 年 2 月 24 日起下调存款类金融机构人民币存款准备金率 0.5 个百分点
5 月 12 日	中国人民银行决定从 2012 年 5 月 18 日起下调存款类金融机构人民币存款准备金率 0.5 个百分点
6 月 7 日	中国人民银行决定自 2012 年 6 月 8 日起下调金融机构人民币存贷款基准利率，一年期存款基准利率由 3.5% 下调到 3.25%；一年期贷款基准利率由 6.56% 下调到 6.31%。同时，调整金融机构存贷款利率浮动区间：将存款利率浮动区间的上限调整为基准利率的 1.1 倍；将贷款利率浮动区间的下限调整为基准利率的 0.8 倍
7 月 5 日	中国人民银行决定自 2012 年 7 月 6 日起下调金融机构人民币存贷款基准利率。其中，金融机构一年期存款基准利率由 3.25% 下调到 3%；一年期贷款基准利率由 6.31% 下调到 6%。同时，将金融机构贷款利率浮动区间的下限调整为基准利率的 0.7 倍

资料来源：中国人民银行。

（二）2012年主要货币政策分析

1. 2012 年主要货币政策制定的背景及程序

2012 年，随着国际收支和人民币汇率逐渐趋向合理均衡，加之欧洲主权债务危机引发国际金融市场动荡，外汇流入减少，外汇占款比上年少增超过 2 万亿元，银行体系流动性供给格局发生较大变化，根据流动性供需形势的变化，中国人民银行于 2012 年 2 月 24 日和 5 月 18 日两次下调存款准备金率各 0.5 个百分点，保持银行体系流动性合理充裕。与两次下调存款准备金率政策相配合，中国人民银行全年累计开展正回购操作 9 440 亿元，开展逆回购操作 60 380 亿元；截至 2012 年末，公开市场逆回购操作余额为 4 980 亿元。针对经济增速有所放缓、物价涨幅趋于回落等情况，中国人民银行分别于 6 月 8 日、7 月 6 日两次下调金融机构人民币存贷款基准利率。其中，1 年期存款基准利率由 3.5% 下降到 3%，累计下调 0.5 个百分点；1 年期贷款基准利率由 6.56% 下降到 6%，累计下调 0.56 个百分点。同时，把利率调整与利率市场化改革相结合，调整金融机构存贷款利率浮动区间：一是将金融机构存款利率浮动区间的上限调整为基准利率的 1.1 倍；二是将金融机构贷款利率浮动区间的下限调整为基准利率的 0.7 倍。上述措施有利于引导资金价格下行，为进一步降低企业融资成本创造了更加有利的政策环境。金融机构自主定价空间进一步扩大，有利于促进其不断通过提高金融服务水平参与市场竞争。存贷款基准利率和利率浮动区间调整后，金融机构对企业贷款利率水平总体逐月降低。[①]

2. 2012 年主要货币政策执行情况

2012 年，中国经济平稳较快增长，金融运行总体平稳。全年实现国内生产总值（GDP）51.9 万亿元，同比增长 7.8%；居民消费价格同比上涨 2.6%，经常项目顺差占 GDP 的比重降至 2.6%。

2012 年末，广义货币供应量 M_2 余额为 97.4 万亿元，同比增长 13.8%，增速比上年末提高 0.2 个百分点。狭义货币供应量 M_1 余额为 30.9 万亿元，同比增长 6.5%。流通中货币 M_0 余额为 5.5 万亿元，同比增长 7.7%。全年现金净投放 3 910 亿元，同比少投放 2 251 亿元。2012 年末，基础货币余额为 25.2 万亿元，同比增长 12.3%，比年初增加 2.8 万亿元。货币乘数为 3.86，比上年末高 0.07。金融机构超额准备金率为 3.3%，比上年末高 1.0 个百分点；其中，农村信用社为 8.2%，比上年末高 0.9 个百分点。[②]

2012 年末，全部金融机构（含外资金融机构）本外币各项存款余额为 94.3 万亿元，同比增长 14.1%，增速比上年末高 0.6 个百分点。人民币各项存款余额为 91.7 万亿元，同比增长 13.3%，增速比上年末略低 0.2 个百分点。外币存款余额为 4 065 亿美元，同比增长 47.8%。从人民币存款部门分布看，住户存款平稳增长，非金融企业存款增速稳步回升。年末，金融机构住户存款余额为 40.6 万亿元，同比增长 16.7%，增速比上年末高 1.0 个百分点。非金融企业人民币存款余额为 32.7 万亿元，同比增长 7.9%。年末，财政存款余额为 2.4 万亿元，比年初减少 1 974 亿元。[③]

2012 年末，全部金融机构本外币贷款余额为 67.3 万亿元，同比增长 15.6%，增速比上年末略低 0.1 个百分点。人民币贷款余额为 63.0 万亿元，同比增长 15.0%，全年增速波动幅度明显低于前两年，比年初增加 8.2 万亿元，同比多增 7 320 亿元。从人民币贷款部门分布看，住户贷款增速企稳回升，年末同比增长 18.6%。非金融企业及其他部门贷款保持较快增长，年末同比增速为 13.7%。分机构看，中资全国性大型银行、区域性中小型银行与农村合作金融机构贷款同比多增较多。从期限看，中长期贷款占比回

① 中国人民银行货币政策分析小组：《中国货币政策执行报告：2012 年第四季度》，2013 年 2 月 6 日。
② 中国人民银行货币政策分析小组：《中国货币政策执行报告：2012 年第四季度》，2013 年 2 月 6 日。
③ 中国人民银行货币政策分析小组：《中国货币政策执行报告：2012 年第四季度》，2013 年 2 月 6 日。

升。在投资回升带动下，建设项目的信贷支持力度逐步加大。年末中长期贷款增长9.0%，其增速自2012年4月以来一直稳定于9%左右，呈平稳增长态势，比年初新增2.9万亿元，在全部贷款中占比为35%，比年内最低点回升2.7个百分点。年末个人住房贷款同比增速为12.9%。金融机构外币贷款余额为6 836亿美元，同比增长26.9%，比年初增加1 451亿美元，同比多增569亿美元。从投向看，对进出口贸易和"走出去"的支持力度较大。其中，进出口贸易融资增加924亿美元，同比多增649亿美元；境外贷款与境内中长期贷款增加517亿美元，同比多增111亿美元。①

2012年全年社会融资规模为15.76万亿元，为历史最高水平，比上年多2.93万亿元，主要是由于信托贷款、企业债券、人民币贷款和外币贷款融资较为活跃，这四类融资合计为12.66万亿元，比上年多3.05万亿元。从构成看，人民币贷款增加较多，但占比下降至历史最低水平；外币贷款新增额明显多于上年；企业债券融资十分活跃，直接融资占比创历史最高水平；信托贷款同比大幅多增。②

2012年6月和7月，中国人民银行连续两次下调存贷款基准利率，并小幅扩大利率浮动区间，金融机构贷款利率进一步下降，并于年末趋于稳定。12月，贷款加权平均利率为6.78%。其中，一般贷款加权平均利率为7.07%；票据融资加权平均利率为5.64%。个人住房贷款利率稳步下行，12月加权平均利率为6.22%。③

2012年，人民币小幅升值，人民币汇率预期总体平稳。2012年末，人民币对美元汇率中间价为6.2855元，比上年末升值154个基点，升值幅度为0.25%。根据国际清算银行的计算，2012年，人民币名义有效汇率升值1.73%，实际有效汇率升值2.22%；2005年人民币汇率形成机制改革以来至2012年12月，人民币名义有效汇率升值23.25%，实际有效汇率升值31.86%。④

（三）政策评价与展望

展望未来一段时期，全球经济有可能继续缓慢复苏，美国已经历一段持续的去杠杆过程，欧洲央行的流动性支持计划也对稳定市场起到了积极作用，从而形成一个总体较为疲弱但相对稳定的外部环境。但是，部分经济体债务负担沉重，"紧财政、宽货币"或成主要发达经济体长期政策选择，加之贸易投资保护主义抬头，新兴经济体面临来自贸易、金融等多方面的挑战。从国内情况看，中国经济有望继续保持平稳较快发展的基本态势。2012年城镇居民人均可支配收入和农村居民人均纯收入实际增速均超过GDP增速。随着收入分配改革推进，消费在拉动经济增长中的作用会趋于增大。此外，中国经济已经历了一段去库存过程，工业生产对需求回升和预期变化更为敏感，也有利于经

---

① 中国人民银行货币政策分析小组：《中国货币政策执行报告：2012年第四季度》，2013年2月6日。
② 中国人民银行货币政策分析小组：《中国货币政策执行报告：2012年第四季度》，2013年2月6日。
③ 中国人民银行货币政策分析小组：《中国货币政策执行报告：2012年第四季度》，2013年2月6日。
④ 中国人民银行货币政策分析小组：《中国货币政策执行报告：2012年第四季度》，2013年2月6日。

济稳定增长。但是，经济企稳的基础还不够稳固，结构不平衡问题仍比较突出，资源环境约束也在明显增强。经济中仍存在多方面导致物价上行的因素。一是劳动年龄人口增长逐步趋缓，劳动密集产品的价格可能会经历一个趋势性上升的过程，同时资源性产品价格也有待逐步理顺。二是全球宽松的货币环境可能延续，输入性通胀压力需关注。[①]

2013 年，中国人民银行将继续实施稳健的货币政策，保持政策的连续性和稳定性，增强调控的针对性、灵活性和前瞻性，适时适度进行预调微调，提高金融服务实体经济的水平，有效防范系统性金融风险，保持金融体系稳定，促进物价总水平基本稳定和经济平稳较快发展。

二、汇率与国际收支相关政策

（一）2012 年主要汇率及国际收支政策一览

2012 年，中国加快转变经济发展方式，外贸、外资和外汇领域的政策调整取得成效，国际收支状况进一步趋向平衡。主要措施包括：

表 5 - 2　　　　　　　　　2012 年主要汇率政策和国际收支政策汇总

时间	政策
1 月 17 日	中国人民银行与阿联酋中央银行签署规模为 350 亿元人民币/200 亿迪拉姆的双边本币互换协议，有效期 3 年，经双方同意可以展期
2 月 3 日	中国人民银行、财政部、商务部、海关总署、国家税务总局和银监会联合发布《关于出口货物贸易人民币结算企业管理有关问题的通知》（银发〔2012〕23 号），明确参与出口货物贸易人民币结算的主体不再限于列入试点名单的企业，对出口货物贸易人民币结算企业实行重点监管名单管理
2 月 8 日	中国人民银行与马来西亚国家银行续签双边本币互换协议，互换规模由原来的 800 亿元人民币/400 亿林吉特扩大至 1 800 亿元人民币/900 亿林吉特，有效期 3 年，经双方同意可以展期
2 月 21 日	中国人民银行与土耳其中央银行签署规模为 100 亿元人民币/30 亿土耳其里拉的双边本币互换协议，有效期 3 年，经双方同意可以展期
3 月 20 日	中国人民银行与蒙古银行签署中蒙双边本币互换补充协议，互换规模由原来的 50 亿元人民币/1 万亿图格里特扩大至 100 亿元人民币/2 万亿图格里特
3 月 22 日	中国人民银行与澳大利亚储备银行签署规模为 2 000 亿元人民币/300 亿澳大利亚元的双边本币互换协议，有效期 3 年，经双方同意可以展期
4 月 14 日	为促进外汇市场发展，增强人民币汇率双向浮动弹性，中国人民银行发布《中国人民银行公告》〔2012〕第 4 号，决定自 2012 年 4 月 16 日起将银行间即期外汇市场人民币兑美元交易价浮动幅度由千分之五扩大至百分之一
6 月 26 日	中国人民银行与乌克兰国家银行签署金额为 150 亿元人民币/190 亿格里夫纳的双边本币互换协议，有效期为 3 年，经双方同意可以展期
7 月 26 日	为加强境外机构人民币银行结算账户管理，促进贸易投资便利化，中国人民银行发布《关于境外机构人民币银行结算账户开立和使用有关问题的通知》（银发〔2012〕183 号）
8 月 31 日	两岸货币管理机构签署《海峡两岸货币清算合作备忘录》。双方同意以备忘录确定的原则和合作架构建立两岸货币清算机制
9 月 24 日	中国人民银行与中国银行澳门分行续签《关于人民币业务的清算协议》
12 月 11 日	根据《海峡两岸货币清算合作备忘录》相关内容，经过评审，中国人民银行决定授权中国银行台北分行担任台湾人民币业务清算行（中国人民银行公告〔2012〕第 18 号）

资料来源：国家外汇管理局。

[①] 中国人民银行货币政策分析小组：《中国货币政策执行报告：2012 年第四季度》，2013 年 2 月 6 日。

（二）2012 年主要汇率政策及国际收支相关政策分析

1. 2012 年汇率及国际收支政策制定的背景和程序

2012 年，在宽流动性、低利率环境下，全球经济增长放缓，国际金融持续动荡。上半年全球经济增长普遍放慢，下半年新兴经济体经济状况有所改善，全球经济出现触底企稳迹象。外需疲弱对我国出口产生了一定影响。欧美主权债务危机的演变更加复杂，金融市场避险情绪交替变化。第一季度，欧债危机暂告缓解，但自 3 月下旬起，欧债危机再次恶化，新兴经济体普遍出现资本外流。9 月以来，欧央行宣布直接货币交易（OMT）计划、美联储启动第三轮和第四轮量化宽松货币政策等措施稳定了金融市场，新兴经济体资本回流压力逐渐增加。2012 年，中国经济平稳较快增长，金融运行总体平稳，全年实现国内生产总值（GDP）51.9 万亿元，同比增长 7.8%，第四季度国内生产总值同比增长 7.9%，结束了此前连续 7 个季度的增速回落态势，最终消费和投资对经济增长的贡献率分别达 51.8% 和 50.4%，经济增长的内生性、自主性进一步增强。居民消费价格同比上涨 2.6%，经常项目顺差占 GDP 的比重降至 2.6%。[1]

为进一步完善人民币汇率形成机制，增强人民币汇率弹性，自 2012 年 4 月 16 日起，中国人民银行将银行间即期外汇市场人民币兑美元交易价浮动幅度由千分之五扩大至百分之一。中国人民银行继续采取措施推动人民币对新兴市场货币直接交易市场的发展，并在银行间外汇市场推出人民币对日元直接交易。

2. 汇率及国际收支政策执行情况

2012 年末，人民币对美元汇率中间价为 6.2855 元/美元，较 2011 年末升值 0.2%，2005 年人民币汇率形成机制改革以来累计升值 31.7%。2012 年，人民币对美元汇率中间价最高为 6.3495 元，最低为 6.2670 元，243 个交易日中 122 个交易日升值、121 个交易日贬值。最大单日升值幅度为 0.26%（162 点），最大单日贬值幅度为 0.33%（209点）。2012 年末，人民币对欧元、日元汇率中间价分别为 1 欧元兑 8.3176 元人民币、100 日元兑 7.3049 元人民币，分别较 2011 年末贬值 1.86% 和升值 11.03%。2005 年人民币汇率形成机制改革以来至 2012 年末，人民币对欧元汇率累计升值 20.40%，对日元汇率累计升值 0.01%。根据国际清算银行的数据，2012 年人民币对一篮子货币的名义有效汇率升值 1.7%，扣除通货膨胀因素的实际有效汇率升值 2.2%；在国际清算银行监测的 61 个经济体货币中，升值幅度分别居第 20 位和第 18 位。2005 年人民币汇率形成机制改革以来，人民币名义和实际有效汇率累计分别升值 23.3% 和 31.9%，在上述61 个经济体货币中，升值幅度分别居第 4 位和第 3 位。[2]

2012 年，经常项目顺差 1 931 亿美元，较 2011 年增长 42%；资本和金融项目逆差

---

① 国家外汇管理局国际收支分析小组：《2012 年中国国际收支报告》，2013 年 4 月 3 日。
② 国家外汇管理局国际收支分析小组：《2012 年中国国际收支报告》，2013 年 4 月 3 日。

168 亿美元，为亚洲金融危机以来首次逆差，上年为顺差 2 655 亿美元；国际收支总顺差 1 763 亿美元，下降 56%，大大低于 2007—2011 年年均顺差 4 552 亿美元的规模。国际收支总顺差 1 763 亿美元，回落至 2004 年的顺差水平，较 2011 年下降 56%。经常项目顺差与 GDP 之比为 2.3%，仍保持在国际认可的合理范围之内。储备资产增幅明显放缓，与 GDP 之比为 1.2%，较 2011 年下降 4.1 个百分点。2012 年，我国国际收支从 1999 年以来的持续"双顺差"转为"经常项目顺差、资本和金融项目逆差"，显示我国国际收支逐渐趋向自主调节、自我平衡。但这与市场主体根据境内外利差、汇差等市场环境变化调整财务运作，由以往的"资产本币化、负债外币化"转向"资产外币化、负债本币化"的顺周期变化密切相关，国际收支自我平衡的基础还不牢固。2012 年，国际收支交易总规模为 7.5 万亿美元，较 2011 年增长 6%；与同期 GDP 之比为 91%，较 2011 年略降 6 个百分点。其中，国际收支口径的货物和服务贸易总规模较 2011 年增长 7%，跨国直接投资（包括外国来华直接投资和我国对外直接投资）交易总规模减少 2%。[1]

2012 年，银行累计办理跨境贸易人民币结算业务 2.94 万亿元，同比增长 41%，其中货物贸易结算金额 2.06 万亿元，服务贸易及其他经常项目结算金额 8 764.5 亿元。全年跨境贸易人民币结算实收 1.30 万亿元，实付 1.57 万亿元，净流出 2 691.7 亿元，收付比由 2011 年的 1:1.7 上升至 1:1.2。2012 年银行累计办理人民币跨境直接投资结算业务 2 840.2 亿元，其中对外直接投资结算金额 304.4 亿元，外商直接投资结算金额 2 535.8 亿元。截至 2012 年末，境内代理银行为境外参加银行共开立人民币同业往来账户 1 592 个，账户余额 2 852.0 亿元；境外企业在境内共开立人民币结算账户 6 197 个，账户余额 500.2 亿元。[2]

（三）政策评价与展望

展望国内外形势，2013 年，国内外经济和金融运行企稳，世界经济进入深度转型调整期，中国国际收支仍有望保持基本平衡，但顺差规模可能有所增加，"促平衡"任务依然艰巨。下一阶段，外汇管理部门将按照党中央、国务院的统一部署，全面深化外汇管理体制改革，推进主体监管和服务贸易外汇管理改革，大力促进资本项目外汇管理便利化；加强外汇宏观总量分析和区域分析，突出重点主体的监测分析，提升外汇监测分析能力和水平；管好用好外汇储备，进一步完善大规模外汇储备经营管理体制；坚守风险底线，不断完善跨境资金流动监管体系，充实和完善政策预案，防范跨境资本双向流动冲击。[3]

---

[1] 国家外汇管理局国际收支分析小组：《2012 年中国国际收支报告》，2013 年 4 月 3 日。
[2] 国家外汇管理局国际收支分析小组：《2012 年中国国际收支报告》，2013 年 4 月 3 日。
[3] 国家外汇管理局国际收支分析小组：《2012 年中国国际收支报告》，2013 年 4 月 3 日。

主要金融市场发展政策

一、银行业市场发展政策

（一）2012 年银行业市场主要发展政策一览

2012 年，面对全球经济增长乏力和国内经济稳中有进的新形势，中国政府加快转变经济发展方式和调整经济结构，继续实施积极的财政政策和稳健的货币政策，不断增强政策的前瞻性、针对性和灵活性，进一步坚持房地产市场调控政策，深入推进地方融资平台规范管理，商业银行整体运行平稳。根据银监会发布的数据，截至 2012 年底，我国银行业金融机构资产总额为 133.6 万亿元，同比增长 17.9%；负债总额为 125.0 万亿元，同比增长 17.8%；净利润为 1.24 万亿元，同比增长 19%；整体加权平均资本充足率为 13.25%，同比上升 0.54 个百分点；不良贷款余额为 1.07 万亿元，比年初增加 234 亿元，不良贷款率 1.56%，同比下降 0.22 个百分点。

表 6-1　　　　　　　2012 年对银行业发展产生影响的主要政策列表

政策及主要内容	颁布机构
先后 2 次下调存款准备金率	中国人民银行
2 次上调存贷款基准利率	中国人民银行
扩大存贷款利率浮动区间	中国人民银行
关于进一步加强预付卡业务管理的通知	中国人民银行
《支付机构预付卡业务管理办法》	中国人民银行
《中国银行间市场债券回购交易主协议》	中国人民银行
《关于进一步扩大信贷资产证券化试点有关事项的通知》	中国人民银行等
《国务院关于进一步支持小型微型企业健康发展的意见》	国务院
《关于农村中小金融机构实施富民惠农金融创新工程的指导意见》	银监会
《关于农村中小金融机构实施金融服务进村入社区工程的指导意见》	银监会
《关于农村中小金融机构实施阳光信贷工程的指导意见》	银监会
《农户贷款管理办法》	银监会
《关于印发绿色信贷指引的通知》	银监会
《关于整治银行业金融机构不规范经营的通知》	银监会
《新资本充足率管理办法》	银监会
《资本工具创新指导意见》（征求意见稿）	银监会
《商业银行实施资本管理高级方法监管暂行细则》	银监会

资料来源：课题组整理。

表 6-2　　　　　　　　　2012 年银行业金融机构发展主要情况

主要指标	2010 年	2011 年	2012 年
总资产（亿元）	94.26 万	111.5 万	133.6 万
总负债（亿元）	88.43 万	104.3 万	125.0 万
净利润（亿元）	7 637	10 412	12 386
资产利润率（%）	1.10	1.30	1.28
资本利润率（%）	19.20	20.40	19.85
净息差（%）	2.50	2.70	2.75
非利息收入占比（%）	17.50	19.30	19.83
成本收入比（%）	35.30	33.40	33.10
核心资本（亿元）	42 985	53 367	64 340
附属资本（亿元）	10 295	14 418	17 585
资本充足率（%）	12.20	12.70	13.25
核心资本充足率（%）	10.10	10.20	10.62
流动性比例（%）	42.20	43.20	45.83
存贷比（%）	64.50	64.90	65.31
人民币超额备付金率（%）	3.20	3.10	3.51
不良贷款余额（亿元）	4 336	4 279	4 929
不良贷款率（%）	1.10	1.00	0.95
贷款损失准备（亿元）	9 438	11 898	14 564
拨备覆盖率（%）	217.70	278.10	295.51

资料来源：课题组整理。

（二）2012 年银行业市场主要发展政策分析

2012 年，在国内经济金融政策的推动下，我国银行业整体呈现稳健发展的态势，商业银行资产负债规模持续增长，净息差有所收窄，利润增速回落，业务创新持续推进，小微企业、涉农金融、绿色信贷等业务发展不断强化，实现了业务的平稳运行。

1. 两次下调存款准备金率，商业银行存贷款平稳增长

2012 年上半年，国内经济下行压力增大，实体经济贷款需求不足，中国人民银行在继续坚持稳健货币政策基础上，前瞻性地加强了政策预调微调。2 月和 5 月，中国人民银行两次下调存款类金融机构人民币存款准备金率各 0.5 个百分点，调整后中国大型金融机构和中小金融机构存款准备金率分别为 20% 和 18%，促进商业银行存贷款平稳适度增长。

两次下降存款准备金率主要原因是为了应对经济增长疲软，以刺激经济复苏。由于上半年国内经济数据低于市场预期，实体经济信贷需求下滑明显，下调存款准备金率将进一步推升货币乘数，拉动货币供应增长，提高银行放贷能力。同时，两次下调存款准备金率强化了流动性放松预期，有助于增强市场对经济复苏的信心，刺激实体经济信贷

需求回升，促进存贷款平稳增长。

在政策推动下，中国经济在第三季度开始温和复苏，信贷需求逐步增强，全年商业银行存贷款实现平稳增长。截至2012年末，全部金融机构（含外资金融机构，下同）本外币贷款余额为67.3万亿元，比年初增加9.1万亿元，同比多增1.2万亿元，同比增长15.6%，增速比上年略低0.1个百分点。其中，人民币贷款余额为63万亿元，比年初增加8.2万亿元，同比多增7 320亿元。2012年末，全部金融机构（含外资金融机构，下同）本外币各项存款余额为94.3万亿元，同比增长14.1%，增速比上年末高0.6个百分点，比年初增加11.6万亿元，同比多增1.8万亿元。其中，人民币各项存款余额为91.7万亿元，同比增长13.3%，增速比上年末略低0.2个百分点，比年初增加10.8万亿元，同比多增1.2万亿元。

2. 两次下调基准利率，商业银行贷款利率总体下行

2012年6月和7月，中国人民银行连续两次下调存贷款基准利率，金融机构1年期存款基准利率较年初共下降0.50个百分点，1年期贷款基准利率较年初共下降0.56个百分点；其他各档次存贷款基准利率及个人住房公积金存贷款利率也做了相应调整。

中国人民银行在两个月内连续两次下调存贷款基准利率主要有以下几方面原因：一是经济增长压力较大，需要通过降低利率来减少企业融资成本，从而刺激经济。二是国内通货膨胀大幅走低，CPI数据落至3%以下，为降息腾挪出政策空间。受贷款基准利率下调影响，商业银行贷款加权平均利率平稳下行。12月，贷款加权平均利率为6.78%，比年初下降1.23个百分点。其中，一般贷款加权平均利率为7.07%，比年初下降0.73个百分点；票据融资加权平均利率为5.64%，比年初下降3.42个百分点。

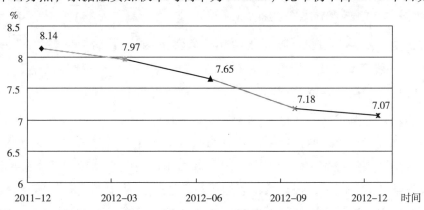

资料来源：2012年货币政策执行报告。

图6-1 2012年商业银行一般贷款加权平均利率走势

3. 利率市场改革提速，商业银行净息差并未明显下降

2012年，中国人民银行加快推进利率市场化改革，两次小幅扩大了存款利率浮动区间。6月，中国人民银行将存款利率浮动上限调整为基准利率的1.1倍，贷款利率下浮

下限降至基准利率的 0.8 倍；7 月，中国人民银行再次将贷款利率浮动下限进一步下调为基准利率的 0.7 倍，存款利率浮动上限仍保持为基准利率的 1.1 倍。

在存款利率上浮空间扩大之后，由于竞争压力和客户结构等因素不同，各商业银行存款定价存在较大差别。工商银行、建设银行、农业银行、中国银行、交通银行五大商业银行基本保持基准利率不变，多数股份制银行根据客户等级和存款规模等因素，选择性地将存款利率上浮 10%，城市商业银行则基本上都将存款利率上浮 10%。

表 6-3　　　　　　　2012 年 1—12 月金融机构人民币贷款各利率区间占比　　　　单位：%

月份	下浮	基准	上浮					
	(0.9, 1.0)	1.0	小计	(1.0, 1.1)	(1.1, 1.3)	(1.3, 1.5)	(1.5, 2.0)	2.0 以上
1	4.79	26.22	69.00	22.33	25.51	8.76	9.22	3.17
2	5.53	27.59	66.88	23.12	23.76	7.98	8.61	3.40
3	4.62	24.95	70.43	21.12	26.99	9.48	9.41	3.43
4	5.03	23.06	71.91	20.76	28.92	10.10	8.98	3.16
5	5.35	24.08	70.57	20.51	28.90	9.73	8.31	3.12
6	7.92	25.08	66.99	19.94	27.87	8.90	7.66	2.63
7	9.51	24.38	66.11	19.74	26.78	9.13	7.61	2.85
8	11.61	22.66	65.73	19.64	26.45	8.30	8.33	3.01
9	11.31	24.57	64.12	20.16	25.18	8.13	7.67	2.98
10	10.88	26.80	62.32	20.15	24.30	7.28	7.53	3.06
11	11.70	25.74	62.56	19.43	24.52	7.64	7.71	3.26
12	14.16	26.10	59.74	18.41	22.87	7.58	7.84	3.04

资料来源：2012 年第四季度货币政策执行报告。

同时，受贷款利率浮动下限变化影响，金融机构执行下浮利率的贷款占比有所上升。12 月，一般贷款中执行下浮利率的贷款占比为 14.16%，比年初上升 7.14 个百分点，这主要是由于社会融资总额不断增大以及直接融资和表外融资比例持续提升，导致商业银行在大、中型企业的议价能力有所下滑所致。从短期看，利率市场化对商业银行贷款利率影响有限：一方面，在经济下行期商业银行存在惜贷情绪，贷款重新定价也要到明年第一季度逐步完成。另一方面，由于银行在社会融资结构中占重要地位，在贷款资源仍较为稀缺的情况下，银行议价能力依然较强。但从中长期看，随着直接融资和金融脱媒的发展，将迫使商业银行对客户更多的让利，尤其是对大型客户，这将对银行的议价能力构成较大挑战。

综合利率市场化对银行存款和贷款利率定价影响来看，短期内，利率市场化对银行净息差影响有限。第四季度商业银行整体净息差环比下降 2 个基点至 2.75%，回落幅度并不大，预计随着降息带来存贷款重定价，明年第一、第二季度有望成为行业净息差的阶段性低点。

%

资料来源：银监会。

图 6-2 2012 年银行业净息差变化

4. 资产证券化新政出台，第三轮试点正式启动

2012 年 5 月，人民银行、银监会、财政部下发《关于进一步扩大信贷资产证券化试点有关事项的通知》，正式重启第三轮信贷资产证券化，首期信贷资产证券化额度为 500 亿元。9 月，国家开发银行以簿记建档、集中配售的方式，向全国银行间债券市场发行规模为 101.6644 亿元的 2012 年第一期开元信贷资产支持证券。

本次资产证券化新政有四大新特点：一是扩大资产证券化基础资产池种类。本次试点的基础范围扩大至涉农贷款、汽车贷款、经清理合规的地方政府融资平台公司贷款、节能减排贷款、战略性新兴产业贷款、文化创意产业贷款、保障性安居工程贷款、汽车贷款等多元化信贷资产。二是参与机构的范围进一步扩大。前一轮试点集中在国家开发银行和大型银行，这次参与试点金融机构包括了城商行、农商行，其中北京银行、台州银行和哈尔滨银行三家城商行被纳入资产证券化试点，额度总计 20 亿元，这有助于引导中小银行积累相关业务的经验。三是强制风险自留。上一轮试点并不强制也不鼓励发起机构持有其资产支持证券，这次试点要求发起机构持有其最低档资产支持证券，每一单的持有比例不低于 5%，持有期限不低于最低档次证券的存续期限。四是强制双评级。前期评级采用单一机构评级方式，此轮试点开始采用双评级，即聘用两家机构来对证券化信贷资产进行评级。

资产证券化重启有助于释放商业银行资本，提高资本充足率，增加银行资产流动性，便利银行资产负债的期限匹配，有利于分散银行体系风险。尽管此轮试点规模仅为 500 亿元，但随着未来业务的扩容，这将对商业银行信贷投放产生一定积极影响，有效缓解资本充足率不足压力。

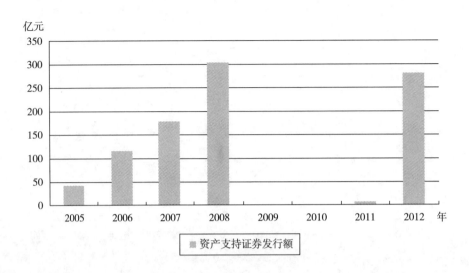

资料来源：WIND。

图6-3 2005年以来中国资产证券发行规模

5. 加强政策引导，商业银行加快关键环节金融业务发展

一是促进银行小微企业金融业务发展。2012年，国务院下发《国务院关于进一步支持小型微型企业健康发展的意见》，文件要求从落实支持小型微型企业发展的各项金融政策、加快发展小金融机构、拓宽融资渠道、加强对小型微型企业的信用担保服务、规范对小型微型企业的融资服务等五个方面，努力缓解小型微型企业融资困难。在国家政策引导下，商业银行小微企业贷款连续4年实现持续增长目标。截至2012年末，主要金融机构及农村合作金融机构、城市信用社和外资银行小微企业人民币贷款余额同比增长16.6%，比大型和中型企业贷款增速分别高8.0个和1.0个百分点；银行业金融机构的小微企业贷款（含小微型企业贷款、个体工商户贷款和小微企业主贷款）余额达14.8万亿元，占全部贷款余额的22.0%。

二是进一步加快涉农金融业务发展。2012年，银监会发布《关于农村中小金融机构实施富民惠农金融创新工程的指导意见》、《关于农村中小金融机构实施金融服务进村入社区工程的指导意见》和《关于农村中小金融机构实施阳光信贷工程的指导意见》等三个文件，全面启动"三大工程"。9月，银监会又下发《农户贷款管理办法》，从农户贷款的管理架构与政策、贷款基本要素、受理与调查、审查与审批、发放与支付、贷后管理、激励与约束等方面出台管理办法，进一步规范银行业金融机构农户贷款管理。同时，中国人民银行利用支农再贷款、再贴现政策引导商业银行扩大涉农信贷投放。2012年8月，中国人民银行在陕西、黑龙江开展试点，将支农再贷款的对象拓宽到设立在市区的涉农贷款占其各项贷款比例不低于70%的四类机构，有效引导和支持以上金融机构扩大涉农信贷投放。

截至2012年末，主要金融机构及农村合作金融机构、城市信用社、村镇银行、财务公司本外币涉农贷款（不含票据融资）余额为17.6万亿元，比年初增加3.0万亿元，同比增长20.7%，比全部贷款（不含票据融资）平均增速高5.6个百分点，实现了增速不低于全部贷款平均增速、增量不低于上年同期的"两个不低于"目标。

三是促进绿色信贷业务发展。2012年2月，银监会发布《关于印发绿色信贷指引的通知》，从组织管理、政策制度及能力建设、流程管理、内控管理与信息披露、监督检查等方面提出指引，要求银行业金融机构应当从战略高度推进绿色信贷，加大对绿色经济、低碳经济、循环经济的支持，防范环境和社会风险，并以此优化信贷结构，推进可持续发展。

（三）政策评价与展望

2013年，国内经济将呈现温和复苏态势，在"稳中求进"的总基调下，拉动经济增长的三驾马车趋稳回升，物价重回上行周期，"稳货币、宽财政"政策组合继续实施，银行业将保持平稳运行的态势。

1. 货币政策保持稳健，合理适度灵活应变，贷款增速放缓

2013年，在稳健的货币政策基调下，货币政策同时存在放松和收紧的压力。一方面，经济增长基础仍需进一步巩固，PMI指数未见明显回升，民间投资还未能较快回升，货币政策"向松微调"完全退出尚早。另一方面，为避免房价大幅上涨、防止投资过热和前瞻管理通胀预期，货币政策也难以过于宽松。2013年的稳健货币政策将是真正意义上的"中性"，但会根据经济运行状况，更加注重增强政策的前瞻性、针对性和灵活性，以处理好稳增长、调结构、控通胀、防风险的关系。整体看，全年存款准备金率和存贷款利率政策或将保持基本稳定，以公开市场操作管理市场流动性将成为政策调控常态。2013年，在稳健的货币政策基调下，商业银行存款增速与2012年大致持平，贷款增速进一步下降，全年新增信贷规模或在9万亿元左右，以对经济增长形成有力支撑。

2. 多重因素促使商业银行利润增速进一步回落

2013年，在多重因素作用下，商业银行利润增长压力较大。一是生息资产增速放缓。当前，商业银行利息收入还是银行收入的主要来源，利润增长依然主要依靠生息资产的增长，但2013年生息资产增速放缓将对银行净利润增长构成较大压力。二是净息差进一步收窄。一方面，利率市场化打开存款上浮空间，面对市场激烈的竞争环境，商业银行存款成本可能继续上升。另一方面，受经济弱势复苏、直接融资占比提升、贷款利率下浮区间扩大等因素影响，商业银行定价能力难以提升，相反受2012年基准利率下调滞后效应影响，利率再定价将拉低上市银行利润增速。三是不良贷款余额的继续反弹后趋稳。尽管地方融资平台和房地产贷款质量继续保持稳定，但受外需冲击较大的沿海地区外向型小企业的不良贷款额仍可能惯性走高，部分产能过剩问题突出行业（如钢贸、光伏航运、造船等）的企业在短期内仍无法摆脱经营的困境，其资产质量走势值得

关注。

3. 重点领域管控持续强化，资产质量基本稳定，风险整体可控

一是地方融资平台贷款管理进一步强化。在经历了 2012 年集中还款的考验后，地方融资平台贷款质量不会出现大的波动。2013 年，监管部门将进一步出台相关政策，按照"总量控制、分类管理、区别对待、逐步化解"的原则，继续推进地方政府融资平台贷款风险管控。整体看，随着国内经济复苏、投资回升、存量平台贷款余额降低以及融资渠道的拓宽，短期内地方融资平台贷款质量不会出现大的恶化，但中长期平台贷款变动趋势仍需关注。二是房地产贷款质量基本稳定。在经历了 2012 年房价回落筑底企稳之后，国内房价上升压力增大。2013 年，国家对房地产市场调控不会放松，特别是在近期出台的"国五条"的影响下，房地产市场总体将平稳运行。商业银行将继续采取较为谨慎的信贷政策和从严的风险管理措施，房地产贷款风险可控，但随着房地产行业的整合，个别中小型开发商或由于资金问题出现不良贷款。三是影子银行风险总体可控。与欧美国家相比，我国各类影子银行业务总体规模较小，杠杆率较低，尽管我国的影子银行潜藏着一定风险，包括理财产品的风险、高利借贷的违约风险、表外风险危及银行表内稳健等，但整体风险可控。2013 年，银监会、证监会等相关政策部门将采用"审慎和限制"为主的原则，加强影子银行监管，防范影子银行风险在整个银行体系扩散和向实体经济蔓延，特别是对银行理财产品、非银行理财产品、信托、民间借贷等影子银行的清理、整顿和规范，从而进一步限制影子银行的规模和增速，有效管控风险。

二、股票市场发展政策

（一）2012 年中国股市主要发展政策一览

表 6 - 4　　　　　　　　　　2012 年中国股市主要发展政策

发布日期	政策名称	发文单位
1 月 4 日	《关于实施〈基金管理公司、证券公司人民币合格境外机构投资者境内证券投资试点办法〉有关事项的通知》	中国人民银行
1 月 30 日	《〈关于修改上市公司重大资产重组与配套融资相关规定的决定〉的问题与解答》	证监会
2 月 8 日	《全国中小企业股份转让系统业务规则（试行)》	全国中小企业股份转让系统有限责任公司
2 月 16 日	《关于证券行业准备金支出企业所得税税前扣除有关政策问题的通知》	财政部
2 月 22 日	证监会正式颁发了首批独立基金销售牌照	证监会
3 月 14 日	《深交所 2011 年个人投资者状况调查报告》	深交所
3 月 25 日	《上海证券交易所交易型开放式指数基金业务实施细则》	上交所
4 月 20 日	《深圳证券交易所创业板股票上市规则》	深交所
4 月 26 日	《国务院关于进一步支持小型微型企业健康发展的意见》	国务院

续表

发布日期	政策名称	发文单位
5月25日	《关于落实〈国务院关于鼓励和引导民间投资健康发展的若干意见〉工作要点的通知》	证监会
6月20日	《证券投资基金运作管理办法》	证监会
7月27日	《关于实施〈合格境外机构投资者境内证券投资管理办法〉有关问题的规定》	证监会
8月23日	《关于规范证券公司参与区域性股权交易市场的指导意见（试行）》	证监会
8月27日	《转融通业务保证金管理实施细则（试行）》、《转融通业务规则（试行）》、《融资融券业务统计与监控规则（试行）》	中国证券金融公司
9月28日	《非上市公众公司监督管理办法》	证监会
10月18日	《证券公司客户资产管理业务试行办法》	证监会
11月12日	《证券公司代销金融产品管理规定》	证监会
11月16日	《关于调整证券公司净资本计算标准的规定（2012年修订）》	证监会
11月16日	《关于修改〈关于证券公司证券自营业务投资范围及有关事项的规定〉的决定》	证监会
12月20日	《关于股份有限公司境外发行股票和上市申报文件及审核程序的监管指引》	证监会
12月25日	经国务院批准，中国人民银行、银监会、证监会积极落实商业银行设立基金管理公司试点范围扩大工作	国务院

资料来源：课题组整理。

（二）2012年股票市场主要发展政策分析

1. 地方养老金入市获得重大突破

2012年1月17日，《中国证券报》报道称酝酿已久的地方养老金入市获得重大突破，南方某省已经获准将1 000亿元基本养老基金转交全国社保基金理事会运营，第一季度将开始投资。[①] 2012年3月19日，社保基金会和广东省政府以及有关方面签订委托投资协议。经国务院批准，全国社会保障基金理事会受广东省政府委托，投资运营广东省城镇职工基本养老保险结存资金1 000亿元。养老金入市开创了养老金投资的多元化渠道，增加了养老金保值增值的方法，也是对养老金制度改革的一个探索。如果能够很好地坚持长期投资、价值投资，并配以严厉的责任追究制度，可以稳定A股市场众多散户的心态，鼓励投资者形成长期价值投资的理念，从而减少股市的大起大落，除此之外，长期资金的注入会间接促使政府加快治理股市制度积弊，对股市政策形成正面影响。

2. 加强场外交易市场建设

2012年1月31日，证监会颁布了《全国中小企业股份转让系统有限责任公司管理

---

① 《千亿地方养老金获批入市，有望一季度开始投资》，载《中国证券报》，2012－01－07。

暂行办法》，规定在证券公司代办股份转让系统的原 STAQ、NET 系统挂牌公司和退市公司及其股份转让相关活动，由全国股份转让系统公司负责监督管理。2012 年 9 月 20 日，全国中小企业股份转让系统有限责任公司正式成立，经营范围包括组织安排非上市股份公司股份的公开转让，为非上市股份公司融资、并购相关业务提供服务，以及为市场参与者提供信息、技术服务。与此相联系，证监会于 2012 年 9 月 28 日发布《非上市公众公司监督管理办法》，确立了"非上市公众公司"的概念，突破了非上市公司（如新三板挂牌公司）股东人数不得超过 200 人的限制，并允许非上市公众公司的股票在"依法设立的证券交易场所"（目前而言就是全国中小企业股份转让系统）公开转让。[①] 2013 年 3 月 19 日，证监会发布公告称，将会在全国中小企业股份转让系统有限责任公司办公地点设行政许可受理窗口，专门受理非上市公众公司申请股票公开转让、定向发行的申请。

3. 券商创新大会发布 11 条政策红利

2012 年 5 月 7 日、8 日证券公司创新发展研讨会在北京召开，提出 11 条推进行业创新举措。10 月 12 日，证监会公布《证券公司参与区域性股权交易市场管理办法（讨论稿)》；10 月 18 日，正式发布《证券公司客户资产管理业务试行办法》；11 月 12 日，公布《证券公司代销金融产品管理规定》；11 月 16 日，发布《关于调整证券公司净资本计算标准的规定（2012 年修订)》，修改《关于证券公司自营业务投资范围及有关事项的规定》等。[②] 综合来看，多元化业务、经纪业务、场外市场是券商业务创新发展的主要方向，而政策红利将成为券商转型的重要推力。同时，政策红利的释放将主要体现在资本监管放松、业务监管放松、行政监管放松等方面。

4. QFII 和 RQFII 额度大幅提高

证监会于 2012 年 4 月 3 日宣布，新增合格境外机构投资者（QFII）投资额度增加 500 亿美元，总投资额度达 800 亿美元。2012 年合格境外机构投资者（QFII）审批速度明显加快，超过 66 家机构获批 QFII 资格，截至 2012 年 11 月 30 日，已有 201 家境外机构获批 QFII 资格，全部 QFII 累计获批 360.43 亿美元投资额度。此外，国家外汇管理局修改 QFII 外汇投资相关规定，将主权基金、央行及货币当局等机构投资额度上限放宽至可超过等值 10 亿美元。2012 年 11 月 14 日，证监会宣布再增加 2 000 亿元人民币的合格境外机构投资者（RQFII）投资额度，至此，RQFII 试点总额度达到 2 700 亿元人民币。海通中国人民币收益基金和汇添富人民币债券基金，成为首批发售的两只 RQFII 产品。

---

① 廖凡：《2012 年的中国证券业监管》，载《中国法治发展报告（法治蓝皮书)》第 11 卷，101 页，社会文献出版社，2013。

② 《2012 年中国证券市场十大新闻》，载《中国证券报》，2012 - 12 - 28。

5. 基金第三方销售正式开闸

2012年2月22日,证监会公布了首批独立基金销售牌照名单,首批上榜的是好买财富、众禄投顾、诺亚财富、东方财富等四家机构,至此,第三方独立基金销售机构增至8家。这意味着在银行、券商和基金公司之外,投资者可以从新的平台投资基金,随着销售机构的增多,也可能获得更多的手续费优惠。基金第三方销售的进入,大大扩展了基金销售的通道,有助于逐渐打破基金销售市场银行独大的局面,进而改善基金业的整个生态链,第三方销售机构的增加还有助于增加消费者的金融体验,享受到更优惠的价格和更完善的售后服务。这是我国金融服务业向民间资本开放的一大步。

6. 转融通业务正式启动

经中国证监会批准,中国证券金融公司于2012年8月27日发布《转融通业务规则(试行)》和《融资融券业务统计与监控规则(试行)》、《转融通业务保证金管理实施细则(试行)》,同日,上海证券交易所、深圳证券交易所发布了《转融通证券出借交易实施办法(试行)》,中国证券登记结算公司发布了《关于暂免收取证券出借及转融通登记结算业务相关费用的通知》、《中国证券登记结算有限责任公司担保品管理业务实施细则(适用于转融通)》等一系列转融通业务配套细则,自2012年8月27日起实施。标志着转融通业务试点正式实质启动。海通证券、银河证券、中信证券等11家证券公司将作为首批借券人,向中国证券金融公司融入资金,为融资融券业务提供新的资金来源,满足证券投资领域的资金需求。转融通业务的正式启动,是完善我国资本市场基础性制度建设的重要举措,对于进一步树立价值投资理念,增强资本市场流动性,将起到积极的推动作用。

(三)政策评价与展望

2012年是中国股票市场创新发展的一年,出台了大量的创新改革措施和发展政策,取得了一定的成效,进一步巩固了我国资本市场健康发展的制度基础。但是也应该看到,我国资本市场目前仍处于新兴加转轨的转变过程之中,发展速度依旧落后于国民经济增长的步伐,目前资本市场的资源配置功能和价格发现功能还没有得到充分的发挥,市场仍然缺乏自主创新的激励机制和约束机制,许多体制性障碍和制度性缺陷的存在仍有待我们去克服。展望2013年,加快多层次资本市场的建设步伐,服务创新型国家建设已经成为资本市场发展的重中之重,同时我们应该进一步加大业务创新和产品创新的力度,提升券商的执业水平和内控机制,逐步放松干预和管制,尊重市场规律和创新动力,做优做强资本市场。

三、保险业市场发展政策

（一）2012 年保险业市场主要发展政策一览

表 6 - 5 　　　　　　　　　　2012 年度中国保险市场主要发展政策

日期	文件名称	发布单位
3 月 30 日	《国务院关于修改〈机动车交通事故责任强制保险条例〉的决定》	国务院
6 月 5 日	《关于贯彻落实〈"十二五期间"深化医药卫生体制改革规划暨实施方案〉的通知》	保监会
6 月 12 日	《关于印发〈全面推广小额人身保险方案〉的通知》	保监会
6 月 15 日	《关于印发〈中国保监会关于鼓励和支持民间投资健康发展的实施意见〉的通知》	保监会
8 月 24 日	《关于开展城乡居民大病保险工作的指导意见》	发展改革委、卫生部、财政部、人力资源和社会保障部、民政部、保监会
9 月 14 日	《关于坚定不移推进保险营销员管理体制改革的意见》	保监会
9 月 14 日	《关于支持汽车企业代理保险业务专业化经营有关事项的通知》	保监会
9 月 17 日	《金融业发展和改革"十二五"规划》	中国人民银行、银监会、证监会、保监会、国家外汇管理局
11 月 12 日	《农业保险条例》	国务院

资料来源：课题组整理。

（二）2012 年保险市场主要发展政策分析

正如保监会项俊波主席所指出的，2012 年是保险市场形势严峻、挑战巨大、经营十分艰难的一年。全行业坚持以科学发展为主题，以加快转变发展方式为主线，开拓创新，真抓实干，稳步推进改革发展各项工作，保险市场呈现稳中有进、进中趋好的发展态势。一是市场运行总体平稳。全年保费收入 1.55 万亿元，同比增长 8%。产险业务继续保持较快发展，保费收入 5 331 亿元，同比增长 15.4%；寿险业务呈现回升态势，保费收入 8 908 亿元，同比增长 2.4%；健康险保费收入 862.8 亿元，同比增长 24.7%；人身意外险保费收入 386.2 亿元，同比增长 15.6%。保险公司总资产 7.35 万亿元，较年初增长 22.9%。二是服务经济社会的能力不断提高。农业保险保费收入 240.6 亿元，同比增长 38.3%，为 1.83 亿户次提供了 9 006 亿元风险保障，向 2 818 万受灾农户支付赔款 148.2 亿元。保险业经办新农合县市数量 129 个，受托管理资金 50.5 亿元。小额保险覆盖 3 200 万人，同比增长 33.3%。出口信用保险承保企业 3.5 万家，保费收入 142.6 亿元，提供风险保障 2 936.5 亿美元，为国家稳定外需作出了贡献。保险资金运用余额 6.85 万亿元，在 23 个省市投资基础设施 3 240 亿元。2012 年，保险公司赔款与给付 4 716.3 亿元，同比增长 20%。在北京 7·21 暴雨、"布拉万"台风等重大灾害事故中，保险业较好地履行了赔付责任。[①]

具体来说，2012 年国家和保险监管部门出台或实施了以下重要发展政策。

1.《金融业发展和改革"十二五"规划》发布，明确行业改革发展目标和任务

2012 年 9 月，经国务院批准，中国人民银行、中国银行业监督管理委员会、中国证券监督管理委员会、中国保险监督管理委员会、国家外汇管理局发布《金融业发展和改革"十二五"规划》（以下简称《规划》）。《规划》提出了"十二五"时期金融业发展和改革的指导思想、主要目标和政策着力点，从改善金融调控、完善组织体系、建设金融市场、深化金融改革、扩大对外开放、维护金融稳定、加强基础设施等七方面，明确了"十二五"时期金融业发展和改革的重点任务。

保险业作为金融行业的重要组成部分，其发展改革也是《规划》的重点内容。《规划》明确要"鼓励保险业机构创新发展，顺应经济社会发展需要和市场需求，初步建成市场体系完善、服务领域广泛、经营诚信规范、风险防范有效、综合竞争力较强的现代保险业，实现发展速度、质量和效益的统一。着力优化保险业组织体系，形成市场主体多元、竞争有序、充满活力的市场格局。推动保险集团公司进一步完善内部治理，加强资源整合，依托保险主业，促进业务协同，提高运营透明度。鼓励发展养老、健康、责任、汽车和农业等专业保险公司，探索发展信用保险专业机构，初步形成专业性保险公司差异化竞争优势。支持中小保险公司创新发展，形成各有优势、各具特色的经营模式。规范发展相互保险组织，试点设立自保公司。规范保险资产管理公司管理体制，支持符合条件的中小保险公司设立公司治理完善、股权结构合理、市场化运作的保险资产管理公司，探索设立专业化保险资产管理机构。鼓励保险中介机构专业化发展，积极推动专属保险代理机构和保险销售公司的建立和发展。支持符合条件的国有资本、民间资本和境外资本投资保险公司。"

《规划》同时明确要"积极培育保险市场更好发挥保险服务功能，不断丰富保险产品，拓宽保险服务领域。大力发展个人寿险、健康保险、养老保险、企业年金业务，以及与住房、汽车消费有关的保险业务。搞好个人税收递延型养老保险试点。总结推广商业保险参与社会保障、医疗保障体系建设的经验和做法。加快发展与公众利益密切相关的环境污染、公众安全等责任保险。逐步建立国家政策支持的巨灾保险体系，完善巨灾风险分散转移和补偿机制。大力提高保险服务水平，规范保险市场秩序，解决销售误导和理赔难等突出问题。鼓励开展资产管理产品创新，稳步开展保险资金投资不动产和未上市企业股权。支持保险资金在风险可控的前提下拓宽投资渠道，依规投资保险类企业、非保险类金融企业和与保险业务相关的养老、医疗、汽车服务等企业股权。健全保险业偿付能力监管体系，强化资本补充和约束机制，健全以风险为导向的分类监管制

[①] 项俊波：《在 2013 年全国保险监管工作会议上的讲话》，2013 - 01 - 24。

度。完善保险公司治理监管制度和标准，显著提高公司治理监管制度的执行力。强化保险资金运用监管，防范投资风险。发挥保险保障基金的重要作用。"

2.《农业保险条例》正式颁布，农业保险制度实现新突破

中国是一个农业大国，"三农"问题在中国经济社会发展中居于"重中之重"的地位。发展农业保险，充分发挥保险机制的作用，分散和转移农业风险，对于提高农业抗风险能力，稳定农业生产，保护农民利益，具有重要意义。国家对发展农业保险高度重视，对建立和发展农业保险提出了明确要求。《农业法》规定"国家建立和完善农业保险制度"。《保险法》也明确"国家支持发展为农业生产服务的保险事业"。根据这些规定，并在总结近年来农业保险发展实践经验的基础上，2012年11月12日，国务院颁布《农业保险条例》。

《农业保险条例》实现了国家支持农业保险措施的规范化、制度化。2007—2011年，中央财政累计给予农业保险费补贴达264亿元。各级财政对主要农作物的保险费补贴合计占应收保险费的比例达80%。可以说，没有国家的财政支持等措施，就没有农业保险的发展。为使国家对农业保险的支持措施规范化、制度化，条例明确：一是国家支持发展多种形式的农业保险，健全政策性农业保险制度。二是对符合规定的农业保险由财政部门给予保险费补贴，并建立财政支持的农业保险大灾风险分散机制。三是鼓励地方政府采取由地方财政给予保险费补贴、建立地方财政支持的农业保险大灾风险分散机制等措施支持发展农业保险。四是对农业保险经营依法给予税收优惠，鼓励金融机构加大对投保农业保险的农民和农业生产经营组织的信贷支持力度。

在给予农业保险政策支持的同时，《农业保险条例》规定了农业保险合同和农业保险业务经营的规则，侧重于保护投保农户的利益：一是为保持农业保险合同的稳定性，规定农业保险合同当事人在合同有效期内，不得因保险标的危险程度发生变化而增加保险费或者解除保险合同。二是为保障受灾农户及时足额得到保险赔偿，规定保险机构接到发生保险事故的通知后，应当及时进行现场查勘、核定损失、支付保险金。三是为保证定损和理赔结果的公开、公平、公正，规定农业生产组织或者村民委员会等单位组织农民投保的，保险机构应当将查勘定损结果和理赔结果予以公示。四是为合理确定保险费率和保险条款，规定保险机构应当在充分听取省级人民政府财政、农业、林业部门和农民代表意见的基础上，公平、合理地拟定农业保险条款和保险费率，并依法报保险监督管理机构审批或者备案。

另外，为防范农业保险经营风险，真正发挥农业保险支农惠农作用，条例明确了以下风险防控规定：一是规定保险机构应当有完善的农业保险内控制度，有稳健的农业再保险和大灾风险安排及风险应对预案，其偿付能力以及农业保险业务的准备金评估、偿付能力报告编制应符合国务院保险监督管理机构的规定。二是为切实保证财政给予的保险费补贴依法使用，规定禁止以虚构或者虚增保险标的、虚假理赔、虚列费用等任何方

式骗取财政给予的保险费补贴。三是对违反条例规定行为的法律责任作了明确规定。《农业保险条例》的颁布，意味着我国农业保险发展开始进入有法可依的新阶段。这是我国农业保险发展具有里程碑意义的一件大事，标志着农业保险持续健康发展的制度基础更加牢固，将为保险业更好地服务"三农"、进一步完善农业支持体系提供有力的制度保障。

3. 大病保险制度基本建立，开辟了保险业服务医疗保障体系建设的新途径

近年来，随着新医改的持续推进，我国全民医保体系初步建立。但目前我国城镇居民医保、新农合的保障水平还比较低，特别是患大病发生高额医疗费用后个人负担仍比较重，存在"一人得大病，全家陷困境"的现象。2012年8月24日，国家发展改革委、卫生部、财政部、人力资源和社会保障部、民政部、保监会等六部委联合出台《关于开展城乡居民大病保险工作的指导意见》，正式推出城乡居民大病保险制度，在基本医疗保障的基础上，对大病患者发生的高额医疗费用给予进一步保障。指导意见明确规定，城乡居民大病保险采取政府主导、商业保险机构承办的方式，也就是从城镇居民医保基金、新农合基金中将划出一定比例资金向商业保险机构购买大病保险。保险公司参与大病医保，在直接获得保费的同时，还可以获得庞大的客户群，极大地提高品牌知名度，为销售商业保险创造条件，并在政府授权下监督医院的医疗行为，逐步积累起对医院的约束经验。所以，指导意见的出台不仅为保险业服务医疗保障体系建设提供了新的模式，也为商业健康保险发展创造了新的机遇。同时，指导意见明确大病保险应遵循收支平衡、保本微利的原则，要求各相关部门加强对保险机构的监管。这也意味着大病保险制度对商业保险机构的风险控制、专业水平、成本控制和服务能力等经营管理水平提出了更高的要求。

4. 交强险对外资公司开放，保险市场对外开放进入新阶段

适应国家总体开放战略，国务院于2012年3月30日发布《关于修改〈机动车交通事故责任强制保险条例〉的决定》，在加入世界贸易组织承诺的基础上进一步扩大保险市场对外开放的范围，允许外资保险公司经营交强险业务。该决定自2012年5月1日起正式施行。此后，外资财险公司纷纷筹备进入交强险市场。10月上旬，外资保险公司承保交强险的第一单签发。

车险在我国财产险业务中占约70%。此前不允许外资保险公司经营交强险，意味着它们基本与车险无缘，因为大部分消费者都选择在一家保险公司同时购买交强险和商业车险。正因如此，外资保险公司开放交强险的呼声颇高。此次开放交强险，合理回应了外资保险公司的诉求。外资保险公司进入交强险市场后，大保险公司由于具备强大的营销和服务网络，受到的影响较小，但中小公司可能受到较大冲击。对消费者而言，外资险企业的加入意味着更多选择和服务的提升。交强险对外资公司开放，是我国保险业对外开放政策的一个重大突破，对于提升保险市场对外开放质量，促进市场竞争，提高服

务水平具有十分重要的意义。

5. 推进保险营销员管理体制改革和保险中介市场转型升级

保险营销员队伍是保险中介市场的重要组成部分。自 1992 年引入个人营销机制以来，保险行业的营销员队伍经历了一个较长的快速发展期，截至 2011 年底，全国共有保险营销员 335.7 万人。保险营销员制度对于促进保险业的发展起了非常重要的作用。但随着社会进步、行业发展和法律体系不断完善，现行保险营销员管理体制关系不顺、管理粗放、队伍不稳、素质不高等问题日益突出，不适应保险行业转变发展方式的需要，不适应经济社会协调发展的时代要求，不适应消费者多样化的保险需求。2010 年保监会就发布了《关于改革完善保险营销员管理体制的意见》，引导市场主体积极改革探索，成效已初步显现。2012 年 9 月 14 日，保监会进一步发布《关于坚定不移推进保险营销员管理体制改革的意见》（以下简称《意见》），再次将营销员体制改革推到台前。《意见》强调了推进保险营销员管理体制改革的必要性和紧迫性，明确了改革的基本原则和工作目标，提出了推进改革的主要任务和政策措施。要求把握好改革时机、力度和节奏，将保险营销员管理体制改革工作不断推向深入。

《意见》提出营销员体制改革的总体要求为："体制更顺、管控更严、队伍更稳、素质更高"；基本原则为"监管引导、市场选择、行业推动、公司负责"。《意见》首次明确了保险营销员管理体制改革的 3 年、5 年和长期目标，并将选择适当时机和地区先行试点，分别实现阶段性目标和整体目标：力争用 3 年左右时间，改变保险营销管理粗放、队伍不稳、素质不高的现状，保险营销队伍素质稳步提升，保险营销职业形象明显改善。用 5 年左右时间，新模式、新渠道的市场比重有较大幅度提升。用更长一段时间，构建一个法律关系清晰、管理责任明确、权利义务对等、效率与公平兼顾、收入与业绩挂钩，基本保障健全、合法规范、渠道多元、充满活力的保险销售新体系，造就一支品行良好、素质较高、可持续发展的职业化保险销售队伍。

《意见》提出了推进改革的六项主要任务和政策措施：一是鼓励探索保险营销新模式、新渠道；二是强化保险公司对营销员的管控责任；三是提升保险营销队伍素质；四是改善保险营销员的待遇和保障；五是建立规范的保险营销激励制度；六是持续深入开展总结和研究工作。

在明确了总体要求和目标措施后，一系列具体改革措施在监管部门的指导下稳步施行，推动保险营销员进行多元转化的试点，包括转为保险公司的销售员工、保险中介公司的销售员工、以保险公司为用人单位的劳务派遣公司员工，以及符合保险法规定的个人保险代理人等。据统计，截至 2012 年上半年，保监会一共批准 13 家保险公司成立了保险销售公司，原保险公司营销员转为保险销售公司员工。2012 年 11 月，建信人寿先行试点营销员体制改革，试点采取代理制与一小时合同制混合的用工体制，并提供五险一金的社会保障。这些试点措施的成效将逐步显现，2012 年必将成为中国保险营销员管理体制改革进程中的重要一年。

在推进保险营销员管理体制改革的同时，保监会按照"堵疏结合、退进并举"的原则，积极推动整个保险中介市场转型发展，提升专业化和规模化水平。具体来说，堵和退，就是严格限制区域性保险代理公司的市场准入，限制增量；通过治理整顿，对现有"散、乱、差"代理机构进行"关、停、并、转"，减少存量。2012年监管部门采取了如下措施推进上述工作：加强中介业务检查、问题通报和督促整改；发布《关于进一步规范保险中介市场准入的通知》，对保险代理、经纪公司的行业背景和注册资本进行限制；发布《关于暂停区域性保险代理机构和部分保险兼业代理机构市场准入许可工作的通知》，决定暂停区域性保险代理公司及其分支机构设立许可以及金融机构、邮政以外的所有保险兼业代理机构资格核准等。疏和进，就是推动中介市场结构调整，通过鼓励、引导保险中介集团化发展，实现保险中介市场的专业化和规模化。在2011年发布《保险中介服务集团公司监管办法（试行）》和《保险代理、经纪公司互联网保险业务监管办法（试行）》的基础上，2012年保监会发布《关于支持汽车企业代理保险业务专业化经营有关事项的通知》，鼓励和支持汽车企业，出资设立保险代理、保险经纪公司，或者与已经设立的保险代理、保险经纪公司合作，由保险代理、保险经纪公司统筹开展汽车保险业务，促进汽车保险中介服务规范化、专业化、规模化发展。2012年3月，保监会有关部门回函民太安保险公估股份有限公司、广州美臣投资管理咨询有限公司、英大长安保险经纪有限公司、北京联合保险经纪有限公司等4家公司，支持其设立保险中介服务集团公司的有关准备工作。这是落实2011年《保险中介服务集团公司监管办法（试行）》，推动保险中介集团化发展的一项重要工作。

保险中介的集团化发展将提升保险中介的规模销售能力和全面服务能力，有助于从根本上解决保险中介市场的"小、散、乱、差"问题，切实保护保险消费者利益，有助于支持营销员管理模式改革，推动保险业产销分离和转型升级，有助于增强保险中介自身的风险防控和化解能力。

6. 税延试点方案初步确定，商业养老保险发展迎来新机遇

2012年，保险监管部门加大与财政、税务等部门及上海市政府的沟通协调力度，就上海个人税延型养老保险试点方案主要内容达成一致意见。税收递延政策将有力激发寿险市场消费需求，对于促进商业养老保险发展、完善多层次社会保障体系具有重要意义。

（三）政策评价与展望

2012年，中国保险业改革、发展和创新持续稳步推进，保险业服务经济社会发展的能力不断提升，对外开放进一步深化，保险市场呈现稳中有进、进中趋好的发展态势。展望2013年，中国保监会主席项俊波在2013年全国保险监管工作会议上明确，全年要坚持稳中求进的工作基调、转方式调结构的主攻方向、市场化的改革取向，在做好日常

各项保险监管工作的同时，要立足行业长远健康发展，坚持远近结合、标本兼治，积极改革创新，着手破解行业共同关注的一些难题。

1. 坚持"稳中求进"的工作基调

2013 年可能是保险业发展最为困难的一年，行业的首要任务是保持业务平稳健康增长，维护市场稳定运行，防止出现系统性区域性风险。同时也要有所作为，善于在复杂多变的形势中捕捉和把握机遇，在改革创新中创造发展条件，促进行业持续健康发展。

2. 坚持转方式、调结构的主攻方向

转方式、调结构不仅是市场主体的责任，也是加强监管的应有之义。要充分利用外部环境复杂、行业经营困难倒逼保险业调整结构、转型升级的新机遇，因势利导，顺势而为，注重发挥监管政策的引导和约束作用，增强市场主体深化结构调整的主动性和创造性，推动行业在转变发展方式上取得实质性进展。

3. 坚持市场化的改革取向

改革是保险业持续健康发展的必由之路。必须处理好监管和市场的关系，更加尊重市场规律，进一步减少行政审批，推进产品定价机制和营销体制等各项改革，充分发挥市场在资源配置中的基础性作用，形成充满活力、富有效率、更加开放的保险市场运行机制，为行业发展注入强大动力。坚决破除一切妨碍科学发展的思想观念和体制机制弊端，构建系统完备、科学规范、运行有效的监管制度体系，使各方面制度更加成熟更加定型。

4. 探索解决保险产品定价机制与监管问题

当前保险市场存在的很多问题，包括销售误导、理赔难等，都与产品不合理有直接或间接关系。目前对保险产品的监管制度和监管模式已经不适应行业发展的需要，亟须进行调整和完善。一是研究修改完善保险产品管理办法，进一步明确产品监管"管什么、怎么管"的问题，进一步明确保险公司在产品方面应承担的责任。二是加强对保险产品的审核，探索建立保险产品预审机制。三是稳步推进费率形成机制改革。四是鼓励和支持创新，满足消费者的多样化保险需求。

5. 探索提升行业竞争力

项俊波主席指出，对现代保险业来说，竞争已经不仅局限于行业内各公司之间的竞争，更重要的是在全面开放环境下国内保险市场与国际保险市场的竞争，在综合经营环境下保险机构与其他金融机构的竞争。要立足发挥保险的功能作用，研究探索如何提升保险业核心竞争力。一是发挥保险的风险管理优势，不断扩大覆盖面，为经济社会发展提供更加全面的风险保障服务。二是发挥长期资产负债管理优势，平滑经济波动对保险资产负债的影响，实现长期稳定的资产回报。三是发挥机构网络和专业人才优势，加强管理服务，在建立多层次社会保障体系中发挥更大作用。同时，针对中小保险公司发展存在的普遍性问题，研究制定相应的监管政策。

6. 进一步争取政策支持

一是争取财政支持政策，包括完善农业保险补贴政策，建立巨灾保险制度等。二是争取税收支持政策，包括消费者购买养老、医疗保险产品税收递延政策，政策性和非盈利性保险业务的税收优惠等。三是推动部分重点领域立法，促进责任保险发展。

四、债券市场发展政策

（一）2012 年债券市场主要发展政策一览

2012 年，"加快发展"成为债券市场突出的特点，公司信用类债券部际协调机制建立，加强市场管理、规范市场行为、推动市场创新、推动市场建设等层面的政策不断出台，取得了较好的政策效果。2012 年我国债券市场规模稳步扩大，产品品种更加丰富，发行方式不断优化，市场交易较为活跃，市场制度和基础设施建设进一步完善，债券市场在我国国民经济中的地位日益突出，积极落实国家宏观经济政策、优化资源配置、推动金融体制深化改革，有力地支持了实体经济的发展。

表 6－6　　　　　　　　　　2012 年债券市场有关政策文件

时间	政策
1 月 4 日	中国人民银行发布关于实施《基金管理公司、证券公司人民币合格境外机构投资者境内证券投资试点办法》有关事项的通知
4 月 6 日	由中国人民银行牵头，国家发展改革委、中国证监会为成员单位的公司信用类债券部际协调机制成立，通过《公司信用类债券部际协调机制议事规则》
5 月 2 日	国家发展改革委发布《关于境内非金融机构赴香港特别行政区发行人民币债券有关事项的通知》，规范非金融机构赴港发债行为
5 月 16 日	中国银行间市场交易商协会发布了新修订的《银行间债券市场非金融企业债务融资工具信息披露规则》
5 月 17 日	中国人民银行联合中国银监会和财政部下发《关于进一步扩大信贷资产证券化试点有关事项的通知》，扩大信贷资产证券化试点
5 月 22 日 至 23 日	上海证券交易所和深圳证券交易所分别发布《上海证券交易所中小企业私募债券业务试点办法》和《深圳证券交易所中小企业私募债券业务试点办法》，中小企业私募债业务试点正式启动
5 月 31 日	在公司信用类债券部际协调机制的作用下，经人民银行备案确认，证券公司短期融资券重启
6 月 6 日	深圳证券交易所发布修订后的《深圳证券交易所公司债券上市规则》
6 月 18 日	中国银行间市场交易商协会发布《非金融企业债务融资工具市场自律处分规则》
7 月 16 日	中国保监会发布《保险资金投资债券暂行办法》，进一步规范保险公司债券投资行为
8 月 1 日	中国银行间市场交易商协会发布《非金融企业债务融资工具注册文件表格体系》
8 月 3 日	中国银行间市场交易商协会发布《银行间债券市场非金融企业资产支持票据指引》，推出非金融企业资产支持票据
9 月 3 日	非金融企业债务融资工具注册信息系统上线（简称孔雀开屏系统）
10 月 9 日	国家发展改革委发布《关于加强企业发债过程中信用建设的通知》
10 月 29 日	经中国人民银行和中国银监会批准，资产管理公司金融债推出
11 月 29 日	深圳证券交易所发布《深圳证券交易所债券交易实施细则》
12 月 3 日	中国人民银行发布第 17 号公告，同意中国银行间市场交易商协会发布《中国银行间市场债券回购交易主协议》

资料来源：课题组整理。

（二）2012 年债券市场主要发展政策分析

1. 建立公司信用类债券部际协调机制，推动债券市场规范发展

根据国务院《关于 2012 年深化经济体制改革重点工作的意见》的要求，2012 年 4 月，中国人民银行牵头、国家发展改革委和中国证监会作为成员单位的公司信用类债券部际协调机制成立，并召开了第一次会议。部际协调机制的建立，有利于形成发展公司信用类债券市场的合力，扩大直接融资，促进债券市场发展。

部际协调机制第一次会议审议通过了《公司信用类债券部际协调机制议事规则》，并就进一步推动公司信用类债券市场改革发展有关问题进行了深入讨论。会议强调，要紧紧抓住金融服务实体经济的本质要求，以扩大直接融资、促进融资结构和经济结构调整、更好地满足各类企业的融资需求为主导任务，遵循债券市场发展规律，在部际协调机制框架下，进一步加强协调合作，共同推动公司信用类债券市场健康发展。会议就促进监管协调、建立公司信用类债券数据信息的共享机制等具体事项达成一致意见。

2. 推动债券产品丰富，促进市场创新

一是扩大信贷资产证券化试点。5 月 17 日，根据国务院批复精神和前期试点经验，中国人民银行、中国银监会和财政部联合下发《关于进一步扩大信贷资产证券化试点有关事项的通知》，正式重启了信贷资产证券化试点工作。2012 年，5 家机构发行了总计约 190 亿元的信贷资产支持证券。与前两个阶段的试点相比，此次试点在监管要求上更为细化和成熟。第一是扩大参与者范围，上海汽车集团财务公司成为首个发行信贷资产支持证券的财务公司；第二是扩大基础资产池的种类，将符合条件的国家重大基础设施项目贷款和合规的地方政府融资平台贷款纳入资产池；第三是明确 5% 的风险自留比例；第四是建立双评级模式；第五是限制单个银行业金融机构投资比例。监管要求在参考国际经验的同时体现了中国特色，此次试点的重启，不仅可以转移银行体系风险，缓解新资本管理办法下银行资本补充压力，还由于信托公司等非银行金融机构的参与，让一些非金融企业也能从中受益，降低中小企业的融资难度。

二是启动中小企业私募债券试点。5 月 22 日至 23 日，上海证券交易所和深圳证券交易所分别发布《上海证券交易所中小企业私募债券业务试点办法》和《深圳证券交易所中小企业私募债券业务试点办法》，标志着中小企业私募债业务试点正式启动。试点明确，中小企业私募债指的是中小微型企业以非公开方式发行的公司债券，发行利率不超过同期银行贷款基准利率的 3 倍，并且期限在 1 年（含）以上。中小企业私募债采取备案制发行，可通过深交所的综合协议交易平台、上交所的固定收益证券综合电子平台进行转让，也可通过证券公司转让。2012 年，中小企业私募债发行总计 94 亿元。中小企业私募债的推出，扩大了资本市场服务实体经济的范围，强化了直接金融与中小企业的有效对接，为解决中小企业融资问题提供了新的探索途径。

三是重启证券公司短期融资券。在公司信用类债券部际协调机制的框架下，监管机构加强协调和合作，为支持证券公司发展，时隔 7 年后，重启证券公司短期融资券发行。经中国人民银行备案确认，招商证券于 5 月 31 日招标发行了 40 亿元的短期融资券，成为重启后第一单证券公司短期融资券。2012 年，总计 5 家证券公司发行了 16 期 561 亿元的短期融资券。其中，中国证券金融股份有限公司短期融资券的发行，使得银行间市场资金通过转融资方式进入股票市场，建立了银行间市场与股市的互通。证券公司短期融资券的重启拓宽了证券公司融资渠道，为证券公司补充流动性提供了低成本的债券融资方式。

四是推出非金融企业资产支持票据。8 月 3 日，中国银行间市场交易商协会发布《银行间债券市场非金融企业资产支持票据指引》，允许非金融企业发行资产支持票据。在制度框架上，重点对资产支持票据的资产类型、风险隔离、交易结构、信息披露和参与各方的权利义务等进行了规范，强化了对投资人的合理保护机制，同时也并未指定交易结构，在基础资产类型、交易结构设计等方面进行了包容性规范，为后续创新预留空间。2012 年非金融企业资产支持票据共计发行 14 只，募集资金 57 亿元。允许非金融企业发行资产支持票据，有利于提升企业存量资产的利用效率，扩宽企业融资渠道，可以支持更多民生领域建设，同时推动债券市场向纵深发展。

五是推出资产管理公司金融债。10 月 29 日，经中国人民银行和中国银监会批准，中国信达资产管理股份有限公司发行 100 亿元金融债券，成为首只资产管理公司金融债。资产管理公司金融债的推出，为资产管理收购不良资产、化解金融风险提供了新的融资渠道，也丰富了银行间债券市场的品种。

3. 强化自律管理，加强市场风险防范

一是构建自律处分规范体系。6 月 18 日，中国银行间市场交易商协会发布《非金融企业债务融资工具市场自律处分规则》，明确了自律处分工作中的权限职责，规范了自律处分前期调查、处分决定和复审等环节的主要流程，按照从轻到重的顺序列明了声誉处分和行为处分措施的层次、规范自律处分的操作程序。自律处分规则是自律管理的制度性保障和基础性安排，通过构建系统完善的自律处分规范体系保证了自律处分程序的正义性和完备性，对规范市场成员行为和维护市场正常秩序可起到重要作用。

二是修订非金融企业债务融资工具中介服务规则和信息披露规则。为适应非金融企业债务融资工具市场的发展变化，交易商协会先后修订了《银行间债券市场非金融企业债务融资工具中介服务规则》和《银行间市场非金融企业债务融资工具信息披露规则》，分别对中介服务的业务规范、行为规范、相关职责、责任意识，以及信息披露内容、程序和标准等方面进行了细化规范。在微观层面上夯实了债券融资工具市场平稳高效运行的基础。

三是注册制改革取得新突破。非金融企业债务融资工具的注册制是以信息披露为核心，中介机构尽职履责、投资者风险自担的市场化发行准入方式。为进一步提升注册工作透明度，更好地体现公平、公正、公开精神，推动市场管理模式进一步市场化，中国银行间市场交易商协会对现行注册制进行了改革和优化，推出中国银行间市场交易商协会发布《非金融企业债务融资工具注册文件表格体系》和非金融企业债务融资工具注册信息系统（简称孔雀开屏系统）。表格体系进一步明确了最低信息披露要求，方便企业、主承销商和相关中介机构编写注册文件和发表专业意见；孔雀开屏系统公开展示债券融资工具注册文件和工作流程，接受市场监督。注册制的改革对推动市场发展具有积极意义：有助于推动我国债券发行管理方式变革，充分践行市场化理念；有助于发挥市场监管作用，构建诚信体系；有助于提升市场效率，提高注册工作质量；有助于完善资本市场信息披露制度建设，更好地保护投资人权益。

四是发展改革委加强发债信用建设。10月9日，国家发展改革委发布《关于加强企业发债过程中信用建设的通知》，就加强企业发债融资过程中的信用建设有关问题作出规定，包括审核中重视发债企业、主承销商的征信记录使用、逐步加强发债企业多方面征信采集，逐步建立申请发债企业及保荐人综合信用承诺制度。对防范企业债券市场风险、切实加强发债企业信用建设，加快建立诚信企业守信受益、失信企业得到惩戒的机制具有重要作用。

4. 齐头并进，推动债券市场对外开放稳步开展

伴随着我国经济、金融体制改革的深入，债券市场对外开放有序推进，它不仅扩展了境外人民币资金的投资渠道，而且有利于进一步增强人民币国际结算的吸引力，同时将有力地推动我国债券市场的建设与成熟。在发行市场，1月，发展改革委、人民银行批复国家开发银行等10家境内银行赴香港发行人民币债券，总额250亿元人民币；5月2日，发展改革委发布了《关于境内非金融机构赴香港特别行政区发行人民币债券有关事项的通知》，境内非金融机构点心债的发行走向常态化和规范化。在交易市场，1月4日，在《基金管理公司、证券公司人民币合格境外机构投资者境内证券投资试点办法》的基础上，中国人民银行发布实施试点办法有关事项的通知（银发〔2011〕321号），规定了试点机构应选择一家同时具有合格境外机构投资者托管人资格和银行间债券市场结算代理人资格的境内商业银行开立境外机构人民币基本存款账户和境外机构人民币专用存款账户，细化了专用存款账户的使用要求，完善了人民币合格境外机构投资者境内证券投资的配套政策，标志着我国债券市场的进一步开放。3月，我国政府批准日本政府购买650亿元人民币中国国债；4月22日，中国人民银行与世界银行在华盛顿签署协议，国际复兴开发银行（IBRD）和国际开发协会（IDA）进入中国银行间债券市场投资，之后进入银行间债券市场的境外机构继续扩容至印度尼西亚央行等机构。截至2012年底，我国债券市场境外投资者包括了境外央行、国际金融机构、主权财富基金、港澳清算行、境外参加行、境外保险机构和人民币合格境外机构投资者七大类型共100家，

合格境外机构投资者和人民币合格境外机构投资者的总额度分别达到 800 亿美元和 2 700 亿元人民币。境外机构投资我国银行间债券市场正稳步推进。

（三）政策评价与展望

1. 债券市场规模稳步增长，融资贡献继续提升

目前，我国正处于进一步深化改革、促进经济结构调整的重要时期，《金融业发展和改革"十二五"规划》指出，在"十二五"期间，要积极发展债券市场，稳步扩大债券市场规模。因此，2013 年债券市场仍将迎来良好的发展机遇。首先，在积极的财政政策和稳健的货币政策背景下，国债规模预计稳步增长；其次，随着城镇化进程的推进，地方政府融资有望在透明化、规范化中得到进一步发展。此外，实体经济的旺盛资金需求将延续公司信用类债券市场的快速发展势头，总体上 2013 年债券市场规模预计稳步增长。同时，随着债券市场规模的稳步增长，市场深度和广度进一步扩大，将进一步提高对实体经济的融资贡献率，优化社会融资结构，改进和提升金融服务实体经济的能力。

2. 公司信用类债券部际协调机制作用将进一步显现

一直以来，促发展、促创新的理念是债券市场有关监管机构的共识。2013 年，在公司信用类债券部际协调机制的作用下，有关监管机构各司其职、戮力同心，将为推动市场发展发挥出更大的政策合力。市场互通互联进一步加强，信息共享更加全面，政策协调和一致性进一步优化，基于市场的制度建设和投资者保护机制将得到完善。以制度建设为保障，包括非金融企业债务融资工具、企业债和公司债等在内的公司信用类债券将得到协调发展，多样化的企业融资需求能得到更好的满足，公司信用类债券市场将在逐步规范中实现可持续发展。

3. 制度建设和基础设施扎实推进

在监管部门、自律组织和市场参与者的共同推动下，市场规范性管理将进一步加强，债券市场制度建设和基础设施将继续扎实推进：发行效率进一步提高，信息披露更加完善；交易规范性进一步加强，收益率曲线更加完善；做市商作用加强，市场流动性上升；市场约束和风险分担机制进一步优化；交易、清算、结算等基础设施方面更加安全高效。此外，随着人民币跨境使用的日益发展和对外开放步伐的稳妥推进，我国债券市场的国际化程度将不断加深，一方面，更多的合格境外机构有机会参与境内市场进行投融资，另一方面，离岸人民币市场将得到更大发展空间，境内外参与主体更加多元化，境内外市场的联动性将进一步显现。

4. 市场创新更加精细化

过去几年，债券市场在产品创新中快速发展，形成了比较完备的政府信用类债券、金融类债券及非金融企业信用类债券的基础产品序列。下一步，市场创新有望向精细化迈进，在市场主体自发力量的推动下，由简单型产品向含权型产品发展，在基础产品结

构上体现更多个性化设计，满足市场多样化需求。同时，债券交易工具和结构设计等方面有望推进，丰富产品深度，提高产品流动性。

五、货币市场发展政策

2012 年，《中国银行间市场债券回购交易主协议（2013 年版）》出台，将促进债券回购业务的规范运行，也为下一步的市场机制创新奠定了制度基础。在促进票据市场规范有序发展方面，监管当局进一步加大对票据业务的监管力度，要求银行完善业务流程，强化制度执行，切实防范票据业务风险。收费定价模式由政府指导定价改为市场调节价格，银行可根据市场需求进行自主定价，提高灵活性和主动性，为商业汇票的市场化提供了条件，对票据市场的业务结构和发展方向带来长远影响。总体来看，2012 年，货币市场继续保持健康、快速发展势头，市场规模进一步扩大，利率低位运行，市场结构进一步优化，货币市场功能进一步发挥。

（一）同业拆借市场

2012 年同业拆借市场没有出台新的政策，市场管理者更加注重市场规范化管理，以信息披露为重点，继续强化市场透明度建设，促进市场健康有序发展。

在既有的同业拆借市场政策框架下，2012 年同业拆借市场快速发展，各类机构利用货币市场主动管理流动性的意识增强，能力提高，市场交易规模较快增长，总交易量和日均交易量继续创出历史新高。全年累计成交 46.70 万亿元，比上年增加 13.26 万亿元，同比增长 39.27%；日均成交突破 1 500 亿元，达到 1 862 亿元，继续保持 2007 年以来的快速增长势头。

从拆借利率走势来说，全年整体运行较平稳，波动幅度较 2011 年明显减小，仅在特殊时点出现短时波动，表现为春节前出现的一波脉冲式上涨及各季末时点出现的小幅上涨。2012 年同业拆借全年加权平均利率[1]为 3.43%，同比下降 54 个基点。同业拆借利率最高点、最低点均没超过 2011 年，2012 年单日最高点为 1 月 18 日的 8.51%，比上年的最高点低 53 个基点；最低点为 5 月 31 日的 2.16%，比上年最低点高 17 个基点；全年利率极差为 635 个基点，同比缩小 70 个基点。

在交易期限方面，仍以短期拆借为主，并且市场占比继续上升。7 天期以内的交易量占市场总交易量的 95.23%，其中隔夜拆借占比进一步上升，占总交易量的 86.25%，同比上升约 5 个百分点。1 个月期以上的交易合计占总成交量的 2.19%，同比下降约 1.5 个百分点。

交易结构中，银行业金融机构交易占比为 86.99%，非银行金融机构交易占比为 13.01%。其中，股份制银行的交易量最大，占整个市场的 41.11%，其次为国有商业银

---

① 以 7 天期利率为代表。

行和城市商业银行，市场占比分别为 14.9% 和 12.93%；与此同时，非银行金融机构在市场中活跃度不断上升，较为活跃的机构为证券公司和企业集团财务公司，交易量分别占整个市场的 4.11% 和 3.69%，市场交易结构不断优化。

（二）债券回购市场

12 月 3 日，人民银行发布 2012 年第 17 公告明确《中国银行间市场债券回购交易主协议（2013 年版）》（以下简称《回购主协议》）将颁布实施。主协议是债券回购的市场的基础性安排，建立健全了债券回购市场协议文本的基本架构，对增强债券市场价格发现功能、助推利率市场化进行具有重要作用，有利于促进回购业务的规范运行，也为下一步的市场机制创新奠定了制度基础。

从我国债券回购市场出发，按照延续性、适应性和前瞻性的原则，新版《回购主协议》对 2000 年发布的《全国银行间债券市场债券回购主协议》和 2004 年发布的《全国银行间债券市场债券买断式回购主协议》进行了修订，细化与完善了框架结构、核心机制安排、风险事件处理和签署方式，引入了质押券可替换、回购债券的盯市估值及动态调整、担保品快速处理、单一协议和终止净额等创新机制，并为新旧版本主协议的平稳有序过渡设置了 12 个月的过渡期。

新版的《回购主协议》突出了以下六个特点：

一是新回购主协议合并原有两份回购主协议。由于质押式回购与买断式回购具有共同的交易目的和类似的交易结构，因此由一份主协议管辖为市场成员的签署和使用提供了便利，有利于市场成员防范交易对手风险。新回购主协议采用了“通用条款 + 特别条款”的“一拖多”的框架式结构，由通用条款、质押式回购特别条款、买断式回购特别条款、适用的补充协议及交易有效约定构成。其中，通用条款规定了适用于质押式和买断式等所有回购交易的要素和机制；特别条款则根据质押式和买断式的不同特点，就违约事件和终止事件的处理、调整、替换、履约保障安排等分别进行了规定。

二是多边加双边的签署方式。这将保证交易的平稳过渡，同时赋予市场成员自主谈判的空间。市场成员在有效签署新回购主协议后，即在签署方与其他各签署方之间生效，即可据此进行质押式或买断式回购交易。市场成员可以根据需要签署双边的补充协议，具体约定第三方估值机构、罚息利率，选择是否适用交叉违约、特定交易违约、调整、履约保障等机制。这为市场成员之间的个性化交易需求提供了便利工具和自主空间，促进银行间债券回购市场向国际通行做法靠近。

三是违约事件认定与处理机制。针对原两份主协议中对违约事件和终止事件的认定处理仅限于支付和交付义务的违约，且对于违约事件的认定和处理缺乏详细的规定，新回购主协议对违约事件和终止事件条款进行了补充，为市场参与者增加了在各种违约事件和终止事件情形下进行处理的合理选择，进一步明确了对违约等事件的认定标准、处理流程及补偿金额，它将有效降低回购业务中的信用风险和法律风险，切实保障诚信守约的交易成员的合法权益。

四是单一协议和终止净额。根据中国法律制度和回购市场发展的实际特点，新版回购主协议参考 NAFMII 主协议和国际通行回购主协议的做法，在买断式回购中引入了单一协议和终止净额制度。除了提高支付效率以外，这些核心机制还赋予了守约方在违约方发生破产等违约情形后提前终止全部买断式回购交易，并按照净风险敞口进行轧差后支付相关款项的权利。此核心机制具有降低金融交易风险，特别是破产情况下因破产管理人的挑拣履行权等引起的相关风险的功能，是金融交易领域一项重要的风险防范机制。

五是回购债券的动态调整机制。在 2000 年版回购主协议中，质押式回购的回购债券被冻结在正回购方账户中，回购双方均无法动用，会导致金融机构在债券交易市场错失良机，抑制了债券的流动性，同时金融机构在货币市场也不能有效发现价格。新回购主协议增加替换、调整机制后，新增的回购债券动态调整机制有效地解决了上述问题，当正回购方需要被冻结的债券去追逐市场债券行情时，正回购方就能和逆回购方协商换出先前被冻结的债券，抓住市场机遇；当第三方资金融出方对质押债券存在风险和流动性偏好时，也可以通过协商的方式，改变调整原质押回购中被冻结的券种，这将在一定程度上盘活机构持有的回购券种，进一步增加回购市场的流动性。

六是履约保障安排机制。新版回购主协议细化和完善了买断式回购交易的履约保障制度，交易一方可根据对全部买断式回购的净风险敞口，要求另一方调整保证金或保证券。该机制可以在回购券值发生较大波动时，有效地监控净风险敞口，极大地增强了买断式回购交易的信用风险控制力度。新的机制安排夯实了买断式回购交易的信用基础，能够更有效地应对市场成员主体多元化、资信差异化的需要，具有更强的可操作性，有助于当事人对买断式回购交易对手方信用风险的差异化管理，从而促使更多信用等级不同、风险承受能力不同的市场主体参与到买断式回购交易中来，必将提高我国银行间市场债券买断式回购交易的交易量与市场规模。

作为债券回购市场运行的基础性制度安排，新版《回购主协议》的发布和推行，有助于进一步完善债券回购交易机制，增强市场流动性，提高市场成员信用风险管理能力，对于维护市场参与者的合法权益，促进我国债券回购市场规范、持续、健康发展奠定良好基础。

(三) 票据市场

1. 2012 年票据市场政策

2012 年票据市场总体运行平稳，交易规模稳步增长，机构参与度保持适度活跃。其中，前三个季度，票据承兑余额及票据融资余额持续扩大，从第四季度起，票据承兑增幅有所趋缓、余额小幅震荡，票据融资余额也逐月下降。受监管政策调整、货币市场利率和票据市场供求关系变化等因素影响，市场利率震荡走低。

1月，中国人民银行印发关于《中国支付体系发展（2011—2015年）的指导意见》。在主要目标中提出，要"完善以票据和银行卡为主体，以电子支付方式为发展方向，适应多种经济活动需要的支付工具体系"。在主要任务中提出，要"建立健全非现金支付工具法规制度。推动《中华人民共和国票据法》、《票据管理实施办法》和《支付结算办法》的修订工作，明确电子票据的法律地位及法律效力"。同时提出，要"继续推动票据业务创新。支持和推动票据影像业务和电子票据的发展，降低票据处理成本、提高票据支付效率，保障票据支付安全。充分发挥电子商业汇票系统效能，研究引入电子票据新品种，推动票据市场统一化、电子化进程。提升纸质票据防伪技术及核验水平，确保票据使用安全"。

2月，中国银监会下发《关于信托公司票据信托业务等有关事项的通知》，要求信托公司不得与商业银行开展各种形式的票据资产转让、受让业务。同时，对存续的票据信托业务，信托公司应加强风险管理，信托项目存续期间不得开展新的票据业务，到期后应立即终止，不得展期。

2月，中国银监会、中国人民银行、国家发展改革委共同发布《商业银行服务价格管理办法（征求意见稿）》，与2003年银监会与发展改革委发布的《商业银行服务价格管理暂行办法》相比，"银行承兑汇票"定价方式由原先实行的政府指导定价调整为市场调节价格。

6月，中国证监会要求京、沪、深三地证监局对辖内券商与银行在票据等业务上的合作加大监管，加强对证券公司报备的在集合理财业务中投资银行承兑汇票业务的审理。

7月，中国人民银行下发《加强票据业务管理的若干规定》（征求意见稿），要求银行加强票据业务内部管理，通过上收经营网点的自主审批权等，杜绝网点对业务全环节的控制，防范票据业务风险。并对空白承兑汇票、票据变造风险提出了管理意见。在转让环节，规定要求银行开展回购式转贴现、再贴现应做成背书；回购式转贴现、再贴现的卖出回购和回购到期均应做成背书。同时要求，纸质商业汇票贴现后，持票银行只能将票据转让给其他银行、财务公司或中国人民银行。

10月，中国银监会办公厅下发《关于加强银行承兑汇票业务监管的通知》，针对近年来，随着银行承兑汇票业务快速增长，票据业务风险隐患逐渐积累，票据相关案件时有发生的现象，提出加强银行承兑汇票业务的监管意见：

一是银行要高度重视银行承兑汇票业务风险，加强客户授信调查，严格审查票据申请人资格、贸易背景真实性及背书流转过程合理性。加强对关键环节的管理，完善业务流程，强化制度执行，切实防范票据业务风险。

二是银行要推动银行承兑汇票业务的审慎发展。要根据自身发展战略、客户结构、风险管理水平和内控能力，合理确定业务规模和发展速度。

三是银行要加强银行承兑汇票业务统一授信管理，科学核定客户票据业务授信规模，防范各种"倒票"违规行为。

四是银行要加强银行承兑汇票业务统一授权管理。

五是银行要完善银行承兑汇票监测和查库制度，加强票据集中保管。已贴现票据必须完成贴现企业向银行的背书，防止银行合法权利悬空。

六是银行要加强银行承兑汇票业务保证金统一管理。

七是银行要加强银行承兑汇票业务交易资金账户统一管理。

八是银行要加强银行承兑汇票查询查复管理。

九是银行要完善考核方式，降低票据业务余额等规模指标考核权重，提高票据业务合规性、操作风险防控等指标权重。要加强员工管理，不断提高员工票据业务能力和合规意识，严禁员工参与各种票据中介和资金掮客活动。要加强票据业务审计，开展票据业务制度、流程及执行有效性的审计评价。

十是各级监管部门要严肃查处银行承兑汇票业务中的违法违规行为，视情况采取暂停市场准入、暂停票据业务等监管措施。对管理不力、屡查屡犯的，除对直接责任人进行严肃问责外，还要追究有关领导责任。涉嫌犯罪的，及时移送司法机关。

2. 2012 年票据市场政策分析

一是监管方面。近年来，经济金融形势复杂多变，市场流动性偏紧，在信贷投放无法满足企业旺盛资金需求的情况下，融资成本相对较低的银行票据业务快速增长，但其风险隐患也逐渐暴露。2012 年，监管部门在 2011 年出台一系列监管政策的基础上，进一步加大对票据业务的监管力度，要求银行完善业务流程，强化制度执行，切实防范票据业务风险。

由于近年银行为绕开信贷规模的约束，通过转让票据收益权借助信托公司、证券公司等通道，将票据资产移出表外的情况十分普遍，票据信托、银证票据合作规模迅速增长，客观上助长了银行多开票，扩大了票据资产规模，扩大了社会融资总规模，进而加剧票据脱离真实贸易背景的状况。为此，2 月，中国银监会下发《关于信托公司票据信托业务等有关事项的通知》，叫停信托公司与商业银行开展的各种形式的票据资产转让、受让业务；6 月，中国证监会加大对辖内券商与银行在票据等业务上的合作的监管；7 月，中国人民银行下发的《加强票据业务管理的若干规定》（征求意见稿）中，对纸质商业汇票贴现后的受让方进行明确规定，制约证券公司、基金公司、信托公司、村镇银行等机构参与票据转贴现业务。三项监管政策出台后，银行的票据转出渠道明显受阻，票据融资业务增幅趋缓，并于 9 月末出现了年内首次下降，环比负增长 2 170 亿元，且由于季末流动性紧张等因素共同作用，转贴现利率有所上升。

针对受宏观形势变化和部分机构内控薄弱等影响，银行票据案件有所增加，且重大案件发生比例上升的现象，监管部门先后下发了加强银行承兑汇票业务管理的监管政策，提醒票据风险，加强案件风险防控，对银行的内部管理提出要求。主要包括加强签发环节的授权、授信管理防止票据"空转"；加强流转环节的背书管理，规范会计记账模式；整合票据业务审核权限和操作流程，降低"挪用保证金"等操作风险；此外，监管机构还不断规范市场中的票据中介进行的票据中转行为，防止各种"倒票"等违规行为。政策出台以后，各家银行纷纷加大了票据的风险审验力度，以及相关的员工培训工作。与前三个季度票据市场规模快速增长、利率持续走低的情况不同，一方面企业为降低融资成本、加快资金周转，继续保持强劲的融资需求和商业汇票签发意愿，另一方面，银行为提高内部管理水平，防范业务风险，开展票据业务更为审慎，使得第四季度票据承兑和融资业务规模逐月下降，利率则稳中有升。

二是市场发展方面。《中国支付体系发展（2011—2015年）的指导意见》中所提到的健全法规制度、推动票据业务创新对提高票据支付效率、控制交易风险，推动票据市场统一化、电子化都将起到积极作用。2012年，电子票据的业务规模也得到了快速增长，电子商业汇票系统全年处理商业汇票业务135万笔，交易金额4.2万亿元，均超过了过去两年的总和，占2009年11月电子商业汇票系统正式运行至今处理业务量和交易金额的53.7%和56.8%。

《商业银行服务价格管理办法（征求意见稿）》中对"银行承兑汇票"收费定价模式的调整，由政府指导定价改为市场调节价格。由于银行承兑汇票在发挥融资功能的同时具有一定信用风险，适用信用风险对等原则，原先万分之五的手续费收益无法覆盖出票银行的正常风险损失，实行市场调节价格后，银行可根据市场需求进行自主定价，提高灵活性和主动性，为商业汇票的市场化提供了条件。

3. 2013年票据市场展望

2013年，在稳健的货币政策的背景下，票据市场各项业务将继续保持平稳发展。市场竞争将日趋激烈，集约经营、合规管理将是票据市场健康发展的基础，错位发展、推动创新将为票据市场的可持续发展注入动力。

六、财富管理市场发展政策

建设银行与波士顿咨询公司联合发布的《2012年中国财富报告：洞悉客户需求致力科学发展》中披露的数据显示，2012年中国私人可投资资产总额超过73万亿元人民币，截至2012年底，预计可投资资产在人民币600万元以上的高净值家庭数量达到174万户。庞大的个人可投资资产规模预示着我国金融市场已经进入财富管理市场。

（一）商业银行理财产品市场

2012年，商业银行理财产品规模继续增长，但增速放缓。中国社科院陆家嘴研究基地财富管理研究中心统计的数据显示：2012年银行理财产品发行数量达到2.91万款，同比增长45.40%，较2011年106.51%的增速明显放缓；2012年银行理财产品的流量规模达 19.01 万亿元人民币，同比增长 12.21%，较 2010 年和 2011 年超过两倍的增速明显放缓。

银监会相关人士在中国银行业理财业务热点问题座谈会上所披露的数据显示：2011 年全国 160 家银行业金融机构通过理财产品为投资者创造收益超过 1 750 亿元，2012 年全国开展理财业务的 180 家主要银行为客户实现投资收益 2 464 亿元。银行理财产品已经成为居民投资理财的重要工具，银行代客理财业务发展迅速。与此同时，银行理财业务中的潜在风险与不规范行为也逐渐显露。2012 年末，华夏银行、建设银行、工商银行等相继陷入理财风波，引发了投资者对银行理财业务的信任危机。

纵观 2012 年，监管层整体对银行理财市场持支持态度，主要体现在监管层在以下两方面放宽了银行理财产品的投资渠道：第一，继号召养老金入市后，证监会主席助理吴利军呼吁更多银行理财资金入市。事实上，银监会在 2012 年 1 月 1 日正式实施的《商业银行理财产品销售管理办法》中已经为银行理财资金入市腾出了一定空间。该办法规定，商业银行应当采用科学、合理的方法对拟销售的理财产品自主进行风险评级，制定风险管控措施，进行分级审核批准。而此次证监会呼吁银行理财资金入市当然是希望越来越多的增量资金通过更多的渠道进入股市。但面对整体疲软的 A 股市场，商业银行方面对于银行理财资金入市的态度更多的是忧虑，其中最大的问题在于股市蕴涵着巨大的风险，有可能连理财本金都会亏损，这给商业银行的声誉带来巨大的负面影响。第二，将银行理财产品纳入券商自营业务投资范围。对于券商来说，无疑是拓宽了券商自营业务的投资渠道，对于银行理财市场来说，则增加了外部资金渠道。

以上两项措施实际上是证监会推出的利好银行理财的言论。作为主要监管机构，2012 年银监会对于商业银行理财市场的监管措施可归纳为以下两点：第一，坚决查处规避监管和监管套利行为，该项措施并没有成文，只是银监会依据 2012 年创新监管工作会议精神形成的窗口指导措施。2012 年 1 月 11 日，银监会通过窗口指导方式叫停票据信托业务。该业务和银信合作类似，可以帮助银行变相绕开信贷规模管控。第二，2012 年 12 月，上海地区出现了数起银行员工私自代销理财产品、信托产品导致客户亏损事件引发纠纷。银监会办公厅紧急下发《关于银行业金融机构代销业务风险排查的通知》，通知从三个方面对银行代销业务作出要求，一是各银行业金融机构应在收到通知之日起 15 日内完成对基层网点人员的排查，重点检查是否存在擅自推荐或销售未经批准的第三方机构产品的现象。二是各银行业金融机构总行应督促其基层网点在收到通知之日起 7 日内开展内部自查，并向上一级分行报送代理销售产品的明细表，总行应在 15 日内形成各分支机构的汇总报告。三是要求各银行业金融机构总行及分支网点应在 30 日内向对口监管部门报送自查报告和代销产品清单明细，银监会及其派出机构将在此基础上，通过明察暗访的形式抽查辖内各银行业金融机构网点，并于抽查工作结束后的 30 日内向银监会提交抽查报告。

受华夏银行代销事件的恶劣影响，2012 年 12 月 12 日，中国银行业协会正式发布《关于加强银行理财产品销售自律工作的十条约定》，要求银行明示理财产品的风险，同时提前对客户的风险承受能力作出评估。银行在销售理财产品时，一旦违反这些约定，将被予以通报。

我们看到，2012 年银行理财产品市场存在两大不规范现象：一是销售不规范，销售人员往往是夸大收益而忽略风险；二是运作不规范，"资金池"类产品被商业银行广泛采用，由于"资金池"中各标的资产的风险系数不同，且各标的资产的占比含糊，给监管带来较大的难度。我们在 2012 年度监管政策动态中就提到银行理财产品"资金池"运作模式应加以规范，不过从实际层面上看，由于监管缺失，此类运作模式大有愈演愈烈之势，还一度被中国银行前董事长肖钢称为"庞氏骗局"。

展望 2013 年，监管层应从以下三方面完善对银行理财市场的监管：一是明确银行理财的法律关系。全国人大财经委副主任吴晓灵多次表示，法律关系不透明具体表现在投资者买金融产品时不太清楚他买的产品是债权关系、股权关系还是信托关系。如果不对一个金融产品的法律关系给予明确界定，就不会有风险承担的明确问责，这对银行非常不利。二是规范"资金池"类产品的运作模式。令人欣喜的是，2013 年 3 月 25 日，银监会下发《关于规范商业银行理财业务投资运作有关问题的通知》（简称"8 号文"），规定每个理财产品单独管理、建账和核算，即"资金来源运用一一对应原则"，使"资金池"运作的"暗箱"透明化，接受市场和公众的监督。未来，还应出台规范"资金池"类产品运作比例的监管措施。三是加强投资者教育与风险提示工作。银监会《关于银行业金融机构代销业务风险排查的通知》的下发较为仓促，且只是一个指导性的文件，2013 年应有相应的细则出台。

（二）券商集合理财产品市场

2012 年对于券商资管来说是划时代的一年，尽管业绩不尽如人意，但受惠于"金融改革"，券商集合理财产品的发行进入快车道，2012 年全年共有 215 只产品进入募集期，较 2011 年增加 107 只，实际成立产品 182 只，较 2011 年增加 71 只。截至 2012 年 12 月 31 日，114 家证券公司受托管理资金本金总额为 1.89 万亿元，而截至当年第三季度末，该数据仅有 9 295.96 亿元。值得一提的是，2012 年底券商资管规模比 2011 年底（2 818.68 亿元）增长了近 7 倍。不过 2012 年 A 股市场整体表现低迷，偏股型券商集合理财产品亏损严重。

2012 年，证监会对券商集合理财产品的整体态度是"放松监管，鼓励创新"。按时间梳理，全年较有影响力的创新措施主要有以下五条：

其一，召开大会，定调创新。2012 年 5 月 7 日，全国证券公司创新发展研讨会召开，《关于推进证券公司改革开放、创新发展的思路及措施（征求意见稿）》公布，涉及 11 个方面的措施支持行业创新，包括提高证券公司理财类产品创新能力、加快新业务新产品创新进程、放宽业务范围和投资方式限制、扩大证券公司代销金融产品范围、支持跨境业务发展、推动营业部组织创新、鼓励证券公司发行上市和并购重组、鼓励证券公司积极参与场外市场建设和中小微企业私募债券试点、改革证券公司风险控制指标体系、探索长效激励机制、积极改善证券公司改革开放创新发展的社会环境。

其二，将期货公司纳入创新范围。7月31日，证监会发布《期货公司资产管理业务试点办法》，规定期货公司资管业务可以投资期货、期权、其他金融衍生品、股票、债券、证券投资基金、集合资产管理计划、央行票据、短期融资券、资产支持证券等。

其三，公布具体的放松管制措施。10月18日，证监会发布修订后的《证券公司客户资产管理业务管理办法》、《证券公司集合资产管理业务实施细则》及《证券公司定向资产管理业务实施细则》，对以下6个方面做了修改，主基调是"放松管制"：一是取消集合计划行政审批，改为事后由证券业协会备案管理。二是适度扩大资产管理的投资范围和资产运用方式。三是调整资产管理的相关投资限制，取消小集合和定向资产管理双10%的限制、豁免指数化集合计划的双10%及相关关联交易投资限制。四是允许集合计划份额分级和有条件转让。五是删除《集合细则》中关于"理财产品连续20个交易日资产净值低于1亿元人民币应终止"的规定。六是允许证券公司自身办理登记结算业务，允许经证监会认可的证券公司为资产管理提供资产托管服务。这六个方面的"放松管制"大大激发了券商创新的积极性。

其四，进一步打开创新空间。11月，证监会发布实施《关于修改〈关于证券公司风险资本准备计算标准的规定〉的决定》、《关于调整证券公司净资本计算标准的规定（2012年修订）》、《关于修改〈关于证券公司证券自营业务投资范围及有关事项的规定〉的决定》三个新规。修订内容可概括为"降二增一"，即风险资本准备计算标准大幅下降、部分净资本扣减标准降低、自营范围增加。这无疑为证券公司创新发展在制度层面打开了更大空间。

其五，建立开放、包容、多元的财富管理行业的重要举措，为基金管理公司以外的其他机构开展公募基金管理业务开辟了渠道。12月30日，证监会发布《资产管理机构开展公募证券投资基金管理业务暂行规定（征求意见稿）》，拟向证券、保险、私募发放公募基金牌照。

监管层高举"松绑券商资管业务"的大旗，鼓励券商集合理财产品创新，使得一批满足客户真实需求的产品相继问世：一是保证金、定期开放的现金管理产品。该产品在与客户签约的前提下，将客户的保证金投资于低风险、流动性较好的货币类资产，以取得比活期存款更高的收益，且不耽误客户正常证券交易，流动性与收益性兼具。二是分级产品。既有传统的优先与劣后的分级模式，也创新出多空分级模式。三是信托产品集合资产管理计划。大集合投资范围增加了中期票据、保证收益及保本浮动收益商业银行理财计划。小集合允许投资证券期货交易所交易的投资品种、银行间市场交易的投资品种以及金融监管部门批准或备案发行的金融产品。

2012年券商集合理财业务的各项创新，对券商管理人的资产管理能力和风险控制能力都提出了更高的要求。爆发式的增长背后隐藏着巨大的风险。2013年随着新任证监会领导人的上任，券商资管创新步伐或将放缓，监管层应更加注重产品风险提示。

（三）信托产品市场

2012年全行业信托资产规模继续保持一个持续高速增长的态势，再次实现历史性跃升。截至2012年底，信托全行业67家信托公司管理的信托资产规模为7.47万亿元。在房地产信托和银信合作发展均受限的背景下，信托资产仍实现55.3%的同比增幅。实现营业收入638.42亿元，同比增长45.32%。合计实现利润总额441.4亿元，同比增长47.83%。至2012年底，信托业资产余额已超过保险业，上升为第二大金融部门。

信托业资产规模屡攀高峰掩盖不了市场对其持续发展动力的担忧：一方面，信托业缺位《金融业发展和改革"十二五"规划》反映出国家层面未认识到信托业务和信托制度这一工具的价值和作用；另一方面，银行、证券公司、证券投资基金管理公司等各类金融机构以及第三方理财公司等纷纷进入理财市场，都将资产管理和财富管理业务作为创新的重点，信托公司面临的市场竞争加剧。这两方面的叠加效应不禁令人对其前景感到担忧。

2012年，监管层频频加码对信托业的监管。与鼓励券商不断创新不同，对信托业的监管主题是不断"窗口叫停"。

1月，"窗口指导"先后叫停票据类信托产品和投资于同业存款的短期理财产品，其目的均是减少信托产品对真实信贷规模的干扰。2011年下半年票据类信托产品的飞速增长，因银信转让、票据、信贷资产转让等业务把信贷资产从表内转移到表外，监管层认为这些做法变相逃避信贷管控，扰乱了宏观调控，而信托在其中起到了一定的作用。银监会于当月11日电话通知各信托公司进行窗口指导，要求其停止（而不是"暂停"）该类产品的发行；同业存款短期理财产品是指银行委托信托公司发行"同业存款单一资金信托计划"，在该信托计划中，信托公司以受托人的名义将信托资金存放在该银行，形成一笔定期存款，即同业存款。这种操作模式，相当于信托资金购买银行的存款产品。

4月，重启"窗口指导"房地产信托。年初各商业银行相继收紧房地产开发贷款，开发商开始借道房地产信托寻求资金，房地产信托产品再度活跃，这使得监管层不得不再度"关照"房地产信托。银监会要求信托公司要严控房地产信托增长规模以及融资风险。

8月，"窗口指导"政信合作规模。银监会非银部召集了十多家信托公司开会，重申信托公司为仍在"名单"内的地方融资平台提供的融资，总量不得超过2011年末的规模，须切实执行"降旧控新"目标。此次被召集过来的信托公司，均是为地方融资平台提供的融资金额增长过于迅猛，余额超过上年底规模的信托公司。不过，此次"窗口指导"只是针对"名单"内的平台，对于已经退出银监会"名单"的融资平台，银监会并未禁止信托公司为其提供融资。地方融资平台潜在风险是境外机构做空我国经济的主要原因，政信合作理财产品背后往往还带有地方政府土地财政担保。未来，对此项业务的监管应进一步加强。

10月，叫停资金池信托业务。信托公司建立资金池的主要目的，主要是出于把现有的风险向后延迟。信托公司此类产品"分食"了银行理财业务，部分银行客户转向信托产品。10月17日，银监会非银部叫停资金池信托业务，如果信托公司报备该类产品，将不再获得通过。对于存量的资金池信托业务，拟定有关文件予以规范。

11月，叫停基建类信托。2012年前3个季度，在"稳增长"的推动之下，信托成为地方融资的主要渠道之一，基建类产品的占比和规模呈不断上升的态势，这引起监管层的高度重视。出于控制风险的考虑，银监会对基建类信托进行了口头指导，暂时不再批新上报的基建项目。

12月，四部委联合发布"463号文"，这是2012年监管层出台的关于信托市场的唯一一份正式文件，也是分量最重的一份文件。2012年，政信合作信托产品大行其道，银监会对其"窗口指导"的影响效果几乎为零。中国信托业协会公布的数据显示，截至2012年末，政信合作业务余额达5千亿元，而第三季度末该数据还仅为3.9千亿元，增幅之快可见一斑。

为了彻底规范政信合作信托业务，2012年12月，财政部联合发展改革委、人民银行和银监会发布《关于制止地方政府违法违规融资行为的通知》（以下简称"463号文"）。"463号文"旨在刹住政府公益性项目采取隐性举债的方式，遏制以政府公益性资产和无形资产变相做大投融资平台的倾向。"463号文"严禁地方政府直接或间接为各类融资平台项目举债，同时规范以回购或者担保承诺等方式举债的行为，并对平台公司的融资行为进一步管理。其中，对地方政府融资平台明确提出不得将政府办公楼、学校、医院、公园等公益性资产作为资本注入融资平台公司；因承担公共租赁住房、公路等公益性项目建设举借需要财政性资金偿还的债务，除法律和国务院另有规定外，不得向非金融机构和个人借款；不得通过金融机构中的财务公司、信托公司、基金公司、金融租赁公司、保险公司等直接或间接融资。"463号文"实际上截断了财务公司、信托公司、基金公司、金融租赁公司和保险公司等机构向各类政府融资平台输血的通道。对信托公司的政信合作项目来说，这无异于"灭顶之灾"。从实际执行效果来看，2013年前两个月，政信合作信托产品近乎绝迹。

不难发现，整个2012年，监管层不停对信托业务进行"打压"。这主要源于信托资产的野蛮式增长及其无所不能的投资渠道。2013年，监管层应注意两个数据：第一，人民银行2012年社会融资规模统计表显示，2012年全年，信托贷款总额（增量数据）为

1.3 万亿元，超过统计表中委托贷款总额（12 841 亿元）；第二，2013 年 3 月基建信托的发行再度回暖，部分曾因监管新规而一度停售的产品也在 3 月"复活"，地方政府融资平台对资金的需求可见一斑，当中风险应引起高度重视。

（四）保险理财产品市场

截至 2012 年底，已经获批的保险资产管理公司（不包括香港）有 16 家，可以开展保险资金委托的有 13 家，已经获批在香港设立资产管理公司的有 4 家。目前保险资产管理公司涉及的业务主要有投连险管理服务、保险资产管理计划、企业年金服务、基础设施不动产债券计划、增值平台服务以及第三方保险资产管理。

从 1984 年至 2011 年长达 27 年的时间里，保险资金投资范围相对狭窄。2012 年是我国资产管理行业群雄逐鹿的一年。保险理财市场也在这一浪潮中得到充足的发展，保险资金投资渠道大大拓宽，类公募基金业务是保险资产管理机构发挥主动资产管理业务的重要突破。当然，这一突破与监管机构的"放松管制"是密不可分的。

2012 年，监管部门密集出台了 13 项保险资管新政，简称"13 条"，涉及保险资产管理范围和保险投资渠道两大方向。"13 条"新政对保险理财业务的创新主要体现在五个方面：其一，增加保险资金投资品种。直接投资方面，增加现代农业产业经营的重点龙头企业、《政府核准的投资项目目录》中经国务院主管部门核准的能源、资源企业的股权。间接投资方面，可投资农业发展、养老产业和保障房这三类基金。其二，可投资境外不动产股权。在境外投资领域，保险资金可投资的品种有望拓展为货币市场类、固定收益类、权益类、不动产类产品，以及以这些基础资产为标的的投资基金，包括证券投资基金、股权投资基金、房地产信托投资基金。其三，打通保险业与银证信的通道。允许基金、券商加入受托管理保险资金的队伍，允许险企投资券商发起设立的集合资产管理计划、信托公司的集合资金信托计划、商业银行发起的信贷资产支持证券及保证收益型理财产品。其四，区分资金配置与投资。保险资金针对各种不同投资机构，根据不同投资风格和投资优劣势让其管理不同的投资组合。此举或可突破目前保险业与其他金融业的交集十分有限的局面。其五，险企可开展公募资管业务。这是保险资管公司期待已久的利好，意味着保险资产管理公司可以像基金公司那样发行基金产品，向公众募集资金。

（五）公募基金市场

虽然 2012 年股票市场整体低迷，但是基金公司管理资产规模并没有因此萎缩，相反，通过产品设计突围，公募基金总规模出现新突破。截至 2012 年末，公募基金管理资产总规模高达 2.87 万亿元，相对于 2011 年末增长了 7 046 亿元，增幅为 32%。

2012 年公募基金资产规模出现突破性增长，主要归功于短期理财产品的快速发行。2012 年共发行了货币市场型基金 43 只，发行总份额为 6 637 亿份，占全年发行总份额的 65%；债券型基金 68 只，发行总份额为 1 692 亿份，占发行市场总份额的 16%，虽然偏股型基金发行了 104 只，但发行总份额仅有 1 183 亿份，占发行市场总额的 12% 。

2012 年，对公募基金的监管思路主要体现在：拓宽销售渠道，打击内幕交易以及允许成立专户子公司。

拓宽销售渠道方面，证监会做了两件大事：一是放开了基金第三方销售机构的审批。2 月 22 日，证监会公布首批第三方基金销售牌照名单，诺亚正行、好买财富、深圳众禄、东方财富四家机构"中选"，这意味着筹划 7 年之久的基金第三方销售正式开闸。二是引入保险公司。11 月 20 日，证监会发布《保险机构销售证券投资基金管理暂行规定（征求意见稿）》，拟引入保险公司、保险经纪公司和保险代理公司等保险机构参与基金销售业务。

对基金公司而言，基金的发行规模如何，除基金自身的声誉外，渠道也占有很大一部分作用。目前，基金销售的最主要渠道是银行。基金公司为此被迫支付较高的渠道费用。第三方销售机构及保险机构的引入有望打破这一格局。

打击内幕交易方面，11 月 15 日，证监会公布《基金管理公司开展投资、研究活动防控内幕交易指导意见》，要求基金管理公司建立完善内幕信息的识别、报告、处理、检查、责任追究及合规审查、培训、考核等重要防控内幕交易制度，强化了基金管理公司相关法律责任。

关于专户子公司，10 月 29 日，证监会正式发布修订后的《证券投资基金管理公司子公司管理暂行规定》，基金公司被允许成立专户子公司后，将可以开展"类信托"业务，并提出"员工持股"计划。当前和今后一段时间，基金管理公司将面临更加激烈的市场竞争。子公司即将开展的专项资产管理业务，使基金管理公司投资领域从现有的上市证券类资产拓展到了非上市股权、债权、收益权等实体资产。

当然，2012 年基金业最大的亮点在于新《基金法》的出台。新《基金法》里有一个最重要的内容，就是把非公开募集的资金也就是我们俗称的"私募基金"或者"阳光私募"纳入了管理范围，从而在法律上确立了其私募基金的法律地位。未来，私募基金公司可以发行公募产品。

（六）私募股权市场

2012 年整个私募股权市场表现惨淡。中国对冲基金数据库统计数据显示，2012 年全年共发行了 874 只产品，其中结构化产品 561 只，非结构化产品 310 只，TOT 产品 3 只，在数量上远超过 2011 年水平。然而，2012 年的私募基金成绩并不理想。私募网统计数据显示，具有一年业绩记录以上的证券类投资非结构化产品数量为 890 只，其 2012 年平均收益率仅为 1.24% ，私募基金业绩大幅跑输于大盘和公募基金。

2012 年阳光私募在创新方面的发展突破较多，主要有四点：发行通道的创新，阳光私募对信托公司的依赖减小；产品的创新，投资商品、股指期货产品数量激增；投资方式创新明显，对冲策略、MOM 等方式备受市场关注；政策的创新，阳光私募被纳入新基金法。

新《基金法》将私募纳入监管，使私募基金有了明确的监管部门和监管依据，改变了此前私募基金处于监管真空的状态。这有利于破除对私募行业运行混乱的偏见，有利于优化真心实意做投资的私募。

（七）第三方理财市场

第三方理财进入我国时间不长但发展很快，第三方理财不代表基金公司、银行或保险公司，而是按客户自身财务状况和理财需求，在个人理财方案里配备各种金融工具。

2012年，市场上涌现出众多第三方理财公司，它们代理销售基金、信托等投资产品，但不需要任何行业准入牌照；从业人员号称理财师，但大多并不具备理财师资质；第三方机构只负责推销理财产品，不承担任何事后责任。第三方理财市场野蛮增长的同时可谓是"乱象丛生"。

这一切乱象的产生主要源于第三方理财市场的监管空白。第三方理财在界定和规范上属于法律真空。我国没有对应的法律部门或者法规对第三方理财机构进行监管。第三方理财产品涉及银行理财、基金、信托、保险、私募等多个种类，相对应涉及银监会、证监会、发展改革委等多个监管部门。一方面，由于第三方理财的产品涉及基金、信托、私募等多个种类，除了证监会出台的《证券投资基金销售管理办法》覆盖到公募基金销售这一块外，其他产品均处于监管真空状态；另一方面，目前还没有一个监管部门愿意也能够主动牵头去全面接管，国内第三方理财市场仍处在一个监管缺失的状态。

七、金融衍生品市场发展政策

（一）2012年金融衍生品市场主要发展政策一览

表 6-7 **2012年金融衍生品市场有关政策**

发布日期	政策名称	文号或发布单位
5月21日	《关于调整银行间外汇市场部分业务管理的通知》	汇发〔2012〕30号
5月21日	在银行间市场推出SHIBOR利率互换定盘、收盘曲线	中国外汇交易中心发布
5月29日	关于发布《全国银行间同业拆借中心利率互换交易确认规则》和《全国银行间同业拆借中心利率互换冲销规则》的公告	中国外汇交易中心
6月7日	《商业银行资本管理办法（试行）》	中国银监会令2012年第1号
8月21日	《中国银行间市场金融衍生产品交易定义文件（2012年版）》发布应用	中国银行间市场交易商协会公告〔2012〕15号
10月12日	《保险资金参与金融衍生产品交易暂行办法》	保监发〔2012〕94号
10月31日	中国证监会拟修订《关于证券公司证券自营业务投资范围及有关事项的规定》	向社会公开征求意见
11月5日	《关于印发企业会计准则解释第5号的通知》	财会〔2012〕19号

资料来源：课题组整理。

（二）2012 年金融衍生品市场主要发展政策分析

2012 年，我国金融衍生品市场制度和基础设施建设加快，新版金融衍生品交易定义文件发布，保险、证券公司获准扩大交易范围，外汇衍生品市场准入简化，新增无本金交割货币掉期，信用风险缓释工具配套政策出台，交易基准建设日益完善，利率互换支付管理、电子化交易确认和冲销启动。2012 年金融衍生品交易规模稳步增长，市场交易进一步活跃。利率交换市场主体地位强化，SHIBOR 利率基准性持续增强；汇率衍生品市场保持高速增长；信用风险缓释工具市场运行平稳。国内金融衍生品市场发展明显滞后于现货市场的发展。2012 年，国内利率和汇率衍生品交易量接近 20 万亿元，与 GDP 的比率远远小于西方发达国家水平。2012 年 1—11 月，银行间各类人民币利率衍生品累计成交 2.7 万亿元，同比增长 3.9%，其中，利率互换成交 2.67 万亿元，债券远期成交 166 亿元，远期利率协议成交 2 亿元。2012 年，银行间人民币汇率衍生品市场保持高速增长，共完成 2.56 万亿美元交易，同比增长 29.2%，其中，人民币远期外汇市场成交 863 亿美元，同比下降 61%；人民币外汇掉期市场成交 2.46 万亿美元，同比增长 39%；人民币外汇货币掉期和期权市场分别成交 55.4 亿美元和 33.2 亿美元。2012 年银行间外币对衍生品市场成交量显著增长，共完成交易 232 亿美元，同比增长 1.6 倍，其中外币对远期市场成交 26 亿美元，同比增长 16.4%；外币对掉期市场成交 207 亿美元，同比增长 2 倍。2012 年，完成信用风险缓释工具交易商、信用风险缓释工具核心交易商和信用风险缓释凭证创设机构资质备案的市场成员数量增长平稳，截至 2012 年末，共有 45 家市场成员备案成为信用风险缓释工具交易商，比上年增加 2 家。共有 26 家市场成员备案成为信用风险缓释工具核心交易商，比上年增加 1 家。29 家市场成员备案成为信用风险缓释凭证创设机构，比上年增加 1 家。

2012 年，我国金融衍生品市场主要的金融政策包括如下六个方面。

1.《中国银行间市场金融衍生产品交易定义文件（2012 年版）》发布应用

2009 年 3 月，交易商协会在中国人民银行和国家外汇管理局的指导下，在场外金融衍生品市场原有的两份主协议基础上，制定发布了《中国银行间市场金融衍生产品交易主协议（2009 年版）》（简称《NAFMII 主协议》）文本，确立了我国场外金融衍生品市场统一的中国标准。随着我国场外金融衍生品市场交易规模的进一步扩大，创新型产品不断推出，市场出现了一些新情况、新问题。原定义文件由于条款约定较为简单、个别条款与市场惯例不符、缺少对部分已成熟市场机制和创新产品的定义等问题，已经难以满足市场发展的需要，市场成员对进一步完善定义文件提出了迫切需求，并提出需要探索建立《NAFMII 主协议》配套文件自我更新的长效机制。为进一步促进我国场外金融衍生品市场的规范、健康发展，维护市场参与者的合法权益，中国银行间市场交易商协会组织市场成员和法律专家在 2009 年版的基础上，制定了《中国银行间市场金融衍生产品交易定义文件（2012 年版）》（以下简称《定义文件》），于 2012 年 8 月 21 日正式由银行间市场交易商协会公告发布。《定义文件》由利率、汇率、债券和信用定义文件等四份文件组成，包括《中国银行间市场利率衍生产品交易定义文件（2012年版)》；《中国银行间市场汇率衍生产品交易定义文件（2012年版)》；《中国银行间市场债券衍生产品交易定义文件（2012年版)》和《中国银行间市场信用衍生产品交易定义文件（2012年版)》。

修订发布的《定义文件》，在文件结构和内容条款上结合市场发展的经验和相关规则的现状，吸收国际成熟经验进行了修订和完善。一是在结构上按利率、汇率、债券、信用等产品拆分成不同子定义文件，方便市场成员引用和定义文件的后续扩展更新；二是对利率、汇率、债券等在我国已有较成熟市场惯例的衍生产品，此次修订侧重于在内容上对原定义文件中需随市场发展而修订的措辞、语义表述进行调整和细化；三是针对信用衍生产品的创新实践晚于2009年版定义文件发布的情况，此次修订对原信用定义文件进行了较大幅度的改动，以适应当前市场发展的需要，并为我国信用衍生产品市场的进一步发展与创新预留了空间；四是此次修订还就现有部分产品制定了交易确认书模板，以进一步提高场外金融衍生产品市场的交易效率。

2. 保险机构获准扩大衍生产品交易范围

为规范保险资金参与金融衍生产品交易，防范资金运用风险，维护保险当事人合法权益，2012年10月12日，中国保监会以保监发〔2012〕94号印发《保险资金参与金融衍生产品交易暂行办法》（以下简称《办法》），明确提出在中国境内依法设立的保险集团（控股）公司、保险公司、保险资产管理公司可以参与包括远期、期货、期权及掉期（互换）在内的境内金融衍生品交易。《办法》包括总则、资质条件、管理规范、风险管理、监督管理5章36条，自发布之日起施行。《办法》强调，保险机构参与衍生品交易不得用于投机目的，仅限于对冲或规避风险，具体包括"对冲或规避现有资产、负债或公司整体风险"、"对冲未来一个月内拟买入资产风险，或锁定其未来交易价格"。保监会将根据市场发展和实际需要，适时发布衍生品具体品种交易规定。

对于保险公司参与衍生品交易的资质，《办法》称，保险集团（控股）公司、保险公司自行参与衍生品交易的，其董事会应知晓相关风险并承担参与衍生品交易的最终责任，同时要建立符合本办法规定的衍生品交易业务操作、内部控制和风险管理制度，并建立投资交易、会计核算和风险管理等信息系统。此外，保险公司还应配备衍生品交易专业管理人员，包括但不限于分析研究、交易操作、财务处理、风险控制和审计稽核等。为有效管控风险，办法还明确规定，保险机构应当建立动态风险管理机制，制定衍生品交易的全面风险管理制度与业务操作流程，建立实时监测、评估与处置风险的信息系统，完善应急机制和管理预案，同时应根据公司风险承受能力，确定衍生品及其资产组合的风险限额，按照一定的评估频率定期复查更新。不仅如此，保险机构应当建立交易对手评估与选择机制，充分调查交易对手的资信情况，评估信用风险，并跟踪评估交易过程和行为。在综合内外部信用评级情况的基础上，保险公司还应为交易对手设定交易限额，并根据需要采用适当的信用风险缓释措施，同时维持一定比例的流动资产，通过现金管理方法监控与防范流动性风险。

3. 证券机构获准扩大衍生产品交易范围

为了明确证券公司证券自营业务的投资范围及有关事项，证监会于 2011 年 4 月 29 日公布《关于证券公司证券自营业务投资范围及有关事项的规定》（以下简称《自营规定》）。实施以来，在拓宽证券公司投资渠道、有效控制证券公司证券自营业务及另类投资的风险等方面发挥了重要的作用。但随着证券公司改革开放、创新发展，《关于证券公司证券自营业务投资范围及有关事项的规定》已不能完全适应客观需要，需要适当调整、充实。为此，证监会于 2012 年 11 月就修订《关于证券公司证券自营业务投资范围及有关事项的规定》向社会各界公开征求意见。

此次修订，根据实际需要对部分内容进行调整、充实，主要作了两个方面的修改：一方面是适应证券公司扩大证券自营业务投资品种范围的现实需要，修改了《自营规定》的附件《证券公司证券自营投资品种清单》，扩大了证券自营品种范围。修改后，证券自营品种增加一类，扩大两类。增加的是在全国中小企业股份转让系统挂牌转让的证券。扩大的两类，一是在境内银行间市场交易的证券，由部分扩大到全部；二是在金融机构柜台交易的证券，由仅限于由证监会批准或备案发行的，扩大到由金融监管部门或者其授权机构批准或者备案发行的，即将银行理财计划、集合资金信托计划等纳入自营投资范围。另一方面是适应证券公司投资金融衍生品的现实需要，明确了证券公司投资金融衍生品的监管政策。考虑到金融衍生品交易比较复杂，风险较高，要求证券公司具备一定的投资决策和风险管理能力，除对冲风险的外，只允许具备证券自营业务资格的证券公司直接从事金融衍生品交易。证监会将通过公开征求意见，全面、充分吸收各方面的意见和建议，对《自营规定》进行修改完善后适时发布。

4. 简化外汇衍生品市场准入

为进一步推动金融服务实体经济，促进外汇市场发展，根据《中国人民银行关于加快发展外汇市场有关问题的通知》（银发〔2005〕202 号）、《中国人民银行关于在银行间外汇市场开办人民币外汇货币掉期业务有关问题的通知》（银发〔2007〕287 号）等有关规定，2012 年 6 月 5 日，国家外汇管理局发文调整银行间外汇市场部分业务管理，调整举措包括简化外汇掉期和货币掉期业务的市场准入管理和增加货币掉期业务的本金交换形式两项。

国家外汇管理局简化外汇掉期和货币掉期业务的市场准入管理。对银行间外汇市场人民币外汇远期、外汇掉期、货币掉期业务实行一次性备案管理。符合条件的境内机构，持规定材料通过中国外汇交易中心向国家外汇管理局一并申请备案上述三项业务交易资格。《国家外汇管理局关于调整银行间外汇市场部分业务管理的通知》实施前已备案获得银行间外汇市场远期交易资格的境内机构，可自动获得外汇掉期、货币掉期交易资格，无须再次申请备案。2012年远期外汇交易大幅下降。银行对客户远期结售汇累计签约3 641亿美元，其中远期结汇和远期售汇分别为1 814亿和1 827亿美元，较2011年分别下降5.9%、5.2%和6.7%，全年企业由净结汇转向净售汇又恢复净结汇，呈现较明显的周期性波动。2012年远期结售汇业务下降除了期权交易兴起的替代因素外，也反映出随着人民币汇率趋向均衡水平，企业的避险保值意愿有所降低。2012年，银行间远期外汇市场累计成交866亿美元（日均4亿美元），较2011年下降59.6%，主要原因是4月取消银行收付实现制头寸下限管理后，银行对客户远期交易的敞口平盘方式回归即期+掉期，银行间远期交易需求减少。外汇局还规定，境内机构在银行间外汇市场开展人民币外汇货币掉期业务，除现有规定外，还可以采取在协议生效日和到期日均不实际交换人民币与外币的本金交换形式。

5. 信用风险缓释工具配套措施制度陆续出台

一是出台《企业会计准则解释第5号》，明确信用风险缓释工具会计处理方法。2012年11月5日，财政部发布《关于印发企业会计准则解释第5号的通知》（财会〔2012〕19号），宣布自2013年1月1日起正式施行《企业会计准则解释第5号》。《企业会计准则解释第5号》根据中国银行间市场交易商协会发布的《银行间市场信用风险缓释工具试点业务指引》相关条款，明确了信用风险缓释工具的相关定义，信用风险缓释工具是指信用风险缓释合约、信用风险缓释凭证及其他用于管理信用风险的信用衍生品。明确了信用保护买方和卖方应当根据信用风险缓释工具的合同条款，按照实质重于形式的原则，判断信用风险缓释工具是否属于财务担保合同。《企业会计准则解释第5号》的相关规定为金融衍生品市场成员开展信用风险缓释工具的会计处理提供了依据，进一步完善了信用风险缓释工具市场运行制度框架，有利于信用风险缓释工具市场规范持续发展。

二是《商业银行资本管理办法（试行）》将于2013年1月1日起施行。2012年6月7日，中国银行业监督管理委员会颁布《商业银行资本管理办法（试行）》。《商业银行资本管理办法（试行）》引入巴塞尔新资本协议的有关原则与内容，加强了对银行业金融机构从事衍生品业务的监管，强化了风险管理的要求，更加重视了对客户类机构的保护，对银行业金融机构衍生品业务起到进一步规范的作用。《商业银行资本管理办法（试行）》的实施将对于发挥信用风险缓释工具资本缓释作用，完善市场信用风险分担机制、提高商业银行资本金运营效率具有重要意义。

6. 金融衍生品市场基础设施不断完善

一是试行利率互换利息支付电子计算服务。与传统证券交易相比，银行间场外衍生品合约条款复杂、标准化程度低，随着市场规模的不断扩大，双方现金支付额计算存异导致的纠纷不断增加，影响了银行间场外衍生品市场的运行效率。中国外汇交易中心借鉴国际市场运行经验，在国内率先推出由第三方提供的支付管理服务。2012 年 7 月 16 日，中国外汇交易中心开始试行利率互换利息支付电子计算服务，替代金融机构之间使用邮件、电话、传真等方式核对支付金额的方式，大幅提高场外金融衍生品合约履行效率。

二是利率交换电子化交易确认与冲销业务正式启动。近年来，电子化交易确认已经成为国际衍生品交易后处理发展的重要趋势，2012 年上半年，中国人民银行正式批准中国外汇交易中心在银行间市场推出利率互换电子化交易确认和冲销业务。利率互换电子化交易确认与冲销业务的启动，有利于降低金融机构在市场交易中的操作风险、信用风险和法律风险，是利率衍生品市场基础设施建设的重要举措。

三是汇率衍生品基准曲线序列基本完成。为满足市场成员对于衍生品估值和风险管理的需求，2012 年 2 月，中国外汇交易中心发布外汇远期曲线。2012 年 5 月 21 日，为进一步发挥 SHIBOR 作为基准利率的作用，中国外汇交易中心在前期试点基础上，发布 SHIBOR 利率互换定盘/收盘曲线。加上已发布的外汇掉期曲线、美元隐含利率曲线和外汇期权隐含波动率曲线，形成了基本完整的衍生品基准曲线序列。

(三) 政策评价与展望

实体经济的快速发展，需要一个产品和金融工具齐全、功能完备、风险可控的金融市场体系，金融衍生品市场是其中不可或缺的重要组成部分。金融衍生品是金融市场发展到一定阶段的产物，是机构投资者和其他市场参与者用来管理风险，规避市场波动风险必不可少的工具。2013 年，金融衍生品政策将：一是继续推动产品创新，完善金融衍生品序列，深化发展信用风险缓释工具市场。二是推动衍生品市场主体多元化，促进市场风险合理分配。三是加强法律制度建设，创造良好市场环境，进一步完善市场监管和自律体系。随着金融市场参与者多元化发展和金融机构综合经营的不断推进，客观上也提出了建立一套全面的场外金融衍生品市场监管法规与规范性文件的要求，需要完善场外金融衍生品市场监管制度框架，制定统一的"场外金融衍生产品交易管理办法"，在统一的管理办法框架下，根据不同金融衍生品的特征制定相应业务指引，分类指导。逐步形成行政监管和自律管理相结合、一线监测为辅助的监管体系。四是完善市场基础设施建设，保障市场运行效率和安全。

八、商品期货市场发展政策

(一) 2012 年商品期货市场主要发展政策分析

表 6 – 8   2012 年商品期货市场有关发展政策

日期	主要政策	发文单位
2012 年 2 月 2 日	《关于修改〈期货市场客户开户管理规定〉的决定》〔2012〕1 号	中国证监会
2012 年 2 月 13 日	《关于公布〈上海期货交易所风险控制管理办法〉修订案和〈上海期货交易所交易细则〉修订案的公告》〔2012〕1 号	上海期货交易所
2012 年 2 月 20 日	《关于发布施行〈大连商品交易所交割细则修正案〉的通知》大商所发〔2012〕27 号	大连商品交易所
2012 年 2 月 20 日	《关于公布〈上海期货交易所套期保值交易管理办法〉修订案的公告》〔2012〕2 号	上海期货交易所
2012 年 3 月 2 日	《关于调整棉花、PTA 指定交割仓库相关费用标准的通告》〔2012〕4 号	郑州商品交易所
2012 年 3 月 13 日	《关于调整棉花、早籼稻期货交易保证金标准和涨跌停板幅度的通知》郑商发〔2012〕55 号	郑州商品交易所
2012 年 3 月 19 日	《关于进一步做好交易所减收手续费相关工作的通知》	中国期货业协会
2012 年 3 月 22 日	《关于调整白糖期货当日开平仓交易手续费收取标准的通知》郑商发〔2012〕60 号	郑州商品交易所
2012 年 4 月 5 日	《关于调整各品种最低交易保证金和涨跌停板幅度的通知》大商所发〔2012〕47 号	大连商品交易所
2012 年 4 月 17 日	《上海期货交易所就白银期货合约及有关规则征求意见》	上海期货交易所
2012 年 4 月 27 日	《关于调整交易手续费收取标准的通知》大商所发〔2012〕76 号	大连商品交易所
2012 年 4 月 27 日	《关于下调各品种交易手续费标准的通知》上期办发〔2012〕64 号	上海期货交易所
2012 年 4 月 27 日	《关于调整交易手续费收取标准通知》郑商发〔2012〕81 号	郑州商品交易所
2012 年 4 月	《特殊单位客户统一开户业务操作指引（暂行）》	中国期货保证金监控中心
2012 年 5 月 4 日	《关于白银期货上市交易有关事项的通知》上期发〔2012〕61 号	上海期货交易所
2012 年 5 月 7 日	《关于特殊单位客户开户业务的通知》大商所发〔2012〕82 号	大连商品交易所
2012 年 5 月 10 日	《关于期货公司变更注册资本或股权有关问题的规定》〔2012〕11 号	中国证监会
2012 年 5 月 15 日	《关于调整部分品种交易保证金标准和涨跌停板幅度的通知》郑商发〔2012〕99 号	郑州商品交易所
2012 年 5 月 16 日	《关于发布施行〈大连商品交易所交割细则〉等实施细则修正案的通知》大商所发〔2012〕89 号	大连商品交易所
2012 年 6 月 11 日	《关于发布〈上海期货交易所特殊单位客户入市操作指引〉的通告》上期办发〔2012〕87 号	上海期货交易所

续表

日期	主要政策	发文单位
2012 年 7 月 10 日	《关于公布菜油、早籼稻、强麦期货合约和相关业务细则的通知》郑商发〔2012〕122 号	郑州商品交易所
2012 年 7 月 20 日	《关于发布施行《〈大连商品交易所异常交易管理办法（试行）〉有关监管标准及处理程序修正案》的通知》大商所发〔2012〕137 号	大连商品交易所
2012 年 7 月 20 日	《关于修订〈郑州商品交易所异常交易行为监管工作指引（试行）〉有关认定标准及处理程序的通知》郑商发〔2012〕132 号	郑州商品交易所
2012 年 7 月 20 日	《关于公布〈上海期货交易所异常交易监控暂行规定〉修订案和〈上海期货交易所异常交易监控暂行规定有关处理标准和处理程序〉修订案的通知》上期发〔2012〕94 号	上海期货交易所
2012 年 8 月 1 日	《关于调整豆粕品种最低交易保证金标准和涨跌停板幅度的通知》大商所发〔2012〕148 号	大连商品交易所
2012 年 8 月 2 日	《关于调整部分品种交易手续费收取标准的通知》大商所发〔2012〕151 号	大连商品交易所
2012 年 8 月 2 日	《关于降低交易手续费收取标准通知》郑商发〔2012〕135 号	郑州商品交易所
2012 年 8 月 2 日	《关于下调各品种交易手续费标准的通知》上期办发〔2012〕105 号	上海期货交易所
2012 年 8 月 16 日	《关于发布施行〈大连商品交易所交易细则〉等实施细则修正案的通知》大商所发〔2012〕171 号	大连商品交易所
2012 年 9 月 1 日	《期货公司资产管理业务试点办法》证监会令第 81 号	中国证监会
2012 年 9 月 3 日	《关于公布有关期货业务细则的通知》郑商发〔2012〕151 号	郑州商品交易所
2012 年 9 月 21 日	《关于发布施行新〈大连商品交易所套期保值管理办法〉的通知》大商所发〔2012〕204 号	大连商品交易所
2012 年 9 月 23 日	《国务院关于第六批取消和调整行政审批项目的决定》国发〔2012〕52 号	国务院
2012 年 9 月 27 日	《期货公司资产管理合同指引》和《期货公司资产管理业务投资者适当性评估程序（试行）》	中国期货业协会
2012 年 10 月 8 日	《关于发布施行〈大连商品交易所违规处理办法〉修正案的通知》大商所发〔2012〕209 号	大连商品交易所
2012 年 10 月 22 日	《关于印发上海期货交易所结算、标准仓单管理和交易等实施细则修订案的公告》〔2012〕10 号	上海期货交易所
2012 年 10 月 24 日	《国务院关于修改〈期货交易管理条例〉的决定》	国务院
2012 年 10 月 29 日	《关于发布施行大连商品交易所标准仓单管理办法等实施细则修正案的通知》大商所发〔2012〕221 号	大连商品交易所
2012 年 10 月 30 日	《关于发布施行〈大连商品交易所风险管理办法〉修正案的通知》大商所发〔2012〕224 号	大连商品交易所

续表

日期	主要政策	发文单位
2012 年 11 月 1 日	《证券期货业信息安全保障管理办法》证监会令第 82 号	中国证监会
2012 年 11 月 22 日	《关于发布施行〈大连商品交易所交割细则〉等实施细则修正案的通知》大商所发〔2012〕235 号	大连商品交易所
2012 年 11 月 28 日	《关于公布郑州商品交易所玻璃期货合约及相关业务细则的通知》郑商发〔2012〕191 号	郑州商品交易所
2012 年 12 月 20 日	《关于发布施行〈大连商品交易所黄大豆 1 号期货合约〉及相关实施细则修正案的通知》大商所发〔2012〕258 号	大连商品交易所
2012 年 12 月 21 日	《关于发布〈期货公司设立子公司开展以风险管理服务为主的业务试点工作指引〉的通知》中期协字〔2012〕129 号	中国期货业协会
2012 年 12 月 25 日	《关于公布菜籽、菜粕期货合约及相关业务细则的通知》郑商发〔2012〕220 号	郑州商品交易所

资料来源：课题组整理。

（二）2012 年商品期货市场主要发展政策分析

1. 期货交易监管政策的实施与调整

面对 2011 年中国期货市场的低迷，中国证监会、中国期货业协会以及国内上海、郑州、大连三家商品期货交易所在 2012 年适时调整期货政策，在加强对中国期货业监管的同时，推出一系列政策促进期货行业迅速复苏。

一是进一步降低期货品种交易手续费，助力期货行业复苏。为贯彻落实中国期货业协会《关于进一步做好交易所减收手续费相关工作的通知》，上海期货交易所于 2012 年 6 月 1 日和 9 月 1 日连续降低铜、铅、线材、螺纹钢、橡胶、燃料油、黄金、锌和铅的交易手续费；于 2012 年 9 月 1 日降低白银的交易手续费。郑州商品交易所自 2012 年 3 月 13 日起，调整棉花、早籼稻期货交易保证金由 10% 到 6%，涨跌停板幅度由 6% 到 4%；自 2012 年 4 月 5 日起，白糖期货合约当日开平仓交易手续费减半收取；自 2012 年 5 月 18 日结算时起，白糖、菜籽油、优质强筋小麦和硬白小麦期货合约交易保证金标准由 8% 调整为 6%，涨跌停板幅度由 5% 调整为 4%；自 2012 年 6 月 1 日起，降低优质强筋小麦、硬白小麦、早籼稻、菜籽油、白糖、精对苯二甲酸（PTA）、棉花、普通小麦、甲醇等上市品种交易手续费。大连商品交易所自 2012 年 6 月 1 日起，降低黄大豆 1 号、黄大豆 2 号、豆粕、玉米、豆油、棕榈油、聚乙烯、聚氯乙烯、焦炭等上市品种交易手续费；自 2012 年 9 月 1 日起，豆油、棕榈油、聚乙烯、聚氯乙烯合约交易手续费标准由 3.5 元/手调整为 2.5 元/手。

二是调整合约设计理念。2012 年以来，国内各商品交易所在证监会的要求指导下，逐步修正了过去"抑制投机"的想法，从改变期货合约设计理念出发，进一步加强市场买卖活跃度。例如，从焦炭 100 吨、甲醇 50 吨的大合约，下降为菜子和菜子粕各 10 吨、玻璃 20 吨的小合约，而尚处于草拟阶段的原油期货也将采取小合约。

三是放松管制，加强监管。2012 年 9 月，国务院取消一些行政审批事项，证监会成为力度最大的部委之一，例如，取消期货公司增资、营业部迁址等审批；取消证券营业部开展 IB 业务的数量限制及协会的 IB 业务资格考试。同时，证监会把一些审批权限下放到协会，采取自律管理形式，例如，证监会允许期货公司设立以风险管理业务为主的子公司，即采取中期协备案审核的管理方式。根据证监会的精神，国内四家期货交易所先后放宽异常交易行为标准，例如，中金所把日内开仓限额从 500 手提高到 1 000 手，持仓标准提高到 300 手。客户异常交易违规行为与期货公司年度分类评价脱钩，不予扣分。2012 年 11 月，在借鉴券商和基金公司的基础上，证监会推出期货监管综合信息系统（FISS 系统），以逐步实现监管工作的系统化、信息化、标准化，提高监管机关与期货公司的工作效率。2012 年，在证监会"放松管制，加强监管"、交易所进一步下调交易手续费、合约以及监控创新等多项措施共同促进下，中国期货市场从 2011 年的低迷中迅速复苏，全国期货市场累计成交量 14.5 亿手，累计成交额 171 万亿元，同比分别增长 37.6% 和 24.44%。

2. 期货新品种创新和业务创新继续推出

一是新品种创新。2012 年，我国期货市场新推出白银、油菜子、菜子粕、玻璃等新合约；国债、期权、原油、鸡蛋等新品种的征求意见稿以及仿真交易等紧锣密鼓开展；铁矿石、碳排放等也被纳入研究视野。这些新品种的陆续推出，不仅进一步丰富了期货产品线，为市场发展扩容了空间，也为相关实体企业提供了更多的避险工具，使得期货市场服务实体经济的功能得到进一步发挥。

二是期货公司资产管理业务创新。2012 年 7 月 31 日，中国证券监督管理委员会发布《期货公司资产管理业务试点办法》，标志着中国期货公司资产管理业务放闸。期货资产管理业务的投资范围包括：期货、期权及其他金融衍生品；股票、债券、证券投资基金、集合资产管理计划、央行票据、短期融资券、资产支持证券等，以及中国证监会认可的其他投资品种。期货资产管理业务开闸，会改变期货公司业务单一的困局，使期货公司收入来源多样化。

三是设立风险管理业务子公司。2012 年 12 月，中国期货业协会发布《关于发布〈期货公司设立子公司开展以风险管理服务为主的业务试点工作指引〉的通知》，表明证监会批准了期货公司设立以风险管理服务为主的子公司，为专业机构和高净值客户开展仓单服务、合作套保、定价服务、基差交易等业务。设立风险管理子公司业务将改变期货公司以往以通道业务为主的局面，并成为期货公司新的利润增长点和盈利模式。

四是其他创新型业务。2012 年 5 月 10 日，证监会发布《关于期货公司变更注册资本或股权有关问题的规定》（以下简称《规定》），标志监管层开始重开外资参股境内期货公司的大门。《规定》的出台放开了外资入股国内期货公司额限制（要求外资最多持股不超过49%），加快了期货公司代理境内企业的海外期货经纪业务。此外，《规定》的出台也与原油期货等国际化期货品种的推出有关。目前国内石油勘探开发及流通体制尚未放开，因此监管层强调在其市场参与主体中必须积极引进境外投资者。2012年4月底，中国期货保证金监控中心正式向各期货公司下发了《特殊单位客户统一开户业务操作指引（暂行）》，首次明确了基金、券商、信托、社保、QFII等机构投资者在商品期货交易所开户的流程与要求。

3. 完善制度建设，夯实期货市场发展的基础

为更好地适应期货市场快速发展和新的变化，相关部门对期货市场制度进行完善。《国务院关于修改〈期货交易管理条例〉的决定》中指出，新版《期货交易管理条例》将于2012年12月1日起执行。新版《期货交易管理条例》扫清了市场创新活动的法律束缚，并鼓励期货公司通过兼并重组或IPO融资做大做强。

中国证监会正式发布的《证券期货业信息安全保障管理办法》（以下简称《办法》）自2012年11月1日起施行。《办法》系统地规范了证券期货业信息安全管理等监管制度，确立了行业信息安全监管的体制，明确了市场主体的信息安全保障责任，提出了信息安全工作的要求。其出台标志着资本市场信息安全保障工作迈上一个新的台阶。

（三）政策评价与展望

1. 2012年期货市场政策实施评估

中国期货业协会最新统计显示，2013年第一季度，全国期货市场累计成交量为453 209 423手，累计成交额为603 907.26亿元，同比分别增长127.76%和90.46%。其中，得益于2012年下半年以来A股市场波动较大，股指期货成交额上升明显，超过全国期货市场的一半以上。3月，全国期货市场交易规模较上月有所上升，以单边计算，当月全国期货市场成交量为183 420 675手，成交额为245 356.77亿元，同比分别增长126.52%和111.65%，环比分别增长62.28%和61.84%。

尽管第一季度成交大增，但期货公司在经纪业务上的收入能力却不断减弱。由于2012年国内各交易所连续降低手续费，范围几乎覆盖所有的期货品种，使得期货公司的收入也按比例减少。同时，期货市场上的恶性竞争更加激烈，手续费收入更显得不足。随着各个期货交易所继续推进激励期货交易的政策，国内商品市场量仓交易规模将有更大的拓展空间。预计年内随着新品种、新业务的逐步实施，期市交易规模将继续维持较高速增长态势。

2. 商品期货市场政策展望

国务院批转发展改革委《关于2013年深化经济体制改革重点工作的意见》，其中明确指出要推进煤炭、铁矿石、原油等大宗商品期货和国债期货市场建设。借助政策"东风"，商品期货品种的发展创新即将驶入快车道。与实体经济的现实需求一拍即合，商品期货市场也将迎来高速发展的"大时代"。

2013 年，期货市场将在监管层的推动下，呈现出较多的创新及突破，期货品种总数有望从 2012 年的 31 个升至 40 个以上。焦煤、动力煤、铁矿石、鸡蛋、土豆等有望接连登场，进一步丰富国内商品期货市场品种体系；商品指数、碳排放权等战略性品种的研发力度得到加强，取得阶段性成果；备受关注的国债期货推出条件已基本成熟，商品龙头原油期货经过一段时间的酝酿以及政策准备，目前合约设计、交易规则、技术系统和风险控制等基本完成，二者均有望于 2013 年亮相；业内最为期待的大宗商品期权推出条件成熟，目前四家期货交易所均进一步深化模拟交易工作，2013 年有望顺利推出，从而彻底改变期货市场现有格局。此外，值得关注的是，黄金、白银期货连续交易业务推出进入倒计时阶段，有望在 6 月中下旬正式面世，这将为商品期货市场发展带来新的机遇。

九、外汇市场与黄金市场发展政策

（一）2012 年外汇市场与黄金市场主要发展政策一览

表 6-9　　　　　　2012 年外汇市场与黄金市场有关政策

发布日期	政策名称	文号或发布单位
1 月 6 日	外币对市场推出单银行平台	中国外汇交易中心
2 月 3 日	《关于出口货物贸易人民币结算企业管理有关问题的通知》	银发〔2012〕23 号
2 月 27 日	《国家外汇管理局关于银行贵金属业务汇率敞口外汇管理有关问题的通知》	汇发〔2012〕8 号
4 月 14 日	扩大外汇市场人民币兑美元汇率浮动幅度	《中国人民银行公告》〔2012〕第 4 号
4 月 16 日	《国家外汇管理局关于完善银行结售汇综合头寸管理有关问题的通知》	汇发〔2012〕26 号
4 月 24 日	《个人本外币兑换特许业务试点管理办法》	汇发〔2012〕27 号
5 月 29 日	《关于发展人民币对日元直接交易市场的公告》	国家外汇管理局公告
6 月 5 日	《关于出口货物贸易人民币结算企业重点监管名单的函》	银办函〔2012〕381 号
7 月 31 日	《关于境外机构人民币银行结算账户开立和使用有关问题的通知》	银发〔2012〕183 号
11 月 29 日	《上海黄金交易所银行间黄金询价业务交易规则》和《银行间黄金询价业务产品指引》	上海黄金交易所
12 月	《关于加强银行业金融机构黄金市场业务管理有关事项的通知》	银办发〔2012〕238 号

资料来源：课题组整理。

（二）2012 年外汇市场与黄金市场主要发展政策分析

2012 年 9 月，国务院批准了由中国人民银行、中国银行业监督管理委员会、中国证券监督管理委员会、中国保险监督管理委员会、国家外汇管理局共同编制的《金融业发展和改革"十二五"规划》。提出"十二五"时期金融市场在资源配置中的基础性作用进一步增强，人民币汇率形成机制进一步完善，人民币资本项目可兑换逐步实现，多层次金融市场体系进一步完善。指出"十二五"时期要推动黄金市场稳步规范发展，改进黄金市场服务体系，完善黄金市场仓储、运输、交割和黄金账户服务体系。

2012年，随着人民币汇率市场化程度不断提升，我国外汇市场深度与广度逐渐扩大。2012年4月，人民银行决定扩大外汇市场人民币兑美元汇率浮动幅度。为了配合此次汇率浮动幅度加大的改革，国家外汇局进一步采取了以下措施：一是完善银行结售综合头寸管理措施，取消对银行收付实现制头寸实行的临时性下限管理，提高银行外汇交易和风险管理的灵活性与主动性。二是扩大个人本外币兑换特许业务试点范围。三是简化外汇掉期和货币掉期业务的市场准入管理。

2012年国内外汇市场人民币对美元双边汇率基本稳定，对一篮子货币多边汇率升值。2012年末，人民币对美元汇率中间价为6.2855元/美元，较2011年末升值0.2%，2005年人民币汇率形成机制改革以来累计升值31.7%。2012年，人民币对欧元、日元汇率中间价累计分别贬值1.9%和升值11%。根据国际清算银行的数据，2012年人民币对一篮子货币的名义有效汇率升值1.7%，扣除通货膨胀因素，实际有效汇率升值2.2%；2005年人民币汇率形成机制改革以来，人民币名义和实际有效汇率累计分别升值23.3%和31.9%。2012年国内外汇市场人民币汇率弹性增强，双向波动明显。2012年243个交易日中，人民币对美元汇率中间价隔日波幅日均44个基点，与2011年基本持平，中间价122个交易日隔日升值，121个交易日隔日贬值。

2012年，国内人民币外汇市场累计成交9.18万亿美元，较上年增长6.2%。其中，银行对客户市场和银行间外汇市场分别成交3.21万亿和5.97万亿美元。即期外汇交易小幅下降。2012年，即期外汇市场累计成交6.14万亿美元，较2011年下降1.8%，在外汇市场交易总量中的比重降至历史最低的66.9%。其中，银行对客户即期结售汇（不含远期履约）累计2.8万亿美元，较2011年增长3.2%；银行间即期外汇市场累计成交3.4万亿美元（日均138亿美元），较2011年下降5.5%。2012年即期外汇交易下降的主要原因，一是年内外汇市场多次出现较明显的单边波动，引发市场紧张情绪，导致交投不活跃和流动性下降；二是跨境贸易、投资等经济活动直接使用人民币在一定程度上减少了国内外汇市场交易需求。银行间外币对交易小幅下降。2012年，9个外币对买卖累计成交折合857亿美元，较上年下降9.5%。其中，即期交易作为最大交易品种累计成交折合622亿美元（日均2.6亿美元），较2011年下降27.4%。在即期交易币种分布上，以美元/港元、欧元/美元为主，而澳元/美元交易连续4年增长，符合国际外汇市场格局和内地与香港之间特有的经济联系。

2012年国际黄金价格宽幅震荡，上海黄金交易所黄金现货交易量有所下降。上海黄金交易所累计成交黄金6 350.2吨，成交金额21 506.34亿元，同比分别下降14.63%和13.18%。其中，夜市时段交易累计成交1 273.8吨，同比减少516.13吨，降幅

28.84%，交易占比为20.06%，较2011年同期减少了4个百分点。商业银行境内各项场外黄金业务总体小幅增长。

2012年国内外汇市场和黄金市场主要金融政策包括如下十个方面。

1. 银行间外汇市场市场化改革推进，人民币兑美元交易波幅扩大至百分之一

《中国人民银行公告》〔2012〕第4号，规定自2012年4月16日起，银行间即期外汇市场人民币兑美元交易价浮动幅度由5‰扩大至1%，即每日银行间即期外汇市场人民币兑美元交易价可在中国外汇交易中心对外公布的当日人民币兑美元中间价上下1%的幅度内浮动。外汇指定银行为客户提供当日美元最高现汇卖出价与最低现汇买入价之差不得超过当日汇率中间价的幅度由1%扩大至2%，其他规定仍遵照《中国人民银行关于银行间外汇市场交易汇价和外汇指定银行挂牌汇价管理有关问题的通知》（银发〔2010〕325号）执行。这是自2007年以来人民币对美元汇率单日波动幅度的再度扩大。此次汇率波幅扩大是在我国国际收支状况逐步改善，人民币汇率趋向合理均衡水平，外汇市场发展更加成熟的背景下推出的，有利于市场供求在汇率形成中发挥更大作用。在人民币汇率基本接近均衡，贸易及经常账户顺差减少，外汇占款下降的背景下，人民币汇率制度改革再次推进，有利于打破人民币单边升值预期，增大市场在人民币汇率机制形成中的作用，增强人民币汇率的弹性。

从人民币兑美元交易波幅扩大之后的市场情况看，人民币兑美元即期汇率扩幅前后的平均波动幅度未出现明显变化。取消收付实现制头寸下限的影响是远期掉期两条曲线最终收敛为一条掉期曲线。人民币兑美元波动率全年呈下跌走势，隐含波动率高于实际波动率，并逐渐向实际波动率回归。1年期隐含波动率区间在2.3%～4.5%，实际波动率区间在2.1%～2.6%。4月16日扩大银行间外汇市场人民币对美元即期交易价浮动幅度后，交易价相对中间价的日间最大波幅全年日均为0.55%，高于2011年0.18%的波幅水平。5月下旬至8月末，交易价持续处于中间价贬值区间波动，9月中旬以后转向持续处于中间价升值区间波动，特别是10月下旬至12月上旬连续出现交易价触及当日中间价1%的浮动区间下限。

2. 增强外汇交易管理的灵活性，完善银行结售汇综合头寸管理

为进一步发展外汇市场，增强银行外汇交易和风险管理的灵活性与主动性，促进人民币汇率的价格发现，国家外汇管理局根据国际收支状况，配合4月16日扩大外汇市场人民币对美元汇率浮动幅度、增加人民币汇率弹性的改革需要，决定完善银行结售汇综合头寸管理，取消2010年11月以来对银行收付实现制头寸实行的临时性下限管理，《国家外汇管理局关于加强外汇业务管理有关问题的通知》（汇发〔2010〕59号）第一条、《国家外汇管理局关于进一步加强外汇业务管理有关问题的通知》（汇发〔2011〕11号）第一条停止执行。并对银行结售汇综合头寸实行正负区间管理，在现有结售汇综合头寸上下限管理的基础上，将下限下调至零以下。标志着强制结售汇制度退出历史

舞台，企业和个人可自主保留外汇收入，提高银行外汇交易和风险管理的灵活性与主动性，促进人民币汇率的价格发现。

3. 发展人民币兑日元直接交易

为促进中国与日本之间的双边贸易，便利人民币和日元在贸易结算中的使用，满足经济主体降低汇兑成本的需要，经中国人民银行授权，中国外汇交易中心自 2012 年 6 月 1 日起在银行间外汇市场完善人民币对日元的交易方式，发展人民币对日元直接交易。规定：银行间外汇市场人民币对日元交易实行直接交易做市商制度，直接做市商承担相应义务，连续提供人民币对日元直接交易的买、卖双向报价，为市场提供流动性；改进人民币对日元汇率中间价形成方式。人民币对日元汇率中间价由此前根据当日人民币对美元汇率中间价以及美元对日元汇率套算形成改为根据直接交易做市商报价形成，即中国外汇交易中心于每日银行间外汇市场开盘前向银行间外汇市场人民币对日元直接交易做市商询价，将直接交易做市商报价平均，得到当日人民币对日元汇率中间价；中国外汇交易中心对银行间外汇市场人民币对日元直接交易的运行进行管理。发展人民币对日元直接交易，有利于形成人民币对日元直接汇率，降低经济主体汇兑成本，促进人民币与日元在双边贸易和投资中的使用，有利于加强两国金融合作，支持中日之间不断发展的经济金融关系。中国人民银行对此予以积极支持。自 2012 年 6 月 1 日人民币对日元启动直接交易以来，市场成交量与流动性均大幅度改善，月均成交均超过 1 000 亿元人民币，10 家直接成交做市商报价积极。

4. 扩大银行贵金属业务汇率敞口平盘范围

为规范贵金属业务外汇管理，国家外汇管理局将已有银行黄金业务汇率敞口平盘的政策适用范围扩大至白银、铂金等其他贵金属，便利银行为客户提供贵金属投资服务品种，支持藏金于民。贵金属业务汇率敞口是指，银行在境内办理以人民币计价的即期贵金属（包括但不限于黄金、白银、铂金）买卖业务后，在境外市场平盘贵金属交易敞口而形成的本外币错配的一种汇率敞口。对于备案后的贵金属业务汇率敞口，银行可视同自身结售汇交易进行平盘。

5. 扩大个人本外币兑换特许业务试点范围

为进一步深化特许业务试点工作，促进试点地区个人本外币兑换特许业务的持续健康发展，国家外汇管理局修订了《个人本外币兑换特许业务试点管理办法》，并从 2012 年 5 月 1 日起施行。自 2009 年 11 月扩大个人本外币兑换特许业务试点以来，特许业务经营机构数量稳步增加，兑换服务水平不断提高，试点工作效果良好。《个人本外币兑换特许业务试点管理办法》是推动人民币外汇市场发展的又一举措。《个人本外币兑换特许业务试点管理办法》的实施，在风险可控的条件下给予特许机构在市场准入、日常经营方面的便利，为其预留未来的发展空间。同时强调事后数据监测，加大事后常规性现场和非现场监管力度，促进特许机构可持续发展。

6. 外币对市场单银行平台正式上线运行

2012 年 1 月 6 日，中国外汇交易中心宣布外币对市场单银行平台正式运行，这是优化外币对市场结构和交易机制的一次尝试。在此模式下，单个做市商可针对不同会员银行进行客户化报价，将交易对手资信和交易金额等定价因素反映在报价点差中，交易采用非匿名集中清算模式。截至 2012 年 12 月 31 日，获准进入该平台交易的会员共有 15 家，交易系统运行平稳，市场交易活跃。

7. 加强银行业金融机构黄金市场业务管理

2012 年 12 月，人民银行下发了《关于加强银行业金融机构黄金市场业务管理有关事项的通知》（银办发〔2012〕238 号，以下简称《通知》），要求开展黄金市场业务的银行业金融机构定期向人民银行报告相关业务情况。《通知》的内容包括建立黄金市场业务的备案管理制度，以及进一步完善黄金市场业务统计监测制度。《通知》的发布对于规范商业银行黄金市场业务，促进场内场外两个黄金市场的有序发展具有重要意义。

8. 开展银行间黄金询价业务

经中国人民银行备案同意，上海黄金交易所于 2012 年 12 月 3 日起试运行银行间黄金询价业务。为此，上海黄金交易所为规范银行间黄金询价业务秩序，保护市场参与者的合法权益，根据《关于促进黄金市场发展的若干意见》（银发〔2010〕211 号）、《上海黄金交易所业务监督管理规则》（银发〔2011〕93 号）、《上海黄金交易所章程》等有关规定，制定了《上海黄金交易所银行间黄金询价业务交易规则》和《银行间黄金询价业务产品指引》。规定经上海黄金交易所核准的市场参与者可通过中国外汇交易中心外汇交易系统以双边询价方式进行黄金交易，并通过上海黄金交易所进行清算与交割。银行间黄金询价业务的准入机构目前为 20 家，入围的机构不仅包括工商银行、建设银行、中国银行、农业银行等国内商业银行，还包括汇丰、渣打、澳新和大华银行的中国有限公司。银行间黄金询价业务的推出，将有利于满足黄金市场投资者多样化的投资需求，进一步丰富市场交易模式，不断深化市场功能，促进形成多层次的黄金市场交易体系。

9. 黄金 ETF 已进入审批阶段

黄金 ETF 的研发早在 3 年前就已经起步。自 2009 年起，华安基金就开始与上交所和黄金交易所共同研究推出黄金 ETF 的可行性。黄金 ETF 是支持上海国际金融中心建设，响应上海市"创新驱动转型发展"号召的举措。黄金 ETF 的运作将涉及我国交易所基金市场与黄金市场的互联互通，已被列为"十二五"时期上海国际金融中心建设规划的主要任务和措施之一。

10. 清理非法黄金交易所

受黄金交易价格上涨较快、投资者投资热情高涨的影响，前两年出现了部分地方、机构自设交易所（黄金交易平台）的现象，这些交易所（黄金交易平台）管理不规范，违法违规问题突出，风险逐步暴露。为了规范黄金市场的发展，2011年下半年，人民银行会同有关部门对非法黄金交易及非法黄金衍生品交易场所进行清理，并于年底发布《关于加强黄金交易所或从事黄金交易平台管理的通知》。通知中明确，除上海黄金交易所和上海期货交易所外，任何地方、机构或个人均不得设立黄金交易所，也不得在其他交易场所内设立黄金交易平台。正在筹建的，应一律终止相关设立活动；已经开业的，要立即停止开办新的业务。整顿之后，黄金市场继续回到规范发展的轨道上。这些管理制度有力地推动了市场的规范，为金融市场创新和发展提供了基础和保障。目前我国黄金市场已经形成了上海黄金交易所黄金业务、上海期货交易所黄金期货业务共同发展的市场格局，这两个市场与黄金产业协同发展。

（三）政策评价与展望

金融业"十二五"规划提出外汇市场要提高外汇和国际收支风险防范能力。2013年初"两会"政府工作报告明确了国际收支状况进一步改善的预期目标。为此，需要按照"扩内需、调结构、减顺差、促平衡"的思路，建立健全可持续的国际收支平衡机制；继续完善人民币汇率形成机制，增加汇率弹性，加快外汇市场发展，进一步发挥市场在国际收支调节中的作用。鉴于外汇管理改革的渐进性，2013年的外汇管理政策将会充分考虑当前全球经济金融形势，继续以服务于实体经济，提高外汇和国际收支风险防范能力为核心，按照转变外汇管理方式的改革思路，进一步完善外汇管理的各个方面。2013年1月，国家外汇管理局召开了全国外汇管理工作会议，其中的工作重点与上述预期基本一致，具体包括：第一，全面深化外汇管理体制改革，大力促进贸易投资便利化。第二，加强外汇宏观总量分析和区域分析，提升外汇监测分析能力和水平。第三，不断完善跨境资金流动监管体系，切实维护国家经济金融安全。第四，扎实推进主体监管，加快外汇管理理念和方式转变。第五，管好用好外汇储备，进一步完善大规模外汇储备经营管理体制。

《金融业发展和改革"十二五"规划》指出，"十二五"时期要推动黄金市场稳步规范发展，改进黄金市场服务体系，完善黄金市场仓储、运输、交割和黄金账户服务体系。"十二五"期间，金交所希望通过产品创新和服务创新进一步壮大，其中包括推出钯金、黄金ETF等创新产品、发展黄金租赁业务、延长交易时间、探索在银行间市场创立场外询价市场等。2013年黄金市场需要加强基础性制度建设。强化对金融机构黄金业务的管理。加强黄金市场的创新，应进一步发展黄金租借市场，不断完善银行间黄金询价交易，提高黄金市场的流动性。鼓励商业银行开展黄金质押融资、黄金衍生品业务。引入更多的机构投资者参与黄金市场，优化黄金市场投资者结构。

金融监管政策

一、中国人民银行主要监管政策

（一）2012 年中国人民银行主要监管政策一览

表 7 - 1　　　　　　　　　　2012 年中国人民银行主要监管政策

发布日期	文件名	文号
2 月 3 日	《关于出口货物贸易人民币结算企业管理有关问题的通知》（中国人民银行、财政部、商务部、海关总署、国家税务总局和银监会联合发布）	银发〔2012〕23 号
2 月 7 日	《关于金融支持旅游业加快发展的若干意见》（中国人民银行、发展改革委、旅游局、银监会、证监会、保监会和外汇局联合发布）	银发〔2012〕32 号
2 月 16 日	中国人民银行办公厅印发《关于 2012 年中国农业银行改革试点县级"三农金融事业部"执行差别化存款准备金率政策有关事项的通知》	银办发〔2012〕24 号
2 月 29 日	《关于进一步做好水利改革发展金融服务的意见》（中国人民银行、发展改革委、财政部、水利部、银监会、证监会和保监会联合发布）	银发〔2012〕51 号
3 月 6 日	《中国人民银行关于管好用好支农再贷款　支持扩大"三农"信贷投放的通知》	银发〔2012〕58 号
3 月 31 日	中国人民银行印发《关于认真组织落实 2011 年县域法人金融机构新增存款一定比例用于当地贷款考核政策和农村信用社改革试点专项票据兑付后续监测考核政策激励约束措施的通知》	银发〔2012〕86 号
5 月 17 日	《关于进一步扩大信贷资产证券化试点有关事项的通知》（中国人民银行、银监会、财政部联合印发）	银发〔2012〕127 号
6 月 5 日	《关于出口货物贸易人民币结算企业重点监管名单的函》（中国人民银行、财政部、商务部、海关总署、国家税务总局和银监会联合下发）	银办函〔2012〕381 号
7 月 31 日	中国人民银行发布《关于境外机构人民币银行结算账户开立和使用有关问题的通知》	银发〔2012〕183 号
8 月 23 日	中国人民银行印发《关于开展拓宽支农再贷款适用范围试点的通知》	银发〔2012〕207 号
9 月 26 日	《中国人民银行关于进一步加强预付卡业务管理的通知》	银发〔2012〕234 号
9 月 27 日	支付机构预付卡业务管理办法	中国人民银行公告〔2012〕第 12 号
12 月 18 日	关于中国银行间市场交易商协会发布《中国银行间市场债券回购交易主协议》的有关事项[①]	中国人民银行公告〔2012〕第 17 号
12 月 31 日	中国人民银行、中国证券监督管理委员会签署《关于加强证券期货监管合作共同维护金融稳定的备忘录》	

资料来源：课题组整理。

[①]　该规章仅有公告号，无文件名。为方便读者了解该公告内容，课题组在此概括了文件内容。

（二）2012 年中国人民银行主要监管政策分析

2012 年，人民银行按照稳中求进的工作总基调，把稳增长放在更加重要的位置，加强和改进金融宏观调控；在监管政策方面，扎实推进金融改革发展，切实维护金融稳定，全面提升金融服务和管理水平。根据《人民银行法》，中国人民银行负责监督管理银行间同业拆借市场和银行间债券市场、监督管理银行间外汇市场；监督管理黄金市场；维护支付、清算系统的正常运行；负责反洗钱的资金监测等。2012 年人民银行的主要监管政策也主要围绕其法定职责和国务院的具体要求展开。

1. 信贷政策

2012 年，人民银行积极运用支农再贷款政策，支持金融机构扩大涉农信贷投放。3月，人民银行下发《关于管好用好支农再贷款 支持扩大"三农"信贷投放的通知》，要求各分支机构进一步发挥支农再贷款引导金融机构扩大涉农信贷投放的积极作用，支持农村经济持续、稳固发展。8月，人民银行下发《关于开展拓宽支农再贷款适用范围试点的通知》，在陕西、黑龙江两省开展试点，在坚持涉农贷款占各项贷款比例不低于70%的发放标准不变的前提下，将试点地区支农再贷款的对象由现行设立在县域和村镇的农商行、农合行、农信社和村镇银行等存款类金融机构法人拓宽到设立在市区的上述四类机构。

2012 年，人民银行累计安排增加支农再贷款额度 681 亿元，主要用于涉农贷款占比较高的西部和粮食主产省（区）。年末全国支农再贷款限额 2 203 亿元，余额 1 375 亿元，比年初增加 281 亿元；当年累计发放支农再贷款 2 090 亿元，比上年增加 382 亿元。从地区分布看，西部地区和粮食主产区支农再贷款限额及余额占全国的比重均超过90%。支农再贷款支持农村金融机构扩大涉农信贷投放取得明显效果，2012 年末，全国农村金融机构涉农贷款余额 5.3 万亿元，同比增长 16.0%。总体看，支农再贷款政策的实施，对引导金融机构扩大涉农信贷投放、改善农村金融服务发挥了积极作用，有助于促进实现粮食生产"九连增"，有力推动了农村社会事业的发展和农村面貌的改善。

2. 深化金融改革

2012 年人民银行继续推动大型商业银行深化改革，农业银行"三农金融事业部"改革试点取得重要进展。推动落实中国出口信用保险公司改革方案。积极稳妥推动珠江三角洲、浙江温州、福建泉州、浙江丽水等地方金融改革试点。中国人民银行还会同发展改革委、旅游局、银监会、证监会、保监会和外汇局联合发布《关于金融支持旅游业加快发展的若干意见》，要求金融机构加强和改进对旅游业的信贷管理和服务；改进和完善旅游业支付结算服务，支持发展旅游消费信贷；中国人民银行会同发展改革委、财政部、水利部、银监会、证监会和保监会联合发布《关于进一步做好水利改革发展金融服务的意见》，要求金融机构大力创新符合水利项目属性、模式和融资特点的金融产品和服务方式，进一步加大对水利建设的金融支持，积极探索建立金融支持水利改革发展的风险分散和政策保障机制等，努力促使金融为实体经济服务。

3. 扩大人民币跨境使用

6月5日，中国人民银行、财政部、商务部、海关总署、国家税务总局和银监会联合下发《关于出口货物贸易人民币结算企业重点监管名单的函》，境内所有具有进出口经营资格的企业均可自主选择以人民币计价、结算和收付。7月31日，中国人民银行发布《关于境外机构人民币银行结算账户开立和使用有关问题的通知》，允许境外机构采用人民币银行结算账户，促进了贸易投资的便利化；跨境贸易人民币结算和外商直接投资人民币结算都因此大幅增长。2012年跨境贸易人民币结算业务全面推开，国际货币合作也进一步扩大。

4. 金融市场监管

2012年人民银行牵头建立了公司信用类债券部际协调机制。5月17日，中国人民银行、银监会、财政部联合印发《关于进一步扩大信贷资产证券化试点有关事项的通知》，进一步完善了信贷资产证券化的管理制度。继续推动银行间债券市场的规范发展。2012年人民银行还推出了银行间市场黄金询价交易，并稳妥做好非法黄金及黄金衍生品交易的处置工作。

5. 金融风险及金融稳定监管

2012年人民银行有效防范了系统性金融风险，加强对民间借贷、房地产、政府融资平台等的监测分析。从全局的、系统的、长期的视角处理好信贷合理增长和银行贷款质量提升之间的关系，目的是既要防止金融风险蔓延，也要防止出现道德风险。12月，中国人民银行、中国证券监督管理委员会签署《关于加强证券期货监管合作　共同维护金融稳定的备忘录》，立足于发挥中国人民银行分支机构覆盖面广的优势，弥补地市级、县级证券期货监管力量的不足，着力提升金融监管效能，共同维护金融稳定。总体上，2012年人民银行加大了对金融风险监测力度，开展了各类金融稳定压力测试，同时推进金融机构的稳健性评估。

6. 征信及其他监管政策

2012年末，人民银行草拟的《征信业管理条例（草案）》已经国务院审议通过。[①]
人民银行还进一步推进了金融统计的标准化和会计财务工作的稳步转型。第二代支付系统、中央银行会计核算数据集中系统（ACS）建设按计划实施，并制定了《支付机构预付卡业务管理办法》，有效地规范了支付机构从事预付卡业务的行为，防范支付风险；对假币"零容忍"专项治理活动取得成效。机构信用代码全国推广工作基本完成。深化反洗钱监管，成为第一个符合反洗钱金融行动特别工作组（FATF）标准的发展中国家。废止了包括《银团贷款暂行办法》等两件规章和《金融信托投资公司委托贷款业务规

[①] 《征信业管理条例》于2012年12月26日国务院第228次常务会议通过，自2013年3月15日起施行（中华人民共和国国务院令第631号）。

定》等 22 件规范性文件。

（三）政策评价和展望

2012 年人民银行的各项金融政策将在 2013 年持续发挥作用。鉴于 2012 年人民银行各项政策已经初具成效，可以预见人民银行在 2013 年将继续上年政策的持续性，牢牢把握"稳中求进"的总基调，把促进金融稳定和促进市场经济发展的政策放在最为重要的位置。

2013 年人民银行的主要监管政策将包括以下几个方面。

1. 信贷政策

人民银行将继续完善信贷政策的导向效果评估，继续引导金融机构加大对国家重点在建续建项目、"三农"、小微企业、现代服务业、新兴产业等的信贷支持。继续完善民生金融，努力支持就业、扶贫、助学等涉及民生的金融工程，落实好差别化住房信贷政策。

2. 金融改革

人民银行将继续推进大型商业银行和其他大型金融企业完善现代金融企业制度。推动农村信用社深化改革，扎实推进农业银行深化"三农金融事业部"改革试点，持之以恒地通过改革完善农村金融服务体系。坚持推进和深化政策性金融机构改革。稳步推进利率市场化改革。进一步完善人民币汇率形成机制。落实中央政策，支持加快发展民营金融机构。深化金融重点领域改革，提高金融服务实体经济的质量和水平将一直是人民银行的工作重点之一。

3. 进一步扩大人民币跨境使用

人民银行将简化跨境贸易人民币结算手续和审核流程，继续支持香港等境外人民币市场发展，鼓励人民币在境外的使用和循环。人民银行还将开展跨境个人人民币业务；稳妥推进人民币合格境外机构投资者（RQFII）试点，积极做好合格境内个人投资者（QDII2）试点相关准备工作。此外，人民银行将继续推动双边本币互换，落实双边本币结算协定。

4. 推动金融市场规范发展

人民银行将继续推动债券产品创新，创新利率风险管理工具，稳步推进信贷资产证券化试点。做好境内金融机构赴香港发行债券，以及境外机构投资银行间债券市场试点的准入和市场监管。进一步强化信息披露和信用评级等约束机制，规范做市商制度、结算代理业务和货币经纪业务。

5. 加强金融风险监测和排查

人民银行将牢牢守住不发生系统性、区域性金融风险的底线，进一步健全系统性和区域性金融风险监测评估和预警体系，完善风险防范处置应对预案；加强对具有融资功能的非金融机构的风险监测；探索开展金融机构稳健性现场评估和银行业风险业务专项现场评估；抓紧推进建立存款保险制度的各项工作。

二、中国银监会主要监管政策

（一）2012 年中国银监会主要监管政策一览

表 7 - 2 2012 年中国银监会主要监管政策

发布日期	文件名	文号
2012 年 2 月 9 日	中国银监会关于整治银行业金融机构不规范经营的通知	银监发〔2012〕3 号
2012 年 2 月 24 日	中国银监会关于印发绿色信贷指引的通知	银监发〔2012〕4 号
2012 年 3 月 31 日	中国银监会关于完善银行业金融机构客户投诉处理机制切实做好金融消费者保护工作的通知	银监发〔2012〕13 号
2012 年 5 月 14 日	中国银监会办公厅关于银行业金融机构加强残疾人客户金融服务工作的通知	银监办发〔2012〕144 号
2012 年 5 月 26 日	中国银监会关于鼓励和引导民间资本进入银行业的实施意见	银监发〔2012〕27 号
2012 年 6 月 7 日	商业银行资本管理办法（试行）	中国银行业监督管理委员会令 2012 年第 1 号
2012 年 6 月 25 日	中国银监会办公厅关于农村中小金融机构实施富民惠农金融创新工程的指导意见	银监办发〔2012〕189 号
2012 年 6 月 25 日	中国银监会办公厅关于农村中小金融机构实施金融服务进村入社区工程的指导意见	银监办发〔2012〕190 号
2012 年 6 月 25 日	中国银监会办公厅关于农村中小金融机构实施阳光信贷工程的指导意见	银监办发〔2012〕191 号
2012 年 9 月 4 日	商业银行实施资本管理高级方法监管暂行细则	银监办发〔2012〕254 号
2012 年 10 月 19 日	中国银监会关于印发《农户贷款管理办法》的通知	银监发〔2012〕50 号
2012 年 12 月 7 日	中国银监会关于商业银行资本工具创新的指导意见	银监发〔2012〕56 号
2012 年 12 月 7 日	中国银监会关于实施《商业银行资本管理办法（试行）》过渡期安排相关事项的通知	银监发〔2012〕57 号

资料来源：课题组整理。

（二）2012 年中国银监会主要监管政策分析

2012 年，中国银监会以"守底线、强服务、严内控、促转型"为工作任务，促进银行业的健康发展。银行业整体态势良好，资产增速、质量和回报率保持平稳，商业银行抵御风险能力、资本实力和经营效率有所上升。截至 2012 年 12 月末，商业银行不良贷款余额 4 929 亿元，同比上升 647 亿元，不良贷款率为 0.95%，同比下降 0.01 个百分点；流动性比例为 45.8%，同比上升 2.7 个百分点；存贷比为 65.3%，同比上升 0.5 个百分点；人民币超额备付金率为 3.5%，同比上升 0.4 个百分点。商业银行全年累计实现净利润 1.24 万亿元，同比增长 18.9%；平均资产利润率为 1.3%，与 2011 年同期持平；平均资本利润率 19.8%，同比下降 0.6 个百分点；加权平均资本充足率 13.3%，同比上升 0.5 个百分点；加权平均核心资本充足率为 10.6%，同比上升 0.4 个百分点（见表 7 - 3）。

表 7 – 3　　　　　　　　　　　商业银行主要监管指标情况表（法人）

时间 项目	2012 年			
	第一季度	第二季度	第三季度	第四季度
（一）信用风险指标				
不良贷款余额（亿元）	4 382	4 564	4 788	4 929
其中：次级类贷款（亿元）	1 801	1 960	2 028	2 176
可疑类贷款（亿元）	1 909	1 934	2 074	2 122
损失类贷款（亿元）	672	670	685	630
不良贷款率（%）	0.94	0.94	0.95	0.95
其中：次级类贷款（%）	0.39	0.40	0.40	0.42
可疑类贷款（%）	0.41	0.40	0.41	0.41
损失类贷款（%）	0.14	0.14	0.14	0.12
贷款损失准备（亿元）	12 594	13 244	13 884	14 564
拨备覆盖率（%）	287.40	290.18	289.97	295.51
（二）流动性指标				
流动性比例（%）	45.66	46.69	45.23	45.83
存贷比（%）	64.53	64.33	65.28	65.31
人民币超额备付金率（%）	3.03	2.74	2.66	3.51
（三）效益性指标				
净利润（本年累计）（亿元）	3 260	6 616	9 810	12 386*
资产利润率（%）	1.43	1.41	1.39	1.28
资本利润率（%）	22.34	22.29	21.54	19.85
净息差（%）	2.76	2.73	2.77	2.75
非利息收入占比（%）	20.55	20.63	19.47	19.83
成本收入比（%）	29.46	29.52	30.46	33.10
（四）资本充足指标				
核心资本（亿元）	55 980	58 754	61 726	64 340
附属资本（亿元）	14 819	15 746	15 853	17 585
资本扣减项（亿元）	3 834	3 919	3 863	4 057
表内加权风险资产（亿元）	449 785	467 221	484 589	506 604
表外加权风险资产（亿元）	71 843	75 284	76 563	76 108
市场风险资本要求（亿元）	315	342	372	388
资本充足率（%）	12.74	12.91	13.03	13.25
核心资本充足率（%）	10.31	10.41	10.58	10.62
（五）市场风险指标				
累计外汇敞口头寸比例（%）	4.25	5.18	4.65	3.92
（六）不良贷款分机构指标				

续表

时间	2012 年							
	第一季度		第二季度		第三季度		第四季度	
机构	不良贷款余额（亿元）	不良贷款率（%）	不良贷款余额（亿元）	不良贷款率（%）	不良贷款余额（亿元）	不良贷款率（%）	不良贷款余额（亿元）	不良贷款率（%）
商业银行	4 382	0.94	4 564	0.94	4 788	0.95	4 929	0.95
大型商业银行	2 994	1.04	3 020	1.01	3 070	1.00	3 095	0.99
股份制商业银行 **	608	0.63	657	0.65	743	0.70	797	0.72
城市商业银行 **	359	0.78	403	0.82	424	0.85	419	0.81
农村商业银行	374	1.52	426	1.57	487	1.65	564	1.76
外资银行	48	0.49	58	0.58	63	0.62	54	0.52

注 * ：为 1—12 月累计净利润。

注 ** ：自 2012 年 9 月起，原深圳发展银行与原平安银行合并为新平安银行，本表数据未作可比口径调整。

资料来源：中国银监会网站。

综上所述，2012 年中国银监会的监管政策主要集中在以下几个方面。

1. 加强对商业银行的资本监管力度，监管标准逐渐与国际接轨

2012 年 6 月，银监会发布《商业银行资本管理办法（试行）》（以下简称《资本办法》），分别对监管资本要求、资本充足率计算、资本定义、信用风险加权资产计量、市场风险加权资产计量、操作风险加权资产计量、商业银行内部资本充足评估程序、资本充足率监督检查和信息披露等进行了规范。总体来看，新的资本监管体系既与国际金融监管改革的统一标准保持一致，也体现了促进银行业审慎经营、增强对实体经济服务能力的客观要求。实施新监管标准将对银行业稳健运行和国民经济平稳健康发展发挥积极作用。

2012 年 9 月，银监会发布的《商业银行实施资本管理高级方法监管暂行细则》明确了实施高级方法银行的标准，并对高级方法的核准工作流程、核准条件、后续监督检查等进行了规定。2012 年 12 月，银监会发布的《关于商业银行资本工具创新的指导意见》，提出了商业银行资本工具创新的基本原则，明确了合格资本工具的认定标准，并提出了推进资本工具创新的相关工作要求。2012 年 12 月，银监会发布了《关于实施〈商业银行资本管理办法（试行）〉过渡期安排相关事项的通知》，明确了过渡期内分年度资本充足率监管要求。2013 年 1 月 1 日，商业银行应达到最低资本要求；国内系统重要性银行还应满足附加资本要求。2013 年末，储备资本要求为 0.5%，其后 5 年每年递增 0.4%。到 2013 年末，对国内系统重要性银行核心一级资本充足率、一级资本充足率和资本充足率的要求分别为 6.5%、7.5% 和 9.5%；对其他银行核心一级资本充足率、一级资本充足率和资本充足率的要求分别为 5.5%、6.5% 和 8.5%。

2. 严格监控系统性和区域性金融风险

2012 年，为防止发生系统性和区域性金融风险，实现银行业安全稳健运行，中国银监会针对银行业风险反弹压力有所增大的趋势，紧紧围绕平台、房地产、流动性、案件、表外业务和信息科技六大重点风险，有针对性地强化监控和各类指导；同时，对新暴露的少数行业信贷风险、少数企业集群风险和少数地区的民间融资、企业担保等风险苗头，在深入调查的基础上，独立判断、谨慎分析、稳妥应对；基本做到了及早监测发现风险、尽早报告预警风险、及时控制处置风险，有效防止了风险的扩散蔓延，消除了系统性和区域性风险苗头。

3. 对各类非银行金融机构的监管也不松懈

2012 年，中国银监会内部下发了《信托公司现场检查指引》、《信托公司现场检查联席会议工作规程》，明确派出机构的职责，规范信托公司现场检查联席会议，提高异地信托业务监管工作有效性，确保信托公司现场检查工作的质量。中国银监会反复强调了信托业的风险管理，加强了对房地产信托风险、平台贷款风险、银信合作风险以及其他信托业务风险的防范，督促信托公司做好各项基础工作。为防范信托业风险，2012 年1 月中旬，中国银监会叫停票据类信托，又通过"窗口指导"方式叫停同业存款类业务。此后，监管层又展开对房地产信托和政信合作的"窗口指导"，并在 2012 年 10 月叫停资金池信托业务。

根据财务公司的业务特点，中国银监会严密监控财务公司流动性监管指标；督促财务公司密切关注所属集团流动资产和负债情况；跟踪研究其所属行业的景气程度，提前预判和防范集团可能发生的流动性风险。此外，中国银监会还督促和引导财务公司围绕集团资金池稳健开展业务，保持合理的集团外负债规模和水平。

在 2011 年金融租赁公司资产质量情况专项检查基础上，2012 年中国银监会督促金融租赁公司加强整改落实，建立健全资产分类制度以及资产质量分类的动态调整机制，准确分类、充足拨备，保障资产分类真实准确。中国银监会还研究推进金融租赁公司分类监管工作。

对于汽车金融公司、货币经纪公司、消费金融公司三类相对较新的机构来说，2012 年中国银监会基本完成了《汽车金融公司风险评级和分类监管办法》（完善稿），完成《货币经纪公司试点管理办法》的修订，启动《消费金融公司试点管理办法》修订，还完成了《非银行金融机构行政许可事项实施办法》及《非银行金融机构行政许可事项申请材料目录及格式要求》的修订工作，为这些机构的合规发展创造制度条件。

4. 继续做好金融消费者宣传、教育和服务工作，成立专业的金融消费者保护机构

2012 年中国银监会一如既往地做好金融消费者宣传教育工作，加强重点业务领域的政策宣传和沟通。针对银行业创新业务发展迅速、变化快、结构复杂和专业性强等特点，组织协调中国银行业协会和银行业金融机构不断加强理财业务、银行卡、电子银

行、衍生品等业务领域的宣传和舆论引导，帮助社会公众树立科学正确的风险观念、理解和及时知晓银监会的监管要求。特别是在创新业务的营销管理、适宜度评估、信息披露、投诉管理和风险揭示等方面着重开展宣传和解读，便于公众掌握和利用好政策法规维护自身的合法权益。

2012 年，银监会成立银行业消费者权益保护局，其主要职能包括制定银行业金融机构消费者权益保护总体战略、政策法规；协调推动建立并完善银行业金融机构消费者服务、教育和保护机制，建立并完善投诉受理及相关处理的运行机制；组织开展银行业金融机构消费者权益保护实施情况的监督检查，依法纠正和处罚不当行为；统筹策划、组织开展银行业金融机构消费者宣传教育工作等。今后该局将在金融消费者保护方面发挥更大的作用。

（三）政策评价与展望

当前我国金融业仍处于比较好的发展时期，我国经济社会发展基本面长期趋好，国内市场潜力巨大，社会主义市场经济体制机制不断完善，工业化、城镇化、信息化、农业现代化同步推进，为银行业以及其他非银行金融机构的发展提供了较好的机遇和有利条件，这可以从以商业银行为首的各类金融机构 2012 年取得的较好盈利情况中得到证实。但同时，监管机构也清醒地看到，在外部冲击和内部转型的压力下，银行等金融机构面临的风险和困难逐渐增多，对风险管理和监管的要求日益提高。

2013 年，中国银监会需要准确把握银行等金融机构的发展基调、服务方向、改革重点、风险防线、创新精髓和监管导向，进一步健全促进宏观经济稳定、支持实体经济发展的现代金融体系，进一步推动银行等金融机构深化改革和发展转型，进一步改进系统性区域性风险的防范措施，促进经济金融发展质量和效率同步提升。2013 年对银行等金融机构（以银行业为主）的监管工作重点如下：

1. 切实防范和化解金融风险

守住不发生系统性和区域性风险底线是首要任务，特别注意防控三类风险。一是严防信用违约风险。对平台贷款风险，继续执行"总量控制、分类管理、区别对待、逐步化解"政策，控制总量、优化结构，支持符合条件的地方政府融资平台和国家重点在建续建项目的合理融资需求；对房地产贷款风险，要认真执行房地产调控政策，落实差别化房贷要求，加强名单制管理和压力测试。对企业集群风险，要加强监测，分门别类采取措施进行防范。对产能过剩行业风险，要坚持有保有压，确保风险可控。二是严控表外业务关联风险。要严格监管理财产品设计、销售和资金投向，严禁未经授权销售产品，严禁销售私募股权基金产品，严禁误导消费者购买，实行固定收益和浮动收益理财产品分账经营、分类管理。三是严管外部风险传染。重点防范民间融资和非法集资等外部风险向银行体系传染渗透。禁止银行业金融机构及员工参与民间融资，禁止银行客户转借贷款资金。2013 年要重点防控好平台、房地产、企业集群和产能过剩行业等领域的信用违约风险，理财、代付以及银证、银基、银保、银信等合作类交叉性业务领域的表外业务关联风险，影子银行、民间融资和非法集资等领域外部风险传染。

2. 引导银行等金融机构积极支持实体经济发展

正确引导信贷投向，重点加强对重点领域和薄弱环节的信贷支持，规范贷款资金使用，确保信贷资金投入实体经济。支持国家重点在建续建项目的合理信贷资金需求。进一步改进小微企业和"三农"金融服务，确保增速不低于当年贷款平均增速。积极支持产业升级、绿色环保和消费、外贸等重点领域，做好城镇化配套金融服务。推动金融资源适度向欠发达地区和老少边穷地区倾斜。督导银行业合理定价、规范收费，严格执行"七不准、四公开"规定，推动降低融资成本。

3. 深入推动银行业改革转型

一是积极推进体制机制改革，提高银行业金融机构集约经营和服务水平。深入研究我国银行业"走出去"发展战略，优化海外布局。稳步推进农信社转制，鼓励农信社和农商行向乡村下沉服务网点。按照商业可持续和"贴近基层、贴近社区、贴近居民"原则，探索建立多种形式的便民服务网络，强化社区金融服务。二是以稳步实施新资本管理办法为契机，推动银行业金融机构完善公司治理、加强内部控制、改进 IT 和绩效考评，科学设定经营目标和考核指标，增强转型发展的内生动力。引导适应利率市场化改革要求，优化存贷款品种、结构和质量，加强利差管理和中间业务成本管理，审慎开展综合化经营试点。三是督促银行业金融机构落实消费者权益保护要求，广泛开展金融消费者宣传教育和"送金融知识下乡"活动。四是鼓励审慎开展金融创新。支持银行业创新支持实体经济的金融产品，加快资本工具创新进程。五是探索创新民间资本进入银行业的方式，鼓励民间资本参与发起设立新型银行业金融机构和现有机构的重组改制。

4. 进一步规范信托业的有序发展

信托公司相比其他各类金融机构，投资范围最为广泛，投资方式最为灵活；在持续的银行信贷规模管控环境下，信托公司满足了企业的融资需求，在 2012 年又取得了快速的发展，信托公司管理的资产规模仅次于银行业。但信托理财计划兑付的高峰期将在 2013 年上半年出现。可以预见，中国银监会将会对信托理财行业的有序发展给予更多的关注。

5. 加强监管政策的梳理、研究

2013 年，中国银监会将全面加强监管队伍的思想建设、组织建设、作风建设和廉政建设，努力加强班子队伍建设，共同打造良好监管文化，持续提高监管队伍的能力和水平，完善微观审慎与宏观审慎有机结合的监管政策体系。2013 年国内外宏观环境更为复杂，监管任务也更为繁重，中国银监会必须坚持持续健康的发展要求，科学把握稳增长、控通胀与防风险的平衡，坚持运用底线思维、逆周期监管和预调微调方法，增强工作的前瞻性和针对性。

三、中国证监会主要监管政策

(一) 2012 年中国证监会主要监管政策一览

表 7 - 4　　　　　　　　　　　2012 年证券业主要监管政策

发布日期	政策名称	发文单位
1 月 10 日	《国务院关于同意建立清理整顿各类交易场所部际联席会议制度的批复》	国务院
1 月 21 日	《关于调整证券资格会计师事务所申请条件的通知》	财政部、证监会
2 月 12 日	《证券公司合规管理有效性评估指引》	中国证券业协会
2 月 23 日	《关于人民法院为防范化解金融风险和推进金融改革发展提供司法保障的指导意见》	最高人民法院
3 月 7 日	《关于完善首次公开发行股票上市首日盘中临时停牌制度的通知》	深交所
3 月 8 日	《关于加强新股上市初期交易监管的通知》	上交所
3 月 12 日	《关于证券公司切实履行职责防范和抑制新股炒作行为的通知》	证监会
3 月 19 日	《证券资信评级机构执业行为准则》	中国证券业协会
4 月 28 日	《关于进一步深化新股发行体制改革的指导意见》	证监会
5 月 4 日	《关于进一步落实上市公司现金分红有关事项的通知》	证监会
5 月 22 日	《关于办理内幕交易、泄露内幕信息刑事案件具体应用法律若干问题的解释》	最高人民法院、最高人民检察院
6 月 19 日	《证券分析师执业行为准则》、《证券研究报告执业规范》	中国证券业协会
6 月 20 日	《关于实施〈合格境外机构投资者境内证券投资管理办法〉有关问题的规定》	证监会
6 月 28 日	《关于完善上交所上市公司退市制度方案的通知》	上交所
6 月 28 日	《关于完善深交所主板中小板退市制度方案的通知》	深交所
7 月 25 日	《证券期货市场诚信监督管理暂行办法》	证监会
9 月 20 日	《证券投资基金管理公司管理办法》	证监会
9 月 24 日	《证券期货业信息安全保障管理办法》	证监会
9 月 26 日	《基金管理公司特定客户资产管理业务试点办法》	证监会
10 月 29 日	《证券投资基金管理公司子公司管理暂行规定》	证监会
12 月 11 日	《证券公司治理准则》	证监会
12 月 13 日	《关于深化基金审核制度改革有关问题的通知》	证监会
12 月 17 日	《关于加强与上市公司重大资产重组相关股票异常交易监管的暂行规定》	证监会
12 月 21 日	《上市公司募集资金管理和使用的监管要求》、《关于股份有限公司境外发行股票和上市申报文件及审核程序的监管指引》	证监会
12 月 28 日	十一届全国人大常委会第三十次会议表决通过修订后的《证券投资基金法》	全国人大常委会

资料来源：课题组整理。

（二）2012年中国证监会主要监管政策分析

1. 证监会加大监管改革创新力度

2012年10月，在国务院第六批行政审批项目集中清理工作中，中国证监会共取消和下放了32个行政审批项目，占国务院部门清理项目总数的10.2%。据统计，自2001年开始，证监会分六批累计取消了136项行政审批项目。同时，证监会还加大打击内幕交易力度，与其他部委紧密合作，形成全方位的综合防控体系。2012年5月召开的金融创新大会更将创新监管推向了高潮，所列明的11项中国证券业的改革重点涵盖了证券公司业务、管理、产品及经营模式等所有方面。为了进一步强化证券经营机构的创新意识和积极性，证监会在2012年上半年更对多达近百项行政许可与审批制度、条令等进行了清理或权力调整与下放，目的就在于给证券经营机构以创新的动力。[①]

2. 新股发行和退市制度改革

2012年3月，中国证监会就新股发行体制改革方案征求意见。4月28日，证监会正式颁布《关于进一步深化新股发行体制改革的指导意见》，重申新股发行体制改革将坚持市场化方向，以充分、完整、准确的信息披露为中心改进发行审核，并提出6点针对性意见。5月18日，证监会对《证券发行与承销管理办法》进行了相应修改。5月23日，证监会发行监管部、创业板发行监管部下发了《关于新股发行定价相关问题的通知》，对新股发行定价的相关事项进行了明确。6月28日，沪、深交易所分别发布《关于完善上海证券交易所上市公司退市制度的方案》、《关于改进和完善深圳证券交易所主板、中小企业板上市公司退市制度的方案》，并根据方案修订相应《股票上市规则》。新股发行中的各种弊端一直是我国资本市场的痼疾，本次新股发行制度改革中首次提出了"老股转让"改革，即所谓存量发行，颇受市场关注。而退市制度则是资本市场一项基础性制度，只有实施有效的退市机制，才能真正促进证券市场中资源的合理有效配置，推动结构调整和产业升级。

3. 加大对证券市场违法违规行为的打击力度

打击内幕交易行为成为2012年证监会加大执法力度的重点。2012年2月23日，最高人民法院出台了《关于人民法院为防范化解金融风险和推进金融改革发展提供司法保障的指导意见》，5月22日，最高人民法院和最高人民检察院联合发布了《关于办理内幕交易、泄露内幕信息刑事案件具体应用法律若干问题的解释》，该司法解释是我国第一部专门针对内幕交易刑事案件认定和处罚方面的法律文件，在内幕交易人员的界定、内幕交易行为的认定以及犯罪情节和处罚标准的裁量等多方面予以详细的规定。在此背景下，内幕交易案件的查处力度大幅增加，2012年上半年，证监会把打击内幕交易案件

[①] 《2012年中国资本市场十大新闻》，载《金融时报》，2013-01-08。

作为稽查执法的重点，新增内幕交易案件 96 起，占新增案件的 53.3%。[1]

4. 加强对投资者的保护和教育

2011 年底，中国证监会投资者保护局正式设立，2012 年初开始正式投入运作。该局的主要职责包括八个方面：拟定证券期货投资者保护政策法规；负责对证券期货监管政策制定和执行中对投资者保护的充分性和有效性进行评估；对证券期货市场投资者教育与服务工作进行统筹规划、组织协调和检查评估；协调推动建立完善投资者服务、教育和保护机制；研究投资者投诉受理制度，推动完善处理流程和运行机制，组织有关部门办理投资者咨询服务事宜；推动建立完善投资者受侵害权益依法救济的制度；按规定监督投资者保护基金的管理和运用；组织和参与监管机构间投资者保护的国内国际交流与合作。据悉，中国证券投资者保护基金有限责任公司也将会被纳入投保局，由其统一管理。[2]

5. 《证券投资基金法》修订通过

2012 年 12 月 28 日，十一届全国人大常委会第三十次会议表决通过修订后的《证券投资基金法》，将于 2013 年 6 月 1 日起施行。修订后的证券投资基金法一是将非公开募集基金纳入调整范围。明确了"公开募集"与"非公开募集"的界限，在基金合同签订、资金募集对象、宣传推介方式、基金登记备案、信息资料提供、基金资产托管等方面，设定与公募基金明显不同的行为规范和制度安排，实施适度、有限的监管。二是促进公募基金向财富管理机构全面升级转型。弱化行政审批，取消基金托管人的任职核准，取消基金管理人设立分支机构核准、5% 以下股东变更核准，以及变更公司章程条款审批等项目，降低基金管理人的市场准入条件，并允许基金管理人通过专业人士持股等方式，来强化激励约束机制。同时为合伙制基金管理人、保险资产管理公司等金融机构及符合条件的私募基金管理人从事公募业务，商业银行之外的其他金融机构从事基金托管业务，留足了法律空间。[3] 三是加强了对基金投资者权益的保护，补充了风险管理和处置措施，增补了法律责任条款，明确了市场禁入规则，加大了处罚力度，促进基金行业向规范化、法制化的方向发展。

6. 不断健全上市公司分红制度

2012 年 5 月，证监会发布《关于进一步落实上市公司现金分红有关事项的通知》，要求上市公司应在章程中进一步完善现金分红政策，细化分红决策流程，并要求董事会专项论证股东回报事宜，充分听取独立董事和中小股东的意见诉求。同时，证监会有关负责人还表示，上述要求将贯穿于 IPO、再融资、并购重组等整个环节，对于未分红的

---

[1] 《2012 年上半年证券期货稽查执法情况》，http://www.csrc.gov.cn/pub/newsite/jcj/gzdt/201208/t20120803_213491.htm，访问时间：2013 年 4 月 4 日。

[2] 《证监会投资者保护局成立，投保基金将纳入投保局》，载《东方早报》，2012 - 01 - 11。

[3] 《证券投资基金法修订通过》，载《上海证券报》，2012 - 12 - 31。

公司，要详细披露未分红的具体原因，并对未分红资金的使用计划作出说明。在现行法律框架下，证监会将充分考虑公司所处发展阶段和行业特性，进一步研究完善上市公司分红与再融资挂钩制，强化外部约束机制作用，完善投资者回报机制。

（三）政策评价与展望

2012 年，中国证券市场监管改革的力度空前，推出了许多新政策和新制度，从《证券投资基金法》的修订到新股发行和退市制度改革，从打击内幕交易到各类交易场所的清理整顿，从健全上市公司分红机制到加强投资者的保护和教育，等等监管政策涉及资本市场改革发展的方方面面，充分体现了监管创新的决心和恒心。资本市场的长期、健康可持续发展，取决于制度的合理、市场的公平以及对于广大中小投资者合法利益的保护。本轮监管创新的全面推动和逐步深化，对于发展中的中国证券市场而言无疑是一个重大利好，随着监管力度的不断加大和监管措施的不断完善，已经并将继续对中国证券市场的制度建设和法治环境产生重大影响。在 2013 年，我国证券市场的监管政策将会步入深入改革的步伐，而重点仍会落脚于新股发行和退市制度改革的继续深化、上市公司治理的不断加强、加大对于证券市场违法违规行为的查处力度和提升投资者教育和保护水平这几个方面上。

四、中国保监会主要监管政策

（一）2012 年中国保监会主要监管政策一览

表 7 – 5 2012 年中国保监会主要监管政策

日期	文件名称	发布单位
1 月 4 日	关于《人身保险公司保险条款和保险费率管理办法》若干问题的通知	保监会
1 月 12 日	关于印发《财产保险公司再保险管理规范》的通知	保监会
1 月 12 日	关于印发《保险公司财会工作规范》的通知	保监会
1 月 12 日	关于加强农业保险理赔管理工作的通知	保监会
1 月 17 日	关于做好保险消费者权益保护工作的通知	保监会
1 月 17 日	中国保监会关于加强和改进财产保险理赔服务质量的意见	保监会
1 月 29 日	关于调整保险业务监管费收费标准等有关事项的通知	保监会
2 月 6 日	关于调整外资保险公司部分行政许可项目有关事项的通知	保监会办公厅
2 月 14 日	关于人身保险业综合治理销售误导有关工作的通知	保监会
2 月 21 日	关于印发《机动车辆保险理赔管理指引》的通知	保监会
2 月 23 日	关于加强机动车辆商业保险条款费率管理的通知	保监会
2 月 27 日	关于印发《人身保险公司年度全面风险管理报告框架》及风险监测指标的通知	保监会
2 月 28 日	关于进一步规范保险专业中介机构激励行为的通知	保监会
3 月 1 日	关于印发《保险公司非寿险业务准备金基础数据、评估与核算内部控制规范》的通知	保监会
3 月 26 日	关于暂停区域性保险代理机构和部分保险兼业代理机构市场准入许可工作的通知	保监会

日期	文件名称	发布单位
3 月 29 日	关于印发《中国第二代偿付能力监管制度体系建设规划》的通知	保监会
4 月 28 日	关于进一步加大力度规范财产保险市场秩序有关问题的通知	保监会
4 月 28 日	关于进一步加强财产保险公司投资型保险业务管理的通知	保监会
5 月 15 日	关于上市保险公司发行次级可转换债券有关事项的通知	保监会
5 月 17 日	关于印发《保险公司非寿险业务准备金回溯分析管理办法》的通知	保监会
5 月 30 日	关于编报保险公司非寿险业务准备金评估报告有关事项的通知	保监会
6 月 12 日	关于印发《全面推广小额人身保险方案》的通知	保监会
6 月 12 日	关于进一步规范保险中介市场准入的通知	保监会
6 月 27 日	关于保险公司加强偿付能力管理有关事项的通知	保监会
7 月 16 日	中国保监会关于印发《保险资金投资债券暂行办法》的通知	保监会
7 月 16 日	中国保监会关于印发《保险资金委托投资管理暂行办法》的通知	保监会
7 月 16 日	关于保险资金投资股权和不动产有关问题的通知	保监会
7 月 16 日	中国保监会关于印发《保险资产配置管理暂行办法》的通知	保监会
7 月 16 日	关于贯彻依法经营依法监管原则切实维护投保人和被保险人权益的通知	保监会
7 月 19 日	关于印发《保险公司薪酬管理规范指引（试行）》的通知	保监会
7 月 25 日	保险公司控股股东管理办法	保监会
8 月 6 日	中国保监会关于印发《关于加强反保险欺诈工作的指导意见》的通知	保监会
8 月 18 日	关于健康保险产品提供健康管理服务有关事项的通知	保监会
9 月 14 日	关于支持汽车企业代理保险业务专业化经营有关事项的通知	保监会
9 月 29 日	中国保监会关于印发《人身保险销售误导行为认定指引》的通知	保监会
10 月 12 日	关于保险资金投资有关金融产品的通知	保监会
10 月 12 日	关于印发《基础设施债权投资计划管理暂行规定》的通知	保监会
10 月 12 日	关于印发《保险资金境外投资管理暂行办法实施细则》的通知	保监会
10 月 12 日	关于印发《保险资金参与金融衍生产品交易暂行办法》的通知	保监会
10 月 12 日	关于印发《保险资金参与股指期货交易规定》的通知	保监会
10 月 23 日	中国保监会关于印发《人身保险公司销售误导责任追究指导意见》的通知	保监会
11 月 2 日	关于贯彻实施《保险公司薪酬管理规范指引（试行）》有关事项的通知	保监会
11 月 2 日	关于贯彻实施《保险公司董事及高级管理人员审计管理办法》有关事项的通知	保监会
11 月 2 日	中国保监会关于报送年度信息披露报告的通知	保监会办公厅
11 月 5 日	中国保监会关于第六批取消和调整行政审批项目的通知	保监会
11 月 7 日	中国保监会关于印发《人身保险业综合治理销售误导评价办法（试行）》的通知	保监会
11 月 21 日	中国保监会关于废止部分规范性文件的通知	保监会
12 月 11 日	关于尽快遏制电销扰民有关事项的通知	保监会
12 月 17 日	国务院关于修改《机动车交通事故责任强制保险条例》的决定	国务院
12 月 25 日	关于印发《中国保监会电子文件传输系统管理暂行办法》的通知	保监会办公厅

资料来源：课题组整理。

（二）2012 年中国保监会主要监管政策分析

1. 投资新政适时出台，保险资金运用市场化改革取得新成效

保险监管部门连续出台《保险资产配置管理暂行办法》等 12 项资金运用监管新政策。投资监管新政坚持市场化方向；"放"手搞改革，加强改革的顶层设计和协调推动力度，建立和完善保险资金运用创新体系，以开放促发展、促改革、促创新；着力"抓"风险防范，实现企业内部管控和加强外部监管的有机结合。综合来说，新政着力在保险资金运用领域放松管制、拓宽范围、完善风险防控机制。

拓宽渠道，增加品种。新政已囊括了业内预期的所有投资工具，包括"允许保险机构开展融资融券、股指期货业务"、"拓宽保险资金境外投资品种和范围"、"拓宽境内股权和不动产投资范围"、"增加无担保债券品种"、"拓宽基础设施债权计划投资领域"等。

打通保险与银证信通道。保险资金的投资范围打破以往体内循环的封闭现状，实现与银行、证券、信托的对接。允许基金、券商加入受托管理保险资金的队伍，允许保险机构投资券商发起设立的集合资产管理计划、信托公司的集合资金信托计划、商业银行发起的信贷资产支持证券及保证收益型理财产品；允许保险资产公司受托管理养老金、企业年金、住房公积金和其他企业委托的资金；保险资管公司可根据受托资金需求，制定投资策略，开发资产管理产品，并以投资组合名义开设相关账户。

更新理念，减少审批。放松管制、加强监管，用机制换审批，主动减少行政审批，取消重大投资、资产管理产品以外的所有审批，建立风险资本约束机制。

保险投资新政将进一步增强保险资金运用的规范性、专业性和灵活性，其实施将对保险公司产生重大影响：首先，资产配置管理在保险投资中的重要性更加凸显。促使保险公司从保险产品源头，厘清保险资金性质，确定相应的投资政策，支持保险产品创新，改善保险公司盈利模式。其次，保险公司投资运作空间进一步增大。再次，更加考验保险公司的投资能力。最后，保险投资风险增大，保险公司的投资风险管理更加重要。

总之，这一系列资金运用监管新政，既与国家的宏观经济政策相一致，又符合保险机构的现实投资需求，在风险可控的前提下推进这些举措，有利于提升保险业服务民生工程和实体经济的力度，有利于支持资本市场改革，促进商业银行、证券公司和基金管理公司业务创新，对于保险市场乃至金融市场发展将产生深远影响。

2. 第二代偿付能力监管体系建设全面启动，保险监管现代化迈出新步伐

2012 年 3 月 29 日，保监会发布《中国第二代偿付能力监管制度体系建设规划》（以下简称《规划》），力争用 3 ~ 5 年，建设一套以风险为导向、符合我国国情、适应新兴保险市场特点的新一代偿付能力监管体系。

偿付能力监管是保险监管的核心，是保护保险消费者利益的关键所在。2003 年至

2007年底，保监会基本搭建起具有中国特色的第一代偿付能力监管制度体系。第一代偿付能力监管制度体系推动保险公司树立了资本管理理念，提高了经营管理水平，在防范风险、促进我国保险业科学发展方面起到了十分重要的作用。近年来，国际国内金融形势发生了巨大变化。从国际看，金融危机之后，国际金融改革一直在快速推进，金融监管国际趋同的步伐明显加快。银行业出台了巴塞尔资本协议Ⅲ，国际保险监管规则也正在进行一场重大变革。国际保险监督官协会（IAIS）于2011年10月出台了新的26项核心监管原则，并且正在研究制定全球统一的保险集团监管共同框架，将偿付能力监管作为核心内容之一；欧盟正在抓紧推进偿付能力Ⅱ，计划2014年实施；美国保险监督官协会（NAIC）启动了偿付能力现代化工程，对偿付能力监管体系进行调整，2012年底左右完成。因此，未来几年是重塑国际保险监管格局的关键时期。从国内看，国内保险市场和资本市场快速发展，对防范风险和监管的要求越来越高，现行偿付能力监管制度体系在某些方面已不能完全适应新形势下的监管需要。在上述背景下，保监会决定启动中国第二代偿付能力监管制度体系的建设工作，出台了建设规划。

《规划》明确了第二代偿付能力监管制度体系的指导思想、组织领导、总体目标、整体框架、基本原则、实施步骤和工作机制。《规划》提出了三个总体目标：一是用三至五年时间，形成一套既与国际接轨又与我国保险业发展阶段相适应的偿付能力监管制度；二是在制度建设的过程中，不断推动保险公司建立健全全面风险管理制度，提高行业风险管理和资本管理水平；三是通过制度建设，不断提升我国偿付能力监管制度体系的国际影响力，提高我国保险业的国际地位。《规划》明确了三个基本原则：一是坚持以国情为基础。二是坚持与国际接轨。三是坚持以风险为导向。《规划》顺应国际保险监管改革的潮流，提出第二代偿付能力监管制度体系采用国际通行的"三支柱"整体框架：第一支柱，资本充足要求。主要是定量监管要求，包括资产负债评估标准、实际资本标准、最低资本标准、资本充足率标准和监管措施等。第二支柱，风险管理要求。主要是与偿付能力相关的定性监管要求，包括公司全面风险管理要求，监管部门对公司资本计量和风险管理的监督检查等。第三支柱，信息披露要求。主要是与偿付能力相关的透明度监管要求，包括对监管部门的报告要求和对社会公众的信息公开披露要求。《规划》同时明确了整个制度建设工作分总结评估、专题研究、形成制度、测试完善、发布实施等五个阶段推进，并确定了调动全行业力量、提高工作透明度、加强国际交流等三项工作机制。

建设第二代偿付能力监管制度体系，对于保护保险消费者利益、促进保险市场稳健运行，提高行业防范化解风险的能力、维护国家经济金融安全，促进行业转变发展方式、增强保险业服务国民经济大局的能力，提高保险监管水平、增强金融监管的协调性，提高我国保险监管的国际地位、增强我国金融业的国际竞争力，促进我国保险业科学健康发展具有十分重要的意义。

3. 四家国有保险公司移交中管，保险监管体制呈现新格局

2012年3月，中国人保集团、中国人寿集团、出口信用保险公司、太平保险集团等四家国有公司党的关系、组织关系等由保监会移交中组部管理。此次调整后上述四家国有保险公司的人事任命权将移交中组部，保监会将主要负责对保险公司的监管。而此前，保监会既管四家国有保险公司人事任命、业务发展，又管规范市场、保护消费者。两项职责的目标存在一定程度的冲突。上述调整实现了保险监管模式的重大转变，从体制上解决了市场监管与行业主管职能不清的问题，保险监管定位更加清晰和明确。有评论认为，就上述四家国有保险企业自身而言，除正式确认"荣升"为副部级单位外，其实质并没有根本改变，其直接（或间接）大股东仍是财政部，明确的出资人依然在一定程度上缺位。因而，此举可能是为金融国资委的成立做准备。

4. 着眼于保护消费者权益，综合治理行业顽疾

保监会项俊波主席上任伊始即明确"把保护消费者利益作为保险监管工作的出发点和落脚点"。监管部门在2012年初就发布《关于做好保险消费者权益保护工作的通知》，部署消费者权益保护工作。2012年全年，从解决消费者反映最集中、最突出的问题入手，开展综合治理销售误导和理赔难专项工作，并以此为契机，建立健全保险消费者权益保护的制度机制。

一是全面推进寿险销售误导治理工作。2012年2月，保监会发布《关于人身保险业综合治理销售误导有关工作的通知》，全面部署寿险销售误导治理工作。此后又陆续发布《人身保险销售误导行为认定指引》、《人身保险公司销售误导责任追究指导意见》、《人身保险业综合治理销售误导评价办法（试行）》等制度。通过这些制度和措施安排，进一步规范销售误导行为的认定和执法标准，强化保险机构的主体责任。各寿险公司对照销售过程中的7大业务环节158个自查点逐一进行自查整改。针对电话销售业务、银行代理保险业务，组织开展专项检查。销售误导行为在一定程度上得到遏制，销售行为的规范性有所增强。

二是扎实开展车险理赔难治理工作。全年加强车险条款费率管理，制定车险理赔管理指引，统一车险理赔流程，规范理赔服务标准。将理赔难纳入监管处罚范围，加大检查和监督力度。车险理赔难治理取得初步成效，理赔周期比上年平均减少了9天，结案率达到109%，未决案件同比减少7%。同时，全面清理财产保险积压未决赔案。

三是完善消费者权益保护的工作机制。开通全国统一的12378保险消费者投诉维权电话热线，全国转人工的呼入量超过7万个。推动保监局局长接待日工作制度化，建立保险社会监督员制度。建立健全保险纠纷调处机制，全国共设立调解机构219个，成功调解纠纷9 280件，为消费者挽回经济损失3.2亿元。妥善解决保险消费者投诉事项，处理各类投诉15 268件。加强正面宣传力度，在央视、央广等媒体播出行业形象广告片。

5. 加强打击保险欺诈力度，为行业创造良好的发展环境

近年来，随着保险市场的快速发展，保险欺诈风险日益凸显，已经严重侵害了保险消费者权益，破坏了金融市场秩序和信用体系建设。保监会在 2009 年 7 月组织开展了打击"假机构、假保单、假赔案"专项行动。该次专项行动，共发现和查处各类假冒保险机构案件 32 起，各类假冒保单 20 万余份，各类虚假赔案 16 000 余件；向公安机关移交并已立案侦查的案件 149 起。2012 年 3—8 月，保险业又配合全国公安机关开展"破案会战"，严厉打击保险诈骗行为。"破案会战"期间，全国保险犯罪案件共立案近 2 500 起，抓获各类犯罪嫌疑人共计 4 000 多人，涉案金额超过 14 亿元，为行业挽回经济损失近 8 亿元。这是保险业第一次全面参与全国性的惩治经济犯罪活动，成效显著，不仅查办了一批长期"骗保险"的犯罪团伙，而且震慑了一大批"吃保险"的不法人员，同时也挤压了"理赔难"的水分，为保险机构提升理赔质量创造了有利条件，净化了保险市场发展环境，巩固了保险业改革发展的成果。在此基础上，保监会于 2012 年 8 月 6 日发布《关于加强反保险欺诈工作的指导意见》，以进一步建立反保险欺诈工作体系，构建反保险欺诈长效机制。

《关于加强反保险欺诈工作的指导意见》明确，反保险欺诈工作的目标任务是构建一个"政府主导、执法联动、公司为主、行业协作"四位一体的反保险欺诈工作体系，反欺诈体制机制基本健全，欺诈犯罪势头得到有效遏制，欺诈风险防范化解能力显著提升。同时，明确提出了当前和今后一个时期行业反欺诈的八项重点工作：一是健全反保险欺诈制度体系；二是严厉打击各类保险欺诈行为；三是提高欺诈风险管理能力；四是强化反保险欺诈监管机制；五是建立行业反欺诈合作平台；六是完善反保险欺诈协作配合机制；七是加强研究、交流与宣传教育；八是构建反保险欺诈长效机制。

（三）政策评价与展望

2013 年是实施"十二五"规划承前启后的关键一年。中国保监会主席项俊波 2013 年 1 月 24 日在全国保险监管工作会议上明确，2013 年的保险监管主要做好以下重点工作。

1. 牢牢守住不发生系统性区域性风险的底线

防范风险既是当前保险监管的紧迫任务，也是关系保险业长远发展的重大问题。要把加强风险防范作为保险监管的重中之重，重点关注寿险满期给付和退保风险、资金运用风险、偿付能力不达标风险、非寿险投资型业务风险、案件风险，以及综合经营中的风险传递，坚决守住风险底线。一是加强风险动态监测和预警。二是研究加强宏观审慎监管。三是增强风险应急处置能力。四是加强监管合作。

2. 进一步加大消费者权益保护工作力度

一是继续推进解决销售误导和理赔难问题。二是健全保险纠纷调处机制。三是促进保险公司提高服务质量和水平。四是开展形式多样的保险知识普及工作。

3. 继续推进改革创新

坚持求真务实的态度，从保护消费者权益和促进行业科学发展的角度出发，把那些具有一定普遍性、迫切需要解决、通过努力能够解决的问题，作为今年改革的重点，力争取得实效。一是制定监管体系顶层设计的具体实施方案。二是建立保险经营和保险机构服务评价体系。三是建立从业人员分级分类管理制度。四是推进行业共享信息平台建设。

4. 力争在规范市场秩序方面取得新的成效

一是抓住突出问题。主要是查处虚列手续费、虚挂应收、虚假批退保费、虚假理赔、不严格执行报批报备的条款费率，以及不真实提取准备金等违法违规问题。继续开展寿险销售误导综合治理，整治违规承诺高收益等非理性竞争行为。以车商代理保险业务为重点，开展兼业代理市场清理整顿工作。加强综合性检查，重点关注股东行为、资金安全、偿付能力以及准备金评估的合理性。切实做好反保险欺诈和反洗钱工作，进一步优化保险业发展环境。二是抓住重点领域和重点公司。加强现场检查的统筹规划，防止出现多头检查、重复检查。重点抓好商业车险、交强险、农业保险和大病保险业务的监管，加强银邮兼业机构监管。将问题较多和业务规模较大公司列为重点监管对象。选择2～3家寿险公司开展内控与合规性检查。深入治理保险领域商业贿赂，认真落实中央纪委转发保监会《关于严厉打击利用保险业务从事商业贿赂行为的通知》，坚决纠正不正当交易行为。三是依法严格及时处罚违法违规行为。制定保险违法违规行为处罚办法，逐步规范查处标准，做到全国一盘棋。对涉嫌犯罪的，坚决移送司法机关。四是强化对高管人员和上级机构的责任追究。坚持查处机构与处罚人员并重，继续强化案件问责，把违法违规问题与高管人员的法律责任及其任职资格挂钩，与公司的机构、产品审批挂钩，提高市场行为监管的针对性和有效性。

5. 加强对保险法人机构的监管

现在保险市场的各类违法违规现象和风险点虽然出现在基层，但根源往往在总公司。总公司的经营指导思想和管控能力，高管人员的法律意识和执行力，直接决定公司能否合规经营、稳健经营。加强法人机构监管，可以起到事半功倍的效果。一是加强偿付能力监管。对偿付能力不达标、资本金不符合监管规定的公司，坚决采取责令增加资本金、限业务、限机构、限薪酬和费用等监管措施。继续推进第二代偿付能力监管体系建设，全面启动各项监管标准制定工作。二是加强公司治理监管。狠抓制度落实，切实推动保险公司治理从"形式规范"向"治理实效"转变。对保险公司内部审计的合规性、全面性、有效性开展专项检查，推动公司提高自我管控水平。探索建立独立董事干预机制。加强对保险公司股东最终控制人的审查和监管，开展股权和关联交易检查。完善信息披露制度，提高保险经营透明度，强化社会监督。坚持监管部门列席保险公司董事会的做法，完善监管部门与保险公司董事会的信息通报机制。三是加强资金运用监管。全面梳理资金运用各项新政策的主要内容和风险点，根据行业的反馈意见进行完善。稳步推进基础设施及不动产债权计划等产品发行制度的市场化改革。引导和支持行业进行产品创新和机制创新。设立保监会资产负债匹配监管委员会，强化资产负债管理的硬约束，相对弱化比例监管。督促公司加强负债管理，提高资产负债匹配水平。参照国际通行标准，研究制定保险资产管理内控标准和风险责任人制度。研究建立贯穿保险资金运用全过程的偿付能力约束体系。四是推进市场准入和退出机制建设。提高市场准入和退出工作的透明度，建立审核委员会制度。抓紧出台并实施保险公司经营范围分级分类管理制度和分支机构准入制度。引入新型投资者，研究私募股权投资基金等新型资本投资的监管办法。加强对市场化兼并重组的研究，完善风险处置机制。

参考文献

[1] 吴晓灵、何海峰：《中国金融政策报告（2012）》，北京，中国金融出版社，2012。

[2] 阙紫康：《多层次资本市场发展的理论与经验》，上海，上海交通大学出版社，2007。

[3] 徐洪才：《中国多层次资本市场体系与监管研究》，北京，经济管理出版社，2009。

[4] 王国刚主编：《建立多层次资本市场体系研究》，北京，人民出版社，2006。

[5] 胡海峰：《多层次资本市场：从自发演进到政府制度设计》，北京，北京师范大学出版社，2010。

[6] 高峦主编：《中国场外交易市场发展报告（2009—2010）》，北京，社会科学文献出版社，2010。

[7] 顾功耘主编：《场外交易市场法律制度构建》，北京，北京大学出版社，2011。

[8] 高峦主编：《中国场外交易市场发展报告（2010—2011）》，北京，社会科学文献出版社，2011。

[9] 夏斌、陈道富：《中国金融战略 2020》，北京，人民出版社，2011。

[10] 国家外汇管理局国际收支分析小组：《2012 年中国国际收支报告》，2013。

[11] 中国人民银行货币政策分析小组：《中国货币政策执行报告（2012 年第四季度）》，2013。

[12] 中国银监会：《中国银行业监督管理委员会 2012 年年报》，2013。

[13] 中国银监会：《中国银行业运行报告（2012 年度）》，2013。

[14] 中国保监会：《2011—2012 中国保险市场年报》，北京，中国金融出版社，2012。

[15] 项俊波：《在 2013 年全国保险监管工作会议上的讲话》，2013 年 1 月。

[16] 李凤雨：《我国证券市场信息披露的现状、问题与对策》，载《金融发展研究》，2012（10）。

[17] 白冰、逯云娇：《中国场外市场发展研究——基于国内外场外交易市场的比较分析》，载《经济问题探索》，2012（4）。

[18] International Monetary Fund，Annual Report 2012，Working Together to Support Global Recovery，July 26，2012.

[19] Bank for International Settlements，BIS Annual Report 2012/2013，June 23，2013.

[20] The World Bank，Global Financial Development Report 2013：Rethink the Role of the State in Finance，December 3，2012.

English Version

Part One

Column Articles and
Thematic Report

CHAPTER 1

Loosening Regulation over Securities Traders for Development of Chinese OTC Market[①]

Wu, Xiaoling

The reform of capital market should aim to build a seamless multi-level capital market. Now, we should delegate powers to securities traders to develop Chinese OTC market, change the inverted pyramid structure of Chinese OTC market and construct the foundation for capital market development.

First, innovative securities traders approved by China Securities Regulatory Commission (CSRC) could set up the OTC market in their operating divisions. Enterprises meeting the following conditions are eligible to do OTC trading at counters of those approved innovative securities traders.

(1) Enterprises should have their financial statements audited by certified public accountants, and report to securities traders on a periodical basis;

(2) Shares or other objects for trading should be registered or put under custody at a specified system;

(3) Establish a qualified investor system to regulate trading players.

Second, the results of trading at counters of securities traders should be submitted in real time to an information system designated by Securities Association of China (SAC) or CSRC. Like multi-level capital markets in USA, build bulletin boards, announce quotations for market-making stocks of securities traders in the information system, and for non-market-making stocks, register without announcing quotations in the information system and let the regulatory department have knowledge of current trading situations and prices. Authorize SAC to supervise the quality of information disclosure. CSRC should be entitled to impose the most severe punishments over enterprises with false information and securities traders with poor supervision

---

① Excerpted from a keynote speech delivered by Ms Wu Xiaoling in January 2013, and the original title is "To Develop Chinese Multi-Level Capital Market". The Chinese Version of the content contained herein has been reviewed by Ms Wu Xiaoling.

on disclosure of information. Presently, so many Chinese listed companies are involved in false behaviors which, to a great extent, could be explained by the fact that, their costs for making false behaviors or violating regulations are too low. Therefore, to build an orderly capital market, realize genuine information disclosure and take responsibility for investors, the most severe punishment system over non-genuine information disclosure should be in place. A "sword" on the head of each violator will be very helpful for maintaining the order of capital market.

Third, we could build internal deal-making platforms or regional on-floor markets on the basis of OTC trading of securities traders. Conditions for stocks to be traded in regional markets could be lower than those on the main board and the second board; now, all local governments hope to construct regional trading places. Conditions for stocks to be traded in regional markets could be lower than that on the main board and second board; now, all local governments hope to construct regional trading places. In addition to the New York Stock Exchange and NASDAQ stock market, USA also has many local on-floor trading markets. Actually, before 1994, China also used to have local financial trading centers which however, lacked standardized development at that time. Today, based on previous lessons, we could establish regional exchanges, but conditions for listing of these regional exchanges should include shareholders' equity or net tangible assets of the company, pre-tax earnings, number of shares held by the public, number of investors holding more than one hundred shares, market value of shares, purchase price per share, number of market makers and governance requirements of the company; the quantity could be different from that in the main board market, but the substantive connotations of these conditions and standards should be the same.

In order to ensure the quality of stocks traded in regional markets, we should require the availability of three or more market makers; if three securities traders dare to make bilateral quotations for a stock, it demonstrates that, the investment value of this stock is good. We should at least develop such a standard in regional stock markets, while these regional markets should be supervised by securities regulatory bureaus, and CSRC should reinforce the supervision on national markets listed publicly and the formation of unified market rules.

Recently, CSRC published regulatory guidelines of non-listed companies, layed a system foundation for OTC market development, including No. 1 – Information Disclosure, No. 2 – Share Transfer Application Documents, and No. 3 – Essential Clauses in Articles of Association of Non-listed Companies. In No. 2-Share Transfer Application Documents, it is required that, application documents should be submitted for CSRC to determine whether shares could be transferred. In my opinion, it is feasible to temporarily put forward such a requirement for more than two hundred application documents of non-listed companies under the administration of CSRC. However, from the perspective of development direction, share transfer application documents should be submitted to securities traders who will serve as the front-line operators and the first responsible persons for fundraiser behaviors and information disclosure of companies in the capital market. CSRC should focus on making rules and standardizing securities traders' behaviors. If a securities trader fails to respect its position as a main market player by performing certain illegal behaviors, it should receive the most severe punishment, and even, its qualification should be canceled in this respect. If we don't treat securities traders as main market players, but instead, ask regulatory authorities to bear too many responsibilities in the market, I believe that the market development will be negative. As market intermediaries, financial institutions' basic function is to connect investors and fundraisers; if financial intermediaries fail to play the role of connection, it will be difficult to develop the financial industry.

CHAPTER 2

Building China's Financial Policy Framework Based on an Open and Major Economy

He, Haifeng

Since 1978, Chinese economy has maintained a rapid growth with remarkable achievements—in 2012, the GDP of China was ranked 2nd in the world, next only to that of USA, while the international trade of China surpassed that of USA, ranked 1st worldwide. This is a result from China's efforts in adapting to the context of globalization and continuously expanding and deepening reform and opening up. According to forecasts of international and domestic institutions, in the next 10-20 years, China is likely to become the world's largest economy. Along with economic development, China's financial reform and development have also scored great achievements-for example, some gross indicators of Chinese financial institutions and financial markets have been ranked at the forefront of the world. However, in regard to whether China can become a truly developed economy, finance as the core of modern economy will be one of necessary conditions, even probably one of sufficient conditions.

From a medium and long-term point of view, China's financial reform and development is faced with a question that demands immediate attention-how to build a financial policy framework in line with a major and open economy. The significance of this question comes from at least three aspects: greater complexity of international financial environment, more challenges in domestic financial development and further research on financial theory and practice. First of all, the recent financial crisis has a huge impact and far-reaching influence. On one hand, America's financial development pattern, which has always been identified as a world model, is actively seeking change as a result of possible failure; on the other hand, due to variance in purpose of economic and financial development, international coordination of monetary and financial policies between developed and developing countries become increasingly difficult-short-term consensus cannot ensure the consistency of medium and long-term goals or behaviors. For China, facing the prevailing international financial organizations, orders, mechanisms and standards, its basic option must be participation, only different in active or inactive-active participation means that China will not only have an opportunity to influence arrangements and settings of these systems, but meanwhile, will be bound to bear more responsibility. Secondly, China's financial development is faced with many challenges of "deep-water area" of reform and opening up. For example, what financial support does the structural adjustment and transformation of China's economic development pattern need and how to offer support? Also, what problems exist in financial operation, corporate governance and risk management? Finally, traditional research on financial theory and practical financial experience are always unable to provide convincing explanations for China's financial transformation and development, and fail to answer what mindset of an emerging power should China's financial policies have.

To build and improve a future-oriented financial policy framework characterized by open economy of a great power, the first question is: what's its foothold or principle? In the author's opinion, we should first stick to the most fundamental function of finance, i. e. financing the funds and capital to accomplish conversion of economic savings to investments. The international financial crisis once again proves that, despite a high-end service industry, finance still needs to treat serving the real economy as its primary task instead of being confined to self-entertainment or low efficiency. In China, both these two situations exist, although the latter has a longer history. For example, compared with America, China's gross savings rate and household savings rate are much higher, which however, could not be converted into capital through financial systems and financial mechanisms in a highly-efficient manner. As a result, America can maintain a low savings rate while China can't. Theoretically, the high savings rate is just a necessary condition for economic growth, but the savings-investments conversion mechanism is vital. According to some research, America's savings conversion efficiency is significantly higher than other developed countries, such as Japan and Germany. Currently, China suffers the pain of transforming development pattern and increasing domestic demand; financial policies determine financial systems and financial markets and further determine the savings-investments conversion efficiency, in view of this, the market-based direct finance should realize more rapid development. Moreover, China's financial policies should also stick to the principle of "internal and external linkage". Recognizing the trend of globalization, when joining WTO in 2001, China promised financial opening conditions far higher than those signed by Japan and Korea. In the context of increasingly accelerated financial internationalization and opening, the internal reform and development of Chinese finance cannot afford delay any more; in the meantime, these are also the foundation for Chinese finance to achieve the purpose of internationalization.

From the perspective of inside China, the author thinks that, the primary premise for becoming a major financial economy and continuously opening up is to speed up the interest rate liberalization. Firstly, as everyone knows, resource allocation through market mechanisms is a guide of China's economic and financial reform, while interest rate is the price of funds of different durations in financial markets. The regulated interest rate cannot reflect the real supply and demand of funds nor realize the efficient and reasonable allocation of financial resources. It's generally believed that, only by realizing the deposit and loan interest rate liberalization could the interest rate liberalization be truly achieved. According to the international experience of interest rate liberalization, spreads in many countries will be continuously narrowed, while all interest rate systems of today's leading developed countries are built upon market-based decisions. For China, the interest rate liberalization can not only realize better allocation of funds but also lay a foundation for the exchange rate formation mechanism and the foreign exchange management system-because the interest rate basically can be deemed as the compared price of internal interest rate in different economies; RMB exchange rate problems, to a great extent, can be attributed to variance in interest rate mechanism between China and a few major economies including America. Of course, at least in the short term, the interest rate liberation will cause a certain impact on China's banking system. [1] Secondly, ease market access to the financial sector. In May 2010, the State Council issued the *Several Opinions of the State Council on Encouraging and Guiding the Healthy Development of Folk Investments*, clearly allowing folk funds to enter the financial field and to set up various small financial institutions. In regard to the number distribution of enterprises, small enterprises account for a large proportion in an economy, which is true both at home and abroad. Practice proves that, small enterprises acquire financial services mainly from local small financial institutions-they are more focused and thus more efficient. [2] Now that the opening up of Chinese finance has become an inevitable trend, it's more required to ease access of folk capital to the financial sector, so as to establish more local small financial institutions, introduce and expand market competition, and resolve financing difficulties of small enterprises. In the long term, this will help Chinese finance form a reasonable hierarchical structure. Finally, encourage financial product innovation. A natural result of interest rate liberalization and eased market access will be market competition expansion, while the main form of competition among financial institutions is product innovation. If we say the financial innovation in Europe and America is excessive, then China's financial

---

① On July 20th 2013, China eased regulation on loan interest rates of financial institutions, which took an important step towards interest rate liberalization; however, the most important is the deposit interest rate liberalization.

② According to FDIC data, by the end of 2010, among 6,790 financial institutions engaged in deposit and loan business, 6,526 institutions are community institutions.

product innovation is quite inadequate-which could be explained by the "divided operation, divided supervision" system to some extent, although the original intention of this system was to promote financial stability and maintain financial stability. Encouraging financial product innovation can not only contribute to the effective competition of Chinese credit, monetary and capital markets but also benefit the construction and development of derivative markets and even provide direct help for the formation of Shanghai International Financial Center. [1]

From an external point of view, since internationalization is an essential part of a financial power, China should make important progress at least in three aspects. The first is RMB internationalization. [2] The worldwide acceptance and use of a currency includes three stages: trade, investment and reserve, that is, realizing the currency's such functions as medium of exchange, unit of account and storage of value around the world. Experience of America and even Britain cannot be simply copies, because historical conditions have changed dramatically and also will not repeat themselves; but we can still see that, military, technology and economy are decisive factors for currency internationalization, wherein economy is the most important one. The currency issued by a great power of open economy is very likely to become an international currency in the end, which seems not to be a question; the question is: what China should do? Despite the availability of excellent central banks, the previous capital export in pounds and the current capital import in dollars show different characteristics of international currencies. If Chinese economy can realize a steady growth, it seems that RMB internationalization can be simplified into a technical policy issue, i. e. internationalized RMB financial products and corresponding financial markets-this once again demonstrates that, the policy of encouraging Chinese financial product innovation is of great strategic significance. The second is international cooperation. Within a predictable quite long period of time, we can only be a taker but not a decider of international financial systems, so a rational and realistic option will be modest learning and active participation. From Asia, Pacific Ocean to the whole world, strengthen the cooperation with various international financial organizations and major economies, and gradually play a greater role. The third is reforming and improving financial supervision. Facing this round of financial crisis, China cannot be immune to the effects. The purpose of financial policies issued by a successful financial power, in addition to driving financial innovation, maintaining the effective operation of financial markets and supporting the

---

① In fact, the construction planning for Shanghai International Financial Center positions the short term target of Shanghai as a global pricing, trading and innovation center of RMB financial products.

② "RMB internationalization" formally appeared in Chinese official documents in July 2008, as a keyword in a specific function of the Exchange Rate Division of the People's Bank of China.

development of real economy, more points to ensuring financial stability. In order to achieve this purpose, the prudent policies with emphasis on macro-financial management have been established, and the authority and functions of the central bank have been reinforced-these are countermeasures against challenges in systematic risk, while the open China should pay more attention to the external impacts on financial stability.

In the next 10-20 years, whether China can become a financial power may not depend entirely on its own will. It should be noted that, China has realized the necessity to build a financial policy framework in line with this purpose-because this has been specified in the *"12th Five-Year" Plan for Development and Reform of the Financial Industry*. However, as for how to build Chinese financial policy framework based on an open and major economy, the author believes that, issues worth our efforts for solutions must be more extensive than the content discussed herein.

CHAPTER 3

Thematic Report: The Developing Chinese Multi-level Capital Market: Problems and Countermeasures

The inception of China's construction of a multi-level capital market fell in the year of 2003. As we all know, there are at least three milestones in the reform and opening-up of China. In 1978, a decision was made on the Third Plenary Session of the 11th CPC Central Committee to "construct a modernized country", raising the curtain of reform and open-up. In 1993, the Third Plenary Session of the 14th CPC Central Committee gave sanction to *Decision of the Central Committee of the Communist Party of China on Some Issues Concerning the Establishment of the Socialist Market Economy*, marking kickoff of the market economy construction in China. In 2003, *Decision of the Central Committee of the Communist Party of China on Some Issues Concerning the Improvement of the Socialist Market Economy* (the *Decision*) was approved on the Third Plenary Session of the 16th CPC Central Committee, with a view to consummate the market economy system of China. The *Decision* proposed "creating a multi-level capital market, perfecting the capital market structure and enriching capital market products", and further required "regulating and developing the main board market and pressing ahead with venture capital and growth enterprises market development". After that, the SME board was launched on Shenzhen Stock Exchange in May, 2004, followed by the second board in October, 2009. Over the last decade, China has made some achievements in developing a multi-level capital market, but the main board-SME board-second board architecture of China has many inherent defects, when compared with those of developed market economies like the USA. For example, the US has the main board market with New York Stock Exchange at its core and the second board with NASDAQ at the center, as well as national and regional markets and OTC markets across the country. Moreover, there is an appropriate transfer mechanism between markets at different levels intended for different companies, to fully satisfy the financing needs of companies of different types, sizes and at different stages of development. In contrast, the gap between the multi-level capital market of the US and China is quite wide and many problems need to be resolved, so as to provide sustainable support to the improvement of the financial system and growth of the real economy of China.

Structure of the Chinese Capital Market

Overview of the Multi-level Capital Market

Normally, the capital market is the market for offering and trading of securities, mainly comprised of the stock market and the bond market. There are significant similarities between the capital market and other markets in the economy, that is, buyers and sellers striking deals efficiently to attain win-win (the maximization of consumer surplus and producer surplus). The capital market provides liquidity for trading of securities, which is its primary value. Hence, most enterprises should be willing to trade property rights in this market (including debt and equity). By multi-level, it means different financial products need to be traded in different market segments to make transactions more efficient, due to differences in transaction properties such as risk profile, which then gives rise to different trading objects, trading rules and supervisory rules, as well as financial asset management channels at different risk levels. On the part of enterprises, SMEs form the largest number in the economy and they come into existence and disappear all the time. Only a small number of them have the opportunity to grow into large enterprises. Usually, the smaller size of an enterprise, the less financing demand, the fewer investors, and thus less demanding about liquidity of securities and transparency of corporate information. As the size of an enterprise grows, so does its financing demand, the number of investors, and the requirement for liquidity of securities and transparency of corporate information. The reality of growth of enterprises tells us that a multi-level capital market is needed to cater to the financing needs of enterprises at different stages. The debt market features lower risk exposure, fewer risk sources and smaller individual difference, while the equity market has more risk sources and bigger individual difference, so the latter demands more sophisticated hierarchy of the capital market theoretically speaking. That's why a multi-level capital market mainly points to a multi-level stock market (Que Zikang, 2007). In practice, multi-level development of the capital market of most countries with a mature market economy also refers to the stock market.

As far as the stock market is concerned, the structure of a multi-level capital market mainly involves the following respects: what levels form the stock market, differences among these levels, the size of each level and correlations among these levels, as well as differences in the regulatory, intermediary and trading rules for the market at each level. In terms of the differentiation criteria of a multi-level capital market, material differences mainly lie in listing standards, regulatory requirements (information disclosure requirements in particular) and trading rules. What we want to emphasize here is that the transfer mechanism is also a key component of the multi-level capital market. Normally, all enterprises would like to enter a market of high liquidity for trading, but the majority of them are reluctant to enter or fall short of the entry requirements, as such a market means high regulatory requirements and costly information disclosure. They may choose to get listed in a lower-level market first such as the OTC market, and then move to a higher-level market when they are ready. That's why it is necessary to create a communication or transfer mechanism among markets at different levels.

What kind of capital market structure makes an appropriate structure? When it comes to different levels of the capital market, an appropriate structure should be a structure wherein lower-level markets feature lower listing standards, lower regulatory requirements, poorer liquidity and more enterprises; while higher-level markets have higher listing standards, higher regulatory requirements, better liquidity and less enterprises. We may describe such a capital market structure as a pyramid structure. The capital market of a pyramid structure exactly matches the structure of enterprises in the economy and coincides with the growth process of enterprises. It may be considered to be a normal and appropriate hierarchical structure for the capital market. On the contrary, an inverted pyramid structure is very probably an inappropriate capital market structure. Of course, how many levels the capital market has also depends on the specific economic structure and industrial structure. Too many or too few levels are both adverse to the efficiency of the capital market.

Inverted Pyramid Structure of the Chinese Capital Market

Evolution and Status Quo

Like most market economies, the Chinese capital market is also divided into the floor market and the OTC market. It has undergone 23-year's ups and downs, starting from the opening of Shanghai Stock Exchange and Shenzhen Stock Exchange, the floor market, in 1990. To date, a multi-level capital market comprised of the main board, SME board, second board and the OTC market has taken shape and is expanding. As of May 20, 2013, there were 2469 listed companies in Chinese capital market, with total market capitalization measured at 28.3 trillion yuan. By the end of 2009, the stock market of China had leapfrogged Japan to become the second largest market in the world, only next to the US market.

To be more specific, the floor market started developing with trial operation of Shanghai Stock Exchange on December 1, 1990. April of 1991 saw the founding of Shenzhen Stock Exchange with the approval of the People's Bank of China. On October 31, 1991, China

Southern Glass Holding Co. , Ltd and Shenzhen Properties & Resources Development (Group) Ltd started public offering, the first time Chinese joint-stock companies issued B shares. Shenzhen Stock Exchange commenced tentative and preparatory work on the second board from 2001 and launched the SME board in May, 2005. China Securities Regulatory Commission (CSRC) kicked off the split share reform on April 29, 2005, and resolved the legacy left by the old system. China launched the QFII program in December, 2002, to allow licensed foreign institutional investors to invest in the Chinese securities market and bring in foreign capital, without realizing full convertibility of Renminbi capital. Trading of Shanghai-Shenzhen 300 Index futures contracts began officially on April 16, 2010, which a sign of optimization of trading instruments of the Chinese stock market. Please see the table below for the number of stocks, total market value, average market value and standard deviation of market value of each floor market as of May 20, 2013.

Table 1. 1	China Floor Market Size		Unit: 100million yuan
	Number of Stocks	Market Value	Average Market Value	Standard Deviation
Second board	355	11, 873	33	34
SME board	701	34, 911	50	72
Main board	1, 413	235, 953	167	805
Shanghai Stock Exchange	944	197, 634	209	978
Shenzhen Stock Exchange	469	38, 319	82	135
Total	2, 469	282, 736	115	614

Source: data collected by the research group.

The OTC market of China is made up of the inter-bank bond market, the agency share transfer system and the bond OTC market. The inter-bank bond market was launched in June, 1997. After more than ten years' rapid development, the inter-bank bond market has become a major component of the Chinese bond market. Most bond transactions take place in the inter-bank bond market and only a small number through exchanges. By bond OTC trading, it means that commercial banks continue bond trading with investors through their business outlets (including e-banking system) and handle related custody and settlement affairs. Commercial banks bulletin buying and selling prices of treasury bonds at their business outlets based on quotations of the national inter-bank bond market every day, to enable individual and corporate investors to buy and sell treasury bonds timely. Monetary and bond surplus and deficiency of commercial banks are balanced through trading in the inter-bank bond market.

Dating back to 1992 and 1993, the agency share transfer system started with STAQ

(Securities Trading Automated Quotations system) and NET (National Electronic Trading system) run by Stock Exchange Executive Council and China Securities Trading System Corporation Ltd, respectively. Corporate shares are traded in these two markets mainly. In 2001, the Securities Association of China initiated the agency share transfer system, to undertake circulation and transfer of companies delisted from Shanghai Stock Exchange and Shenzhen Stock Exchange. Supported by local governments, more than 200 regional property right exchanges were set up across all provinces and in major cities. To avoid redundant construction of property right exchanges at low level, regional cooperation was conducted to create regional markets. For example, the Property Right Common Market of the Yangtze River opened in 1997. In 2002, the Northern Property Right Common Market was founded. In June, 2007, nine provinces and regions within the pan-Pearl River Delta region signed the *Pan-Pearl River Delta Regional Property Right Exchange Cooperation Framework*, to make joint effort on building a cross-province regional property right common market.

From January, 2006, unlisted joint-stock enterprises in Zhongguancun Science Park began to be listed in the agency share transfer system. The functions of this system were enhanced, to provide agency share transfer services to former STAQ and NET listed companies, companies delisted from Shanghai Stock Exchange and Shenzhen Stock Exchange and unlisted joint-stock enterprises in Zhongguancun Science Park. This is called the Third Board market. In September, 2011, the pilot program of share transfer of unlisted joint-stock companies was expanded to bring Shanghai Zhangjiang, Tianjin Binhai and Wuhan Donghu, among other national high-tech parks, into the list of pilot parks for share transfer, besides Beijing Zhongguancun. By the end of 2012, 200 companies from these parks were listed. Now unlisted joint-stock companies in Zhongguancun Science Park are referred to as the New Third Board market, as they are high-tech enterprises. National SME Share Transfer System was inaugurated as a national stock exchange with the approval of the State Council on January 16, 2013. This is a landmark event in the nationwide OTC market development, indicating the beginning of a boom of the Chinese OTC market. Meanwhile, it also shows that a pyramid-shaped multi-level capital market structure is coming into being. The national share transfer system is still using the technical system to put into operation under the agency share transfer pilot program of Zhongguancun. As the system and the rules improve, the coverage of the pilot program will be widened, to perhaps include all national high-tech parks first and then to encompass all qualified SMEs across the country.

Characteristics of the Chinese Multi-level Capital Market

First, the hierarchical structure is inadequate. The floor market of China is divided into the main board, SME board and second board, but these three only differ in metrics of listing standards, and are not much different in terms of regulatory requirements (disclosure requirements in particular), listing and delisting rules and trading rules, and can hardly constitute a multi-level capital market in the real sense. The OTC market of China includes the inter-bank bond market, national OTC market, regional OTC market and bank counter market. As far as stock trading is concerned, there is no OTC market in China in the real sense. Among existing unlisted company equity dealers around the country, the agency share transfer system, Shanghai United Property Rights Exchange Zhangjiang Branch and the equity trust trading market of Tianjin Property Rights Exchange Binhai New District are all making great effort to create a third board market linked to the main board and second board, but the "online communication and offline settlement" mechanism is inadequate to realize automated trading within the system and financing functionality is absent. The inter-bank bond market serves as the OTC market for bonds. With limited investors and low liquidity, most enterprises cannot conduct bond financing through this market.

We may draw a comparison with the American market as to the aforesaid problem of inadequate hierarchy. The American securities market is made up of three parts (Xu Hongcai, 2009). First, there is the main board market, including two national stock exchanges (New York Stock Exchange (NYSE) and American Stock Exchange (AMEX)) and several regional stock exchanges (Chicago Stock Exchange, Boston Stock Exchange, Cincinnati Stock Exchange, Pacific Stock Exchange and Philadelphia Stock Exchange, etc). NYSE is the largest stock exchange in the world in terms of market value, with about 1867 listed companies and total market capitalization of US $16.6 trillion as of March, 2013. Average daily transaction volume hit US $153 billion in 2008. Second, there is the NASDAQ stock market (National Association of Securities Dealers Automated Quotations system). It provides a trading floor to stocks that scatter all over the country, with insufficient liquidity, and cannot be listed on NYSE or AMEX. NASDAQ is subdivided into Global Select Market, National Market and Small Cap Market. As it largely improves the efficiency, liquidity and fairness of the OTC market, it has grown into one of the leading securities markets in the USA. Third, there is the American OTC market comprised of Over the Counter Bulletin Board (OTCBB) and pink sheets market. As each level differs in trading rules, regulatory rules and listing standards, most enterprises can find a market best suited to their conditions and therefore financing efficiency is largely heightened.

Second, the inverted pyramid structure is to blame. Property right trading centers serving as the equity OTC market in China are mainly designed for regional industrial parks. Hence, their trading networks are not interconnected, and their settlement systems are not integrated, making trading inefficient. Only a small number of enterprises are listed in this market, while the majority of companies seek listing on stock exchanges. This gives rise to the phenomenon of "hordes of troops and horses try to go through a single-log bridge". Let's take the American stock market in 2004 as an example. NASDAQ counted 3229 listed companies, while NYSE with a longer history had 2293 merely and AMEX 575 only. NASDAQ has incubated and sent a lot of high-performing companies to NYSE. China doesn't have a low-level market to incubate and discover outstanding companies. It is difficult to control the uneven quality of applicants for listing. Even substantive regulations cannot prevent fraud and cheating. CSRC is very cautious about the approval of listing. It usually takes a company three to five years from preparation to success in listing. There are more than 18 million enterprises of all sizes in China, but the number of listed companies only accounts for 0.077% of all, that is, less than one out of every one thousand. Among these unlisted companies, 99.6% are SMEs and the majority of them have difficulty in financing.

Third, the OTC market of the bond market has been lagging behind. As issuing bonds can bring tax saving and financial leverage to enterprises, the bond market should be a better way of financing than the equity market. The corporate bond market of China has been underdeveloped. In spite of explosive growth of the credit bond market last year, a very small number of enterprises are using this financing tool, mostly being large central enterprises and local state-owned enterprises, while the mass SMEs still have difficulty in financing. This situation has much to do with backwardness of China's OTC market. The development and financing of American SMEs cannot go without NASDAQ, and 95% of bonds in the USA are traded on this largest OTC market, and its bond financing value takes up half of the entire direct financing market. Moreover, the American bond market is mainly comprised of corporate bonds, while other bonds of the same kind, even municipal bonds, treasury bonds or asset-backed bonds, don't have outstanding balance as large as corporate bonds. Furthermore, large state-owned enterprises form the mainstay of the Chinese stock market as exchanges have high listing standards, but these enterprises prefer equity financing. As a result, the bond market has been lagging behind.

Fourth, differentiated trading systems for different markets are absent, and in particular, a stock broker system doesn't exist. In the view of Wang Guogang (2006), a stock broker system is a multi-level flexible basic system. Different markets should have differentiated trading systems. The unitary exchange market of China leads to total absence of a stock broker mechanism. As for the OTC market, due to weak liquidity, market makers and other brokers can bring liquidity, and their market making effect has direct impact on liquidity of securities. In China, however, market making is not effective, due to limited variety of investors in the interbank bond market, limited types and maturity options of bonds, a small number of bonds, and absence of a linkage mechanism among underwriters, open market dealers and market makers. As for the OTC equity market, there is no market maker mechanism at all.

Last, a delisting and transfer mechanism among different markets is absent. A Delisting and transfer mechanism can equip the market with sort of elimination and upgrade/downgrade mechanism and create a healthy cycle among different levels of the capital market. In the USA, a rigorous delisting and transfer mechanism is in place to assure the quality of NASDAQ listed companies through the survival of the fittest. Besides NASDAQ Global Select Market, Global Market and Capital Market, OTCBB at a lower level is also connected to NASDAQ. Free transfer is allowed between different levels inside NASDAQ, by means of voluntary application and forced transfer.

Drawbacks of the Inverted Pyramid

We have pointed out in the preceding section the inappropriateness of the inverted pyramid structure, the most marked characteristic of China's capital market. To be more specific, the resulting drawbacks are reflected in two respects: financing difficulty and structural imbalance of the real economy and dissimilation of the exchange market.

Speaking of the influence of the capital market on the real economy, it may lead to problems in investment and financing matching, distorted price of money, and imbalance of the entire economy. In the multi-level capital market of China, the absence of lower-level markets makes it impossible to match demand and supply of capital. On one hand, it makes financing through the stock market inaccessible to hordes of companies that don't meet the listing standards of exchanges. On the other hand, the price of money is distorted as a huge mass of money cannot find investment channels. As we may see, idle capital is mostly deposited in banks and becomes a source of low-cost capital to banks. In the meantime, numerous enterprises have to go for usurious loans. Banks harvest rocketing profits and indirect financing has been dominating the market, while growth of the direct financing market has been hampered. State-owned banks dominate the banking sector of China and these state-owned banks are subject to the sway of the government more or less and tend to use the capital in government-invested projects. This can stimulate economic expansion, but the quality of economic growth is hardly bettered. As the return on investment drops, no change happens to financing channels, which is bound to make the economy skewed towards imbalance step by step.

As for the impact of the inverted pyramid structure on the existing market, it may give rise to distortion in supply and demand and the rent-seeking behavior. This has significant negative effect on the exchange market as the OTC market is very small in size and void of a delisting and transfer mechanism. First of all, the absence of a price discovery mechanism reversely forces lots of companies to seek listing on stock exchanges and CSRC to conduct substantive regulation. Meanwhile, a large number of companies that want to get listed would try everything possible for listing, creating much room for rent-seeking. As approval procedures are time-consuming and listing costs are high, many outstanding enterprises give up listing on stock exchanges, while substandard companies would do whatever it takes. The result isthat a great deal of capital cannot find investment channels and a drama of high offering price, high P/E ratio and high subscription rate has been going on in the Chinese stock market for quite long. Many listed companies harbour a distorted intent, and the stock market has become a sheer money scooper.

In a word, a multi-level capital market is the way out for the Chinese capital market, and consummating the OTC market will gradually change the present inverted pyramid structure. This is the foundation to resolve all problems in China's capital market. The next section will dig into the reasons for backwardness of the Chinese OTC market.

Reasons for Backwardness of the Chinese OTC Market

Evolution of National OTC Market
STAQ and NET

The notion of Corporate Share first appeared around 1990. The former Commission for Economic Restructuring promulgated *Opinions on Regulating Joint-stock Companies* on May 15, 1992. Back then, joint-stock companies were only allowed to conduct directed placement targeting legal persons and internal employees entitled to ownership. The *Company Law* of the PRC came into effect on July 1, 1994 and announced no more approval to corporate share placement. There were 6000-odd companies totally involved in directed placement then across the country. The background at that time was: national share and corporate share were established in the course of restructuring in order to maintain state ownership of these enterprises, as most listed companies were reorganized from state-owned enterprises. Meanwhile, due to a concern that circulation of private and public stocks in the same market might jeopardize the dominance of the public ownership system, public equity was prohibited from circulating in the secondary market. Stocks allowed to circulate in the secondary market were divided into private stocks and foreign stocks. As equity transfer and trading were disallowed, corporations were sometimes unable to recover or cash in their investment. For this reason, some experts and scholars suggested setting up a corporate share circulation market.

The pilot program of internal circulation of corporate shares was launched on July 1, 1992. STAQ was designated for corporate share circulation. On April 28, 1993, NET corporate share market went into operation. By the end of 1993, there were ten companies listed in STAQ and seven in NET, with nearly 500 members, 32000 institutional investors with accounts, and cumulative transaction value of 22 billion yuan. Hereto, the STAQ and NET corporate share markets came into being and STAQ and NET were referred to as the Two Nets system.

At the early stage of the pilot program, institutional investors knew little about the corporate share market and were rarely engaged. Following the opening of NET, people began to take an optimistic view of its outlook. After that, both the STAQ and NET markets recorded big rallies. The number of stockholders with STAQ accounts shot up from more than 1,400 to nearly 2,400 over half a month from mid-April to end-April, 1992 (exceeding 6,000 by end-May). People began to see the enormous potential and investment opportunity in the corporate share market. Numerous individual stockholders opened accounts by other means and flooded into the corporate share market. As the rule on "being limited to transfer between corporations" was unworkable, it was not uncommon that stock exchanges simply turned a blind eye. The so-called corporate share was nothing but an empty shell in many regions. In the market targeting corporate investors originally, 90% outstanding shares were held in the hands of natural persons.

Due to incompetent supervision and other factors, there were only 17 listed companies in STAQ and NET. STAQ and NET respectively received an order from CSRC to "suspend approval of listing of new corporate share" on May 20, 1993. CSRC issued an announcement on suspending approval of listing of new stocks officially on June 21, 1993.

In 1997, NET was renamed China Government Securities Depository Trust & Clearing Co. Ltd. And its function changed accordingly, with "stock trading" removed from its main business scope. Moreover, an application was filed with CSRC for transferring the corporate shares listed in NET to Shanghai Stock Exchange and Shenzhen Stock Exchange. In April, 1998, the government took an action to crack down on the illegal OTC market. The State Council proposed six methods in a related document to deal with the aftermath properly: first, the companies repurchase their own shares; second, the companies let other companies purchase the shares; third, the matters are settled through merger and acquisition; fourth, the stocks are converted into bonds; fifth, the stocks are recommended for listing in the A-share market; and sixth, the existing stockholders continue holding the shares. On September 9 and 10, 1999, STAQ and NET posted trading suspended announcements under the excuse of traffic control for rehearsal of national day celebration and machine maintenance, respectively, and haven't resumed trading to date.

Old Third Board

The shutdown of STAQ and NET and delisting of main board companies triggered petitions from a group of stockholders and threatened the stability and development of the capital market. A proper delisting mechanism was needed badly. In order to resolve the legacy of problems left by share transfer of companies delisted from the main board and the Two Nets system, the Securities Association of China released *Interim Measures for Agency Share Transfer Service by Securities Dealers* in June, 2001, and appointed six securities dealers, Shenyin&Wanguo included, as agencies to handle share transfer of the companies listed in STAQ and NET. By the agency of Shenyin&Wanguo, Hangzhou Nature Technology Co. Ltd was the first to enter into the agency share transfer system on July 16, 2001, marking birth of the third board market. PT Narcissus became the first main-board-delisted company to enter into the agency share transfer system at the end of 2001. At its heels, other delisted companies and companies from the Two Nets got listed one after another.

The third board market did a roaring trade at the beginning, with stock prices hitting limit up every day. On one hand, CSRC sensed huge stress and gave out one warning after another. The speculation fever in the third board market cooled down after more than twenty days. Due to poor liquidity, the boom of the third board market was short-lived. Later on, as we may see, lots of ST companies would rather be suspended from trading in the main board than be listed in the third board. On the other hand, companies in the third board encountered huge difficulty in transfer to the main board and were marginalized and unfrequented in the capital market for many years. For this reason, CSRC put into action a horizontal transfer mechanism, to allow companies in the third board to get listed on stock exchanges directly without approval of CSRC as long as they meet the listing standards, but a listing agreement must be signed with securities dealers and register of members of delisted companies must be submitted to chief securities dealers. Thereby the delisting mechanism of the third board market started running normally.

The third board market expanded rapidly in 2004. The number of delisted companies plus companies from the Two Nets in the third board market increased to 57. The third board basically served as the dust bin of companies delisted from the main board and was filled with junk stocks.

New Third Board and Beijing Stock Exchange

In order to underpin the strategy of "invigorating the country through science and education" and address financing problems of high-tech enterprises, CSRC and the Management Council of Zhongguancun Science Park put into operation an agency share transfer system for unlisted companies in Zhongguancun Science Park on January 23, 2006, which was called the new third board. 77 high-tech enterprises in Zhongguancun Science Park were listed in the new third board. On August 11, 2009, Join-Cheer became the first company from the new third board to get listed in the SME board of Shenzhen through IPO.

The birth of the new third board propelled development of the OTC market to some extent. Due to its system design, however, there are some lingering problems, such as weak negotiability, poor financing capacity, small membership and low public awareness.

The State Council gave permission to the expansion of unlisted joint-stock companies in August, 2012. In light of the principle of master planning, phasing in and steady progress, the pilot program was expanded to add Shanghai Zhangjiang Hi-Tech Park, Wuhan Donghu New Technology Development Zone and Tianjin Binhai High-Tech Zone first, besides Zhongguancun Science Park. National SME Share Transfer System Co. , Ltd was incorporated in Beijing in September, 2012, as the future trading platform of the OTC market. National SME Share Transfer System of the Securities Association of China was inaugurated on January 16, 2013. As the operation management body of a national OTC market, it was called Beijing Stock Exchange in the industry.

248 enterprises in Zhongguancun participated in the agency share quotation and transfer pilot program of Zhongguancun as of January 14, 2013, of which 182 got listed, according to statistics. Combined with 25 listed companies from Shanghai Zhangjiang, Tianjin Binhai and Wuhan Donghu, more than 200 companies have gotten listed in the new third board so far.

Evolution of Local OTC Market

Tianjin Equity Exchange (TJS)

The State Council approved of Tianjin's setting up a national unlisted public company equity trading market in Binhai New District in March, 2008. In September of the same year, Tianjin Equity Exchange (TJS) was registered and positioned as a national OTC market, the Chinese version of NASDAQ. It is commendable that TJS pioneered incorporation of the market maker rule into system design, in contrast to the agency share transfer system of Zhongguancun which continues to strike deals by means of bargaining and matching. In accordance with the rules of TJS, any institutional investor, partnership business with independent corporate capacity and independent economic organization with investment license may apply for market maker registration with TJS. Meanwhile, the "equity breakdown and continuous trading" policies of TJS started to take on typical features of an OTC market. Nevertheless, securities dealers are barred from participating as TJS is not under the jurisdiction of CSRC. Without involving securities dealers, the market maker team is unlikely to grow big, neither is the market. CSRC was not involved in this process as the setup of TJS was applied for with and approved by the State Council directly. Hence, there are some problems in the development of TJS and the new third board of CSRC and listing of TJS-listed companies in the new third board.

Henan Technology Stock Exchange

In May, 2010, the Ministry of Industry and Information Technology of the PRC picked five property right exchanges in Henan, Beijing, Shanghai, Chongqing and Guangdong to launch the pilot program of regional SME property right trading market. Among them, the pilot program of Henan copied the entire model of Shanghai Stock Exchange and Shenzhen Stock Exchange. November 12, 2010 witnessed the roaring opening of China Regional (Henan) SME Property Right Trading Market. On the date of opening, the turnover hit 150 million yuan and the stock prices of 41 listed companies mostly skyrocketed by more than 100%, some even tenfold. However, only six business days later, the Department of Industry and Information Technology of Henan made an announcement of "Suspending Trading and Related Activities". As of the date of closing, there were 22,000 account holders. CSRC accused Henan Technology Stock Exchange of going against the *Securities Law* and the *Company Law* by being engaged in stock dealings actually under the name of property right trading and lodged a report to the State Council. Apart from Tianjin and Zhengzhou, many regions, such as Chongqing, Shanghai and Changchun, were also itching to develop local OTC markets. It is noteworthy that the *Company Law* of the PRC defines "a legal trading floor as an exchange or other places approved by the State Council", so the legality of many local OTC markets may be called into question, if examined against the *Company Law* technically.

Reasons for Backwardness of the Chinese OTC Market

Inadequacies of Laws and Rules

The nascent Chinese OTC market was equipped with neither laws and rules made by legislative and regulatory authorities, nor market rules developed by enterprises spontaneously. STAQ and NET came into existence before the *Company Law* and the *Securities Law* were promulgated and even before CSRC was founded. As a result, the corporate share market sowed a bad seed from the outset. For example, Henan Technology Stock Exchange was closed for violations of the *Securities Law* and the *Company Law* by being engaged in stock dealings actually under the name of property right trading.

The Endorsement System for Securities Issuance and the Fragmented Regulatory System

The OTC market should have relatively low admittance criteria and strict supervision and information disclosure, but the Chinese OTC market is practising the endorsement system, which not only is inefficient, but also shuts out many enterprises. Due to historical factors, TJS is not under the jurisdiction of CSRC, so securities dealers are barred from participating in trading activities of TJS. As we all know, without involving securities dealers, the market maker team is unlikely to grow big, neither is the market. TJS-listed companies also have difficulty in listing in the new third board.

Confusing Orientation of Policies

The OTC market should have been oriented towards the development of a multi-level capital market, but the old third board was designed to maintain the stability of the capital market, to provide a share transfer solution to delisted companies and companies from the Two Nets and to address the problem in perfecting the delisting mechanism.

Absence of Well-designed Mechanism

The OTC market is currently deficient in mechanism design, which is reflected in grave absence of listing standards, trading mechanism and transfer mechanism.

In terms of listing standards, the listing standards of the new third board of China are stricter than those of the foreign markets. Recommendation from chief securities dealer is required and five conditions must be met at the same time: first, two full years of existence; second, prominent main business and sustainable profitability; third, sound corporate governance and proper operation; fourth, legality and compliance of share offering and transfer; and finally, letter of confirmation from Beijing People's Government on the eligibility for the unlisted company share quotation and transfer pilot program.

Table 2.1   Comparisons of OTC Listing Standards of Other Countries (Regions)

Market Type		Listing Requirements
USA	OTCBB	Register with SEC, submit required information disclosure documents; recommended by at least one dealer
	Pink Sheets	Submit Form 211; at least one market maker willing to make quotation
Japan	JASDAQ (S)	Net assets worth more than JPY200 million; net income before tax worth more than JPY100 million; more than 100,000 outstanding shares; more than 300 stockholders; market value of outstanding shares worth more than JPY500 million (date of listing)
	JASDAQ (G)	Positive net assets
	Green Sheet	Have growth potential; recommended by at least one securities dealer
Taiwan, China	Emerging Stock Exchange	Public offering companies; recommended for listing by at least two securities dealers
	Broker Market	No requirement

Source: Bai Bing, Lu Yunjiao. A Study of China's OTC Market Development-Based on Comparative Analysis of Domestic and Foreign OTC Markets [J]. Inquiry into Economic Issues, 2012, 4. Securities associations of different countries, postdoctoral workstation of GF Securities.

In terms of trading mechanism, the new third board of China adopts the traditional transfer agreement mode, which leads to low success rate of transactions, time-consuming matching and poor liquidity. The OTC markets of most developed countries use the traditional market making mechanism or a hybrid trading mechanism, wherein the participation of market makers can stimulate market liquidity, shorten transaction time and improve market efficiency.

Table 2.2 **Comparisons of Floor Market and OTC Trading Mechanisms of Other Countries (Regions)**

	Market Type	Trading Mechanism
USA	NYSE	Bid trading
	NASDAQ	Hybrid trading
	OTCBB, Pink Sheets	Traditional market maker
Japan	Tokyo Stock Exchange, Osaka Securities Exchange	Bid trading
	Mothers (TSE)	Bid trading
	Hercules (QSE)	Bid trading
	JASDAQ	Hybrid trading
	Green Sheet	Traditional market maker
Taiwan, China	Taiwan Stock Exchange	Bid trading
	GreTai Securities Market	Bid trading
	Emerging Stock Exchange	Competitive market maker

Source: Bai Bing, Lu Yunjiao. A Study of China's OTC Market Development-Based on Comparative Analysis of Domestic and Foreign OTC Markets [J]. Inquiry into Economic Issues, 2012, 4. Postdoctoral workstation of GF Securities.

In terms of transfer mechanism, under the present rules, transfer from the old/new third board to the SME/second board is almost the same as listing of new stocks. Both require a set of endorsement procedures. The delisting mechanism of the main board is practically useless. Listing eligibility has become some valuable shell resource. Without a transfer and delisting mechanism, the market cannot effectively play the role of resource allocation through the survival of the fittest and the fat profits from main board IPO put the OTC market in the shade.

Reflections on Regulation of the Chinese Capital Market

Information Disclosure Status Quo of China's Securities Market

The securities market is a market overflowing with information, so information disclosure is vital to the securities market. While allowing investors to make informed investment decisions, information disclosure serves as an important supervisory means to effectively guarantee fairness and truthfulness of the securities market and better protect the interests of investors. China has developed a multi-level, three-dimensional securities issuance and trading system comprised of the main board, SME board, second board, new third board and the OTC market and has formed a plural network made up of Shanghai Stock Exchange, Shenzhen Stock Exchange, Beijing Stock Exchange and regional equity trading centers. However, in terms of system construction, the information disclosure system has been built by CSRC and stock exchanges primarily on the basis of the laws of other countries and is not very practicable, in contrast to the full-fledged securities issuance and trading system. Some problems in the course of development and thoughts about regulation need reexamining.

Content of Information Disclosure

The State Council Securities Committee and its executive organization (China Securities Regulatory Commission) were the regulatory bodies of China's securities market at the beginning[1]. On April 22, 1993, the State Council Securities Committee released *Provisional Regulations on the Administration of Share Issuance and Trading*, Section Six of which specifically sets out the rules on information disclosure by listed companies and requires listed companies to disclose, in a timely manner, any major event that may have material impact on stock prices and is unknown to investors. On June 10, 1993, CSRC promulgated *Rules for the Implementation of Information Disclosure by Companies Offering Shares to the Public*[2], which provides for the content and standards of information disclosure by listed companies and more detailed requirements for on-going information disclosure. In addition, CSRC has also defined the content and format of interim and annual reports of listed companies and other requirements.

Generally speaking, information disclosure of the securities market mainly includes information disclosure for securities issuance, on-going information disclosure and provisional reports on major events. To be more specific, information disclosure for securities issuance refers to application papers submitted to the regulatory authority and information disclosure to investors at the time of initial public offering or pubic offering of new shares of a company. On-going information disclosure requires listed companies to disclose any change in business status, financial status, controlling shareholders, significant shareholders and top management in accordance with the laws and regulations, so as to update investors on related developments of the securities market and allow them to adjust investment policies timely and protect their legitimate rights and interests. Provisional reports on major events refer to information disclosure made by listed companies to investors and the public in the case of major events in accordance

---

[1] In April, 1998, the State Council Securities Committee was merged into China Securities Regulatory Commission and handed over its responsibilities to the latter as well.

[2] On January 30, 2007, CSRC put into force *Administrative Measures on Information Disclosure by Listed Companies*, and *Rules for the Implementation of Information Disclosure by Companies Offering Shares to the Public* was repealed on the same day.

with the laws and regulations.

The Legal System of Information Disclosure

The legal system governing information disclosure of the capital market of China consists of three layers.

On the first layer are some important laws governing information disclosure, mainly the *Securities Law* and the *Company Law*. Trading of Securities, Section Three of the *Securities Law* provides rules for information disclosure at the time of listing and on-going information disclosure after listing of securities (including provisional reports), as well as accountability rules for defects in information disclosure, if any. Section Five and Section Seven of the *Company Law* set out the procedures of share issuance of joint-stock companies and issuance of corporate bonds, respectively, and require relevant offering papers to be made available to the public.

On the second layer are some administrative regulations relating to information disclosure. The information disclosure rules on issuance and trading of corporate bonds, public offering of shares and listing and trading of stocks, and issuance and trading of shares of foreign companies listed in mainland China are outlined in light of *Regulations on Corporate Bonds*[①], *Provisional Regulations on the Administration of Share Issuance and Trading* and *Regulations of the State Council on Domestic Listing of Foreign-oriented Stocks by Share-holding Companies*.

On the third layer are rules set by relevant departments, including *Standards for Content and Format of Information Disclosure by Companies Offering Securities to the Public*, *Compilation Rules for Information Disclosure by Companies Offering Securities to the Public*, *Explanatory Announcement on Information Disclosure by Companies Offering Securities to the Public*, *Standards for Content and Format of Annual Reports of Securities Companies*, *Measures for Disclosure of Securities and Futures Regulatory Information* (for Trial Implementation), *Regulations on the Takeover of Listed Companies*, and *Administrative Measures on Information Disclosure by Listed Companies*. In addition, the trading rules formulated by Shanghai Stock Exchange and Shenzhen Stock Exchange also contain provisions on information disclosure issues.

The Regulatory System of Information Disclosure

Information disclosure in the capital market of China is currently subject to a two-layer regulatory system, CSRC and stock exchanges.

As stipulated under the *Securities Law* and relevant provisions for information disclosure management, CSRC has legislative power concerning the securities and futures market and has

---

① *Regulations on Corporate Bonds* came into effect on August 2, 1993, and Article 26 and 27 therein were revised on January 8, 2011.

the right to inquire into and impose a penalty for any offense against the laws and regulations concerning securities and futures. In accordance with the *Administrative Measures on Information Disclosure by Listed Companies* promulgated by CSRC, the information disclosure obligor shall be subject to punishment under Article 193 of the *Securities Law*, where he or she fails to meet the information disclosure obligation in the allotted time, or discloses any information that proves to carry any false records, misleading statements or material omissions, and he or she fails to send relevant reports in the allotted time or sends any report that proves to carry any false records, misleading statements or material omissions. In addition, No. 11 Decree of CSRC in 2011 released *Identification Doctrine of Administrative Liability for Legal Offenses in Information Disclosure*, which details circumstances of legal offenses in information disclosure, identification doctrine of liability of information disclosure obligor for legal offenses in information disclosure, persons liable for legal offenses in information disclosure and identification doctrine of their liability.

Meanwhile, stock exchanges, as organizations practicing self-discipline in stock trading, are liable for management of information disclosure while formulating rules on information disclosure. For example, Shanghai Stock Exchange promulgated *Shanghai Stock Exchange Rules for Listing of Corporate Bonds* and *Guidelines of Shanghai Stock Exchange on Securities Issuance*. Listed companies in breach of the information disclosure rules may be given a notice of criticism or an official rebuke, or any other form of penalty, and serious cases shall be reported to CSRC. It is noteworthy that stock exchanges perform supervision out of self-discipline and they don't enjoy administrative power and have no right to impose punishment or enforce the law on listed companies that are found with defects in information disclosure. Besides, some industrial associations also have information disclosure management obligation. For example, the Chinese Institute of Certified Public Accountants may punish accountants or accounting firms that provided false information or committed any other legal offense.

Evolution of the Verification System of China's Securities Market

The verification system for securities offering in China experienced the evolution from the administrative endorsement system to the approval channel system and then to the sponsor system. The administrative endorsement system reigned the early stage of the securities market. The approval channel system was adopted after the *Securities Law* came into effect in 1998. The sponsor system was put into operation officially in early 2004.

The Administrative Endorsement System

Under the administrative endorsement system (or the quota endorsement system), securities offering totally depends on the endorsement of competent authority. The endorsement procedures consist of three steps. First, CSRC allocates quotas. The competent authority in charge of securities determines annual gross value of securities offering based on economic development master plan and industrial policies of the government and assigns a total quota to each province/city and ministry/commission, which then allocate the quota among enterprises under their jurisdiction. Second, local governments or the ministries/commissions pick out primary candidates. Once the offering quota or the number of companies offering securities is determined, local governments or the ministries/commissions pick out primary candidates according to applications sent by companies, and CSRC reviews the list. Third, CSRC gives approval to offering. There are preliminary examination and reexamination. Staff members of the Division of Securities Offering of CSRC conduct preliminary examination of issuers recommended by the provinces/cities and ministries/commissions. Reexamination is done by the Public Offering Review Committee of CSRC.

The Approval Channel System

The approval channel system was adopted for securities offering after the *Securities Law* came into effect in December, 1998. On one hand, the offering quota system was abolished and the philosophy of recommending one when one is ready was applied. On the other hand, with respect to the time of application for offering, enterprises are required to conduct restructuring before offering and are disallowed to apply for offering shares until one year after listing. Meanwhile, government endorsement was replaced by recommendation by securities dealers. Once an issuer's application is approved by the provincial government or relevant department of the State Council, chief underwriter shall file a recommendation report to CSRC and CSRC shall verify it.

The Sponsor System

The sponsor system was put into operation officially in early 2004. A company must be recommended by a qualified sponsor for public offering and listing of securities. Article 11 of the*Securities Law* states: "issuers applying to make a public share offering or to issue convertible corporate bonds by way of underwriting in accordance with the provisions of the law or to make a public offering of other securities which require a sponsor as provided by the laws and administrative regulations shall appoint a qualified organization to act as a sponsor. A sponsor shall comply with business rules and industry norms and the principles of honesty and trustworthiness and due diligence to conduct due diligence review on the application documents and information disclosure of the issuer and supervise the conduct of the issuer." Article 49 of the *Securities Law* writes: "an organization which is qualified to act as a sponsor shall be appointed as a sponsor for listing applications for shares, convertible corporate bonds or other securities which require a sponsor as stipulated by the laws and administrative regulations. " The sponsor system is superior to the approval channel system in that, among other things, the sponsor continues to have supervision and guidance obligation for a period of time after listing of a company it has recommended and is liable for any malpractice of the company during the period of supervision.

Reflections on China's Verification System for Listing of Securities

The Information Disclosure System

The information disclosure system of the securities market of China is being built and perfected. The laws and regulations have encompassed relatively complete market coverage and standards, but have inadequacies in terms of completeness, truthfulness and timeliness.

Speaking of completeness, many listed companies don't fully disclose the evolution of issuers in related transactions before becoming joint-stock companies nor all major events involved in related transactions. This compromises transparency of the market and justice of transaction prices and means. Moreover, social responsibility performance of listed companies is not reflected in the prospectus, which reveals the incompleteness of information disclosure to a certain extent.

In truthfulness, any fraud practiced by listed companies by taking advantage of information disclosure, in the form of insider trading, false or misleading representations, and so on, with the aim of attaining fat profits, is explicitly prohibited by the laws or regulations, but such frauds happen from time to time in reality[1], owing to information asymmetry between the investors and listed companies.

In timeliness, many listed companies may conceal major events from disclosure in annual reports, interim reports or quarterly reports or don't disclose information timely. This often sways rational judgment and adjustment to investment decisions of investors. As far as truthfulness and timeliness are concerned, aside from these problems incurred by information asymmetry, profit-driven unethical conduct of intermediaries also adds fuel to the flame.

We want to highlight here that *Measures for Supervision and Administration of Public Unlisted Companies (Exposure Draft)* issued by CSRC on June 15, 2012 has cleared the barriers in building a national unified OTC market, but at the same time information disclosure problems in the OTC market have become the focus of social concern. Theoretically, supervision over the OTC market should be focused on information disclosure by listed companies, but consistent

---

① The Supreme Court of the PRC promulgated *Stipulations about Trial of Civil Compensation Cases Arising from False Representation in the Securities Market* in January, 2003.

information disclosure policies are yet to be implemented for the OTC market of China. The share transfer system of Beijing Stock Exchange (the new third board) and regional equity trading markets adopt different rules. Hence, in terms of system design, a set of multi-level differentiated information disclosure rules need to be designed for the OTC markets at different levels and mandatory information disclosure and voluntary information disclosure should be combined. At the early stage of market development in particular, it is acceptable to lower information disclosure standards as appropriate to meet the financing needs of SMEs and to seek balance in information disclosure between listed companies and investors, between different investors and between listed companies, which might be able to reduce overall information disclosure costs of the OTC market.

The Sponsor System

We have the following findings from a retrospect of the evolution of the verification system for securities offering in China. First, at the infant stage of the securities market, listing opportunity is a rare resource to companies, so the administrative endorsement system has its historic meaning. However, it was replaced by the approval channel system soon, due to improper and unprofessional conduct and frequent occurrence of black case work and other malpractices. Next, the imprint of the planned economy left on the approval channel system has given rise to many problems in practice. For example, securities dealers are subject to restrictions on the number of channels and the number of companies recommended when recommending listing candidates to CSRC. This is unfavorable to market competition. Moreover, the main responsibility of securities dealers is for listing recommendation, not for guarantee. Their rights and obligations are limited to the pre-listing stage and terminate upon success of listing. This may tempt securities dealers to fabricate information, at relatively low legal risk, to ensure successful listing of the recommended companies. Finally, the sponsor system appeared. Against the backdrop of "emerging + reshuffling" of the securities market of China, it is also facing the transition from totally centralized supervision to a registration system that coordinates centralized supervision and self-discipline supervision along with establishment of the second board, the new third board and OTC market system. Reflections are needed on these aspects.

As a matter of fact, the sponsor system in China contains many problems that need to be resolved in practice. First of all, the duties of sponsors and sponsor representatives are not clearly divided. In practice, sponsors often intervene in normal work of sponsor representatives and compromise their independence, but assume no sponsor-related responsibility. Next, the duties of sponsors and issuers are not clearly defined. Usually, information sources of sponsors are under the control of issuers, but the problem of information asymmetry between issuers and sponsors still exists. Finally, the boundary between the duties of sponsors and other intermediaries is blurred and muddled. Securities offering and listing is the result of joint efforts made by issuers, securities dealers, attorneys, auditors and evaluators. As referrer, sponsors cannot fulfill the obligation of good faith in place of other intermediaries. Hence, it is extremely difficult to make clear the boundary of responsibilities should any offense occur.

To resolve the problems existing in the verification system of the securities market of China, widening supervisory channels, in particular, giving full play to the role of finance and economics media and market participants in monitoring listed companies, might have more importance and direct effect. As for the practice in other countries, the Enron scandal in the USA is a perfect proof of this. Hence, the Board, finance and economics media, market participants, CSRC and the court should all act as watchdogs over the securities market. None of these five is dispensable.

Vision and Advice for Development of China's Multi-level Capital Market

Goal and Vision

A multi-level capital market system that is mutuallycomplementary and promotive is being built over recent years to drive development of China's capital market. In October, 2003, *Decision of the Central Committee of the Communist Party of China on Some Issues Concerning the Improvement of the Socialist Market Economy* (the *Decision*) was approved on the Third Plenary Session of the 16th CPC Central Committee, and clearly states "to drive reform and open-up and steady development of the capital market and step up direct financing; to create a multi-level capital market, perfect the capital market structure and enrich capital market products; to regulate and develop the main board market and press ahead with venture capital and growth enterprises market development". The *Decision* expatiates on the policies relating to the development of a multi-level capital market in a clear and definite manner for the first time. On January 31, 2004, *Some Opinions of the State Council on Promoting the Reform, Open-up and Steady Development of the Capital Market* (known as the *Nine Policies*) were promulgated. As a programmatic document that sets the development direction of the capital market, the *Nine Policies* proposes unequivocally "to create a multi-level capital market that caters to the financing needs of different types of enterprises step by step", and breaks down this goal into specific tasks, "to continue regulating and developing the main board market and gradually improve the listed company structure of the main board market; to phase in construction of the second board market, consummate venture capital mechanism, and widen the financing channels of SMEs; to actively explore and consummate a share transfer system under unified supervision." The

Compendium of the 11th Five-Year Plan (2006—2010) in 2005 restates some key requirements, for "creating a multi-level capital market, perfecting the function of the market, widening entry channels of capital and raising the percentage of direct financing", for example. President Hu's report at the 18th Party Congress in 2012 reiterates in a clear-cut tone the requirements for "deepening the reform of the financial system, consummating a modern financial system that contributes to stability of the macro economy and underpins development of the real economy and accelerates development of the multi-level capital market. "

All point to the goal of China's developing a multi-level capital market, that is, a plural and completely open capital market system comprised of the main board, the second board and the OTC market and characterized by clear division of duties, sophisticated hierarchy, all-around coordination and interactive connections.

A survey of the evolution and present status of other countries reveals that a multi-level capital market is not a universal phenomenon in all countries. A multi-level capital market usually appears in those large countries with a vast territory and an unbalanced economy and more often than not evolves along with the rising of the large nations. The rising of the USA is closely tied to successful and rapid development of its multi-level capital market. A sound and highly efficient capital market is the motive power of innovation and growth of high-tech enterprises, the foundation and support to enhance independent innovative capacity of enterprises and the most effective means and tool to promote venture capital development. The experience of the USA in developing its multi-level capital market is learned by other countries widely. Like the USA, China also has an extensive territory and unbalanced regional economy, plus rich enterprise resources and diversified investors. Hence, speaking of its vision, China might be the only country in the world that has the potential to develop a gigantic capital market like that of the USA, in consideration of the fundamental factors at the real economy level that determine development of the capital market, though China's capital market can not stand comparison with that of the USA for the time being.

Hence, in the foreseeable future, the multi-level capital market of China will march into a new epoch of quicker development and accelerated liberalization and globalization and will play a pivotal role in the rising of the Chinese economy. Of course, this requires us to make a series of improvements in policies and systems.

Latest Developments

As previously discussed, we know that China has erected a rudimentary multi-level capital market comprised of the main board (Shanghai Stock Exchange and Shenzhen Stock Exchange), the second board and varied OTC markets, including the new third board and regional equity exchanges and property right exchanges. Moreover, the systems and rules needed for the development of the multi-level capital market are being drafted and polished. For example, the reform of the new share offering system and the delisting mechanism in 2012 became a key part of system construction of the multi-level capital market.

In March, 2012, CSRC solicited public opinions on the reform plan for the new share offering system. On April 28, CSRC issued *Guidelines for Further Deepening the Reform of the New Share Offering System*, reiterating that the reform of the new share offering system will adhere to the direction of liberalization and revamp verification of offering by centering on adequate, complete and accurate information disclosure, and proposed six pertinent pieces of advice. On May 18, CSRC revised *Measures for the Administration of Securities Offering and Underwriting* accordingly. On May 23, the Offering Supervision Division and the Second Board Offering Supervision Division of CSRC issued the *Circular of Problems Relating to Offering Price of New Shares*, wherein some matters concerning offering price of new shares are clarified. On June 28, Shanghai Stock Exchange and Shenzhen Stock Exchange released the *Proposal for Optimizing the Delisting System of Listed Companies of Shanghai Stock Exchange* and the *Proposal for Improving and Optimizing the Delisting System of Listed Companies of the Main Board and SME Board of Shenzhen Stock Exchange*, respectively, and both amended *Stock Listing Rules* accordingly.

All kinds of malpractices in new share offering have been pertinacious in the capital market of China. In the reform of the new share offering system this time, the reform of Transfer of Existing Shares was put forward for the first time, so-called secondary offerings, which attracted much attention of the market. The delisting mechanism is a fundamental system of the capital market. Only with an effective delisting mechanism, can we foster proper and effective configuration of resources in the securities market, drive restructuring and industrial upgrading and promote development of the multi-level capital market. On 2013 National Work Meeting on Securities and Futures Supervision, Guo Shuqing, the then Chairman of CSRC, proposed, "to further deepen the reform of the offering and delisting system, put into practice an information-disclosure-centric verification philosophy, revise and optimize rules and provisions such as measures for the management of initial public offering of stocks; continue to refine the pricing mechanism of new shares, urge relevant market participants to perform their duties diligently, and tighten supervision over intermediaries; to conduct financial inspection on companies undergoing IPO verification and spur intermediaries to perform their duties with great diligence; to resolutely crack down on performance disguise, packaging for listing and false disclosure, and inflict severe punishments on any offence against the laws and regulations in accordance with the laws, inclusive of but not limited to false records, misleading representations and major omissions, or helping issuers in excessive packaging and conspiring in fraud; to enforce the new reform measures for the delisting mechanism actively and steadily, keep consummating relevant supporting systems and rules and liberalization mechanism and realize routinization of delisting. "

Advice for Related Policies

Based on our observation and analysis, we have put forward the following advice for developing and optimizing the multi-level capital market of China, which mainly consists of three aspects: market development, the regulatory system and optimization of the legal system.

Market Development: Minimize Administrative Intervention and Enhance Market Efficiency

International experience shows that the government usually doesn't intervene in the OTC market directly, but manages it by formulating rules or adopting other indirect measures. Too much administrative intervention in the OTC market might cause rising trading costs and a waste of regulatory resources, and increase the costs and lower the efficiency of financing of the mass SMEs. Moreover, since the OTC market is mainly intended for mature investors who have certain preference for venture capital and risk tolerance, it is unnecessary to overprotect them through administrative regulation. For many years, we have been managing the OTC market through sort of "one-size-fits-all" administrative intervention and taken to cracking down on or even closing the market in the case of any problem. This approach not only wrecks the natural law of market development, but also stifles innovation motivation and effectiveness of resource configuration. Hence, to develop the OTC market, we should focus on fostering and optimizing the market mechanism, enhancing the efficiency of resource configuration by the market, respecting the sense of autonomy of market players and constructing a market-based management mechanism.

Guided by this philosophy, we need to perfect two aspects at present.

First of all, a registration mechanism is the trend of the regulation of securities offering. Though the approval mechanism can help prevent offering of inferior securities and promote healthy development of the emerging market, there has been a more and more intense appeal for the transition from offering regulation to registration, for new share offering decided by the market rather than by the government, along with further development of the securities market of China. So far, some regional equity trading centers, such as Shanghai Equity Exchange, have accomplished the reform of the registration mechanism in offering regulation. As for the new third board, however, listing and financing verification still takes the form of administrative license by CSRC and an approval document issued by CSRC is something must-have. Apparently, the approval mechanism is still a dominant way of securities offering regulation in China and CSRC enjoys substantive regulation power. In fact, an inherent reason for poor connectivity between the OTC market and the main board market is exactly the barrier and contradiction in offering regulation. This is also a core issue when it comes to how to improve the transfer mechanism.

Next, it is about the transfer mechanism. As previously discussed, substantive regulation by CSRC is required for initial public offering of stocks of Chinese enterprises. Listed companies of the new third board are non-public companies, so they cannot switch to the main board or the second board until becoming public companies with the approval of the Public Offering Review Committee. Apparently, there are serious limitations and inadequacies in the transfer mechanism of China's multi-level capital market. It lacks really effective and convenient transfer system arrangement. Given the present circumstance, first of all, we need to intensify the reform of the present delisting mechanism, improve completeness and operability of the delisting mechanism and optimize all sorts of mechanisms for "procedural delisting". The key is to double execution effort on the basis of system optimization. In China, there was much room of game for institutions in delisting operation in the past due to the absence of procedural automatic delisting. The resulting shell resource premium makes it hardly possible for the stock price of a listed company to go below its net asset value. For this reason, automatic delisting driven by asset value higher than market value is unlikely to happen. This leads to low elimination rate and high growth rate of the securities market of China. Second, we must quicken the pace of design of a real transfer mechanism. Against the backdrop of the transition of offering regulation from the approval system to the registration system, on one hand, a transfer system between national OTC market and regional OTC market needs to be set up; on the other hand, a trading mechanism between the OTC market and the floor market needs to be put in place.

The Regulatory System: Optimize the Regulatory System and Attach Importance to Risk Prevention

First of all, it is necessary to create a regulatory model that combines centralization and autonomy. The OTC market of China has long been excluded from the national regulatory system. The regulatory structure is somewhat muddled. The main board, second board and new third board are under the jurisdiction of CSRC, while local property right exchanges and equity trading centers have been mostly built with the support of local governments and are affiliated to local Financial Service Office or State-owned Assets Supervision and Administration Commission, beyond the jurisdiction of CSRC. Hence, to ensure proper running of the multi-level capital market, it is necessary to create a highly efficient and low-cost market regulatory system and to abide by the rule of combining centralized regulation by CSRC and autonomy of industrial associations and OTC exchanges.

Second, it is necessary to perfect the market maker system. With a competitive and compulsory two-way public offer system in force, market makers can evaluate and judge the value of listed companies and market trends by right of their advantages in information, capital and talent and provide two-way quotations for stock trading and buy/sell stocks. On January 18, 2013, CSRC released *Interim Measures for the Administration of National SME Share Transfer System Co.*, *Ltd*, which states clearly that the new third board market is going to bring in the market maker system. This is a significant breakthrough in trading mechanism. The availability of the market maker system is highly significant to heighten market liquidity, realize price discovery, motivate securities dealers and stabilize the market.

Third, it is necessary to strengthen information disclosure. Information disclosure is an effective means and the most economical way of supervision over the securities market. The OTC market and the main board market differ in functional positioning and market operation. Hence, they should have differentiated information disclosure rules. It is necessary to simplify information disclosure format and reduce information disclosure costs. For example, listed companies of the OTC market may be required to disclose annual and semiannual reports only, but the focus of disclosure should be on financial status of companies and business performance analysis and projections by the management. Meanwhile, more effort is needed to ensure accuracy and truthfulness of information disclosure to prevent insider trading and fraud from happening. We want to add that the legal liabilities of listed companies and securities service institutions and individuals that provide listing and transfer, among other services, for example, chief underwriter, law firm and accounting firm, should be clarified.

Fourth, it is necessary to build a highly efficient and consistent clearing and settlement system. Each component of the capital market of China currently has different clearing and settlement systems and rules. Shanghai Stock Exchange and Shenzhen Stock Exchange do settlement with China Securities Depository and Clearing Corporation Limited, so does the new third board. Other OTC markets, such as Shanghai Equity Exchange and Tianjin Equity Exchange, have developed some in-house registered depository and clearing system to complete settlement. Currently, centralized clearing (i. e. , unified settlement and clearing) is a trend of the international market. After the subprime lending crisis gave rise to default in OTC credit swap contracts, some foreign markets, the US included, are moving towards "OTC trading and floor clearing", to have clearing houses of the floor market centralize the settlement of OTC transactions. The OTC market and the futures market of the USA are linked mainly by centralized clearing. ① We should follow the international trend, integrate the existing settlement platform resources, quicken the pace of setting up a centralized clearing house and clearing system for the OTC market and be sure to control risks, reduce costs and improve efficiency.

Optimization of the Legal System: Optimize the Legal System and Intensify Sanctions

First of all, it is necessary to optimize the legal system. The legal system is vital to investor protection. The difference in the legal system is the most important factor to the difference in the extent of protection offered to investors. In the on-going reform, we need to, on one hand, establish the legal status of the OTC market by revising the *Securities Law* and lay down general provisions for the OTC market and OTC trading behavior, to make it perfectly justifiable; on the other hand, we need to refine legislations about civil liability for misrepresentations, insider trading and market manipulation, among other deeds, in the *Securities Law*. Looking into the clauses of the *Securities Law*, we may find that administrative liability and criminal liability carry dominant weight, while the provisions about civil liability for compensation for damages to investors are too general to be operable. The Supreme Court promulgated *Stipulations about Trial of Civil Compensation Cases Arising from False Representation in the Securities Market* in 2003, but definite judicial interpretations are absent with respect to civil compensation for insider trading and market manipulation. Hence, continued effort is required to consummate civil liability legislations concerning the capital market, vest civil litigious right in investors, and make specific and operable legal provisions or judicial interpretations concerning trial and jurisdiction, form of procedure, doctrine of liability fixation and recognition of damages.

Next, we should intensify sanctions in the administration of justice. First, we need to put to rights the existing defects in the present representative litigation system, clarify procedures and methods chosen by litigation representatives, draw on the upsides of the US's group litigation system, adopt the doctrine of "explicit quitting and implicit joining in" and treat those who don't choose automatic withdrawal from group litigation within the notice period of the court as members of group litigation automatically. This means ruling of the court is valid for those who haven't registered their interests as well. Second, it is advisable to abolish the preceding procedure of civil compensation cases of the securities market, defend due litigious right of investors, ease the difficulty in litigation and protect basic rights and interests of investors. Third, the burden of proof on the prosecution should be reversed in securities-related lawsuits, to intensify the burden of proof on listed companies, controlling shareholders, securities dealers

---

① Shake-up of Exchanges Coming to the End, Commodity OTC Market to Adopt Centralized Clearing and Settlement [J]. The Economic Observer, 2013, 1.

and other securities service providers. In this way, they may weigh the hazard of their infringement act and the severity of legal liability when they do so. This is a reflection and a requirement of safeguarding the fundamental rights and interests of investors and maintaining the order of the capital market.

References

[1] Que Zikang. Theory and Experience of A Multi-level Capital Market [M]. Shanghai: Shanghai Jiao Tong University Press, 2007.

[2] Xu Hongcai. A Study of China's Multi-level Capital Market System and Regulation [M]. Beijing: Economy and Management Publishing House, 2009.

[3] Wang Guogang, Chief Editor. Researches on Creation of a Multi-level Capital Market [M]. Beijing: People's Publishing House, 2006.

[4] *Evolution of China's Third Board Market* [J/OL]. http://wenku.baidu.com/view/a976f74333687e21af45a938.html.

[5] Bai Bing, Lu Yunjiao. A Study of China's OTC Market Development-Based on Comparative Analysis of Domestic and Foreign OTC Markets [J]. Inquiry into Economic Issues, 2012, 4.

[6] Li Fengyu. Status Quo, Problems and Countermeasures of Information Disclosure of China's Securities Market [J], Journal of Financial Development Research, 2012, 10.

[7] A Retrospect of Evolution of the Verification System for Securities Offering of China [OL], http://www.9ask.cn/.

[8] A Brief Discussion on the Sponsor System for Securities Offering [OL], http://www.9ask.cn/.

[9] Hu Haifeng. A Multi-level Capital Market: From Spontaneous Evolution to Government System Design [M]. Beijing: Beijing Normal University Press, 2010.

[10] Que Zikang. Theory and Experience of A Multi-level Capital Market [M]. Shanghai: Shanghai Jiao Tong University Press, 2007.

[11] Gu Gongyun, Chief Editor. Legal System Construction for the OTC Market [M]. Beijing: Peking University Press, 2011.

Part Two

China's Financial Policies
in 2012

CHAPTER 4

Macro Financial Policy

Monetary Policy

Highlights of Monetary Policy in 2012

In 2012, the People's Bank of China (PBC) continued its prudent monetary policy and intensified efforts by making policies better targeted, more flexible and more forward-looking, while also making fine-tunings and taking pre-emptive measures as appropriate in good time, in response to changes in the economic picture. Major monetary policies formulated and promulgated in the year are outlined in the table below:

Table 4. 1   Summary of Monetary Policy Operations by the PBC in 2012

Date	Policy
18 February	The PBC decided to lower the RMB deposit required reserve ratio of deposit-holding financial institutions by 0. 5 percentage points, effective from 24 February 2012.
12 May	The PBC decided to lower the RMB deposit required reserve ratio of deposit-holding financial institutions by 0. 5 percentage points, effective from 18 May 2012.
7 June	The PBC decided to cut the RMB benchmark deposit and lending rates of financial institutions, lowering the 1-year benchmark deposit rate from 3. 5 percent to 3. 25 percent and the 1-year benchmark lending rate from 6. 56 percent to 6. 31 percent; and simultaneously to adjust the floating bands of deposit and lending rates of financial institutions, with the ceiling for deposit rates adjusted to 110 percent of the benchmark deposit rate, and the floor for lending rates adjusted to 80 percent of the benchmark lending rate, effective from 8 June 2012.
5 July	The PBC decided to cut the RMB benchmark deposit and lending rates of financial institutions, lowering the 1-year benchmark deposit rate from 3. 25 percent to 3 percent and the 1-year benchmark lending rate from 6. 31 percent to 6 percent; and simultaneously to adjust the floor for the floating bands of lending rates of financial institutions to 70 percent of the benchmark lending rate, effective from 6 July 2012.

Source: The People's Bank of China.

Analysis of Monetary Policy in 2012

Background and Procedures for Monetary Policy-making in 2012

In 2012, as China's balance of payments and RMB exchange rate got closer to its equilibrium level, coupled with turmoil in the international financial markets set off by the European sovereign debt crisis, foreign exchange inflows contracted and the funds outstanding for foreign exchange decelerated by more than 2 trillion yuan compared with that of 2011. Major changes happened to liquidity supply in the banking system. In response to liquidity supply and demand dynamics, the PBC lowered the deposit reserve requirement ratio on February 24 and May 18, 2012, each time by 0.5 percentage points, to keep liquidity in the banking system at a sufficient level. In line with two cuts in the deposit reserve requirement ratio, the PBC conducted 944 billion yuan of repos and 6,038 billion yuan of reverse repos on cumulative basis in the year. At end-2012, the balance of open market reverse repo operations registered 498 billion yuan. In response to the slowing economy and the moderated rise in commodity prices, the PBC cut the RMB benchmark deposit and lending rates of financial institutions on June 8 and July 6, lowering the 1-year benchmark deposit rate from 3.5 percent to 3 percent and the 1-year benchmark lending rate from 6.56 percent to 6 percent, down by 0.50 percentage points and 0.56 percentage points respectively on a cumulative basis. Meanwhile, interest rate adjustments were combined with the reform of interest rate liberalization, and the floating bands of deposit and lending rates of financial institutions were adjusted simultaneously, with the ceiling for deposit rates adjusted to 110 percent of the benchmark deposit rate, and the floor for lending rates adjusted to 70 percent of the benchmark lending rate. These measures were expected to promote a decline in fund price and to create a more favorable policy environment for reducing financing costs for companies. Financial institutions will also be encouraged to further improve their financial services in market competition as they enjoy more discretionary pricing power. Following these adjustments to the benchmark deposit and lending rates and the floating bands of interest rates, the lending rates financial institutions offered to companies declined month by month. [1]

Execution of Monetary Policy in 2012

In 2012, the Chinese economy stabilized amidst moderate growth and the financial system performed soundly in general. In the whole year, GDP increased 7.8 percent year on year to 51.9 trillion yuan; the consumer price index was up 2.6 percent year on year; and the current

---

[1]　Monetary Policy Analysis Group of the People's Bank of China, *China Monetary Policy Report: Quarter Four of 2012*, 6 February 2013.

account surplus as a share of GDP dropped to 2. 6 percent.

At end-2012, outstanding M_2 registered 97. 4 trillion yuan, up 13. 8 percent year on year. This growth was 0. 2 percentage points higher than that at end-2011. Outstanding M_1 stood at 30. 9 trillion yuan, an increase of 6. 5 percent year on year. Currency in circulation M_0 totaled 5. 5 trillion yuan, up 7. 7 percent year on year. The net amount of cash put into circulation in the whole year posted 391 billion yuan, 225. 1 billion yuan less year on year. At end-2012, outstanding balance of base money registered 25. 2 trillion yuan, an increase of 12. 3 percent year on year and 2. 8 trillion yuan from that at the beginning of 2012. The money multiplier stood at 3. 86, which was 0. 07 higher than that at end-2011. The excess reserve ratio of financial institutions stood at 3. 3 percent, 1. 0 percentage point higher than that at end-2011, and that of rural credit cooperatives (RCCs) stood at 8. 2 percent, 0. 9 percentage points higher than that at end-2011. [1]

At end-2012, outstanding balance of deposits in domestic and foreign currencies of all financial institutions (including foreign-funded financial institutions) stood at 94. 3 trillion yuan, up 14. 1 percent year on year. Such growth represented an acceleration of 0. 6 percentage points compared with that at end-2011. Outstanding balance of RMB deposits registered 91. 7 trillion yuan, up 13. 3 percent year on year. Such growth was 0. 2 percentage points lower than that at end-2011. Outstanding balance of deposits in foreign currencies posted USD406. 5 billion, an increase of 47. 8 percent year on year. Broken down by sectors, the growth of household deposits was flat, whereas that of non-financial institutions accelerated steadily. At end-2012, outstanding balance of household deposits held in financial institutions stood at 40. 6 trillion yuan, up 16. 7 percent year on year. This represented an acceleration of 1. 0 percentage point over end-2011. Outstanding balance of RMB deposits of non-financial institutions totaled 32. 7 trillion yuan, up 7. 9 percent year on year. At end-2012, outstanding balance of fiscal deposits reached 2. 4 trillion yuan, down 197. 4 billion yuan from the beginning of 2012. [2]

At end-2012, outstanding balance of loans in domestic and foreign currencies of all financial institutions reached 67. 3 trillion yuan, up 15. 6 percent year on year. This growth was 0. 1 percentage points lower than that at end-2011. Outstanding balance of RMB loans stood at 63. 0 trillion yuan, up 15. 0 percent year on year. Through out the year, the growth rate fluctuated by an obviously narrower range compared with the previous two years. The outstanding

① Monetary Policy Analysis Group of the People's Bank of China, *China Monetary Policy Report: Quarter Four of 2012*, 6 February 2013.

② Monetary Policy Analysis Group of the People's Bank of China, *China Monetary Policy Report: Quarter Four of 2012*, 6 February 2013.

value added 8. 2 trillion yuan to that at the beginning of 2012, representing an acceleration of 732 billion yuan year on year. Broken down by sectors, at end-2012, loans to the household sector increased 18. 6 percent year on year, indicating steady acceleration. Loans to non-financial institutions and other sectors grew by 13. 7 percent year on year. Broken down by institutions, loan growth of Chinese-funded large banks operating nationwide, Chinese-funded small and medium local banks, and rural cooperative financial institutions accelerated significantly year on year. Broken down by maturities, the percentage of medium-and long-term loans rebounded. Driven by recovering investments, credit support extended to construction projects was intensified. At end-2012, medium-and long-term loans grew by 9. 0 percent year on year. This growth rate has been standing around 9 percent since April of 2012 and showing a steady upward tendency. Newly extended medium-and long-term loans since the beginning of 2012 registered 2. 9 trillion yuan. Medium-and long-term loans accounted for 35 percent of the total extended loans of all maturities, representing a 2. 7 percentage point rebound from the nadir of the year. At end-2012, residential mortgage loans increased 12. 9 percent year on year. Outstanding balance of foreign-currency loans of financial institutions reached USD683. 6 billion, up 26. 9 percent year on year. This was USD145. 1 billion more than that at the beginning of 2012, an acceleration of USD56. 9 billion year on year. In terms of the purpose of loans, the support to imports and exports and the Go Out policy was intensified. Trade financing of imports and exports increased by USD92. 4 billion, an acceleration of USD64. 9 billion year on year. Overseas loans and domestic medium-and long-term loans climbed by USD51. 7 billion, accelerating by USD11. 1 billion year on year. [1]

All-system financing aggregates hit a record high of 15. 76 trillion yuan in 2012, an increase of 2. 93 trillion yuan from 2011. This was mainly driven by strong activity infinancing of trust loans, corporate bonds, RMB loans and foreign-currency denominated loans, combined to reach 12. 66 trillion yuan, adding 3. 05 trillion yuan to that of 2011. In terms of its composition, RMB loans registered bigger growth, but its share of the total tumbled to a historic low. Foreign currency-denominated loans accelerated noticeably compared with 2011. Financing via corporate bonds was highly active and direct financing accounted for an all-time high share of the total. Trust loans saw an immense acceleration year on year. [2]

The PBC lowered the benchmark deposit and lending rates in June and July of 2012 and

---

[1] Monetary Policy Analysis Group of the People's Bank of China, *China Monetary Policy Report: Quarter Four of 2012*, 6 February 2013.

[2] Monetary Policy Analysis Group of the People's Bank of China, *China Monetary Policy Report: Quarter Four of 2012*, 6 February 2013.

slightly widened the floating bands of deposit and lending rates. The lending rates of financial institutions were cut further and stabilized by end-2012. In December, the weighted average lending rate stood at6. 78 percent. The weighted average interest rate of ordinary loans registered 7. 07 percent. The weighted average bill financing rate posted 5. 64 percent. The weighted average residential mortgage rate edged down to 6. 22 percent in December. ①

In 2012, RMB appreciated mildly and expectations regarding the RMB exchange rate were generally stable. At end-2012, the central parity of the RMB against the US dollar was 6. 2855 yuan per US dollar, up 154 basis points and 0. 25 percent over end-2011. The BIS estimated that in 2012, the nominal effective RMB exchange rate appreciated 1. 73 percent and the real effective exchange rate appreciated 2. 22 percent; from the beginning of the exchange rate reform in 2005 to December 2012, the nominal effective exchange rate of the RMB appreciated 23. 25 percent and the real effective exchange rate appreciated 31. 86 percent. ②

Policy Evaluation and Outlook

Going forward, the world economy might continue its slow recovery. The de-leveraging process has been going on in the USA for quite a while. The European Central Bank's liquidity backstop initiative has taken positive effect on the stability of the market. These combined constitute a generally weak but relatively stable external environment. However, some economies are heavily indebted. "Tighten fiscal policy and loosen monetary policy" might become a long-term choice of major developed economies. Coupled with rising trade and investment protectionism, emerging economies will be facing a mix of challenges in trade, finance and so on.

As for domestic economic operation, the Chinese economy is expected to continue growing at a moderately quick but steady pace. Price-adjusted real growth of both per capita disposable income of urban households and per capita cash income of rural households outpaced that of GDP in 2012. As the reform of income distribution moves forward, consumption will make greater contribution to driving economic growth. The Chinese economy has undergone a period of de-inventory. Industrial production will become more sensitive to strengthening demand and any change in expectations, which is also favorable to steady economic growth. However, the foundation for economic stabilization is not solid enough, problems with structural imbalance still appear acute and resource and environmental constraints are obviously intensifying. A

---

① Monetary Policy Analysis Group of the People's Bank of China, *China Monetary Policy Report*: *Quarter Four of 2012*, 6 February 2013.

② Monetary Policy Analysis Group of the People's Bank of China, *China Monetary Policy Report*: *Quarter Four of 2012*, 6 February 2013.

combination of factors in the economy might drive up commodity prices. First, with slowing growth of the working-age population, the prices of labor-intensive products might take on an upward tendency. Meanwhile, the prices of resource products need to be rationalized. Second, worldwide monetary easing is likely to persist, so imported inflation pressure deserves attention. [①]

In 2013, the PBC will continue its prudent monetary policy to maintain continuity and stability of the policy, make macro control better targeted, more flexible and more forward-looking, conduct fine-tunings and take pre-emptive measures as appropriate in good time, empower the financial system to better serve the real economy, effectively guard against systematic financial risks, keep the financial system stable and work for overall stable commodity prices and steady and moderate growth of the economy.

Exchange Rate and Balance of Payments Policy

Highlights of Exchange Rate and Balance of Payments Policy in 2012

In 2012, China accelerated transformation of the growth pattern and made concrete achievements in foreign trade, foreign investment and foreign exchange. China's balance of payments (BOP) became more balanced. Major measures are detailed below:

Table 4. 2   **Highlights of Exchange Rate and BOP Policy in 2012**

Date	Policy
17 January	The PBC signed a bilateral local currency swap agreement with the Central Bank of the UAE. The size of the swap facility is 35 billion yuan/20 billion dirham. The currency swap agreement will expire in three years and can be extended upon mutual consent.
6 February	The PBC, jointly with the Ministry of Finance, the Ministry of Commerce, the General Administration of Customs, the State Administration of Taxation, and the China Banking Regulatory Commission, issued the *Notice on Issues Concerning RMB Settlement of Export of Goods by Domestic Enterprises* (PBC Document [2012] No. 23), to expand the participants in RMB settlement of export of goods from the pilot enterprises to all enterprises that are eligible to engage in export/import business, and launched the focused-supervision list of enterprises in RMB settlement for goods export.
8 February	The PBC renewed the bilateral local currency swap arrangement with Bank Negara Malaysia, and increased its size from 80 billion yuan/40 billion ringgit to 180 billion yuan/90 billion ringgit. The new currency swap agreement will expire in three years and can be extended upon mutual consent.

---

① Monetary Policy Analysis Group of the People's Bank of China, *China Monetary Policy Report: Quarter Four of 2012*, 6 February 2013.

Continued

Date	Policy
21 February	The PBC signed a bilateral local currency swap agreement with the Central Bank of the Republic of Turkey. The size of the swap facility is 10 billion yuan or 3 billion Turkish liras. The effective period of the arrangement will be three years and can be extended upon mutual consent.
20 March	The PBC signed a bilateral local currency swap supplemental agreement with the Bank of Mongolia. The size of the swap facility was increased from 5 billion yuan/1 trillion MNT to 10 billion yuan/2 trillion MNT.
22 March	The PBC signed a bilateral local currency swap agreement with the Reserve Bank of Australia. The size of the swap facility is 200 billion yuan/AUD30 billion. The currency swap agreement will expire in three years, but can be extended upon mutual consent.
14 April	In view of the development of China's foreign exchange market, to enhance the flexibility of the RMB exchange rate in both directions, the PBC released *PBC Announcement* ([2012] No. 4) and announced that it would widen the floating band of the RMB trading price against the US dollar on the interbank spot market from 0. 5 percent to 1 percent, effective from April 16, 2012.
26 June	The PBC signed a bilateral local currency swap agreement with the National Bank of Ukraine. The size of the swap facility is 15 billion yuan/19 billion hryvnia. The effective period of the arrangement will be three years and can be extended upon mutual consent.
31 July	In order to strengthen management of RMB bank accounts of overseas institutions and to facilitate international trade and investment, the PBC issued the *Notice on the Opening and Use of RMB Bank Accounts by Overseas Institutions* (PBC Document [2012] No. 183) .
31 August	The Memorandum on *Cross-Straits Currency Clearing Cooperation* was signed by monetary authorities on both sides of the Taiwan Straits. The two parties agreed to establish a cross-Straits currency clearing mechanism based on the principles and cooperation framework as specified in the Memorandum.
24 September	The PBC and the Macao Branch of Bank of China renewed the *Agreement on the Clearing of RMB Business.*
11 December	The PBC, based on the *Memorandum on Cross-Straits Currency Clearing Cooperation*, authorized the Taipei Branch of Bank of China to serve as the clearing bank of RMB business in Taiwan Region (PBC Document [2012] No. 18) .

Source: State Administration of Foreign Exchange.

Analysis of Exchange Rate and Balance of Payments Policy in 2012

Background and Procedures for Exchange Rate and Balance of Payments Policy-making in 2012

In the context of liquidity easing and low interest rates, the world economy slowed down and the international financial market continued oscillating in 2012. All economies in the world softened generally in the first half of 2012, but emerging economies strengthened a bit in the second half and the global recession showed a sign of bottoming out. Muted external demand undermined China's exports. As the European and American sovereign debt crisis turned more complicated, risk aversion in the financial market changed alternately. In the first quarter, the European debt crisis was declared to have been relieved temporarily, but it took a turn for the worse again from late March. Emerging economies experienced massive outflows of capital widely. Since September, the Outright Monetary Transactions (OMT) program launched by the ECB and the third and fourth round of quantitative easing initiated by the Federal Reserve stabilized the financial market and emerging economies faced climbing pressure from reversal of capital flows. In 2012, the Chinese economy stabilized amidst moderate growth and the financial system performed soundly in general. China's GDP increased 7.8 percent year on year to 51.9 trillion yuan in the whole year and increased 7.9 percent in the fourth quarter, putting an end to the moderation in GDP growth for seven consecutive quarters. Ultimate consumption and investments contributed 51.8 percent and 50.4 percent respectively to economic growth, indicating strengthening endogenous and self-sufficient economic drivers. The consumer price index was up 2.6 percent year on year and the current account surplus as a share of GDP dropped to 2.6 percent. [①]

To further improve the RMB exchange rate regime and enhance the RMB exchange rate flexibility, the PBC expanded the floating band of the RMB trading price against the US dollar on the inter-bank spot foreign exchange market from 0.5 percent to 1 percent, effective from April 16, 2012. The PBC continued with its effort to promote direct trading of the RMB against the emerging market currencies and initiated direct trading between the RMB and the Japanese yen on the inter-bank foreign exchange market.

Execution of Exchange Rate and Balance of Payments Policy

At end-2012, the central parity of the RMB against the US dollar was 6.2855 yuan per US dollar, up 0.2 percent over end-2011. From the reform of the RMB exchange rate regime in 2005, the RMB has appreciated by a cumulative 31.7 percent against the US dollar. In 2012, the central parity of the RMB against the US dollar peaked at 6.3495 yuan per dollar and reached a trough of 6.2670 yuan per dollar. It appreciated on 122 out of the 243 trading days and depreciated on the remaining 121 trading days, with the largest intraday appreciation at 0.26 percent (or 162 points), and the sharpest intraday depreciation at 0.33 percent (or 209 points). At end-2012, the central parity of the RMB against the euro registered 8.3176 yuan per euro, a depreciation of 1.86 percent from end-2011, and the central parity of the RMB against the Japanese yen stood at 7.3049 yuan per 100 Japanese yen, an appreciation of 11.03 percent from end-2011. Beginning from the reform of the RMB exchange rate regime in 2005 to end-2012, on a cumulative basis the RMB appreciated 20.40 percent against the euro and 0.01

---

① Balance of Payments Analysis Group, State Administration of Foreign Exchange, *China Balance of Payments Report* 2012, 3 April 2013.

percent against the Japanese yen. The BIS estimated that in 2012, the nominal effective RMB exchange rate against a basket of currencies appreciated 1.7 percent and the real effective exchange rate excluding inflation factor appreciated 2.2 percent, ranking the 20th and the 18th among the currencies of 61 economies monitored by the BIS. From the beginning of the RMB exchange rate reform in 2005, the nominal and real effective exchange rate of the RMB appreciated 23.3 percent and 31.9 percent on cumulative basis, ranking the fourth and the third among the aforesaid 61 currencies, respectively. [1]

In 2012, the current account surplus surged by 42 percent from 2011 to USD193.1 billion; the capital and financial account deficit posted USD16.8 billion, the first deficit since the Asian financial crisis, compared with a surplus of USD265.5 billion last year; and the surplus in the balance of payments totaled USD176.3 billion, down 56 percent, far below the annual average surplus of USD455.2 billion from 2007 to 2011. This amount marked a 56 percent slump from that of 2011, back to the size of surplus in 2004. The current account surplus as a share of GDP was 2.3 percent, still within the reasonable range accepted by the international community. Growth of reserve assets moderated obviously and its share of GDP at 1.2 percent lost 4.1 percentage points from that of 2011. In 2012, China's BOP posted a surplus in current account and a deficit in capital and financial account for the first time from a continued twin surplus since 1999. This signals that China's BOP is moving towards self-adjustment and self-balance. However, this is closely related to financial operations by market players in response to changes in the market environment such as interest rate spread and exchange rate spread between home and abroad and also to the cyclical change from "assets in local currency and debts in foreign currencies" to "assets in foreign currencies and debts in local currency". Self-balance of BOP is built on a shaky ground. In 2012, China's BOP totaled USD7.5 trillion, an increase of 6 percent from that of 2011; and its share of GDP over the same time frame was 91 percent, down 6 percentage points from that of 2011. Among the total BOP, trade of goods and services grew 7 percent from that of 2011, while cross-border direct investments (including foreign direct investments and outbound direct investments) declined by 2 percent. [2]

In 2012, RMB settlement of cross-border trade handled by banks aggregated 2.94 trillion yuan, up 41 percent year on year. This included 2.06 trillion yuan in trade of goods and 876.45 billion yuan in trade of services and other items under the current account. Actual RMB receipts

---

① Balance of Payments Analysis Group, State Administration of Foreign Exchange, *China Balance of Payments Report* 2012, 3 April 2013.

② Balance of Payments Analysis Group, State Administration of Foreign Exchange, *China Balance of Payments Report* 2012, 3 April 2013.

and payments in cross-border trade in 2012 totaled 1. 30 trillion yuan and 1. 57 trillion yuan, making a net outflow of 269. 17 billion yuan and bringing the receipt-to-payment ratio from 1 : 1. 7 in 2011 up to 1 : 1. 2. In 2012, RMB settlement of cross-border direct investments handled by banks reached 284. 02 billion yuan on cumulative basis, including 30. 44 billion yuan of outbound direct investments and 253. 58 billion yuan of foreign direct investments. As of end-2012, domestic correspondent banks opened 1, 592 RMB vostro accounts for overseas participating banks, with account balance at 285. 20 billion yuan; and overseas companies opened 6, 197 RMB settlement accounts with domestic banks, with account balance worth 50. 02 billion yuan. [1]

Policy Evaluation and Outlook

Looking forward to 2013, the Chinese and global economy and financial markets are expected to perform in a stable manner and the world economy will enter into a period of deep restructuring. China's BOP is expected to stay balanced, but the size of surplus might expand. To foster equilibrium will remain to be a tough mission. Going forward, SAFE will continue to follow the overall arrangements of the CPC Central Committee and the State Council, deepen the reform of the foreign exchange administration regime in an all-around manner, propel the reform of subject supervision and foreign exchange management for trade of services and facilitate foreign exchange management of capital account; strengthen foreign exchange macro analysis and regional analysis, underscore monitoring and analysis of key subjects and enhance foreign exchange monitoring and analysis competency and standard; manage and utilize foreign exchange reserves properly, further refine the operation and management system of large-sized foreign exchange reserves; defend the risk bottom line, consummate the cross-border capital flow monitoring system, enrich and perfect policies and contingency plans and guard against shocks from cross-border capital flows, in either direction. [2]

---

[1] Balance of Payments Analysis Group, State Administration of Foreign Exchange, *China Balance of Payments Report* 2012, 3 April 2013

[2] Balance of Payments Analysis Group, State Administration of Foreign Exchange, *China Balance of Payments Report* 2012, 3 April 2013.

CHAPTER 5

Highlights of Financial Market Development Policy

Market Development Policy of the Banking Sector

Highlights of Market Development Policy of the Banking Sector in 2012

In 2012, with the global economy losing growth momentum and the domestic economy stabilizing amidst growth, the Chinese government accelerated transformation of economic growth pattern and economic restructuring, continued its proactive fiscal policy and prudent monetary policy; made policy-making more forward-looking, better targeted and more flexible; took a hardline stance towards macro control of the housing market; pressed ahead with regulation of local financing platforms; and helped commercial banks perform soundly in general. According to CBRC statistics, as of the end of 2012, total assets of banking institutions increased 17. 9 percent year on year to 133. 6 trillion yuan; total liabilities amounted to 125. 0 trillion yuan, a year on year growth of 17. 8 percent; net profits posted 1. 24 trillion yuan, up 19 percent year on year; the weighted average capital adequacy ratio stood at 13. 25 percent, up 0. 54 percentage points year on year; outstanding non-performing loans registered 1. 07 trillion yuan, adding 23. 4 billion yuan to that at the beginning of 2012. The NPL ratio was 1. 56 percent, marking a 0. 22 percentage point retreat year on year.

Table 5. 1   Major Policies Having Impact on Development of the Banking Sector in 2012

Policy and Content	Issued by
Lowered the deposit reserve requirement ratio on two occasions	The PBC
Raised the benchmark deposit and lending rates on two occasions	The PBC
Expanded the floating bands of deposit and lending rates	The PBC
Circular on Tightening Management of Prepaid Card Business	The PBC
Administrative Measures for Prepaid Card Business of Payment Institutions	The PBC

Continued

Policy and Content	Issued by
Master Agreement on Bond Repurchase Transactions in the Inter-bank Market of China	The PBC
Notice on Relevant Matters Concerning Further Expanding the Pilot Program of Credit Asset Securitization	The PBC and others
Opinions of the State Council on Further Supporting the Healthy Development of Small and Micro Enterprises	The State Council
Guidelines on Small-/Medium-sized Rural Financial Institutions' Implementing Innovative Financial Projects for the Benefit of Farmers and the Agriculture	CBRC
Guidelines on Small-/Medium-sized Rural Financial Institutions' Implementing the Project of Financial Services to the Countryside and Communities	CBRC
Guidelines on Small-/Medium-sized Rural Financial Institutions' Implementing the Sunshine Credit Project	CBRC
Administrative Measures for Loans to Farmers	CBRC
Notice of CBRC on Issuing Green Credit Guidelines	CBRC
Notice on Putting to Rights Malpractices of Banking Institutions	CBRC
New Administrative Measures for Capital Adequacy Ratio	CBRC
Guidelines of CBRC on Innovations in Capital Instruments (Exposure Draft)	CBRC
Interim Provisions for Commercial Banks' Supervision over Capital Management with Advanced Methods	CBRC

Source: data collected by the research group.

Table 5.2　　　　　**Development of Banking Institutions in 2012**　　Unit: 100 million yuan

Key Indicator ＼ Year	2010	2011	2012
Total assets	942,600	1,115,000	1,336,000
Total liabilities	884,300	1,043,000	1,250,000
Net profit	7,637	10,412	12,386
ROA	1.10%	1.30%	1.28%
ROE	19.20%	20.40%	19.85%
Net interest margin	2.50%	2.70%	2.75%
Proportion of non-interest income	17.50%	19.30%	19.83%
Cost-to-income ratio	35.30%	33.40%	33.10%
Core capital	42,985	53,367	64,340
Tier 2 capital	10,295	14,418	17,585
Capital adequacy ratio	12.20%	12.70%	13.25%
Core capital adequacy ratio	10.10%	10.20%	10.62%
Liquidity ratio	42.20%	43.20%	45.83%
Loan-deposit ratio	64.50%	64.90%	65.31%
RMB excess reserve ratio	3.20%	3.10%	3.51%
Outstanding NPLs	4,336	4,279	4,929
NPL ratio	1.10%	1.00%	0.95%
Loan loss provision	9,438	11,898	14,564
Provision coverage ratio	217.70%	278.10%	295.51%

Source: data collected by the research group.

Analysis of Market Development Policy of the Banking Sector in 2012

In 2012, driven by domestic economic and financial policies, the banking sector of China developed soundly in general and commercial banks performed in a stable manner, with continuous growth of assets and liabilities, narrower net interest margin, moderated profit growth, further progress in business innovations, and strengthened services to small and micro enterprises, agriculture-related finance and green credit.

The deposit reserve requirement ratio was lowered on two occasions and deposits and loans of commercial banks grew steadily

In the first half of 2012, the Chinese economy faced increasing downside pressure and loan demand of the real economy was subdued. The PBC continued its prudent monetary policy and strengthened fine, pre-emptive and forward-looking policy tunings. In February and May, the PBC lowered the RMB deposit reserve requirement ratio of deposit-holding financial institutions, each time by 0.5 percent age points, and adjusted the deposit reserve requirement ratio of large-sized and small-/medium-sized financial institutions to 20 percent and 18 percent, respectively, and facilitated steady and moderate growth of loans and deposits of commercial banks.

The two cuts in the deposit reserve requirement ratio were made mainly in order to cope with economic slowdown and to stimulate economic revival. As the Chinese economic figures in the first half of 2012 fell short of market expectations and loan demand of the real economy slumped, lower deposit reserve requirement ratio was expected to buoy up the money multiplier, drive growth of money supply and enhance the lending capacity of banks. Meanwhile, the two cuts in the deposit reserve requirement ratio could heighten the expectation regarding liquidity loosening, boost the market's confidence in economic recovery, stimulate loan demand of the real economy and promote steady growth of deposits and loans.

Thanks to the policy stimulus, the Chinese economy started reviving in a mild way from the third quarter, loan demand looked up gradually and commercial banks saw stead growth of loans and deposits throughout the year. As of the end of 2012, outstanding loans in domestic and foreign currencies of all financial institutions (including foreign-funded financial institutions, the same hereinafter) reached 67.3 trillion yuan, adding 9.1 trillion yuan to that at the beginning of 2012 and representing an acceleration of 1.2 trillion yuan year on year. It was a 15.6 percent growth year on year, 0.1 percentage points lower than that of 2011. Outstanding RMB loans stood at 63.0 trillion yuan, adding 8.2 trillion yuan to that at the beginning of 2012 and representing an acceleration of 732 billion yuan year on year. At end-2012, outstanding deposits in domestic and foreign currencies of all financial institutions (including foreign-fundedfinancial institutions, the same hereinafter) posted 94.3 trillion yuan, up 14.1 percent year on year.

Such growth represented an acceleration of 0.6 percentage points over end-2011. The outstanding value was 11.6 trillion yuan more than that at the beginning of 2012, an acceleration of 1.8 trillion yuan year on year. Outstanding RMB deposits registered 91.7 trillion yuan, up 13.3 percent year on year. Such growth was 0.2 percentage points lower than that at end-2011. The outstanding value was 10.8 trillion yuan more than that at the beginning of 2012, an acceleration of 1.2 trillion yuan year on year.

Following two cuts in benchmark interest rates, lending rates of commercial banks slid in general

The PBC cut the benchmark deposit and lending rates in June and July of 2012, lowering the 1-year benchmark deposit rate and the 1-year benchmark lending rate of financial institutions by 0.50 percentage points and 0.56 percentage points on a cumulative basis from the beginning of 2012. Other deposit and lending rates and residential mortgage loan rates were adjusted accordingly.

The PBC lowered the benchmark deposit and lending rates in two consecutive months for the following reasons. First, given the huge pressure upon economic growth, it was necessary to cut interest rates to reduce financing costs of companies and thereby give a stimulus to the economy. Second, inflation receded sharply and CPI dropped to below 3%, which made room for interest rate cuts. Dragged by lower benchmark lending rates, the weighted average lending rates of commercial banks trended down in a steady manner. The weighted average lending rate stood at 6.78 percent in December, down 1.23 percentage points compared with the beginning of 2012. The weighted average interest rate of ordinary loans registered 7.07 percent, which was 0.73 percentage points lower than that at the beginning of 2012. The weighted average bill financing rate posted 5.64 percent, down 3.42 percentage points compared with the beginning of 2012.

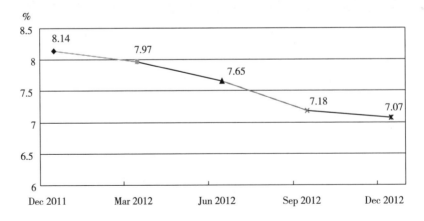

Source: 2012 Monetary Policy Executive Report.

Figure 5.1   The Curve of Weighted Average Rate of Ordinary Loans of Commercial Banks in 2012

The market-based interest rate reform was implemented at a quicker pace, but net interest margin of commercial banks didn't drop noticeably

In 2012, the PBC stepped up its effort to press ahead with the market-based interest rate reform at a quicker pace and expanded the floating band of deposit rates slightly on two occasions. In June, the PBC adjusted the ceiling for the floating band ofdeposit rates to 110 percent of the benchmark deposit rate, and lowered the floor for the floating band of lending rates to 80 percent of the benchmark lending rate. In July, the PBC lowered the floor for lending rates further to 70 of the benchmark lending rate, while the ceiling for deposit rates remained unchanged.

After the ceiling for the floating band of deposit rates was raised, commercial banks began to have vastly different deposit pricing, due to difference in competition pressure and client mix. The five major commercial banks, Industrial and Commercial Bank of China, China Construction Bank, Agricultural Bank of China, Bank of China and Bank of Communications, kept the benchmark interest rates almost unchanged, while most joint-stock commercial banks added 10% to the benchmark deposit rates selectively based on client class and size of deposit, and almost all city commercial banks added 10 percent to the benchmark deposit rates as well.

Table 5.3   **Shares of Loans with Rates Floating at Various Ranges**

of the Benchmark Rate, January through December, 2012   Unit: %

Month	Lower than the Benchmark	At the Benchmark	Higher than the Benchmark					
	(0.9, 1.0)	1.0	Subtotal	(1.0, 1.1)	(1.1, 1.3)	(1.3, 1.5)	(1.5, 2.0)	Above 2.0
Jan.	4.79	26.22	69.00	22.33	25.51	8.76	9.22	3.17
Feb.	5.53	27.59	66.88	23.12	23.76	7.98	8.61	3.40
Mar.	4.62	24.95	70.43	21.12	26.99	9.48	9.41	3.43
Apr.	5.03	23.06	71.91	20.76	28.92	10.10	8.98	3.16
May.	5.35	24.08	70.57	20.51	28.90	9.73	8.31	3.12
Jun.	7.92	25.08	66.99	19.94	27.87	8.90	7.66	2.63
Jul.	9.51	24.38	66.11	19.74	26.78	9.13	7.61	2.85
Aug.	11.61	22.66	65.73	19.64	26.45	8.30	8.33	3.01
Sep.	11.31	24.57	64.12	20.16	25.18	8.13	7.67	2.98
Oct.	10.88	26.80	62.32	20.15	24.30	7.28	7.53	3.06
Nov.	11.70	25.74	62.56	19.43	24.52	7.64	7.71	3.26
Dec.	14.16	26.10	59.74	18.41	22.87	7.58	7.84	3.04

Source: Monetary Policy Executive Report, quarter four, 2012.

Affected by the adjustment to the floor for the floating band of lending rates, the share of loans extended by financial institutions with rates lower than the benchmark rate climbed up. In December, the share of ordinary loans with rates lower than the benchmark rate advanced by 7. 14 percentage points from the beginning of 2012 to 14. 16 percent. This was mainly because the ever expanding all-system financing aggregates and continuously climbing shares of direct financing and off-balance sheet financing undermined the bargaining power of commercial banks with large-/medium-sized enterprises. In the short run, interest rate liberalization has limited impact on lending rates of commercial banks. On one hand, amidst economic downturn, commercial banks are in a reluctant mood to extend loans. Repricing of loans won't be completed until the first quarter of 2013. On the other hand, given the scarcity of loan resources, banks still play a pivotal role in the social financing framework and enjoy strong bargaining power. In the medium-to-long run, however, along with the development of direct financing and financial disintermediation, commercial banks will be forced to grant more interest concessions to clients, especially to key accounts. This poses a big challenge to the bargaining power of banks.

To summarize the impact of interest rate liberalization on the pricing of deposit and lending rates of banks, in the short run, interest rate liberalization has limited impact on net interest margin of banks. Overall net interest margin of commercial banks recorded a 2 basis points dip quarter on quarter to 2. 75 percent in the fourth quarter. A trough of net interest margin of the banking sector at the current phase is estimated to appear in the first and second quarter of 2013 along with repricing of deposit and lending rates triggered by interest rate cuts.

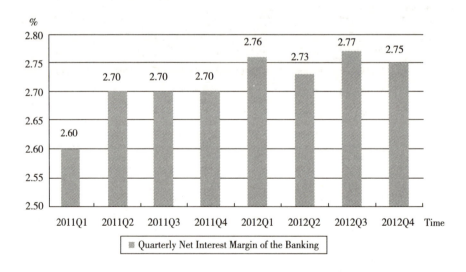

Source: CBRC.

Figure 5. 2　Net Interest Margin Change of the Banking Sector, 2012

The new policy regarding asset-backed securities was put into effect and the third round of pilot program was launched

In May, 2012, the PBC, China Banking Regulatory Cominission (CBRC) and the Ministry of Finance issued the *Notice on Relevant Matters Concerning Further Expanding the Pilot Program of Credit Asset Securitization*, kicking off the third round of credit asset securitization officially. A quota of 50 billion yuan was given for credit asset securitization at phase I. In September, China Development Bank (CDB) issued the first tranche of Kaiyuan credit asset-backed securities of 2012, to a total value of 10, 166, 440, 000 yuan, in the nationwide interbank bond market in the form of bookkeeping and centralized allotment.

The new ABS policy this time takes on four new features. First, the variety of underlying asset pool for ABS has been expanded. The applicable scope of the pilot program has been widened this time to cover diversified credit assets, including lending to the agricultural sector, auto loan, corporate loan of financing platforms of local governments ratified after investigation, energy-saving and emission-reduction loan, loan for strategic emerging industries, loan for cultural creativity industries and loan for affordable housing projects. Second, the applicable scope of participants has also been extended. The first round of the pilot program was focused on CDB and large banks. Financial institutions participating in this pilot program include city commercial banks and rural commercial banks. Bank of Beijing, Taizhou Bank and Harbin Bank are included in the ABS pilot program and granted a total quota of 2 billion yuan. This can help small-/medium-sized banks accumulate practical business experience. Third, risk self-retention is compulsory. In the previous round, originators were neither forced nor encouraged to hold their ABS. This time, originators are required to hold the lowest-level ABS at a minimum of 5% in each tranche, for no shorter than the duration of the lowest-level ABS. Fourth, dual rating is compulsory. Rating was done by a single institution in the previous round. This time dual rating is adopted. Two institutions are engaged for ABS rating.

The relaunch of ABS can help unleash the capital of commercial banks, enhance capital adequacy ratio, improve asset liquidity, facilitate matched maturity of assets and liabilities and spread systematic risks of banks. Though the total value in this round is 50 billion yuan merely, it will have certain positive effect on credit extension of commercial banks and effectively ease the pressure from low capital adequacy along with business expansion in the future.

Being more policy-oriented, commercial banks accelerated financial business development in key fields

First, banks expanded business with small and micro enterprises. In 2012, the State Council issued *Opinions of the State Council on Further Supporting the Healthy Development of*

100 million yuan

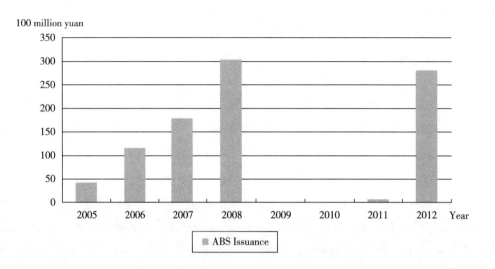

Source: WIND.

Figure 5.3   China ABS Issuance Since 2005

Small and Micro Enterprises (the *Opinions*). The Opinions call for double effort to alleviate the difficulty of small and micro enterprises in financing, by implementing all financial policies in support of the development of small and micro enterprises, quickening the development of small financial institutions, widening financing channels, improving credit guaranty for small and micro enterprises and regulating financing services to small and micro enterprises. Guided by the government's policies, loans extended by commercial banks to small and micro enterprises have kept growing for four consecutive years. As of end-2012, outstanding RMB loans extended by major financial institutions, rural cooperative financial institutions, urban credit cooperatives, and foreign-funded banks to small and micro enterprises rose 16.6 percent year on year, 8.0 and 1.0 percentage points more than those extended to large-and medium-sized enterprises. Outstanding loans extended by banking institutions to small and micro enterprises (including loans to small and micro enterprises, to individually-owned businesses and to owners of small and micro enterprises) totaled 14.8 trillion yuan, representing 22.0 percent of total loan balance.

Second, the development of agriculture-related finance quickened further. In 2012, CBRC released *Guidelines on Small-/Medium-sized Rural Financial Institutions' Implementing Innovative Financial Projects for the Benefit of Farmers and the Agriculture*, *Guidelines on Small-/Medium-*

sized Rural Financial Institutions' Implementing the Project of Financial Services to the Countryside and Communities, and *Guidelines on Small-/Medium-sized Rural Financial Institutions' Implementing the Sunshine Credit Project*, kicking off the three major projects officially. In September of the same year, CBRC released *Administrative Measures for Loans to Farmers*, which outlines the management framework and policies for loans to farmers, basic elements of loans, acceptance and investigation, examination and approval, release and payment, post-loan management, incentive and constraints, to regulate loans extended to farmers by banking institutions. Meanwhile, the PBC encouraged commercial banks to expand credit support to the agriculture and farmers through the re-lending and rediscount policy in favor of the agriculture. In August, 2012, the PBC initiated a pilot program in Shanxi and Heilongjiang, to broaden the applicable scope of re-lending in favor of the agriculture to four categories of institutions that are based in cities and have rural and agricultural loans accounting for no less than 70 percent of all loans. This policy effectively encouraged and supported these financial institutions to expand credit facility to the agriculture and farmers.

As of end-2012, domestic and foreign currency-denominated rural loans and agricultural loans (excluding bill financing) extended by major financial institutions, rural cooperative financial institutions, urban credit cooperatives, village and township banks, and financial companies increased by 3. 0 trillion yuan from early 2012, or 20. 7 percent year on year, to hit 17. 6 trillion yuan, outpacing the average growth rate of all loans (excluding bill financing) by 5. 6 percentage points. Therefore, two preset goals were fulfilled, i. e. , the growth rate no lower than the average growth rate of all loans, and the increment no lower than that of a year ago.

Third, the development of green credit was geared up. In February, 2012, CBRC released *Notice of CBRC on Issuing Green Credit Guidelines*, which sets out guidelines on organization management, policy making and ability building, process management, internal control and information disclosure, and supervision and examination; and requests banking institutions to boost green credit from a strategic perspective, expand credit support to green economy, low-carbon economy, and circular economy, guard against environmental and social risks, and thereby optimize the credit structure and drive sustainable development.

Policy Evaluation and Outlook

The Chinese economy is expected to revive in a moderate manner in 2013. Set against the general tone of growth amidst stability, the three carriages driving economic growth are expected to stabilize and rebound and commodity prices are expected to resume an upside trajectory. The mix of stabilizing monetary policy and loosening fiscal policy will continue to be in force and the banking sector will keep running soundly.

The monetary policy will remain prudent, appropriate, flexible and resilient and the growth of loans will decelerate

In 2013, with prudence being the general tone of monetary policy, the pressure to loosen and tighten monetary policy will exist concomitantly. On one hand, the foundation of economic growth needs to be consolidated. It is premature to loosen fine-tunings of monetary policy, as no marked improvement is seen in PMI and private investments fail to rally quickly. On the other hand, it is inappropriate to go too far to loosen monetary policy, in order to avoid a surge in housing prices, prevent investment fever and manage inflation in a forward-looking manner. By prudent monetary policy for 2013, it actually means "neutral". Depending on the running status of the economy, double effort is needed to make policies more forward-looking, better targeted, and more flexible, so as to properly address the relationships among stability, restructuring, inflation control and risk aversion. In general, the deposit reserve requirement ratio and deposit and lending rates are expected to remain stable throughout the year, and managing market liquidity through open market operations will become a normal state of policy regulating. In 2013, against the backdrop of prudent monetary policy, the growth of deposits in commercial banks is expected to basically stay flat with that of 2012, while the growth of lendings is estimated to slow down further. The value of new loans in the year is estimated at circa 9 trillion yuan, to prop up economic growth forcefully.

A combination of factors is expected to drag down profit growth of commercial banks

In 2013, due to the combined influence of a set of factors, commercial banks will face considerable pressure to achieve profit growth. First, the growth of interest-bearing assets will gear down. At present, interest income is still the major source of income to commercial banks and profit growth is still dependent on the growth of interest-bearing assets to a large extent. In 2013, however, the slow-down of interest-bearing assets will impose considerable pressure on net profit growth of banks. Second, net interest margin will narrow further. On one hand, interest rate liberalization lifts the ceiling for floating of deposit rates. In the face of intense competition, commercial banks might see rising deposit costs. On the other hand, restricted by weak economic recovery, bigger share of direct financing, lowered floor for floating of lending rates and other factors, commercial banks are unlikely to heighten their pricing power. On the contrary, due to the time lag in the effect of lowered benchmark rates last year, interest rate repricing is expected to drag down profit growth of listed banks. Third, outstanding NPLs are expected to stabilize after a rebound. The quality of local financing platform loans and residential mortgage loans will remain sound, but the value of NPLs to export-oriented small enterprises in the coastal regions hit hard by sagging external demand might rise as a result of inertial force.

Enterprises in some industries plagued by massive overcapacity (like steel trade, photovoltaic and shipping, shipbuilding) are unlikely to extricate themselves from the trouble in the short term and the quality of their assets deserves attention.

The control over key fields will be tightened, asset quality will remain stable and risks will be controllable as a whole

First, the management of local financing platform loans will be tightened. After riding out the test of bulk repayment in 2012, local financing platforms are unlikely to experience volatile quality of loans. In 2013, the authority is going to promulgate relevant policies and press ahead with risk control over government-backed local financing platform loans in light of the principle of "total amount control, classified management, differentiation, and gradual dissolving". In general, the quality of local financing platform loans is unlikely to deteriorate badly in the short term, given recovery of the Chinese economy, upturn of investments, lower outstanding loans of the platforms in stock and widened financing channels, but the middle-to-long-term movement of loans of the platforms does deserve close attention. Second, the quality of residential mortgage loans will remain stable. After hitting the bottom and stabilizing in 2012, China's housing prices will undergo increasing upside pressure. In 2013, the government is going to continue to take a firm hand on the housing market. Owing to the recently released "five regulations" in particular, the housing market is expected to perform soundly as a whole. Commercial banks will continue to adopt prudent credit policy and tight risk control. The risk in residential mortgage loans will be controllable. With integration of the housing industry, however, some small-/medium-sized developers might have NPLs. Third, the risk in the shadow banking system will stay within a controllable level generally. Compared with European countries and the USA, all kinds of shadow banking businesses in China are characterized by small size and low leverage ratio. The overall risk is controllable, though certain risk is hidden in shadow banks, including risk in wealth management products, in default on usurious loans, and in off-balance-sheet business that may put the balance sheet of banks at stake. In 2013, CBRC and CSRC, among other policymakers, are going to abide by the rule of prudence and restriction, tighten supervision over shadow banks, take strict precautions against proliferation of the risk in shadow banks over the entire banking system and spread into the real economy, and pay special attention to clear out, put to rights and regulate shadow banking businesses such as banking wealth management products, non-banking wealth management products, trust and private lendings, so as to restrict the scale and growth of shadow banks and keep all risks under effective control.

Stock Market Development Policy

Highlights of China's Stock Market Development Policy in 2012

Figure 5. 4　　Highlights of China's Stock Market Development Policy, 2012

Date	Title of Policy	Issued by
4 January	*Notice on Relevant Matters Concerning the Implementation of the Pilot Measures for Domestic Securities Investment Made by RMB Qualified Foreign Institutional Investors of Fund Management Companies and Securities Companies*	The PBC
8 January	*Interim Measures for the Administration of National SME Share Transfer System Co. , Ltd*	CSRC
11 January	*Notice on Issues Concerning Individual Income Tax on Individuals' Income from the Transfer of Restricted Shares of Listed Companies after Securities Institutions' Completion of Technology and System Preparations*	The Ministry of Finance, State Administration of Taxation
30 January	*Q&A about the Decision on Amending the Provisions on the Material Asset Reorganization and Ancillary Financing of Listed Companies*	CSRC
8 February	*Business Rules of National SME Share Transfer System (for Trial Implementation)*	National SME Share Transfer System Co. , Ltd
23 February	CSRC announced the first list of independent fund distribution licenses	CSRC
27 February	*Notice on Issues Regarding the Deduction of Reserve Expenditures in the Securities Sector before the Payment of Enterprise Income Tax*	The Ministry of Finance
14 March	*Shenzhen Stock Exchange Individual Investor Survey Report 2011*	Shenzhen Stock Exchange
25 March	*Shanghai Stock Exchange Detailed Rules for Implementation of ETF Business*	Shanghai Stock Exchange
20 April	*Shenzhen Stock Exchange Growth Enterprise Market Listing Rules*	Shenzhen Stock Exchange
26 April	*Opinions on Further Supporting the Healthy Development of Small and Micro Enterprises*	The State Council
25 May	*Notice on Key Points in Implementing Several Opinions of the State Council on Encouraging and Guiding the Healthy Development of Private Investment*	CSRC
20 June	*Administrative Measures for the Operation of Securities Investment Funds*	CSRC
27 July	*Provisions on Issues Concerning the Implementation of the Administrative Measures for Securities Investment Made in China by Qualified Foreign Institutional Investors (QFII)*	CSRC
27 August	*Rules for the Management of Margins in Refinancing (for Trial Implementation) , Refinancing Business Rules , and Statistical and Monitoring Rules for Margin Trading and Short Selling*	China Securities Finance Corporation Limited
31 August	*Guiding Opinions on Regulating Securities Companies' Participation in Regional Equity Trading Markets (for Trial Implementation)*	CSRC

Continued

Date	Title of Policy	Issued by
18 October	*Trial Implementation Measures for the Customer Asset Management Business of Securities Companies*	CSRC
11 October	*Measures for the Supervision and Administration of Non-listed Public Companies*	CSRC
12 November	*Provisions on the Administration of Proxy Sale of Financial Products by Securities Companies*	CSRC
16 November	*Provisions on Adjusting the Basis of Calculation of Net Capital of Securities Companies*	CSRC
18 November	*Decision on Amending the Provisions on the Investment Scope for Proprietary Trading of Securities Companies and Related Matters*	CSRC
21 December	*Regulatory Guidelines on Document Submission and Review Procedure for Overseas Stock Issuance and Listing of Joint Stock Companies*	CSRC
25 December	With the approval of the State Council, the PBC, CBRC and CSRC actively expanded the pilot program of setting up fund management companies by commercial banks.	The State Council

Source: data collected by the research group.

Analysis of China's Stock Market Development Policy in 2012

Breakthrough was made in local pension funds' investment in the stock market

News of *China Securities Journal* dated January 17, 2012 covered that breakthrough was made in local pension funds' long-simmering investment in the stock market. A province in south China was approved to vest National Council for Social Security Fund with the authority to run 100 billion yuan basic pension fund and to start investment in the first quarter of 2012. [1] On March 19, 2012, a trust investment agreement was concluded among National Council for Social Security Fund, Guangdong provincial government and other parties concerned. With the approval of the State Council, National Council for Social Security Fund was entrusted by Guangdong provincial government to invest and manage the 100 billion yuan balance of basic pension insurance for urban employees of Guangdong province. Putting pension funds into the stock market opened up diversified investment channels of pension funds and broadened the ways of value preservation and appreciation for pension funds. It also made an exploration into the reform of the pension fund system. If long-term investment and value investment are upheld, and a rigorous accountability mechanism is in place, we will be able to pacify the mass retail

[1] Investment of 100 Billion Yuan Local Pension Funds in the Stock Market Approved, Estimated to Begin in the First Quarter [J]. China Securities Journal, 2012, 1.

investors in the A-share stock market and encourage investors to develop the notion of long-term value investment, so as to minimize violent ups and downs of the stock market. Moreover, a dose of long-term fund into the market could indirectly urge the government to cleanse the deep-rooted evils in the stock market and then have positive influence on policy of the stock market.

OTC market construction was solidified

On January 8, 2012, CSRC issued *Interim Measures for the Administration of National SME Share Transfer System Co., Ltd.* National SME Share Transfer System Co., Ltd is authorized to oversee and manage listed and delisted companies of the former STAQ and NET systems, which were under the agency share transfer system of securities companies, and their share transfer activities. On September 20, 2012, National SME Share Transfer System Co., Ltd was incorporated, with its business scope covering organizing and arranging public share transfer of unlisted joint-stock companies, providing services related to financing and M&A of unlisted joint-stock companies, and offering information and technical services to market participants. Concomitantly, CSRC issued *Measures for Supervision and Administration of Public Unlisted Companies* on October 11, 2012, wherein the concept of "public unlisted company" is defined, the limit to the number of stockholders of unlisted companies (new third board listed companies for example) to 200 persons is lifted, and public transfer of stocks of public unlisted companies on a "legally established securities trading place" (equivalent to National SME Share Transfer System for the moment) is allowed. [①] On March 19, 2013, CSRC released an announcement, saying that service windows for administrative licensing will be open to the public at the offices of National SME Share Transfer System Co., Ltd, to process applications for public transfer of stocks and private placement of public unlisted companies.

11 policy dividends were declared on the Brokerage Innovation Conference

May 7 and 8 of 2012 witnessed the opening of the Brokerage Innovation Conference in Beijing and the declaration of 11 measures to encourage innovations in the industry. On October 12, CSRC released *Administrative Measures for Securities Companies' Participation in Regional Equity Trading Markets (Exposure Draft)*. On October 18, *Trial Implementation Measures for the Customer Asset Management Business of Securities Companies* came into effect officially. On November 12, *Provisions on the Administration of Proxy Sale of Financial Products by Securities Companies* were promulgated. On November 16, *Provisions on Adjusting the Basis of Calculation of Net Capital of Securities Companies (Revised in 2012)* came out and *Provisions on the*

① Liao Fan. Regulation of China's Securities Industry 2012, Annual Report on China's Rule of Law No. 11 (Bluebook of Rule of Law) [M]. Social Sciences Academic Press, 2013.

Investment Scope for Proprietary Trading of Securities Companies and Related Matters were amended. [1] To sum up, diversification, brokerage and OTC are main directions of innovative development of securities companies, and policy dividends will give an important impetus to the transformation of securities companies. Meanwhile, policy dividends will be mainly reflected in loosening capital control, business supervision and administrative regulation.

The quotas for QFII and RQFII investments were raised immensely

CSRC announced on April 3, 2012 to add another 50 billion US dollars to the current level of investment quota, making the total QFII investment quota at 80 billion US dollars. QFII licensing was quickened obviously in 2012, with more than 66 QFII licenses granted. As of November 30, 2012, 201 foreign institutions received QFII licenses, and were granted investment quotas worth of 36.043 billion US dollars cumulatively. Moreover, State Administration of Foreign Exchange revised the provisions concerning QFII-related foreign exchange investments and raised the ceiling for the investment quota of sovereign funds, central banks and monetary authorities to top the equivalent of one billion US dollars. On November 14, 2012, CSRC announced an additional 200 billion yuan investment quota for RQFII, making total investment quota under the pilot program of RQFII at 270 billion yuan. Haitong China Renminbi Income Fund and the Renminbi Bond Fund of China Universal Asset Management became the first two RQFII products offered.

Third-party fund sales were initiated

On February 22, 2012, CSRC announced the first list of independent fund distribution licenses. On the list were four institutions, Howbuy, Zhonglu Investment Consulting, NOAH Private Wealth Management and Eastmoney, which increased the total number of third-party independent fund sales agencies to eight. This gives more options to investors to access new fund investment platforms, besides banks, securities companies and fund firms. Along with increasing sales agencies comes the chance to enjoy more concessions in commission rates. The entry of third-party fund sellers has largely widened fund sales channels and helped gradually break the monopoly of banks on fund sales. Thereby the entire ecological chain of the fund industry can be optimized. The participation of third-party sales agencies can also improve the financial experience of consumers and allow them to enjoy more competitive prices and better aftersale services. This marks a big step towards the open-up of the financial service industry to private capitals.

---

① 2012 Top Ten Breaking News of China' Securities Market [J]. China Securities Journal, 2012, 12.

Re-financing business was launched officially

Endorsed by CSRC, China Securities Finance Corporation Limited promulgated *Refinancing Business Rules* (*for Trial Implementation*), *Statistical and Monitoring Rules for Margin Trading and Short Selling* (*for Trial Implementation*) and *Rules for the Management of Margins in Refinancing* (*for Trial Implementation*), on August 27, 2012. On the same day, a basket of supporting business rules on refinancing were unveiled, including *Implementation Measures for Refinancing Securities Lending* (*for Trial Implementation*) by Shanghai Stock Exchange and Shenzhen Stock Exchange, and *Notice on Temporary Exemption from Payment of Fees Related to Depository and Clearing for Securities Lending and Refinancing*, and *Detailed Rules for the Implementation of Collateral Management Business* (*Applicable to Refinancing Business*) by China Securities Depository & Clearing Corporation Limited, effective from August 27, 2012. These marked official implementation of the pilot program of refinancing. 11 securities companies, including Haitong Securities, Galaxy Securities and CITIC Securities, were appointed the first securities lenders, to inject fund into China Securities Finance Corporation Limited, provide a new source of fund for margin trading and short selling, and meet the funding demand of the securities investment sector. The kick-off of refinancing business is a significant step to consummate the fundamental institutional construction of China's capital market and can help foster a value investment philosophy and increase capital market liquidity.

Policy Evaluation and Outlook

The year of 2012 marked a year of innovative development of China's stock market and saw an avalanche of innovative reform actions and development policies being rolled out, achieving tangible results, and further consolidating the institutional foundation for the healthy development of China's capital market. Meanwhile, we should realize that the capital market of China is still at a nascent and transitional stage. Its development still lags behind the growth pace of the national economy. The resource configuration function and price discovery function of the capital market are yet to be brought into fullest play. The market is still void of an incentive mechanism and constraint mechanism for independent innovations. Countless institutional obstacles and systematic defects exist and need our effort to overcome. Looking forward to 2013, our top priorities are to quicken the pace of building a multi-level capital market and develop a service innovative country. Meanwhile, we should make double effort on business innovations and product innovations, enhance the professional competence and internal control mechanism of securities companies, gradually loosen intervention and regulation, respect the law of the market and the innovative power, and optimize and strengthen the capital market.

Market Development Policy of the Insurance Industry

Highlights of Market Development Policy of the Insurance Industry in 2012

Table 5. 5   Highlights of China's Insurance Market Development Policy

Date	File Name	Issued by
30 March	Decision of the State Council on Amending *Regulations on Compulsory Traffic Accident Liability Insurance for Motor Vehicles*	The State Council
5 June	Notice on Implementing the *Plan and Implementation Scheme for Deepening the Healthcare System Reform During the 12th Five-Fear*	CIRC
12 June	Notice on Issuing the *Plan for Roll-out of Petty Personal Insurance*	CIRC
15 June	Notice on Issuing the *Implementation Opinions of China Insurance Regulatory Commission on Encouraging and Supporting the Healthy Development of Private Investment*	CIRC
24 August	Guiding Opinions on the Supplementary Insurance of Major Diseases for Urban and Rural Residents	National Development and Reform Commission, the Ministry of Health, the Ministry of Finance, the Ministry of Human Resources and Social Security, the Ministry of Civil Affairs, and CIRC
14 September	Opinions on Unswervingly Pressing ahead with Reform of the Insurance Salesmen Management System	CIRC
14 September	Notice on Matters Related to Supporting Car Sellers to Specialize in Insurance Agency Business	CIRC
17 September	The 12th Five-Year Plan for the Development and Reform of the Financial Industry	The PBC, CBRC, CSRC, CIRC and SAFE
12 November	Agricultural Insurance Regulations	The State Council

Source: data collected by the research group.

Analysis of Market Development Policy of the Insurance Industry in 2012

As warned by Xiang Junbo, Chairman of China Insurance Regulatory Commission (CIRC), the year of 2012 was a year the insurance market faced grave situations, overwhelming challenges and huge difficulties. Upholding the theme of scientific development, the whole industry focused on transforming growth pattern, made exploration and innovation, held the reins and did solid work, and pressed ahead with all tasks of reform and development in an earnest manner. As a result, the insurance market showed a trend of growth amidst stability and improvement amidst growth. First, the market performed stably in general. Total premium income of the year amounted to 1. 55 trillion yuan, representing a year-on-year growth of 8 percent. Property insurance kept growing at a relatively quick pace and achieved premium income of 533. 1 billion yuan, up 15. 4 percent year on year; life insurance rebounded and derived premium income of 890. 8 billion yuan, up 2. 4 percent year on year; premium income from health insurance posted 86. 28 billion yuan, a 24. 7 percent year on year growth; and premium income from life accident insurance grew 15. 6 percent year on year to 38. 62 billion yuan. Total assets of insurance companies hit 7. 35 trillion yuan, a surge by 22. 9 percent from the beginning of 2012. Second, the capacity for serving the economy and society was heightened. Premium income from agricultural insurance amounted to 24. 06 billion yuan, up 38. 3 percent year on year. It provided risk cover worth of 900. 6 billion yuan to 183 million households and indemnified 28, 180, 000 disaster-stricken rural households for a total loss of 14. 82 billion yuan. The insurance industry was taking care of New Rural Cooperative Medical System of 129 counties and cities and had 5. 05 billion yuan fund under management. Petty insurance covered 32 million persons, up 33. 3 percent year on year. Export credit insurance covered 35, 000 companies, derived premium income of 14. 26 billion yuan, provided risk cover worth of 293. 65 billion yuan and made contribution to stabilization of external demand. The outstanding balance of insurance fund employed was 6. 85 trillion yuan, including 324 billion yuan invested in infrastructure in 23 provinces and cities. In 2012, total claim and benefit payments of insurance companies amounted to 471. 63 billion yuan, representing a year-on-year growth of 20 percent. The insurance industry performed compensation liability in a satisfactory manner in some major disasters and accidents, such as Beijing 7 · 21 Rainstorm and Typhoon Bolaven. ①

To be more specific, the government and CIRC instituted or put into operation the following important development policies in 2012:

The 12th Five-Year Plan for the Development and Reform of the Financial Industry outlined the targets and tasks for the reform and development of the industry

Endorsed by the State Council, the PBC, CBRC, CSRC, CIRC and SAFE released *The 12th Five-Year Plan for the Development and Reform of the Financial Industry* (the *Plan*) in September, 2012. The *Plan* puts forward the guidelines, key targets and the gist of policies for the development and reform of the financial industry during the 12th Five-Year, and makes clear top priorities in the reform and development of the financial industry during the 12th Five-Year

---

① Xiang Junbo: *Speech on* 2013 *National Insurance Regulation Work Meeting*, January 24, 2013.

from improving financial macro control, perfecting the organization system, constructing the financial market, deepening the financial reform, expanding open-up, maintaining financial stability and consolidating the infrastructure.

The development and reform of the insurance industry, as an essential component of the financial industry, is a key part of the *Plan*. As provided for under the *Plan* clearly, "it is necessary to encourage innovative development of insurance institutions, conform to the needs of economic and social development and market demand, erect a modern insurance industry characterized by a complete market system, wide-ranging services, good faith, effective risk prevention and strong comprehensive competitive strength, and achieve unity of development speed, quality and efficiency. Effort is required to optimize the insurance industry organization system, draw a market picture of diversified participants, orderly competition, and great vitality, to urge insurance groups to further consummate corporate governance, strengthen integration of resources, promote business synergy on the basis of the main insurance business and enhance operation transparency. It is advisable to develop insurance companies specialized in pension insurance, heath insurance, liability insurance, car insurance and agricultural insurance, explore credit insurance institutions and cultivate differentiated competitive advantage in specialized insurance companies. Support is given to innovative development of small-/ medium-sized insurance companies and to form competitive and distinctive business models. Mutual insurance companies can be developed and self-insurance companies can be piloted. The management system of insurance asset management companies should be well-designed. Qualified small-/medium-sized insurance companies are encouraged to set up insurance asset management companies with good corporate governance, proper equity structure and efficient market operations. Specialized insurance asset management organizations can be founded tentatively. Specialization of insurance intermediaries is encouraged. Establishment and development of exclusive insurance agents and insurance sales firms shall be propelled. Investment in insurance companies by eligible state-owned capital, private capital and foreign capital is encouraged. "

The *Plan* further proposes "to develop the insurance market, give play to its insurance service function better, enrich insurance products, and widen insurance service scope; to develop personal life insurance, health insurance, pension insurance, and corporate annuity, as well as insurance related to housing and car consumption; to do well in the pilot program of income tax-deferred pension; to summarize and spread the experience and best practice in commercial insurance' participation in social security and health insurance system construction; to accelerate the development of liability insurance for environmental pollution and public security that is closely related to public interests; to phase in a government-backed catastrophe insurance system and consummate catastrophic risk diversification, transfer and compensation mechanism; to immensely improve insurance service, safeguard order of the insurance market, and solve serious problems such as misleading statements in sales and difficulty in claims; to encourage innovations in asset management products, and invest insurance funds in real estate and equity of unlisted companies in a steady manner; to give backing to insurance funds to widen investment channels under the condition of controllable risk and invest in equity of insurance companies, non-insurance financial enterprises, and elderly care, healthcare and car service businesses that are relevant to insurance; to perfect the regulatory system over solvency of the insurance industry, reinforce capital replenishment and constraints and consummate a risk-oriented classified regulatory system; to polish the regulatory system and standards over governance of insurance corporations, and prominently heighten execution of the corporate governance regulatory system; and to keep a close watch on the use of insurance funds, take precautions against investment risks and give play to the pivotal role of the insurance protection fund. "

Agricultural Insurance Regulations **were promulgated, marking a new breakthrough in the agricultural insurance system**

China is an agricultural country. The problems with the agriculture, farmers and the countryside are still of the utmost importance in the economic and social development of China. It is of paramount importance to develop agricultural insurance, give full play to the insurance mechanism, diversify and transfer agricultural risks, because it can heighten the anti-risk capacity of the agriculture, stabilize agricultural production and protect the interests of farmers. The government has always put a premium on agricultural insurance and clarified the requirements for setting up and developing agricultural insurance. As provided for under the *Agriculture Law*, "the government shall set up and perfect an agricultural insurance system. " The *Insurance Law* also makes it clear that "the government supports insurance undertakings that serve agricultural production. " Pursuant to these provisions, the State Council released *Agricultural Insurance Regulations* on November 12, 2012, by summing up the practical experience in developing agricultural insurance over recent years.

Agricultural Insurance Regulations (the *Regulations*) legalize and routinize the measures in support of agricultural insurance. From 2007 to 2011, central finance earmarked a cumulative amount of 26. 4 billion yuan as subsidy for agricultural insurance premium. The combined premium subsidy for main crops granted by public finance at all levels accounted for 80% of receivable premium. It may well be said that without the financial support of the government, the development of agricultural finance would have been impossible. In order to legalize and routinize the measures in support of agricultural insurance, the *Regulations* state clearly. First, the government endorses the development of all types and forms of agricultural insurance, so as to consummate a policy-driven agricultural insurance system. Second, for agricultural insurance that complies with relevant rules, the Finance authority shall give subsidy for premium and a public finance-backed catastrophic risk diversification mechanism shall be put in place for agricultural insurance. Third, local governments are encouraged to support the development of agricultural insurance by earmarking premium subsidy from local public finance, and setting up a public finance-backed catastrophic risk diversification mechanism for agricultural insurance, among other measures. Fourth, tax incentives shall be granted to agricultural insurance business to encourage financial institutions to expand credit support to farmers and organizations in agricultural production that have agricultural insurance.

While supporting agricultural insurance in policies, *Agricultural Insurance Regulations* also set forth the rules on agricultural insurance contract and agricultural insurance business operation, which are skewed towards protecting the interests of insured farmers. First, in order to maintain the stability of agricultural insurance contract, the parties are disallowed to raise premium or terminate the insurance contract during the valid term of the contract, because of any change in the risk exposure of the object. Second, to make sure disaster-stricken farmers get compensation timely in full, insurance companies are required to do site survey, evaluate loss and pay insurance benefit timely upon receiving the notice of an insurance accident. Third, to guarantee open, fair and impartial loss evaluation and claim, insurance companies are required to make public the results of loss evaluation and claim if organizations in agricultural production or villagers' committees have organized farmers to acquire agricultural insurance. Fourth, to set premium rate and lay down insurance clauses appropriately, insurance companies are required to frame agricultural insurance clauses and premium rate in a fair and reasonable manner, after hearing out the views and opinions of the Finance, Agriculture and Forestry authority of the provincial government and farmer representatives, and submit these to CIRC for approval or recordkeeping.

In addition, in order to guard against risks in agricultural insurance business, and enable agricultural insurance to give concrete support and benefit to farmers, the *Regulations* provide for the following rules on risk prevention and control. First, insurance companies are required to put in place a sound agricultural insurance internal control system, robust agricultural re-insurance and catastrophic risk arrangement and contingency plan, and their solvency and reserve evaluation and solvency reporting for agricultural insurance must comply with the rules set by

CIRC under the State Council. Second, to guarantee legal use of premium subsidy provided by public finance, any form of fraud for getting premium subsidy, inclusive of but not limited to fabrication or false addition of insurance object, false claim and falsely stated fees, is strictly forbidden. Third, legal liabilities for any offense against the regulations are provided for clearly.

The promulgation of *Agricultural Insurance Regulations* marks the entry of agricultural insurance in China into a new stage of the rule of law. It is a milestone in the development of agricultural insurance in China and flags solidified institutional foundation for sustainable and sound development of agricultural insurance. It will empower the insurance industry from institutions to better serve the agriculture, farmers and the countryside, and improve the agriculture support system.

A rudimentary major disease insurance system was established to open up a new way for the insurance industry to serve the health insurance system

In recent years, along with progress in the new healthcare system reform, a universal health insurance system has taken shape in China. Currently, health coverage provided by Basic Medical Insurance for Urban Residents and New Rural Cooperative Medical System is at a low level. The financial burden on patients is intolerable when high medical expenses are incurred by major diseases. The phenomenon of "one person taken ill, the whole family impoverished" still exists. On August 24, 2012, National Development and Reform Commission, the Ministry of Health, the Ministry of Finance, the Ministry of Human Resources and Social Security, the Ministry of Civil Affairs, and CIRC released *Guiding Opinions on the Supplementary Insurance of Major Diseases for Urban and Rural Residents* (*Guiding Opinions*). Thereby, the major disease insurance system for urban and rural residents was launched officially. On top of basic medical insurance, patients receive additional reimbursement for high medical expenses incurred by major diseases. It is clearly stated under the *Guiding Opinions* that major disease insurance for urban and rural residents is sponsored by the government and run by commercial insurance institutions. A portion of money is taken out from the Basic Medical Insurance for Urban Residents and New Rural Cooperative Medical System fund to purchase major disease insurance from commercial insurance institutions. By participating in major disease insurance, insurance companies can get access to a massive client base while receiving income from premium directly. Then, they can build up their brand awareness tremendously and pave the way for selling commercial insurance. Authorized by the government to superintend the conduct of hospitals, they can accumulate experience in how to restrain hospitals. Therefore, the promulgation of the *Guiding Opinions* not only unfolds a new model for the insurance industry to serve the health insurance system, but also creates a new opportunity for the development of commercial health insurance. Meanwhile, the *Guiding Opinions* lay down the rules of breakeven and thin profit for major disease insurance, and require all competent authorities to strengthen supervision over insurance institutions. This also means the major disease insurance system has heightened the requirements for risk control, professional competence, cost control and service capacity of commercial insurance institutions.

The open-up of compulsory insurance to foreign enterprises brought open-up of the insurance market to the next level

In conformity with the overall open-up strategy of the country, the State Council released *Decision on Amending Regulations on Compulsory Traffic Accident Liability Insurance for Motor Vehicles* (the *Decision*) on March 30, 2012. On the basis of the commitment made for entry into WTO, the insurance market was wider open, to allow foreign insurance companies deal in compulsory insurance. The *Decision* came into effect from May 1, 2012. Thereafter, foreign property insurance companies made preparations actively for entry into the compulsory insurance market. In early October, the first compulsory insurance policy was issued by a foreign insurance company.

Car insurance takes up approximately 70% of the property insurance market of China. Foreign insurance companies were disallowed to deal in compulsory insurance before, which means they were basically kept out of car insurance business, because the majority of consumers tend to buy compulsory insurance and commercial car insurance from the same insurance company. Exactly for this reason, foreign insurance companies cried out for access to compulsory insurance business. The open-up of the compulsory insurance market this time is a positive response to the appeal of foreign insurance companies. The entry of foreign insurance companies into the compulsory insurance market has little impact on large insurance companies because they boast a powerful marketing and service network, but it might give a hard blow to small-/ medium-sized companies. To consumers, foreign insurance companies bring more options and better services. The open-up of the compulsory insurance market to foreign companies is a critical breakthrough in the open-up of China's insurance industry and is of vital importance to improve the open-up quality of the insurance market, promote market competition and enhance services.

The reform of the insurance salesmen management system and transformation and upgrade of the insurance intermediary market were pushed forward

Insurance sales force is a key component of the insurance intermediary market. Since the individual marketing mechanism was initiated in 1992, the insurance sales team developed rapidly and the number of insurance salesmen totaled 3,357,000 persons in China as of the end of 2011. The insurance salesmen system made great contribution to the development of the insurance industry. Along with advancement of the society, development of the industry and perfection of the legal system, however, some problems emerged in the present insurance salesmen management system, for example, awkward relations, loose management, unstable team and low caliber. It disaccords with the need of the insurance industry for the transformation of growth pattern, the contemporary requirement for concerted development of the economy and the society and diversified insurance demand of consumers. In 2010, CIRC released *Opinions on Reforming and Improving the Insurance Salesmen Management System*, with a view to guide market players to make exploration into the reform actively, and it took some effect. On September 14, 2012, CIRC released *Opinions on Unswervingly Pressing Ahead with Reform of the Insurance Salesmen Management System* (the *Opinions*), to put the reform of the salesmen system on the agenda again. The *Opinions* lays emphasis on the necessity and urgency to press ahead with the reform of the insurance salesmen management system, makes clear the basic rules and targets of the reform, and puts forward main tasks and measures for pushing forward the reform. It requires a good command of the timing, intensity and pace of the reform and deepening the reform of the insurance salesmen management system.

The *Opinions* sets forth general requirements for the reform of the insurance salesmen management system: "streamlined system, tighter control, more stable team and higher caliber". The basic rules are "supervision and guidance, choice of the market, driven by the industry and responsibility on companies". The *Opinions* maps out the three-year, five-year and long-term targets of the insurance salesmen management system reform for the first time. A pilot program is scheduled to be launched in a right region at the right time, and the targets will be phased in. The present situation of loose management, unstable team and low caliber of insurance salesmen will be changed over three years. The quality of insurance salesmen will be enhanced step by step and the profession of insurance sales will leave a better impression. In five years, new models and new channels will enjoy a much bigger market share. Over a longer period of time, a new insurance sales system will be built, which is characterized by well-defined legal relations, clear-cut management responsibilities, rights commensurate with obligations, equal importance of efficiency and equality, performance-related pay, sound basis, legality and compliance, diversified channels and strong vitality, and a professional insurance sales team of good moral, high caliber and sustainability will be brought up.

The *Opinions* outlines six main tasks and measures for pressing ahead with the reform. First, encourage exploration into new insurance marketing models and channels; second, emphasize the responsibility of insurance companies for the management of salesmen; third, enhance the quality of insurance salesmen; fourth, provide better pay and social security to insurance salesmen; fifth, set up a proper insurance marketing incentive mechanism; and sixth, summarize experience and do research in depth.

After the overall requirements, targets and measures were made clear, a series of reform steps were taken under the leadership of the authority. A pilot program of diversified transfer of insurance salesmen was launched, for example, turned into salesmen of insurance companies, salesmen of insurance intermediaries, contract workers employed by insurance companies, and individual insurance agents compliant with the provisions of the *Insurance Law*. According to statistics, by the first half of 2012, CIRC approved of 13 insurance companies' setting up insurance sales companies, and the former salesmen of the insurance companies were reemployed by the insurance sales companies. In November, 2012, CCB Life Insurance pioneered the reform of the salesmen management system, by adopting a hybrid employment system combining agency and hourly contract mechanism, and providing a social security package comprised of five insurances plus housing fund. These pilot measures will take effect gradually. The year of 2012 is bound to become a crucial year in the reform of the insurance salesmen management system of China.

While pressing ahead with the reform of the insurance salesmen management system, CIRC actively drove transformation and development of the whole insurance intermediary market and enhanced specialization and scale of services, by following the rule of "combining dredging and blocking, advance and retreat". To be more specific, by blocking and retreat, it means tightening market access control over regional insurance agents and putting a limit to increment. The existing small-sized, poorly managed and dispersed agents were shut down, suspended, merged or reorganized to reduce the number. In 2012, the authority took the following actions to perform the aforesaid tasks: intensified inspection over intermediary business, made public problems identified and pressed for corrections; released *Notice on Further Regulating Market Access to Insurance Intermediaries*, to impose restrictions on the industrial background and registered capital of insurance agents and brokers; released *Notice on Suspending Market Access to Regional Insurance Agents and Some Sideline Insurance Agents*, and decided to suspend licensing regional insurance agents and their branches and qualification approval of all sideline insurance agents bar from financial institutions and post offices. By dredging and advance, it means propelling restructuring and advancing specialization and scale of the insurance intermediary market by encouraging and guiding insurance intermediaries to form business groups. On the basis of *Measures for the Supervision of Insurance Intermediary Service Groups* (*for Trial Implementation*) and *Measures for the Supervision of Online Insurance Services of Insurance*

Agents and Brokers (for Trial Implementation) promulgated in 2011, CIRC further released *Notice on Matters Related to Supporting Car Sellers to Specialize in Insurance Agency Business* in 2012, to encourage and support car sellers to found insurance agents and brokers, or to cooperate with existing insurance agents and brokers to have them provide car insurance service, so as to realize compliance, specialization and mass development of car insurance intermediary services. In March, 2012, CIRC, together with other competent authorities, gave a reply to Mintaian Insurance Surveyors&Loss Adjusters, Guangzhou Meichen Investment and Management Consulting Co., Ltd., Yingda Changan Insurance Brokers Co., Ltd. and Beijing Union Insurance Broker Co., Ltd., endorsing these four companies' preparations for setting up insurance intermediary service groups. This is important to carry out *Measures for the Supervision of Insurance Intermediary Service Groups (for Trial Implementation)* in 2011 and drive the development of insurance intermediary service groups.

The development of insurance intermediary business groups is expected to enhance mass sales capacity and all-around service capability of insurance intermediaries, root out the problems with small-sized, poorly managed, and dispersed insurance intermediaries, protect the interests of insurance consumers, support the reform of salesmen management model, drive separation of insurance production and marketing, propel transformation and upgrade and help build up the ability of insurance intermediaries in risk prevention and mitigation.

The pilot program of income tax-deferred pension was fixed and heralded a new opportunity for commercial pension insurance

In 2012, CIRC doubled its effort on communication and coordination with the Finance and Taxation authority and Shanghai municipal government and reached agreement on the main content of the pilot program of income tax-deferred pension for Shanghai. The income tax-deferred pension policy is of cardinal significance because it can stimulate consumption demand for life insurance, propel commercial pension insurance development and consummate a multi-level social security system.

Policy Evaluation and Outlook

The reform, development and innovation of China's insurance industry continued progressing in a steady manner in 2012. The ability of the insurance industry in serving economic and social development was enhanced, open-up was deepened, and the insurance market showed a trend of growth amidst stability and improvement amidst growth. Looking forward to 2013, Xiang Junbo, Chairman of CIRC, pointed out clearly on 2013 National Insurance Regulation Work Meeting the general tone of advancement amidst stability, the direction of transformation and restructuring and the market-oriented reform, and required aligning short-term targets with long-term goals, seeking both temporary and permanent solutions, driving reform and innovation actively and endeavoring to resolve some knotty problems of common concern in the industry, for the sake of healthy development of the industry in the long run, while doing well in everyday insurance regulation.

Stick to the general tone of advancement amidst stability

The year of 2013 might be the most challenging year to the insurance industry. Top priorities of the industry are to maintain steady and healthy growth, keep the market running soundly, and prevent systematic and regional risks. Meanwhile, it is also important to make things happen, be good at spotting and seizing opportunities in the ever changing and complex environment, create the conditions for development through reform and innovation and fuel sustainable and sound development of the industry.

Stick to the direction of transformation and restructuring

Transformation and restructuring not only is the responsibility of market players, but also obligates the authority to tighten regulation. It is necessary to make the most of the emerging opportunity when the insurance industry is forced to execute restructuring, transformation and upgrade by the complex external environment and the difficulty in doing business. It is advisable to adapt to and follow the trends, give play to the steering and restricting function of regulatory policies, sharpen the initiative and creativity of market players in deepening restructuring, and make tangible progress in transformation of growth pattern of the industry.

Stick to the market-oriented reform

Reform is the route one must take to realize sustainable and sound development of the insurance industry. It is necessary to properly address the relationship between regulation and market, respect the law of the market more, simplify administrative approval, propel the reform of product pricing mechanism and marketing system, give full play to the fundamental role of the market in resource configuration, form a vibrant, efficient and more open insurance market running mechanism and inject power into the industry. It is necessary to eradicate any drawback in ideology, systems and mechanisms that may hinder scientific development, construct a complete, scientific, proper and efficient regulatory system and make all systems and elements more mature and well-established.

Try to solve problems in the insurance product pricing mechanism and regulation

Many problems exist in the insurance market, such as misleading statements in sales and difficulty in claims, and all of them have something to do with inappropriate products directly or indirectly. The present regulatory system and model of insurance products is not fit for the development of the industry and need adjusting and optimizing immediately. First, it is worth considering to revise and perfect the measures for the management of insurance products, clarify "what and how" to manage, and make clear the responsibilities insurance companies bear with respect to products. Second, it is necessary to tighten review of insurance products and create an insurance product preview mechanism. Third, it is necessary to push forward the reform of the rate formation mechanism. Fourth, it is necessary to encourage and support innovations and meet diversified insurance needs of consumers.

Enhance competitiveness of the industry

When it comes to the modern insurance industry, competition is no longer limited to competition among companies in the same industry; more importantly, there is the competition between the domestic and the international insurance market in a fully open environment and the competition between insurance institutions and other financial institutions in an integrated business environment, said Xiang Junbo. It is necessary to give therein to the function of insurance, and explore how to build up core competitive strength of the insurance industry. First, capitalize on the advantage of insurance in risk management, expand coverage and provide an all-around shelter from risks for economic and social development. Second, capitalize on the advantage in long-term asset and liability management, iron out the impact of economic fluctuations on insurance assets and liabilities and achieve reliable long-term return on assets. Third, capitalize on the advantage in service network and talent pool, strengthen management services and make greater contribution to the construction of a multi-level social security system. Meanwhile, regulatory policies targeting common problems with small-/medium-sized insurance companies must be formulated.

Shoot for more supportive policies

First, shoot for fiscal supportive policy, for example, perfecting the subsidy policy for agricultural insurance, and creating a catastrophe insurance system. Second, strive for tax supportive policy, including tax-deferred policy for consumers who purchase pension and health insurance products, and tax incentives for policy-backed and non-profit insurance business. Third, drive legislation in some key fields and propel the development of liability insurance.

Bond Market Development Policy

Highlights of Bond Market Development Policy in 2012

In 2012, "quicker development" came as a marked feature of China's bond market. An inter-ministry coordination mechanism for corporate credit bonds was built. A basket of policies were instituted to strengthen market management, regulate market behavior, stimulate market innovation and drive market construction and achieved satisfactory results. In 2012, the size of

China's bond market continued enlarging, the variety of products was enriched, means of issuance were optimized, market trading was active and the market system and infrastructure were bettered. The bond market gained importance in the national economy. By implementing macroeconomic policies, optimizing resource configuration and deepening the reform of the financial system, the bond market forcefully propped up the real economy.

Table 5. 6　　　　　　　　　　**Bond Market Policies in 2012**

Date	Policy
4 January	The PBC issued *Notice on Relevant Matters Concerning the Implementation of the Pilot Measures for Domestic Securities Investment Made by RMB Qualified Foreign Institutional Investors of Fund Management Companies and Securities Companies.*
6 April	Led by the PBC, an inter-ministry coordination mechanism for corporate credit bonds was established, with NDRC and CSRC as members, and *Rules of Order for the Inter-ministry Coordination Mechanism for Corporate Credit Bonds* was endorsed.
2 May	NDRC issued *Notice on Matters Concerning the Issue of RMB Bonds in the Hong Kong Special Administrative Region by Domestic Non-financial Institutions*, to regulate the conduct of bond issuance by non-financial institutions in Hong Kong.
16 May	National Association of Financial Market Institutional Investors released the newly revised *Rules for Information Disclosure on Debt Financing Instruments of Non-financial Enterprises on the Interbank Bond Market.*
17 May	The PBC, together with CBRC and the Ministry of Finance, released *Notice on Relevant Matters Concerning Further Expanding the Pilot Work of Credit Asset Securitization*, to expand the pilot work of credit asset securitization.
23 May	Shanghai Stock Exchange and Shenzhen Stock Exchange issued *Pilot Measures of Shanghai Stock Exchange for the Issuance of Private Placement Bonds of Small and Medium Enterprises* and *Pilot Measures of Shenzhen Stock Exchange for the Issuance of Private Placement Bonds of Small and Medium Enterprises*, kicking off the pilot program of private placement bonds of SMEs officially.
31 May	Under the action of the inter-ministry coordination mechanism for corporate credit bonds, securities companies restarted short-term financing bills after filing records with and getting permission from the PBC.
5 June	Shenzhen Stock Exchange released the revised *Shenzhen Stock Exchange Listing Rules for Corporate Bonds.*
18 June	National Association of Financial Market Institutional Investors released *Self-regulatory Disciplinary Rules for the Debt Financing Instrument Market of Non-financial Enterprises.*
19 July	CIRC released *Interim Measures for the Investment of Insurance Funds in Bonds*, to regulate the behavior of insurance companies in bond investment.

Continued

Date	Policy
1 August	National Association of Financial Market Institutional Investors released *Registration Files and Forms for Debt Financing Instruments of Non-financial Enterprises* and the registration information system for debt financing instruments of non-financial enterprises (referred to as the Unfolding Peacock Tail system in brief).
3 August	National Association of Financial Market Institutional Investors released *Guidelines for Asset-backed Notes of Non-financial Enterprises on the Interbank Bond Market*, launching asset-backed notes of non-financial enterprises.
9 October	NDRC released *Notice on Strengthening Enterprise Credit Construction during Issuance of Bonds*.
29 October	With the permission of the PBC and CBRC, asset management companies launched financial bonds.
29 November	Shenzhen Stock Exchange released *Detailed Rules of Shenzhen Stock Exchange for the Trading of Bonds*.
3 December	The PBC issued Announcement No. 17, giving permission to National Association of Financial Market Institutional Investors to promulgate *Master Agreement for Bond Repurchase Transactions on the Interbank Market of China*.

Source: data collected by the research group.

Analysis of Bond Market Development Policy in 2012

An inter-ministry coordination mechanism for corporate credit bonds was established to drive well-regulated development of the bond market

Led by the PBC, an inter-ministry coordination mechanism for corporate credit bonds was established, with NDRC and CSRC as members, and the first meeting was convened in April, 2012, as required by the State Council under *Opinions on Priorities in Deepening Economic Reform in* 2012. The inter-ministry coordination mechanism was established to help join forces develop the corporate credit bond market, expand direct financing and give an impetus to the bond market.

Rules of Order for the Inter-ministry Coordination Mechanism for Corporate Credit Bonds was endorsed on the first meeting of the inter-ministry coordination mechanism and in-depth discussions were held on pushing forward the reform and development of the corporate credit bond market and relevant issues. The meeting accentuated the importance to be steadfast to the essential requirement for the financial industry to serve the real economy, give priority to expand direct financing, drive financing and economic restructuring and better satisfy the financing demand of all enterprises, respect the law of the bond market, strengthen coordination and collaboration and jointly promote healthy development of the corporate credit bond market, under the framework of the inter-ministry coordination mechanism. Agreement was reached on the meeting on strengthening regulation and coordination, creating a corporate credit bond data sharing mechanism and other matters.

Effort was made to enrich bond products and inspire innovations

First, the pilot work of credit asset securitization was expanded. Based on the reply given by the State Council and the experience from previous pilot effort, the PBC, together with CBRC and the Ministry of Finance, released *Notice on Relevant Matters Concerning Further Expanding the Pilot Work of Credit Asset Securitization* on May 17, officially restarting the pilot work of credit asset securitization. In 2012, five institutions issued credit asset-backed securities worth of 19 billion yuan in total approximately. Compared with the previous two pilot phases, the regulatory requirements were refined and better thought out this time. First of all, the applicable scope of participants was broadened. SAIC Finance became the first financial company to issue credit asset-backed securities. Second, the variety of underlying asset pool was expanded to include qualified loans for major infrastructure projects of the government, and compliant loans of local financing platforms. Third, 5% risk retention was clearly stipulated. Fourth, a dual rating model was built. Fifth, a limit was set to the investment share of a single banking institution. The regulatory requirements have drawn upon international experience while having Chinese characteristics. The relaunch of the pilot program can not only transfer the risks in the banking system, ease the capital replenishment pressure on banks under the new capital regulations, but also allow some non-financial enterprises to benefit therefrom and alleviate the difficulties in financing for SMEs, thanks to the participation of non-banking financial institutions like trust companies.

Second, the pilot program of private placement bonds of SMEs was initiated. On May 23, Shanghai Stock Exchange and Shenzhen Stock Exchange issued *Pilot Measures of Shanghai Stock Exchange for the Issuance of Private Placement Bonds of Small and Medium Enterprises* and *Pilot Measures of Shenzhen Stock Exchange for the Issuance of Private Placement Bonds of Small and Medium Enterprises* (the *Pilot Measures*), kicking off the pilot program of private placement bonds of SMEs officially. As specified in the *Pilot Measures*, private placement bonds of SMEs are corporate bonds non-publicly issued by micro, small and medium-sized enterprises, at an interest rate no more than triple benchmark lending rates of banks during the same time frame, with maturity no less than one year. SME private placement bonds are issued on a record-filing basis and can be transferred via the integrated agreement trading platform of Shenzhen Stock Exchange, or the integrated electronic platform for fixed-income securities of Shanghai Stock Exchange, or through securities companies. In 2012, SME private placement bonds issued were worth 9.4 billion yuan in total. The launch of SME private placement bonds expanded the range of services the capital market provides to the real economy, strengthened effective linkage between direct finance and SMEs and explored new possibilities and ways to solve the financing problems faced by SMEs.

Third, short-term financing bills of securities companies were relaunched. Under the framework of the inter-ministry coordination mechanism for corporate credit bonds, the regulatory authority strengthened coordination and cooperation and restarted issuance of short-term financing bills of securities companies seven years later in order to shore up the development of securities companies. After filing records with and getting permission from the PBC, China Merchants Securities issued short-term financing bills worth of 4 billion yuan through open bid on May 31 and it became the first short-term financing bill issuance by a securities company after it was relaunched. In 2012, five securities companies issued 16 short-term financing bills worth of 56. 1 billion yuan in total. Among them, the issuance of short-term financing bills by China Securities Finance Corporation Limited helped pump the fund on the interbank market into the stock market through refinancing and achieved connectivity between the interbank market and the stock market. The relaunch of short-term financing bills of securities companies widened the financing channels of securities companies and provided them with a low-cost bond financing means to replenish liquidity.

Fourth, asset-backed notes (ABNs) of non-financial enterprises were launched. On August 3, National Association of Financial Market Institutional Investors released *Guidelines for Asset-backed Notes of Non-financial Enterprises on the Interbank Bond Market*, giving permission to non-financial enterprises to issue ABNs. In terms of the regulatory framework, asset types, risk segregation, trading structure, information disclosure and rights and obligations of all parties of ABNs were specified and a proper investor protection mechanism was accentuated. In the meantime, trading structure was not specified. Inclusive specifications were made on underlying asset types, trading structure design and other aspects, to leave room for innovation later. In 2012, non-financial enterprises issued 14 ABNs and raised 5. 7 billion yuan in total. The permission to the issuance of ABNs by non-financial enterprises can enhance the utilization of inventory assets of enterprises, expand financing channels, support more projects concerning people's livelihood and deepen the development of the bond market.

Fifth, financial bonds of asset management companies were launched. On October 29, endorsed by the PBC and CBRC, China Cinda Asset Management Co. , Ltd. issued a financial bond worth of 10 billion yuan and it became the first financial bond issued by an asset management company. The launch of financial bonds of asset management companies opened up a new financing channel for asset management companies to acquire non-performing assets and dissolve financial risks and also enriched the variety of products available on the interbank bond market.

Self-discipline was accentuated and market risk prevention was strengthened

First, a set of self-regulatory disciplinary rules were framed. On June 18, National Association of Financial Market Institutional Investors released *Self-regulatory Disciplinary Rules for the Debt Financing Instrument Market of Non-financial Enterprises*, to clarify the rights and obligations in self-regulatory discipline, specify the process of self-regulatory discipline, including preliminary investigation, decision on disciplinary action and review, set forth hierarchical disciplinary actions for reputational punishment and behavioral punishment in ascending order of severity, and frame operational procedures for self-regulatory discipline. Self-regulatory disciplinary rules represent institutional assurance and basic arrangement for self-discipline, guarantee justice and integrity of self-regulatory disciplinary procedures by establishing a complete self-regulatory disciplinary system and are important to regulate the behavior of market members and maintain market order.

Second, the rules for intermediary services and information disclosure on debt financing instruments of non-financial enterprises were revised. To adapt to the latest developments and changes of the debt financing instrument market of non-financial enterprises, National Association of Financial Market Institutional Investors revised *Rules for Intermediary Services on Debt Financing Instruments of Non-financial Enterprises on the Interbank Bond Market* and *Rules for Information Disclosure on Debt Financing Instruments of Non-financial Enterprises on the Interbank Bond Market*, to specify business rules, code of conduct, relevant responsibilities and sense of responsibility related to intermediary services, as well as information disclosure content, procedures and standards. It consolidated the base for stable and efficient running of the debt financing instrument market at a micro level.

Third, new breakthrough was made in the reform of the registration system. Information disclosure is the kernel of the registration system of debt financing instruments of non-financial enterprises. Market access is predicated on due diligence of intermediaries and participation of investors at their own risk. To enhance transparency of registration work, better demonstrate the spirit of fairness, justice and openness, and drive market-based management, National Association of Financial Market Institutional Investors revamped and optimized the existing registration system and released *Registration Files and Forms for Debt Financing Instruments of Non-financial Enterprises* and the registration information system for debt financing instruments of non-financial enterprises (referred to as the Unfolding Peacock Tail system in brief). The forms system further clarified the minimum information disclosure requirements, to make it easier for enterprises, chief underwriters and other intermediaries concerned to prepare registration files and express professional opinions. The Unfolding Peacock Tail system demonstrates registration files and work flows of debt financing instruments to the public and accept market supervision. The reform of the registration system is a constructive thing to drive market development for the following reasons. First, it can propel the reform of bond issuance management styles in China and put into practice a market-oriented philosophy fully. Second, it can bring into play the supervisory function of the market and construct a credit system. Third, it can help improve market efficiency and the quality of registration work. Fourth, it can help consummate the capital market information disclosure system and better protect the rights and interests of investors.

Fourth, NDRC strengthened credit construction during issuance of bonds. On October 9, NDRC released *Notice on Strengthening Enterprise Credit Construction during Issuance of Bonds* and made provisions for some matters concerning enterprise credit construction during issuance of bonds, for example, review with special attention to bond issuers, use of credit investigation records of chief underwriters, collection of multi-facet credit information of bond issuers, and establishment of a comprehensive credit commitment system for bond issuers and sponsors. It is important to take precautions against risks in the corporate bond market, reinforce enterprise credit construction during issuance of bonds and create a mechanism wherein enterprises of good faith enjoy benefit while enterprises of bad faith get punished.

Concerted efforts were made to drive open-up of the bond market in a steady manner

As the economic and financial system reform in China goes deeper, open-up of the bond market is pushed forward progressively. It has not only expanded the investment channels of overseas Renminbi capital, but also helped heighten the appeal of Renminbi in international clearing, while driving construction and development of the bond market of China. In the issuance market, in January, NDRC and the PBC approved of 10 domestic banks' issuing RMB bonds in Hong Kong, China Development Bank included, at a total value of 25 billion yuan. On May 8, NDRC issued *Notice on Matters Concerning the Issue of RMB Bonds in the Hong Kong Special Administrative Region by Domestic Non-financial Institutions*. Thereafter, issuance of dim sum bonds by domestic non-financial institutions became regularized and normalized.

In the trading market, on January 4, the PBC issued *Notice on Relevant Matters Concerning the Implementation of the Pilot Measures for Domestic Securities Investment Made by RMB Qualified Foreign Institutional Investors of Fund Management Companies and Securities Companies* ([2011] No. 321). The Notice requires the pilot institutions to choose one domestic commercial bank qualified as a custodian of qualified foreign institutional investors and as a clearing agent of the interbank bond market simultaneously to open RMB basic deposit account and RMB special deposit account for foreign institutions. It specifies the requirements for the use of such special deposit account, refines supporting policies for domestic securities investment made by RQFII and marks further open-up of China's bond market. In March, the Chinese government approved of the Japanese government's buying 65 billion yuan national debts of China. On April 22, the PBC and the World Bank Group concluded an agreement in Washington. International Bank for Reconstruction and Development (IBRD) and International Development Association (IDA) began investment in China's interbank bond market. Thereafter, foreign institutions granted access to the interbank bond market continued expanding, to include Bank Indonesia, among others. As of end-2012, 100 foreign institutional investors entered China's bond market in seven categories, namely, foreign central bank, international financial institution, sovereign wealth fund, Hong Kong and Macao clearing bank, foreign participating bank, foreign insurance institution and RQFII. QFII and RQFII investment quotas totaled 80 billion US dollars and 270 billion yuan, respectively. Investments of foreign institutions in China's interbank bond market are progressing soundly.

Policy Evaluation and Outlook

The bond market is expected to expand in size in a steady manner and make greater contribution to financing

China is at a crucial stage of deepening the reform and driving economic restructuring. As set forth under the *12th Five-Year Plan for the Development and Reform of the Financial Industry*, during the period 12th Five-Year Plan, China shall step up effort to develop the bond market and expand the size of the bond market progressively. Hence, the bond market will embrace a promising development opportunity in 2013. First of all, against the backdrop of active fiscal policy and prudent monetary policy, national debts are estimated to keep growing at a solid pace. Next, along with progress in urbanization, local government financing is expected to gain further development amidst transparent and proper management. Moreover, given the real economy's buoyant demand for fund, the corporate credit bond market is expected to maintain the growth momentum. In general, the size of the bond market is estimated to grow at a steady pace in 2013. With that, the market depth and breadth will extend further. It will make bigger contribution to financing for the real economy, optimize social financing structure and improve and heighten the ability of the financial industry in serving the real economy.

The function of the inter-ministry coordination mechanism for corporate credit bonds will manifest itself more prominently

To promote development and innovation has always been the common understanding among relevant authorities in charge of the bond market. In 2013, under the action of the inter-ministry coordination mechanism for corporate credit bonds, relevant authorities shall perform their respective duties, make concerted efforts, and join forces to fuel development of the market. Market interconnection will be enhanced, information sharing will be more inclusive, policy coordination and consistency will be optimized and market-based institutional construction and investor protection mechanism will be improved. Assured by institutional construction, all corporate credit bonds, including debt financing instruments of non-financial enterprises, enterprise bonds and corporate bonds, will achieve concerted development, diversified financing demand of enterprises will be better satisfied and the corporate credit bond market will realize sustainable development along with improved management.

Institutional construction and infrastructure will be pushed forward solidly

Driven by joint efforts of regulatory bodies, self-discipline organizations and market participants, a well-regulated market will be strengthened and institutional construction and infrastructure of the bond market will be pushed forward solidly. Issuance efficiency will be improved and information disclosure will be bettered. Good practice of trading will be promoted and the yield curve will be improved. Market makers will play a more important role and market liquidity will be heightened. Market constraints and risk sharing mechanism will be optimized. Trading, clearing and settlement infrastructure will be made safer and more efficient. Moreover, along with increasing cross-border use of RMB and advancement in open-up, China's bond market will be globalized in greater depth. On one hand, more QFIIs will have the chance to participate in investment and financing in the Chinese market. On the other hand, the offshore RMB market will enjoy bigger growth potential, domestic and foreign participants will feature stronger diversity, and the synergy between the domestic and international market will become more salient.

Market innovations will be more detail-oriented

In recent years, product innovations in the bond market thrived. A relatively complete array of basic products have been developed, including government credit bonds, financial bonds and credit bonds of non-financial enterprises. Next, market innovations are expected to be more detail-oriented. Driven by spontaneous effort of market players, the market will move from simple products to option-embedded products. The basic product structure will embody more individualized design elements to cater to diversified market demand. Meanwhile, progress is expected to be made in bond trading instruments and structural design. Product depth will be enriched and product liquidity will be heightened.

Money Market Development Policy

Master Agreement for Bond Repurchase Transactions on the Interbank Market of China

(*2013*) was released in 2012. It is expected to facilitate conduct of bond repurchase transactions in a well-regulated manner and lay the institutional foundation for innovations to be made in the market mechanism next. For the purpose of well-regulated and orderly development of the bill market, the authority doubled its effort to tighten regulation of bill transactions and required banks to perfect their business process, enforce the rules and take concrete precautions against risks associated with bills. The fee pricing model was changed from government-guided pricing to market-regulated pricing. Banks have full discretion in pricing depending on market demand, which can beef up their flexibility and initiative, and pave the way for liberalization of commercial drafts. It has far-reaching influence on the structure and development direction of the bill market. In general, in 2012, the money market maintained healthy and rapid growth momentum, with further expansion of market size, low interest rates and optimized market structure, and played its role better.

Interbank Borrowing Market

No new policy came out in the interbank borrowing market in 2012. The market administration attached more importance to proper market management and continued improving market transparency with information disclosure at the core, to drive healthy and orderly development of the market.

Under the framework of the existing policies for the interbank borrowing market, the interbank borrowing market boomed in 2012. All institutions showed stronger awareness of and sharpened up their skills in preemptive liquidity management by taking advantage of the money market. The market trading volume swelled rapidly, and total turnover and average daily turnover continued hitting all-time highs. Cumulative turnover of the year reached 46.70 trillion yuan, representing an increase of 13.26 trillion yuan, or 39.27 percent, year on year; average daily turnover topped 150 billion yuan to hit 186.2 billion yuan, indicating continued rapid growth since 2007.

Interbank offered rates appeared calm throughout the year of 2012, with obviously narrower extent of fluctuations compared with 2011. Only transient fluctuations occurred on special occasions, as shown in a pulse of rise before the Spring Festival and a marginal increase at the end of each quarter. The weighted average interest rate of interbank borrowings in 2012[①] posted 3.43 percent, down 54 basis points year on year. Neither the peak nor the nadir of interbank offered rates in 2012 went beyond that of 2011. The intraday peak value in 2012, 8.51 percent, occurred on January 18, 53 basis points lower than that of 2011; the nadir, 2.16 percent,

---

① 7-day interest rate is used for reference.

occurred on May 31, 17 basis points higher than that of 2011; the extreme interest rate spread in the year was 635 basis points, 70 basis points narrower than a year ago.

In terms of maturity, short-term borrowings still dominated the interbank borrowing market, with a continuously expanding market share. Transactions within seven days took up 95. 23 percent of total turnover. The share of overnight borrowings continued growing, accounting for86. 25 percent of total turnover, up circa 5 percentage points year on year. Transactions with maturity longer than one month accounted for 2. 19 percent of total turnover, down circa 1. 5 percentage points year on year.

In terms of trading structure, transactions of banking institutions took up 86. 99 percent, while that of non-banking financing institutions took up the rest 13. 01 percent. To be more specific, joint-stock banks took up the biggest share, 41. 11 percent of total turnover of the entire market. Next, state-owned and city commercial banks accounted for 14. 9 percent and 12. 93 percent, respectively. In the meantime, the activity of non-banking financial institutions was on the advance. Securities companies and financial companies of business groups performed quite actively, representing 4. 11 percent and 3. 69 percent of total turnover of the entire market, respectively. The trading structure was optimized.

Bond Repo Market

The PBC issued Announcement No. 17 of 2012 on December 3, announcing *Master Agreement for Bond Repurchase Transactions on the Interbank Market of China* (the *Repo Master Agreement*) coming into effect. Master agreement, as a fundamental arrangement for the bond repo market, outlines and polishes the basic framework of the text of the bond repo agreement. It can heighten the price discovery function of the bond market, propel interest rate liberalization, facilitate well-regulated conduct of repo transactions and lay the institutional foundation for innovations to be made in the market mechanism next.

Based on the reality of the bond repo market of China, and in light of the principles of continuity, suitability and farsightedness, the new *Repo Master Agreement* revised *Master Agreement for Pledge-style Bond Repos on the Interbank Bond Market of China* released in 2000 and *Master Agreement for Buyout Bond Repos on the Interbank Bond Market of China* released in 2004, refined and consummated the framework, core mechanisms and arrangements, risk event handling methods and ways of signing. Some innovative mechanisms were embedded, for example, swap of pledged bonds, mark to market, valuation and dynamic adjustment of repurchased bonds, fast disposal of collaterals, single agreement and close-out netting. Moreover, a 12-month transitional period was provided to ensure orderly and steady transition from the old to the new master agreement.

The new *Repo Master Agreement* highlights six features as follows:

First, the two old master agreements are merged into the new *Repo Master Agreement*. As pledge-style repos and buyout repos share the same trading purpose and a similar trading structure, one governing master agreement makes signing and use more convenient for market members and can help market members guard against counterparty risk. The new *Repo Master Agreement* adopts a "one plus many" framework, i. e. , "general provisions plus special provisions", and is comprised of general provisions, special provisions for pledge-style repos, special provisions for buyout repos, applicable supplementary agreement and stipulations on transaction validity. Among them, general provisions specify the elements and mechanisms applicable to all repo transactions, including pledge-style and buyout repos. Special provisions specify rules on handling default events and termination events, adjustment, swap, performance guarantee arrangement and other issues, based on differences between pledge-style and buyout repos.

Second, a multilateral plus bilateral signing approach is adopted. This can assure smooth transition of transactions and leave room of discretionary negotiations to market members. After market members sign the new *Repo Master Agreement* in a valid manner, it takes effect between one signatory and all of the other signatories, and thereby pledge-style or buyout repo transactions can be conducted. Market members may sign a bilateral supplementary agreement as necessary to prescribe in details third-party valuation agency, penalty rate, and whether cross default, default under specified transaction, adjustment and performance guarantee are applicable. This provides a convenient tool and discretion to meet individualized trading demand of market members and places the interbank bond repo market on a par with international common practice.

Third, the default event identification and handling mechanism is updated. Under the two old master agreements, identification and handling of default events and termination events are limited to defaults on payment and delivery obligations, and there are no detailed provisions for identification and handling of default events. The new *Repo Master Agreement* includes additional clauses on default events and termination events, to provide market participants with due choices under different circumstances of default events and termination events, and clarify identification criteria, handling process and compensation for default events. It effectively mitigates credit risk and legal risk in repos and protects the legitimate rights and interests of members who act in good faith.

Fourth, single agreement and close-out netting are adopted. In view of the nature of the Chinese legal system and the development of the repo market, the new *Repo Master Agreement* has drawn upon the master agreement of NAFMII and the common practice of international repo master agreement, and incorporated single agreement and close-out netting mechanisms into buyout repos. While enhancing payment efficiency, these core mechanisms vest the non-defaulting party with the right to terminate all buyout repo transactions earlier and receive payment after netting against net risk exposure, in case of bankruptcy of the defaulting party and other circumstances of defaults. This core mechanism is able to mitigate risks in financial transactions, particularly risks associated with selective performance of receiver in bankruptcy. It is a crucial countermeasure against risks in financial transactions.

Fifth, a dynamic adjustment mechanism is adopted for repurchased bonds. In the 2000 version of repo master agreement, repurchased bonds under pledge-style repos are frozen in the account of the positive buy-back party and cannot be used by either party. As a result, financial institutions might miss valuable opportunity in the bond trading market and liquidity of bonds is undermined. Moreover, financial institutions are unable to discover prices in the money market effectively. After swap and adjustment mechanisms are added to the new *Repo Master Agreement*, the new dynamic adjustment mechanism for repurchased bonds can solve the aforesaid problems effectively. When the positive buy-back party needs the frozen bonds to chase the bond market trends, the positive buy-back party can negotiate with the counter buy-back party to swap the frozen bonds and seize the market opportunity. When a third-party cash lender has risk and liquidity preference for pledged bonds, it is possible to change and adjust the types of bonds frozen in the previous pledge-style repos through negotiation. This can revitalize the types of repurchased bonds held by institutions to some extent and further heighten liquidity of the repo market.

Sixth, a performance guarantee arrangement is adopted. The new *Repo Master Agreement* has refined and perfected the performance guarantee mechanism for buyout repos. One party may demand the counterparty to adjust the cash deposit or bonds in security depending on the net risk exposure in all buyout repos. This mechanism can effectively monitor net risk exposure and largely strengthen credit risk control in buyout repo transactions in case of violent fluctuations in the value of repurchased bonds. The new mechanism has consolidated the credit base of buyout repo transactions and is able to cope with diversified subjects and differentiated credit standing of market members more effectively. It is more operable, and can help the parties manage counterparty credit risk in buyout repos in a differentiated manner, so as to encourage more market subjects with different credit rating and risk tolerance to get involved in buyout repo transactions. It is bound to step up the turnover of buyout repos and the size of the interbank bond market of China.

As a fundamental institutional arrangement for the bond repo market, the new *Repo Master Agreement* has been promulgated and put into force to revamp the bond repo transaction mechanisms, increase market liquidity, and enhance the credit risk management capability of market members. It has laid a solid foundation for protecting the legitimate rights and interests of market participants and driving well-regulated, sustainable and sound development of China's bond repo market.

Bill Market

Bill Market Policy in 2012

The bill market performed soundly in 2012 in general, with steady growth of trading volume and fairly active participation of institutions. Outstanding balance of bill acceptance and bill financing grew continuously all through the first three quarters. From the fourth quarter onwards, the growth of bill acceptance business moderated, and outstanding balance waved mildly, while outstanding balance of bill financing dropped month by month. Market interest rates declined amidst oscillations due to the impact of adjustment to regulatory policies, changes in interest rates of the money market and supply and demand dynamics of the bill market.

In January, the PBC released *Guiding Opinions on China Payment System Development* (2011—2015). As proposed therein, the main target is to "consummate a payment instrument system that mainly uses bills and bank cards, evolves towards electronic payment methods and adapts to the demand of diverse economic activities." The main tasks are "to institute and refine the laws and regulations on non-cash payment instruments, proceed with revisions to the *Law of the People's Republic of China on Negotiable Instruments*, *Measures for the Implementation of Administration of Negotiable Instruments* and *Measures for Payment and Settlement*, and establish the legal status and legality of electronic negotiable instruments." In the meantime, it calls for effort "to continue driving innovations in negotiable instruments, support and propel the development of imaging business and electronic negotiable instruments, reduce operating costs of negotiable instruments, enhance payment efficiency and guarantee payment security with negotiable instruments, give full play to the functionality of the electronic commercial draft system, introduce new types of electronic negotiable instruments, make progress in unification and electronic technology of the negotiable instrument market, upgrade anti-counterfeiting technology and verification of paper-based negotiable instruments and ensure safe use of negotiable instruments."

In February, CBRC released *Notice on Relevant Issues Concerning the Trust Business of Trust Companies for Bills*. Trust companies are disallowed to transfer or receive any bill asset to or from commercial banks in any form or by any means. Meanwhile, for existing bills in trust, trust companies are expected to tighten risk control, are disallowed to take in new bills for the duration of the existing bills in trust and must terminate the dealing immediately upon maturity and extension is forbidden.

In February, CBRC, the PBC and NDRC jointly released *Measures Governing Service Prices of Commercial Banks (Exposure Draft)*. Compared with *Interim Measures Governing Service Prices of Commercial Banks* released by CBRC and NDRC in 2003, the pricing model of "banker's acceptance bill" is changed from government-guided pricing to market-regulated pricing.

In June, CSRC ordered its branches in Beijing, Shanghai and Shenzhen to tighten supervision over cooperation on bills between securities companies and banks under their jurisdiction, and to reinforce review of investment banker's acceptance bills under collective wealth management business filed by securities companies.

In July, the PBC released *Provisions for Tightening Management of Bills (Exposure Draft)*, and ordered banks to tighten internal control of bills, withdraw the discretionary approval right of banking outlets to put a stop to their control over the whole business process and guard against risks associated with bills. It also gave advice for risks in alterations of blank acceptance bills and other negotiable instruments. As for the conduct of transfer, it required banks to take the form of endorsement for repo interbank discount and re-discount; and to take the form of endorsement for sale of repo and repo-to-maturity of repo interbank discount and re-discount. Meanwhile, it required that banks holding discounted paper-based commercial drafts could only transfer such drafts to other banks, financial companies or the PBC.

In October, the General Office of CBRC issued *Notice on Strengthening Supervision of Banker's Acceptance Bills*. Along with booming banker's acceptance business in recent years, risks underlying bills have accumulated and legal cases involving bills happened from time to time. With this in mind, CBRC proposed the following opinions on strengthening supervision of banker's acceptance bills:

First, banks should take seriously the risks in banker's acceptance bills, strengthen client credit check, examine the qualification of bill applicants, truthfulness of trade background and appropriateness of endorsement process strictly, tighten control over key steps, perfect the business process, enforce the rules and take concrete precautions against risks associated with bills.

Second, banks should develop bill acceptance business in a prudent manner, and decide on business scale and development speed appropriately depending on their development strategy, client base, risk management and internal control capability.

Third, banks should drive unified credit line management for bill acceptance business, measure and determine clients' credit line for bills in a scientific manner and prevent any form of illegal scalping.

Fourth, banks should reinforce unified authorization for bill acceptance business.

Fifth, banks should perfect the monitoring and inventory-taking system of banker's acceptance bills, and strengthen centralized storage of bills. For discounted bills, banks must get endorsement from discounting companies to materialize their legitimate rights.

Sixth, banks should strengthen unified management of cash deposit for bill acceptance business.

Seventh, banks should strengthen unified management of transaction fund accounts for bill acceptance business.

Eighth, banks should strengthen management of inquiry of banker's acceptance bills and inquiry response.

Ninth, banks should optimize the performance assessment system, by lowering the weight of some indicators like outstanding balance of bills, and raising the weight of other indicators like compliance of bills and control of operational risks. Banks should tighten personnel management, sharpen the skills and compliance awareness of the staff engaged in bills, and prohibit the staff from getting involved in any form of bill intermediary or capital broker activity. Banks should tighten the audit of bills, and audit and evaluate the bill business system, process and effectiveness of execution.

Tenth, the authority shall crack down on any misdeed and offense against the laws and regulations in banker's acceptance bills, and take regulatory actions circumstantially, for example, to deny market access or suspend the bill business. In the case of dereliction of management duty or recidivism, not only the person directly accountable shall be blamed, but also the leaders concerned shall be held liable. If a crime is suspected, the case shall be referred to the judicial organ timely.

Analysis of Bill Market Policy in 2012

First, with respect to regulation, the economic and financial situation has been volatile and complicated, market liquidity has turned tighter and credit facility has failed to satisfy the strong demand of enterprises for fund in recent years. Under these circumstances, the relatively low-cost bill financing business of banks has boomed, but with it hidden risks have emerged. In 2012, the authority intensified regulation of bills on the basis of a series of policies released last year, and ordered banks to perfect their business process, enforce the rules and take concrete precautions against risks associated with bills.

In recent years, it has become a common practice of banks to move bill assets out of balance sheet by assigning the income right in bills to trust companies or securities companies, among others, in order to circumvent the restriction on the size of credit facility. Consequently, bill trust and cooperation between banks and securities companies on bills thrived and put a premium on bill drawing by banks. This augmented the size of bill assets and all-system financing aggregates and then aggravated the situation of bills divorced from true trade background. In view of the facts, CBRC issued *Notice on Relevant Issues Concerning the Trust Business of Trust Companies for Bills* in February, and ordered trust companies to stop transferring or receiving any bill asset to or from commercial banks in any form or by any means. In June, CSRC tightened supervision over cooperation on bills between securities companies and banks under its jurisdiction. In July, the PBC released *Provisions for Tightening Management of Bills* (*Exposure Draft*), wherein the assignee after discounting of paper-based commercial drafts is specified clearly, to restrict activities of securities companies, fund firms, trust companies and village and township banks in interbank discount of bills. After these three policies came into effect, the outlets of banks' bills were blocked obviously, and the growth of bill financing moderated. It dropped for the first time in the year in September, with a negative month-on-month growth of 217 billion yuan. Moreover, interbank discount rate climbed up due to the combined action of tight liquidity at the end of the quarter and other factors.

In view of increasing incidence of legal cases related to banks' bills and a bigger percentage of serious cases owing to changes in macro situation and vulnerable internal control of some institutions, the authority issued policies for tightening management of banker's acceptance bills, warned of risks associated with bills, strengthened risk prevention and control against legal cases and raised requirements for internal management of banks. Main policies include strengthening authorization for drawing bills and credit extension to prevent "invented circulation" of bills; tightening endorsement management during circulation, and regulating accounting model properly; and integrating review power and operational process for bills and mitigating operational risks such as embezzlement of cash deposit. Moreover, the authority kept under control the bill transfer behavior of intermediaries in the market to prevent any form of illegal scalping. After these policies came into effect, all banks intensified bill-related risk examination and staff training. In contrast to rapid growth of the bill market and declining interest rates in the first three quarters, the bill acceptance and financing business receded month by month in the fourth quarter, while interest rates trended up amidst stability, because on one hand, enterprises continued to show strong financing demand and enthusiasm for commercial drafts in order to lower financing costs and accelerate capital turnover; and on the other hand, banks became more cautious about drawing bills in order to improve internal management and take precautions against business risks.

Second, with respect to market development, *Guiding Opinions on China Payment System Development* (2011—2015) points out the positive effect of a sound legal system and incentives to innovations in bills on improving payment efficiency with bills, controlling transaction risks, and making progress in unification and electronic technology of the bill market. In 2012, electronic negotiable instruments also boomed. The electronic commercial draft system processed 1,350,000 commercial draft transactions and registered total turnover of 4.2 trillion yuan in the year, both exceeding the sum totals of the previous two years. These two figures represent 53.7 percent and 56.8 percent of the total number of transactions and aggregate turnover from November of 2009 when the electronic commercial draft system went into operation to date.

Under the *Measures Governing Service Prices of Commercial Banks* (*Exposure Draft*), the pricing model of "banker's acceptance bill" is changed from government-guided pricing to market-regulated pricing. As banker's acceptance bills entail certain credit risk while providing a means of financing, the rule of credit risk reciprocity is applicable. The income derived from handling charge at 0.5‰ cannot cover normal risk loss in issuing banks. After market-regulated pricing is adopted, banks have full discretion in pricing depending on market demand, which can beef up their flexibility and initiative, and pave the way for liberalization of commercial drafts.

2013 Bill Market Outlook

Looking forward to 2013, against the backdrop of prudent monetary policy, the bill market is expected to keep running soundly in all respects. Market competition is estimated to heat up. Intensive business and compliance management will be the foundation for healthy development of the bill market, and differentiation and innovation will inject the energy of sustainable growth into the bill market.

Wealth Management Market Development Policy

According to some figures disclosed under *2012 China Wealth Report: Explore Customers' Needs for Scientific Development* co-released by Boston Consulting Group and China Construction Bank, total personal assets available for investment in China exceeded 73 trillion yuan in 2012. As of end-2012, the number of high net worth families with assets available for investment above six million yuan was estimated at 1,740,000. Such enormous personal assets available for investment indicate that China's financial market has evolved into a wealth management market.

Wealth Management Product Market of Commercial Banks

In 2012, wealth management products of commercial banks continued expanding, at a lower pace, though. In 2012, 29, 100 banks' wealth management products were issued, which was a year-on-year growth of 45. 40 percent, but decelerated sharply compared with 106. 51 percent growth in 2011; the turnover of banks' wealth management products hit 19. 01 trillion yuan, up 12. 21 percent year on year, also indicating sharp slowdown compared with double growth in 2010 and 2011, according to statistics released by the Wealth Management Research Center, Lujiazui Institute of Chinese Academy of Social Sciences.

As disclosed by some researchers of CBRC on the workshop on hot topics concerning wealth management business of China's banking sector, in 2011, 160 banking institutions across the country created more than 175 billion yuan proceeds for investors by providing wealth management products, and in 2012, 180 major banks engaged in wealth management business realized return on investment worth of 246. 4 billion yuan for their clients. Banks' wealth management products have become important instruments of investment and wealth management for residents and the wealth management business of banks was thriving. In the meantime, hidden risks and malpractices in banks' wealth management business have emerged. A streak of scandals in wealth management business of Hua Xia Bank, China Construction Bank and Industrial and Commercial Bank of China exposed at the end of 2012 triggered a crisis of investor faith in banks' wealth management business.

Throughout 2012, the authority was supportive of banks' wealth management business in general, as reflected in loosened control over investment channels of banks' wealth management products in the following two respects. First, following the call for investing pension funds in the stock market, Wu Lijun, the Assistant to Chairman of CSRC, called for investing more funds under banks' wealth management business in the stock market. As a matter of fact, CBRC has already made some room for the investment of funds under banks' wealth management business in the stock market in the *Measures for the Administration of Sale of Wealth Management Products of Commercial Banks* (the *Measures*) brought into effect officially on January 1, 2012. As provided for under the *Measures*, commercial banks shall apply scientific and reasonable methods to independent risk rating for the wealth management products they plan to sell, map out risk control measures and practice classified review and approval. In the appeal for investing the funds under banks' wealth management business in the stock market this time, CSRC of course wishes to see more and more funds flowing into the stock market through more channels. Given the depressed A-share market, however, the attitude of commercial banks towards investing the funds under their wealth management business in the stock market is more about worry than anything else. The biggest problem lies in the huge risks hidden in the stock market, which might cause a loss of the principal of wealth management products. In that case, the reputation of commercial banks will be undermined badly. Second, banks' wealth management products were incorporated into the investment scope for proprietary trading of securities companies. On the part of securities companies, this undoubtedly broadens the investment channels of proprietary trading, while to the bank wealth management market, it means additional external funding channels.

These two policies mentioned above are actually signals given by CSRC in favor of banks' wealth management business. The regulatory measures of CBRC, as a major regulatory body, concerning the wealth management market of commercial banks in 2012 can be boiled down to two points as follows. First, crack down on evasion of regulation and regulatory arbitrage. This measure is an unwritten window instruction developed by CBRC in accordance with the keynote of 2012 Innovative Regulation Work Meeting. On January 11, 2012, CBRC put a stop to bill trust by means of window instruction. Like cooperation between banks and trust companies, bill trust can also help banks circumvent the control over the size of credit facility. Second, in December, 2012, a number of disputes between banks and their clients arose inShanghai from losses incurred by unauthorized sale of wealth management products and trust products by employees of banks on commission. The General Office of CBRC issued *Notice on Risk Screening for Commission Sale of Banking Institutions* (the *Notice*) immediately. The *Notice* puts forward three requirements for commission sale of banks. First, all banking institutions shall finish screening the staff of grassroots banking outlets within 15 days from the date the *Notice* is received, with focus on unauthorized recommendation or sale of third-party products, if any. Second, the head offices of all banking institutions shall urge their grassroots banking outlets to perform self-examination within seven days after the *Notice* is received and to submit a detailed list of products being sold on commission to the branches at the higher level. Then the head offices shall consolidate the inputs from all branches to present a summary report within 15 days. Third, the head offices and branches of all banking institutions shall submit the self-examination reports and the detailed lists of products being sold on commission to the competent authority within 30 days. Based on these submissions, CBRC and its agencies will then randomly check the outlets of banking institutions under their jurisdiction, openly or secretly, and file a spot check report to CBRC within 30 days after completion of spot check.

Due to the appalling impact of the commission sale scandal of Hua Xia Bank, China Banking Association officially released *Ten Conventions on Strengthening Self-discipline of Banks in Sale of Wealth Management Products* on December 12, 2012, and ordered banks to explicitly inform the risks in wealth management products and to evaluate the risk tolerance of clients in advance. Any bank that violates any of these conventions during sale of wealth management products shall be criticized openly.

As we may see, two major malpractices existed in the bank wealth management product market in 2012. First, there is malpractice in sales. Salesmen tend to exaggerate proceeds but belittle risks. Second, there is malpractice in operations. "Cash pool" products are widely used by commercial banks. It is very difficult for the authority to regulate such cash pools as the underlying assets therein differ in risk factor and the percentage of each underlying asset is indefinite. We have mentioned in 2012 dynamics of regulatory policies that the "cash pool" operation model of banks' wealth management products needs proper control. In practice, however, this operation model is gaining ground due to absence of proper regulation and was even called the "Ponzi Scheme" by Xiao Gang, the former Chairman of the Board of Bank of China.

Looking forward to 2013, the authority should perfect regulation of the bank wealth management market from the following three aspects. First, clarify the legal relation in bank wealth management. Legal relation is not transparent as investors have no idea whether the financial product they are buying involves creditor's rights, equity or trust relation, said Wu Xiaoling, Deputy Director of NPC's Finance and Economics Committee, on several occasions. If the legal relation involved in a financial product is not well-defined, it is impossible to make clear accountability for assumption of risk. This works quite to the disadvantage of banks. Second, regulate the operation model of "cash pool" products properly. Delightedly, CBRC released *Notice on Issues Concerning Regulation of Investment Operations of Wealth Management Business of Commercial Banks* (File No. 8 in brief) on March 28, 2013, which requires separate management, bookkeeping and accounting for each wealth management product. That is, the "rule of one to one correspondence is applied to the source of fund", to make "cash pool" operations "in the dark" transparent and exposed to the supervision of the market and the public. In the future, it is advisable to put into force regulations on the percentage of each category of "cash pool" product. Third, strengthen investor education and risk warning. *Notice on Risk Screening for Commission Sale of Banking Institutions* was issued by CBRC, and is just a directive document. In 2013, detailed rules should be promulgated accordingly.

Collective Wealth Management Product Market of Securities Companies

The year of 2012 is an epoch-making year to the asset management business of securities companies. In spite of subpar performance, issuance of collective wealth management products by securities companies was pulled into the fast lane, thanks to the financial reform. 215

products started fund raising in 2012, adding 107 to the number in 2011. 182 products came into existence, adding 71 to that of 2011. As of December 31, 2012, 114 securities companies had a total principal of 1. 89 trillion yuan under their management, compared to 929. 596 billion yuan at the end of the third quarter. It is noteworthy that total asset under management of securities companies at end-2012 increased nearly sevenfold from the end of 2011 (281. 868 billion yuan). Nevertheless, the A-share market remained subdued throughout 2012 and collective wealth management products of securities companies skewed towards stocks suffered huge losses.

CSRC took an attitude of "loosening regulation and encouraging innovation" towards collective wealth management products of securities companies in 2012. The five most influential innovative measures in the year are described as follows in chronological order:

First, convene a conference and set the general tone of innovation. On May 7, 2012, Brokerage Innovation Conference was held and *Ideas and Measures for Driving Reform and Open-up, Innovation and Development of Securities Companies (Exposure Draft)* was released. Eleven policies supporting innovation in the industry were mapped out, including sharpening up the innovation ability of securities companies in wealth management products, accelerating innovation in new services and products, loosening restrictions on business scope and investment methods, broadening the range of financial products allowed to be sold by securities companies on commission, supporting cross-border business development, driving innovation organized by business offices, encouraging offering, listing, M&A and reorganization of securities companies, encouraging securities companies to take an active part in OTC market construction and the pilot program of private placement bonds of micro, small and medium enterprises, reforming the risk control indicator system of securities companies, exploring long-term effective incentive mechanism, and improving the social environment for reform and open-up, innovation and development of securities companies.

Second, include futures companies in innovation. On August 3, CSRC released *Measures for the Pilot Program on the Asset Management Service of Futures Companies*, which allows the asset management business of futures companies to invest in futures, options, other financial derivatives, stocks, bonds, securities investment funds, collective asset management schemes, central bank bills, short-term financing bills, and asset-backed securities.

Third, release specific measures for loosening regulation. On October 19, CSRC released the revised *Measures for the Customer Asset Management Business of Securities Companies, Detailed Rules for the Implementation of Collective Asset Management Business of Securities Companies* and *Detailed Rules for the Implementation of Targeted Asset Management Business of*

Securities Companies. Under the tenet of "loosening regulation", revisions were made in six aspects. First, abolish administrative endorsement of collective schemes and adopt record-filing management by the Securities Association of China afterwards. Second, duly expand the investment scope and asset usage under asset management. Third, readjust investment restrictions on asset management, and rescind the two 10% restrictions on small collective and targeted asset management, the two 10% restrictions on exemption indexation collective schemes and the restriction on relevant investment in related transactions. Forth, give permission to classified and conditional transfer of units under collective schemes. Fifth, delete the clause, "a wealth management product of which the net asset value has been lower than 100 million yuan for 20 consecutive trading days shall be terminated", from *Detailed Rules for Collective Schemes.* Sixth, allow securities companies to conduct registration and clearing on their own and allow securities companies authorized by CSRC to provide asset custody service for asset management. "Loosening regulation" in these six aspects has largely whetted the enthusiasm of securities companies for innovation.

Fourth, create more room for innovation. On November 18, CSRC put into effect *Decision on Amending the Provisions on the Basis of Calculation of Risk Capital Reserves of Securities Companies*, *Provisions on Adjusting the Basis of Calculation of Net Capital of Securities Companies* (*Revised in* 2012) and *Decision on Amending the Provisions on the Investment Scope for Proprietary Trading of Securities Companies and Related Matters.* The content revised can be summarized as "two lowering and one adding", i. e., lowering the basis of calculation of risk capital reserves largely, lowering some standards for net capital deduction and adding content to the scope of proprietary trading. This undoubtedly creates more room for innovation and development of securities companies in institutions.

Fifth, frame open, inclusive and diversified key measures for the wealth management industry and provide institutions other than fund management firms with access to management of publicly offered funds. On December 30, CSRC released *Interim Provisions on the Management of Publicly Offered Securities Investment Funds by Asset Management Institutions* (*Exposure Draft*) and planned to grant publicly offered fund license to securities companies, insurance companies and private equity funds.

Thanks to the authority's effort to uphold the flag of "loosening control over asset management business of securities companies" and encourage innovation in collective wealth management products of securities companies, a lot of products well-designed to meet the material needs of clients came into being. First, there are cash management products that require cash deposit and are open regularly. Under the condition of a contract signed with clients, cash deposit from clients is invested in monetary assets characterized by low risk and high liquidity. These products can derive proceeds higher than that demand deposit could have derived, without holding up regular trading of securities of clients. Hence, they are attractive in terms of both liquidity and return. Second, there are classified products. There is not only the conventional classification model by putting good ones preceding poor ones, but also the innovative long-short classification model. Third, there are collective asset management schemes of trust products. The investment scope of big collective schemes has been expanded to include mid-term notes, yield-guaranteed and principal-guaranteed plus floating yield wealth management schemes of commercial banks. Small collective schemes are allowed to invest in instruments traded on stock and futures exchanges, instruments traded on the interbank market and financial products issued with the endorsement of or after registration with the financial authority.

All innovations in collective wealth management business of securities companies made in 2012 have raised higher requirements for the asset management skills and risk control capability of the management of securities companies. Behind explosive growth are huge hidden risks. With the new CSRC chairman's assumption of office in 2013, innovation in asset management business of securities companies might slow down and the authority is expected to give more weight to product risk warning.

Trust Product Market

The size of trust assets of the whole industry continued growing at a high speed and achieved a historic leap again in 2012. As of end-2012, 67 trust companies in the entire industry had 7. 47 trillion yuan trust assets under their management. In spite of brakes on real estate trust and cooperation between banks and trust companies, trust assets still recorded 55. 3 percent year on year growth, operating revenue gained 45. 32 percent growth year on year to hit 63. 842 billion yuan, and total profit posted 44. 14 billion yuan, up 47. 83 percent year on year. At end-2012, outstanding assets of the trust sector exceeded that of the insurance sector and it became the second largest financial sector of China.

Though the size of trust assets hit one record high after another, the market's concern about its sustainability couldn't be appeased. For one, absence of the trust industry from the *12th Five-Year Plan for the Development and Reform of the Financial Industry* shows the government is not aware of the value and function of the trust instrument and the trust system. For the other, all financial institutions, including banks, securities companies and securities investment fund management companies, and third-party wealth management companies flood into the wealth management market and all of them regard asset management and wealth management as the key to innovation. Trust companies are faced with more intense market competition. The combined effect of these two factors casts a shadow over its prospect.

In 2012, the authority put increasing weight on the regulation of the trust industry. While encouraging securities companies to make innovations unremittingly, to the trust industry, the authority issued one order after another to "stop window service".

In January, "window instruction" was given to put a stop to bill trust products and short-term wealth management products invested in interbank deposits, with a view to mitigate the disturbance from trust products to actual credit scale. In the second half of 2011, bill trust products soared. As bank-to-trust transfer, bills and credit asset transfer moved credit assets out of balance sheet, the authority thought these dealings evaded credit control and upset macro control, and trust played a part. CBRC gave window instruction to all trust companies by phone on January 11 and ordered them to stop (not suspend) issuing this kind of products. Short-term wealth management products of interbank deposits refer to "single capital trust scheme for interbank deposits" banks commission trust companies to issue. Under this trust scheme, trust companies put trust capital under the name of trustee in the bank, which is a term deposit, or interbank deposit. This operation model is equivalent to purchasing deposit products of banks with trust capital.

In April, "window instruction" for real estate trust was restarted. Commercial banks tightened loans for real estate development in early 2012, so developers began sourcing fund from real estate trust. As a result, real estate trust products were revitalized and the authority had to "care" about real estate trust once again. CBRC ordered trust companies to control the growth speed of and financing risks in real estate trust strictly.

In August, "window instruction" for the scale of cooperation between government-backed financing platforms and trust companies was issued. The Department of Non-banking Financial Institutions of CBRC called together ten-odd trust companies for a meeting and reiterated that the total volume of financing trust companies provide to local financing platforms still on the "list" must not exceed the volume at end-2011 and the target of "reducing existing volume and controlling added volume" must be put into action earnestly. All of the trust companies invited to the meeting were trust companies with the volume of financing they have provided to local financing platforms growing too quickly and with outstanding balance exceeding that of end-2011. The "window instruction" this time targeted platforms still on the "list" only. As for delisted financing platforms, CBRC doesn't prohibit trust companies from providing financing to them. The latent risk in local financing platforms is the main reason foreign institutions are going short for the Chinese economy. A concomitant of cooperative wealth management products between the government and trust companies is usually the guarantee for land finance of local governments. In the future, regulation of this business should be tightened further.

In October, cash pool trust business was called off. Trust companies create cash pool primarily for the purpose of postponing existing risks. This product line of trust companies cannibalizes the wealth management business of banks and some bank clients have turned to trust products. On October 17, the Department of Non-banking Financial Institutions of CBRC put a stop to cash pool trust business. If a trust company files a record for this kind of product, it shall be denied. As for existing cash pool trust business, some paper work needs to be done to bring it under control.

In November, infrastructure trust was called off. In the first three quarters of 2012, driven by the keystone of "steady growth", trust became one of the major channels of local financing. The percentage and scale of infrastructure products showed a continuous uptrend. This drew the attention of the authority. For the sake of risk control, CBRC gave an oral instruction for infrastructure trust and suspended approval of new infrastructure projects.

In December, four ministries and commissions co-released *File No. 463*. It is the only official file released by the authority concerning the trust market in 2012 and also the most important one. In 2012, cooperative trust products between the government and trust companies prevailed and CBRC's "window instruction" almost had no effect. As of end-2012, outstanding balance of cooperative business between the government and trust companies reached 500 billion yuan, compared to 390 billion yuan merely at the end of the third quarter, according to data released by China Trustee Association. We may see how fast it grew.

In order to regulate cooperative trust business between the government and trust companies to the core, on the last day of 2012, the Ministry of Finance, NDRC, the PBC and CBRC co-released *Notice on Suppressing Local Governments' Illegal Financing Activities* (the *Notice*, also referred to as File No. 463). The *Notice* is intended to put a brake on implicit indebtedness by the government for public projects and to suppress the inclination to expand investment and financing platforms under the disguise of public assets and intangible assets of the government. The *Notice* prohibits local governments from running into debt for all sorts of financing platform projects directly or indirectly, regulates the behavior of borrowing in the form of repurchase, guarantee or commitment and manages the financing activities of the platform companies. Government-backed local financing platforms are disallowed to contribute public assets, such as government office buildings, schools, hospitals and parks, as capital to financing platform companies. For debts that have been incurred because of public undertakings, such as public rental housing and roads, and need to be paid back with the help of fiscal funding, borrowing from non-financial institutions or individuals is forbidden, unless otherwise specified under the laws and stipulations of the State Council. Direct or indirect financing through financial companies, trust companies, fund firms, finance lease companies and insurance companies among financial institutions is prohibited. *File No. 463* has actually cut off the capital pump from financial companies, trust companies, fund firms, finance lease companies and insurance companies to all sorts of government-backed financing platforms. This is undoubtedly a catastrophe to cooperative trust projects between the government and trust companies. As for the result of execution, cooperative trust products between the government and trust companies were almost extinct in the first two months of 2013.

Apparently, throughout 2012, the authority was "cracking down on" trust business nonstop, mainly because of unchecked growth of trust assets and omnipotent investment channels. In 2013, the authority needs to pay attention to two figures. First, according to all-system financing aggregates of 2012 provided by the PBC, trust loans (increment) totaled 1.3 trillion yuan in 2012, more than the total amount of entrusted loans in the statistical table (1,284.1 billion yuan). Second, offering of infrastructure trust recovered in March, 2013, and some products suspended because of the new rules revived in March. We may see how thirst government-backed local financing platforms are for fund. The risks therein warrant our close attention.

Insurance Wealth Management Product Market

As of end-2012, there were 16 licensed insurance asset management companies (excluding Hong Kong SAR), 13 were allowed to entrust insurance capital and 4 were approved to set up asset management companies in Hong Kong SAR. Insurance asset management companies currently deal in investment-linked insurance management service, insurance asset management scheme, corporate annuity service, infrastructure and real estate bond plan, value-added platform service and third-party insurance asset management.

The investment scope of insurance capital remained limited for as long as 27 years from 1984 to 2011. In the year of 2012, the asset management industry of China boomed with ambitious and competitive players. Driven by this tidal wave, the insurance wealth management market also became full-fledged. The investment channels of insurance capital were largely widened. Quasi-public fund marked a critical breakthrough in the initiative of insurance asset management institutions in asset management business. Of course, this breakthrough is inseparable from the authority's "loosening regulation".

In 2012, the authority released 13 new policies on insurance asset management intensively, shortened as 13 Provisions, which fall into two major categories, insurance asset management and insurance investment channels. 13 Provisions have innovated the insurance wealth management business as reflected in the following five respects. First, the variety of investments accessible to insurance capital is enriched. In terms of direct investment, equity in leading enterprises engaged in modern agriculture, and energy and resource enterprises approved by relevant department of the State Council under the *Catalogue of Investment Projects Approved by the Government* is added. As for indirect investment, investment in three types of funds is allowed, agricultural development, elderly care and affordable housing. Second, investment in overseas real estate equity is allowed. With respect to overseas investment, the allowable investment scope of insurance capital is expected to be broadened to cover money market, fixed-income, equity, and real estate products, as well as investment funds with these underlying assets as the objects, including securities investment fund, equity investment fund, and real estate trust investment fund. Third, the insurance industry is given access to banking, securities and trust sectors. Funds and securities companies are allowed to act as custodian of insurance capital. Insurance companies are allowed to invest in collective asset management schemes launched by securities companies, collective capital trust schemes run by trust companies and credit asset-backed securities and yield-guaranteed wealth management products initiated by commercial banks. Fourth, capital allocation is differentiated from investment. Different investment institutions are engaged to manage different investment portfolios of insurance capital depending on their investment style and strength and weakness in investment. This policy might change the present situation of very limited intersection between the insurance industry and other financial sectors. Fifth, insurance companies are allowed to tap into asset management business through public offerings. This long-awaited good news means insurance asset management companies are able to offer funds like fund firms and raise fund publicly.

Public Fund Market

In spite of the overall slump of the stock market in 2012, the total assets under management (AUM) of fund firms didn't shrink. Instead, the size of publicly offered funds expanded to a new record high through innovatively designed products. At end-2012, the total AUM of publicly offered funds hit 2.87 trillion yuan, a year on year growth of 32 percent from 704.6 billion yuan at end-2011.

The explosive growth of AUM of publicly offered funds in 2012 can be primarily attributed to fast issuance of short-term wealth management products. In 2012, 43 money market funds were issued, offering a total of 663.7 billion units, accounting for 65 percent of the total number of units outstanding in the year. 68 bond funds were issued, offering a total of 169.2 billion units, accounting for 16 percent of the total number of units outstanding. 104 stock funds were issued, offering 118. 3 billion units only, which took up 12 percent of the total number of units outstanding.

In 2012, the keystone of public fund regulatory policy can be described as: widening sales channels, cracking down on insider trading and giving permission to start-up of segregated account business subsidiaries.

To broaden sales channels, CSRC took two bold moves. First, it lifted the restriction on third-party fund sales institutions. On February 22, CSRC announced the first list of third-party fund distribution licenses. Four institutions were "awarded" the license, NOAH, Howbuy, Zhonglu and Eastmoney. Third-party fund sales that had simmered for seven years were kicked off finally. Second, it brought in insurance companies. On November 20, CSRC released *Interim Administrative Provisions on the Sale of Securities Investment Funds by Insurance Institutions (Exposure Draft)* and planned to involve insurance companies, insurance brokers and insurance agents in fund sales.

To fund firms, the size of fund offering is heavily dependent on the accessibility of channels, besides the reputation of funds. Banks are dominating the most important channel of fund sales currently. Hence, fund firms are compelled to pay high commission. The entry of third-party sales institutions and insurance institutions is likely to put an end to this situation.

To crack down on insider trading, on November 20, CSRC released *Guiding Opinions on the Prevention and Control of Insider Trading in Investment and Research Activities Conducted by Fund Management Companies* and ordered fund management companies to put in place a robust insider trading prevention and control system to consummate identification, reporting, processing, examination and investigation of liability of insider information, as well as compliance audit, training and performance assessment. As a result, it enforced legal liability on fund management companies.

As for segregated account business subsidiaries, on October 31, CSRC released the revised *Interim Provisions on Administration of Subsidiaries of Securities Investment Fund Management Companies.* With the permission to set up subsidiaries engaged in segregated account business, fund companies will be able to conduct quasi-trust business, and put forward employee stock ownership plans. At present and in the days to come, fund management companies are expected to face more intense market competition. The segregated asset management business to be started by subsidiaries will allow fund management companies to diversify their investments from the existing assets of publicly traded securities into physical assets, such as unlisted equity, creditor's rights and income right.

Of course, the most eye-catching event in the fund industry in 2012 is the newly released

Law of the People's Republic of China on Securities Investment Fund (the new *Fund Law*). The most important content of the new *Fund Law* is to bring non-publicly offered fund, referred to as "private equity fund" or "sunshine private equity" in practice, under administration, so as to establish the legal status of private equity funds. In the future, private equity fund managers will be allowed to offer products for subscription by public investors.

Private Equity Market

The private equity market appeared bleak in 2012. 874 products were offered in 2012, including 561 structured products, 310 non-structured products and 3 trust of trusts (TOT) products, far exceeding the numbers in 2011, according to data of China Hedge Fund Database. However, the performance of private equity funds in 2012 was disappointing. 890 securities investment non-structured products with more than one-year track records posted average rate of return at 1.24 percent merely in 2012, according to statistics of simu360.com. The performance of private equity funds was dwarfed by that of the stock market and publicly offered funds.

Many innovations and breakthroughs were made in sunshine private equity in 2012, as reflected in: innovation in offering channels, and less reliance of sunshine private equity on trust companies; innovation in products and booming investment commodities and stock index futures products; prominent innovation in investment patterns, and strong interest in hedge policies and MOM, among others; innovation in policies and inclusion of sunshine private equity in the new *Fund Law*.

After the new *Fund Law* brings private placement under regulation, the competent authority in charge of private equity funds and the basis of regulation are made clear and the void of supervision over private equity funds is filled. This can help dispel the biased preconception that the private equity fund industry is out of order and optimize private equity funds that take investment honestly and seriously.

Third-Party Wealth Management Market

Third-party wealth management business has been developing rapidly though it started in China not long ago. Third-party wealth management doesn't stand for fund firms, banks or insurance companies, but involves a portfolio of financial instruments selected into personal wealth management plans tailored to the financial position and wealth management requirements of specific clients.

Numerous third-party wealth management companies emerged in the market in 2012. They sell fund, trust and other investment products on commission, but are not licensed to access any industry. The jobholders claim to be wealth management specialists, but most of them are not qualified for wealth management at all. Third-party institutions only sell wealth management products, but assume no aftersale liability. While growing unchecked, the third-party wealth management market is, we may say, in chaos.

All the chaos mainly stem from the absence of supervision over the third-party wealth management market. Third-party wealth management is neither defined nor prescribed for in the law. There is no corresponding law-enforcing authority or rules to regulate third-party wealth management institutions. Third-party wealth management involves banks' wealth management, fund, trust, insurance, private equity and other products, corresponding to CBRC, CSRC, NDRC and other competent authorities. On one hand, among fund, trust, private equity and many other products involved in third-party wealth management business, only the sale of publicly offered funds is mentioned under the *Administrative Measures for the Sale of Securities Investment Funds* released by CSRC, while all of the other products are beyond regulation. On the other hand, no authority is willing and able to take the lead to take over the full regulatory responsibility, so the third-party wealth management market of China is totally unattended.

Financial Derivatives Market Development Policy

Highlights of Financial Derivatives Market Development Policy in 2012

Table 5. 7　　　Highlights of Financial Derivatives Market Policy in 2012

Date	Title of Policy	File No. or Issued by
6 April	Launched the interest rate swap confirmation and write-off services on the interbank market	China Foreign Exchange Trade System
21 May	*Notice on Adjusting Administration of Some Businesses on the Interbank Foreign Exchange Market*	SAFE [2012] No. 30
21 May	Launched Shibor interest rate swap fixing and closing curves on the interbank market	China Foreign Exchange Trade System
8 June	*Administrative Measures for the Capital of Commercial Banks (for Trial Implementation)*	CBRC No. 1 Decree, 2012
21 August	*China Interbank Market Financial Derivatives Transactions Definition Document (2012 Version)* was released and applied	NAFMII Announcement [2012] No. 15
12 October	*Interim Measures for the Participation of Insurance Funds in the Trading of Financial Derivatives*	CIRC [2012] No. 94
1 November	CSRC decided to amend the *Provisions on the Investment Scope for Proprietary Trading of Securities Companies and Related Matters*	Exposure draft
5 November	*Notice on Issuing Interpretation No. 5 of the Accounting Standards for Business Enterprises*	MOF [2012] No. 19

Source: data collected by the research group.

Analysis of Financial Derivatives Market Development Policy in 2012

China accelerated the construction of financial derivatives market framework and infrastructure in 2012. The new version of financial derivatives transactions definition document was released. Insurance and securities companies were authorized to broaden their trading scope. Market admission management for foreign exchange derivatives was simplified. Non-principal delivery currency swap business was added. The policy for credit risk mitigation instruments was released. Trading benchmark construction was progressing well. Interest rate swap payment management and electronic confirmation and write-off services were launched. The trading volume of financial derivatives grew at a steady pace and market activity strengthened further in 2012. The dominant role of interest rate swaps in the market was consolidated and the status of Shibor as benchmark was solidified further. The exchange rate derivatives market continued growing rapidly. The credit risk mitigation instruments market performed soundly. The domestic financial derivatives market obviously lagged behind the spot market. In 2012, the turnover of domestic interest rate and exchange rate derivatives hit 20 trillion yuan approximately and its share of GDP was far smaller than that of western developed countries. From January to November, 2012, aggregate turnover of all kinds of interbank RMB interest rate derivatives increased 3. 9 percent year on year to 2. 7 trillion yuan, including 2. 67 trillion yuan for interest rate swaps, 16. 6 billion yuan for bond forwards, and 200 million yuan for forward rate agreements. In 2012, the interbank RMB exchange rate derivatives market maintained high speed growth, with a total turnover of 2. 56 trillion US dollars, up 29. 2 percent year on year. Among this total, the turnover of the RMB/foreign exchange forward market posted 86. 3 billion US dollars, a decrease of 61 percent year on year. The turnover of the RMB/foreign exchange swap market amounted to 2. 46 trillion US dollars, representing an increase of 39 percent year on year. The turnover of the RMB/foreign exchange currency swap and options market amounted to 5. 54 billion and 3. 32 billion US dollars, respectively. The trading volume of the interbank foreign currency pair derivatives market achieved marked growth in 2012, with a total turnover of 23. 2 billion US dollars, a year on year increase by 1. 6 times. Among this total, the turnover of the foreign currency pair forward market increased 16. 4 percent year on year to 2. 6 billion US dollars; and the turnover of the foreign currency pair swap market amounted to 20. 7 billion US dollars, representing double growth year on year. In 2012, the number of market members that have completed qualification record-filing for credit risk mitigation instrument trader, credit risk mitigation instrument core trader and credit risk mitigation warrant institutor increased steadily. As of end-2012, after proper record-filing, 45 market members were qualified for credit risk mitigation instrument trader, adding two to the number of last year; 26 for credit risk mitigation instrument core trader, adding one to that of last year; and 29 for credit risk mitigation warrant institutor, adding one to that of last year.

Main financial policies for the financial derivatives market of China in 2012 are described as follows:

China Interbank Market Financial Derivatives Transactions Definition Document (2012 Version) **was released and applied**

In March, 2009, NAFMII formulated and released *China Interbank Market Financial Derivatives Master Agreement* (2009 Version) (*NAFMII Master Agreement*) under the guidance of the PBC and SAFE on the basis of two existing master agreements for the OTC financial derivatives market, and framed unified Chinese standards for the OTC financial derivatives market. With the expanding trading volume of China's OTC financial derivatives market, innovative products kept coming forth, and some new circumstances and problems occurred in the market place. The old definition document cannot meet the development need of the market, owing to relatively simple clauses and stipulations, some clauses incompliant with market practice and lack of definitions of some mature market mechanisms and innovative products, among other defects. Market members cried for refining the definition document and proposed to create a long-term effective mechanism for automatic update of the documents matching *NAFMII Master Agreement*. To further promote healthy and compliant development of China's OTC financial derivatives market and protect the legitimate rights and interests of market participants, NAFMII organized market members and legal experts to formulate *China Interbank Market Financial Derivatives Transactions Definition Document* (2012) (the *Definition Document*) based on the 2009 Edition and promulgated it officially on August 21, 2012. The *Definition Document* is comprised of four documents, namely, *China Interbank Market Interest Rate Derivatives Transactions Definition Document* (2012), *China Interbank Market Exchange Rate Derivatives Transactions Definition Document* (2012), *China Interbank Market Bond Derivatives Transactions Definition Document* (2012) and *China Interbank Market Credit Derivatives Transactions Definition Document* (2012).

The *Definition Document* has been revised and polished by incorporating the experience from the market development and the status quo of relevant rules into the structure, content and clauses of the document and drawing upon international good practice. First, in terms of structure, the document is subdivided into four subfiles on interest rate, exchange rate, bond and credit, respectively, to make easier quoting by market members and subsequent extension and update to the definition document. Second, for derivatives with relatively mature market practice, i. e. , interest rate, exchange rate and bond, revisions are focused on rephrasing and refining the wording and expressions in the old definition document in pace with market development. Third, as the innovation practice relating to credit derivatives took place after the promulgation of the 2009 Edition, material revisions were made to the old credit definition document this time, to meet the contemporary market development need and reserve room for further development and innovation of the credit derivatives market. Forth, transaction confirmation templates for some products were formulated this time, to make transactions of the OTC financial derivatives market more efficient.

Insurance institutions were authorized to broaden derivatives trading scope

In order to regulate the participation of insurance funds in the trading of financial derivatives, guard against risks in fund use, and protect the legitimate rights and interests of insurance parties, on October 12, 2012, CIRC released Interim Measures for the Participation of Insurance Funds in the Trading of Financial Derivatives (CIRC [2012] No. 94) (the *Measures*), and stated that insurance group (holding) corporations, insurance companies and insurance asset management companies incorporated domestically in accordance with the law are allowed to participate in domestic financial derivatives trading, including forwards, futures, options and swaps (exchange) . The *Measures* are comprised of 36 articles in five sections, namely, general provisions, eligibility criteria, management specifications, risk management and supervision, and come into force upon promulgation. As highlighted under the *Measures*, insurance institutions' participation in derivatives trading is limited to hedging or risk aversion purposes, including "hedging against or evading risks in existing assets, liabilities or the company as a whole", "hedging against risks in assets to be bought in within the coming month or locking in future transaction prices", and must not be speculative. CIRC shall release derivative-specific trading rules in due course depending on market development and actual needs.

As for the eligibility of insurance companies for participating in the trading of derivatives, the *Measures* require that when insurance group (holding) corporations and insurance companies participate in the trading of derivatives at their discretion, the board of a company must be aware of associated risks and assume ultimate responsibility for participating in the trading of derivatives. Meanwhile they are required to map out operation, internal control and risk management rules for derivatives trading in conformity with the *Measures* and build investment and trading, accounting and risk management information systems. In addition, insurance companies must be provided with managers specialized in derivatives trading, inclusive of but not limited to analysis and research, transaction operation, financial operation, risk control and audit. In order to effectively control risks, the *Measures* require expressly insurance institutions to create a dynamic risk management mechanism, formulate total risk management system and operation flows for derivatives trading, build information system for real-time monitoring, evaluation and handling of risks, consummate emergency response mechanism and contingency management plan, determine risk limit to derivatives and the asset portfolios based on the risk tolerance of the company and do review and update regularly at a fixed frequency of evaluation. Moreover, insurance institutions should create a counterparty evaluation and selection mechanism, perform due diligence on the credit standing of the counterparty, evaluate credit risk and track and evaluate trading process and behavior. On the basis of combining internal and external credit rating, insurance companies should set a trading limit to the counterparty, adopt appropriate credit risk mitigations as necessary, and meanwhile reserve a certain proportion of current assets and monitor and control liquidity risk through cash management.

Securities institutions were authorized to broaden derivatives trading scope

CSRC released *Provisions on the Investment Scope for Proprietary Trading of Securities Companies and Related Matters* (the *Provisions*) on April 29, 2011, with a view to clarify the investment scope for proprietary trading of securities companies and related matters. Thereafter, the Provisions have played an important part in expanding the investment channels of securities companies and effectively controlling the risks in proprietary trading and alternative investments of securities companies. Along with reform and open-up, innovation and development of securities companies, however, the Provisions are no longer suited to meet actual needs and need revising and substantiating. For this purpose, CSRC asked for advice publicly about amending the *Provisions* on November 1, 2012.

Some content was modified or enriched as necessary. Revisions were primarily made in two respects. First, the *List of Investment Products for Proprietary Trading of Securities Companies* attached to the *Provisions* was revised to expand the variety of investments for proprietary trading to meet the actual needs of securities companies for expanding the investment scope for proprietary trading. After that, one category was added and two categories were expanded for proprietary trading. Securities listed in the National SME Share Transfer System were added. Two categories were expanded. For one, securities traded on the domestic interbank market were expanded from partial to all. For the other, securities traded over the counter of financial institutions were expanded from those issued with the sanction of or after record-filing with CSRC only to those issued with the sanction of or after record-filing with financial authority or its authorized institutions, which means wealth management schemes of banks and collective capital trust plans are added to the investment scope for proprietary trading. Second, the regulatory policy for investment of securities companies in financial derivatives was clarified to meet the actual needs of securities companies for investment in financial derivatives. In consideration of the complexity and high risk of the trading of financial derivatives, securities companies are required to have certain investment decision-making and risk control power. Bar from risk hedging, only securities companies eligible for proprietary trading are allowed to participate in the trading of financial derivatives directly. CSRC shall solicit public opinions and take in all suggestions and comments fully and then release the revised and polished *Provisions* in due time.

Market admission management for foreign exchange derivatives was simplified

To allow the financial sector to serve the real sector better and promote the development of the foreign exchange market, SAFE released a document about adjusting the administration of some businesses of the interbank foreign exchange market on June 5, 2012, in light of *Notice of the People's Bank of China on Relevant Issues Concerning Accelerating the Development of Foreign Exchange Market* ([2005] No. 202), *Notice of the People's Bank of China on Issues about Opening RMB and Foreign Currency Swap Business in the Interbank Market* ([2007] No. 287) and other rules. Adjustments include simplifying market admission management for foreign exchange swap and currency swap businesses and adding the mode of principal exchange for currency swap business.

SAFE decided to simplify market admission management for foreign exchange swap and currency swap businesses and adopt one-time record-filing management for RMB/foreign exchange futures, foreign exchange swap and currency swap on the interbank foreign exchange market. Eligible domestic institutions may submit the required files and apply for record-filing with SAFE through China Foreign Exchange Trade System to be qualified for these three businesses together. Those domestic institutions that completed record-filing and became qualified for forwards trading on the interbank foreign exchange market before *Notice on Adjusting Administration of Some Businesses on the Interbank Foreign Exchange Market* came into force may obtain the qualification automatically for foreign exchange swap and currency swap businesses and don't need to apply for record-filing again. Foreign exchange forward trading slumped in 2012. Foreign exchange forward settlement and sale contracts signed between banks and clients were worth 364.1 billion US dollars cumulatively, with the value of foreign exchange forward settlement and sale at 181.4 billion and 182.7 billion US dollars, respectively, down 5.9 percent, 5.2 percent and 6.7 percent from 2011, respectively. Throughout the year, marked cyclical fluctuations were seen, with enterprises moving from net settlement to net sale and then back to net settlement of foreign exchange. The slump in forward settlement and sale of foreign exchange in 2012 indicates enterprises are less enthusiastic about hedging, with RMB exchange rate moving towards an equilibrium level, besides the alternative factor of emerging option trading. Cumulative turnover of the interbank foreign exchange forward market hit 86. 6 billion US dollars in 2012 (average daily turnover of 400 million US dollars), representing a slump by 59. 6 percent from 2011. The main reason for this is that banks adopt the spot + swap mode again for squaring open positions in forward transactions of clients and the demand for interbank forward transactions has sagged after the lower limit to positions under cash basis of accounting for banks was abolished in April. As specified by SAFE, in conducting RMB/foreign exchange currency swap business on the interbank foreign exchange market, domestic institutions may choose not to physically exchange RMB and foreign currency principal either on the date when the agreement comes into force or on the date when the agreement expires, unless otherwise specified in the existing rules.

Matching policies for credit risk mitigation instruments were released in succession

First, *Interpretation No. 5 of the Accounting Standards for Business Enterprises* was released to clarify accounting methods of credit risk mitigation instruments. On November 5, 2012, the Ministry of Finance (MOF) issued *Notice on Issuing Interpretation No. 5 of the Accounting Standards for Business Enterprises* ([2012] No. 19) and declared *Interpretation No. 5 of the Accounting Standards for Business Enterprises* effective from January 1, 2013. *Interpretation No. 5 of the Accounting Standards for Business Enterprises* have clarified the definition of credit risk mitigation instruments, pursuant to relevant provisions under *Guidelines for the Pilot Operation of Credit Risk Mitigation Instruments in the Interbank Market* (the *Guidelines*) released by NAFMII. The term "credit risk mitigation instruments" as mentioned in the *Guidelines* shall refer to credit risk mitigation agreements, credit risk mitigation warrants and other credit derivatives used for managing credit risks. It is made clear that protection buyer and seller shall make judgment whether a credit risk mitigation instrument is a financial guaranty contract, based on the contract terms of the credit risk mitigation instrument, and in light of the rule of substance over form. Relevant provisions under *Interpretation No. 5 of the Accounting Standards for Business Enterprises* provide members of the financial derivatives market with the accounting standards for credit risk mitigation instruments, perfect the operational framework of and are conducive to sound and sustainable growth of the credit risk mitigation instruments market.

Second, *Administrative Measures for the Capital of Commercial Banks (for Trial Implementation)* shall come into force on January 1, 2013. On June 7, 2012, CBRC issued *Administrative Measures for the Capital of Commercial Banks (for Trial Implementation)* . *Administrative Measures for the Capital of Commercial Banks (for Trial Implementation)* incorporate relevant rules and content of *The New Basel Capital Accord*, tighten supervision over derivatives dealings of banking institutions, underline risk management requirements, give more weight to protection of client institutions and can help bring derivatives dealings of banking institutions under proper administration. The promulgation of *Administrative Measures for the Capital of Commercial Banks (for Trial Implementation)* is a significant event as it can give play to the capital mitigation functionality of credit risk mitigation instruments, improve credit risk sharing mechanism and enhance the capital operation efficiency of commercial banks.

Infrastructure of the financial derivatives market was further improved

First, electronic computation service for interest payment under interest rate swaps was put into practice on a trial basis. Compared with the trading of traditional securities, the contract terms of interbank OTC derivatives are complicated and seldom standardized. With the ever expanding market size, more and more disputes have arisen from discrepant computation of cash payment amount between two parties and impaired the operational efficiency of the interbank OTC derivatives market. By drawing upon the practical experience of the international market, China Foreign Exchange Trade System pioneered third-party payment management service. On July 16, 2012, China Foreign Exchange Trade System started trial run of electronic computation service for interest payment under interest rate swaps to replace the payment amount check mode by email, telephone and fax among financial institutions, and largely heightened the performance efficiency of OTC financial derivatives contracts.

Second, interest rate swap electronic confirmation and write-off services were launched. In recent years, electronic confirmation has become an important international trend in post-transaction processing of derivatives. In the first half of 2012, the PBC gave official sanction to China Foreign Exchange Trade System to launch interest rate swap electronic confirmation and write-off services on the interbank market. Interest rate swap electronic confirmation and write-off can help financial institutions reduce operational risk, credit risk and legal risk in trading and is a crucial move during the infrastructure construction of the interest rate derivatives market.

Third, an array of exchange rate derivatives benchmark curves was almost completed. To satisfy market members' demand for derivatives valuation and risk management, in February, 2012, China Foreign Exchange Trade System launched foreign exchange forward curve. On May 21, 2012, to give better play to the role of Shibor as benchmark rates, China Foreign Exchange Trade System unveiled Shibor interest rate swap fixing and closing curves on the basis of earlier pilot work. Plus the already released foreign exchange swap curve, US dollar implicit interest rate curve and foreign exchange option implicit volatility curve, an almost complete array of derivatives benchmark curves has come into being.

Policy Evaluation and Outlook

Rapid growth of the real economy necessitates a financial market system of complete products and financial instruments, full-fledged functions and controllable risks, and the financial derivatives market is an indispensable part thereof. Financial derivatives are the product of development of the financial market and are must-have tools that can be used by institutional investors and other market participants to manage risks and evade the risks from market volatility. In 2013, with respect to the policies for financial derivatives, first, effort will be carried on to drive product innovations, perfect the array of financial derivatives, and deepen the development of the credit risk mitigation instruments market. Second, effort will also be made to promote diversity of subjects of the derivatives market and spread market risks reasonably. Third, it is necessary to strengthen the legal system construction, create a sound market environment, and perfect the market regulation and self-discipline system. Along with progress in the diversification of participants of the financial market and integrated business of financial institutions, it is an objective requirement to develop a complete set of regulations and specifications for the OTC financial derivatives market, consummate the regulatory framework of the OTC financial derivatives market and formulate consistent *Administrative Measures for the Trading of OTC Financial Derivatives*. Under the framework of these consistent administrative measures, specific business guidelines shall be developed and classified guidance shall be given in line with the features of different financial derivatives. A regulatory system that combines administrative regulation and self-regulation and is supported by front-line monitoring shall come into being progressively. Fourth, the market infrastructure construction will be pushed forward to guarantee operational efficiency and safety of the market.

Commodity Futures Market Development Policy

Highlights of Commodity Futures Market Development Policy in 2012

Table 5.8　　Commodity Futures Market Development Policy in 2012

Date	Policy	File No. and Issued by
2 February	*Decision on Amending the Administrative Provisions on Opening Accounts for Investors in the Futures Market*	CSRC [2012] No. 1
13 February	*Announcement on Releasing the Amendment to Administrative Measures of Shanghai Futures Exchange for Risk Control and the Amendment to Detailed Trading Rules of Shanghai Futures Exchange*	Shanghai Futures Exchange [2012] No. 1
20 February	*Notice on Promulgating and Enforcing the Amendment to Detailed Delivery Rules of Dalian Commodity Exchange*	Dalian Commodity Exchange [2012] No. 27
20 February	*Announcement on Releasing the Amendment to Administrative Measures of Shanghai Futures Exchange for Hedging Transactions*	Shanghai Futures Exchange [2012] No. 2

Continued

Date	Policy	File No. and Issued by
2 March	*Notice on Adjusting Standard Rates for Cotton and PTA Designated Delivery Warehouse*	Zhengzhou Commodity Exchange [2012] No. 4
13 March	*Notice on Adjusting Standard Margin and Limit Up/Limit Down for Futures Trading of Cotton and Early Indica Rice*	Zhengzhou Commodity Exchange [2012] No. 55
19 March	*Notice on Doing Well in Exchanges' Reduction of Handling Charges*	China Futures Association
22 March	*Notice on Adjusting Standard Handling Charges for Intraday Open/Close Position of White Sugar Futures*	Zhengzhou Commodity Exchange [2012] No. 60
5 April	*Notice on Adjusting Minimum Margin and Limit Up/Limit Down for All Types of Commodities*	Dalian Commodity Exchange [2012] No. 47
17 April	*Shanghai Futures Exchange Asking for Advice on the Silver Futures Contract and Relevant Rules*	Shanghai Futures Exchange
27 April	*Notice on Adjusting Standard Handling Charges*	Dalian Commodity Exchange [2012] No. 76
27 April	*Notice on Lowering Standard Handling Charges for All Types of Commodities*	Shanghai Futures Exchange [2012] No. 64
27 April	*Notice on Adjusting Standard Handling Charges*	Zhengzhou Commodity Exchange [2012] No. 81
April	*Operation Guide for Centralized Account Opening for Special Institutional Clients (for Trial Implementation)*	China Futures Margin Monitoring Center
4 May	*Notice on Issues Concerning Silver Futures Trading*	Shanghai Futures Exchange [2012] No. 61
7 May	*Notice on Account Opening for Special Institutional Clients*	Dalian Commodity Exchange [2012] No. 82
10 May	*Provisions on Issues Concerning Changes in the Registered Capital or Equity of Futures Companies*	CSRC [2012] No. 11
15 May	*Notice on Adjusting Standard Margin and Limit Up/Limit Down for Some Types of Commodities*	Zhengzhou Commodity Exchange [2012] No. 99
16 May	*Notice on Promulgating and Enforcing the Amendment to Detailed Delivery Rules of Dalian Commodity Exchange and Other Implementation Rules*	Dalian Commodity Exchange [2012] No. 89
11 June	*Notice on Releasing Operation Guide of Shanghai Futures Exchange on Market Entry of Special Institutional Clients*	Shanghai Futures Exchange [2012] No. 87
10 July	*Notice on Releasing Rapeseed Oil, Early Indica Rice and Strong Gluten Wheat Futures Contracts and Relevant Trading Rules*	Zhengzhou Commodity Exchange [2012] No. 122

Continued

Date	Policy	File No. and Issued by
20 July	*Notice on Promulgating and Enforcing the Amendment to Regulatory Specifications and Operation Procedures Related to Administrative Measures of Dalian Commodity Exchange for Abnormal Transactions (for Trial Implementation)*	Dalian Commodity Exchange [2012] No. 137
20 July	*Notice on Amending Identification Specifications and Operation Procedures Related to Guidelines of Zhengzhou Commodity Exchange for Supervision of Abnormal Transactions (for Trial Implementation)*	Zhengzhou Commodity Exchange [2012] No. 132
20 July	*Notice on Releasing the Amendment to Interim Provisions of Shanghai Futures Exchange on Monitoring Abnormal Transactions and the Amendment to Operation Specifications and Procedures Related to Interim Provisions of Shanghai Futures Exchange on Monitoring Abnormal Transactions*	Shanghai Futures Exchange [2012] No. 94
1 August	*Notice on Adjusting Minimum Margin and Limit Up/Limit Down for Soybean Meal*	Dalian Commodity Exchange [2012] No. 148
2 August	*Notice on Adjusting Standard Handling Charges for Some Types of Commodities*	Dalian Commodity Exchange [2012] No. 151
2 August	*Notice on Lowering Standard Handling Charges*	Zhengzhou Commodity Exchange [2012] No. 135
2 August	*Notice on Lowering Standard Handling Charges for All Types of Commodities*	Shanghai Futures Exchange [2012] No. 105
16 August	*Notice on Promulgating and Enforcing the Amendment to Detailed Trading Rules of Dalian Commodity Exchange and Other Implementation Rules*	Dalian Commodity Exchange [2012] No. 171
1 September	*Measures for the Pilot Program on the Asset Management Service of Futures Companies*	CSRC [2012] No. 81
3 September	*Notice on Releasing Detailed Futures Trading Rules*	Zhengzhou Commodity Exchange [2012] No. 151
21 September	*Notice on Promulgating and Enforcing the New Measures on Administration of Hedging at Dalian Commodity Exchange*	Dalian Commodity Exchange [2012] No. 204
23 September	*Decision of the State Council on the Sixth List of Administrative Approval Items to be Abolished or Adjusted*	The State Council [2012] No. 52
27 September	*Guidelines for Asset Management Contract of Futures Companies and Investor Suitability Evaluation Procedures for Asset Management Business of Futures Companies (for Trial Implementation)*	China Futures Association
8 October	*Notice on Promulgating and Enforcing the Amendment to Punishment Measures of Dalian Commodity Exchange for Violations of Rules*	Dalian Commodity Exchange [2012] No. 209

Continued

Date	Policy	File No. and Issued by
22 October	*Announcement on Issuing the Amendment to Implementation Rules of Shanghai Futures Exchange on Settlement, Standard Warrant Management and Trading*	Shanghai Futures Exchange [2012] No. 10
24 October	*Decision of the State Council on Amending Regulations on Futures Trading*	The State Council
29 October	*Notice on Promulgating and Enforcing the Amendment to Rules for Standard Warrants of Dalian Commodity Exchange and Other Implementation Rules*	Dalian Commodity Exchange [2012] No. 221
30 October	*Notice on Promulgating and Enforcing the Amendment to Dalian Commodity Exchange Risk Management Measures*	Dalian Commodity Exchange [2012] No. 224
1 November	*Measures for the Management of Information Security and Assurance in the Securities and Futures Industries*	CSRC [2012] No. 82
22 November	*Notice on Promulgating and Enforcing the Amendment to Detailed Delivery Rules of Dalian Commodity Exchange and Other Implementation Rules*	Dalian Commodity Exchange [2012] No. 235
28 November	*Notice on Releasing Zhengzhou Commodity Exchange Glass Futures Contract and Detailed Trading Rules*	Zhengzhou Commodity Exchange [2012] No. 191
20 November	*Notice on Promulgating and Enforcing the Amendment to Dalian Commodity Exchange No. 1 Soybean Futures Contract and Relevant Implementation Rules*	Dalian Commodity Exchange [2012] No. 258
21 November	*Notice on Releasing Guidelines for the Pilot Work for Futures Companies' Opening Subsidiaries to Focus on Risk Management Services*	China Futures Association [2012] No. 129
25 November	*Notice on Releasing Rapeseed and Rapeseed Meal Futures Contracts and Detailed Trading Rules*	Zhengzhou Commodity Exchange [2012] No. 220

Source: data collected by the research group.

Analysis of Commodity Futures Market Development Policy in 2012

Enforcement and Adjustment of Regulatory Policy for Futures Trading

In view of the depressed futures market of China in 2011, CSRC, China Futures Association, Shanghai Futures Exchange, Zhengzhou Commodity Exchange and Dalian Commodity Exchange adapted their policies for futures duly in 2012, and launched a series of policies to boost the futures industry while reinforcing regulation.

First, handling charges for futures trading were lowered further to give an impetus to revival of the futures industry. To carry out *Notice on Doing Well in Exchanges' Reduction of Handling Charges issued by China Futures Association*, Shanghai Futures Exchange lowered the handling charges for copper, lead, wire rod, deformed steel bar, rubber, fuel oil, gold and zinc on June 1 and September 1, 2012, in a row; and then lowered the handling charge for silver on September 1, 2012. Zhengzhou Commodity Exchange lowered the margin for cotton and early indica rice futures trading from 10 percent to 6 percent and limit up/limit down from 6 percent to 4 percent from March 13, 2012; cut the handling charges for intraday open/close position of white sugar futures contract by half from April 5, 2012; reduced the standard margin for white sugar, rapeseed oil, high-quality strong gluten wheat and hard white wheat futures contracts from 8 percent to 6 percent and limit up/limit down from 5 percent to 4 percent from settlement on May 18, 2012; and then cut the handling charges for high-quality strong gluten wheat, hard white wheat, early indica rice, rapeseed oil, white sugar, PTA, cotton, common wheat and methyl alcohol from June 1, 2012. Dalian Commodity Exchange lowered the handling charges for No. 1 soybean, No. 2 soybean, soybean meal, corn, bean oil, palm oil, polyethylene, polyvinyl chloride and coke from June 1, 2012; and then lowered the standard handling charges from 3.5 yuan per lot to 2.5 yuan per lot for bean oil, palm oil, polyethylene and polyvinyl chloride contracts from September 1, 2012.

Second, contract design concept was changed. Since 2012, at the request and instruction of CSRC, the commodity exchanges in China have gradually corrected the entrenched idea of "suppressing speculation" and boosted trading activity by changing the design concept of futures contracts. For example, big contracts such as 100 ton coke and 50 ton methyl alcohol were downsized to small contracts, for example, 10 ton rapeseed and rapeseed meal respectively, and 20 ton glass. Crude oil futures in the pipeline will also adopt small contract.

Third, control was loosened, but regulation was strengthened. In September, 2012, the State Council abolished some administrative approval items and CSRC was one of the ministries and commissions to effect the boldest change. For example, approval of capital increase and relocation of business office of futures companies was abolished. The quantity limit to introducing broker (IB) business by business offices of securities companies and IB competency test of China Futures Association were cancelled. Meanwhile, CSRC delegated some approval authority to China Futures Association to promote self-regulation. For example, CSRC approved of futures companies' opening subsidiaries to focus on risk management services, for which record-filing and review by China Futures Association is required. In line with the guiding opinion of CSRC, all of the four futures exchanges in China loosened the criteria for abnormal transactions. For example, China Financial Futures Exchange raised the intraday open position limit from 500 lots to 1000 lots and the position holding standard to 300 lots. Abnormal transactions and violations of clients are delinked to annual classification and rating of futures companies and no penalty point is given. In November, 2012, by drawing upon the experience of securities companies and fund firms, CSRC launched the Futures Integrated Supervisory System (FISS), to realize systematic, information-based and standardized supervision and improve the work efficiency of the regulatory body and futures companies. In 2012, driven by CSRC's effort to "loosen control and strengthen regulation", and a mix of measures adopted by the exchanges, for example, reduction in handling charges, and innovations in contracts and monitoring, the futures market of China revived quickly from the recession in 2011. The trading volume of the futures market totaled 1.45 billion lots, and the trade amount aggregated 171 trillion yuan, up 37.6 percent and 24.44 percent, respectively.

Continued innovations in futures product categories and business

First, innovations were made in new categories. In 2012, new contracts for silver, rapeseed, rapeseed meal and glass were launched on the futures market. Exposure drafts for new categories such as treasury bonds, options, crude oil and egg and simulated trading were progressing well. Iron ore and carbon credit were also studied. These new categories not only enriched the futures product lines, but also expanded the potential for market development, provided more hedging instruments to relevant business entities and allowed the futures market to serve the real economy better.

Second, innovations were made in the asset management business of futures companies. On August 1, 2012, CSRC issued *Measures for the Pilot Program on the Asset Management Service of Futures Companies*, and raised the curtain on the asset management business of futures companies. The investment scope of asset management business of futures companies covers futures, options and other financial derivatives; stocks, bonds, securities investment funds, collective asset management schemes, central bank bills, short-term financing bills, asset-backed securities and other investments approved by CSRC. The startup of futures asset management business will lift futures companies out of the predicament of single business and diversify their sources of income.

Third, subsidiaries focused on risk management services were allowed to be set up. In December, 2012, China Futures Association issued *Notice on Releasing Guidelines for the Pilot Work for Futures Companies' Opening Subsidiaries to Focus on Risk Management Services*, which declares that CSRC has approved of futures companies' opening subsidiaries to focus on risk management services, and to provide specialized institutions and high net worth clients with warrant service, joint hedging, pricing service and basis trading service. The startup of risk management subsidiaries will change the channel-centric business model of futures companies and create new growth pole of profit and new profit model.

Fourth, other innovative services were launched. At the night of May 14, 2012, CSRC released *Provisions on Issues Concerning Changes in the Registered Capital or Equity of Futures Companies* (the *Provisions*), which indicates the authority begins to reopen the door for foreign shareholding in domestic futures companies. The *Provisions* removed the cap to foreign shareholding in domestic futures companies (no more than 49 percent as required) and accelerated overseas futures brokerage business of domestic futures companies. Moreover, the promulgation of the *Provisions* is also related to international futures categories like crude oil. The domestic oil prospecting, exploiting and circulation system is yet to be opened up. Hence, the authority emphasized the importance to attract foreign investors to join in the market. At the end of April, 2012, China Futures Margin Monitoring Center circulated *Operation Guide for Centralized Account Opening for Special Institutional Clients (for Trial Implementation)* among all futures companies and clarified the process and requirements for opening accounts at commodity futures exchanges for institutional investors, including funds, securities companies, trust companies, social security and QFII.

Improvement in institutional construction and solid base for the development of the futures market

To better adapt to rapid development of and new changes in the futures market, relevant authorities refined the rules on the futures market. *Decision of the State Council on Amending Regulations on Futures Trading* declares the new version *Regulations on Futures Trading* effective from December 1, 2012. The new version clears the legal restraints on innovations and encourages futures companies to grow bigger and stronger through M&A, reorganization or IPO financing.

Measures for the Management of Information Security and Assurance in the Securities and Futures Industries (the *Measures*) released by CSRC came into force from November 1, 2012. The *Measures* have specified information security management and other regulations for the securities and futures industries, established the framework of information security supervision, clarified the responsibilities of market players for information security and assurance, and set forth information security requirements. It takes information security and assurance of the capital market to a new level.

Policy Evaluation and Outlook

Evaluation of Futures Market Policy Enforcement in 2012

In the first quarter of 2013, the trading volume of the futures market totaled 453, 209, 423 lots and the trade amount registered 60, 390. 726 billion yuan, up 127. 76 percent and 90. 46 percent year on year, respectively, according to latest statistics of China Futures Association. Thanks to sharp fluctuations of the A-share market since the second half of 2012, the turnover of stock index futures surged and took up more than half of the entire futures market. In March, the trading volume of the futures market climbed up from the preceding month. On unilateral calculation basis, the trading volume of the futures market posted 183, 420, 675 lots and the trade amount was 24, 535. 677 billion yuan, up 126. 52 percent and 111. 65 percent year on year, and 62. 28 percent and 61. 84 percent month on month, respectively.

In spite of the surge in trade in the first quarter, the profitability of futures companies in brokerage business was on the wane. The cuts in handling charges by the exchanges in 2012 almost covered all futures categories and led to decreasing income of futures companies accordingly. Meanwhile, competition on the futures market intensified and income from handling charges seemed even more insufficient. As all futures exchanges proceed with the incentives for futures trading, the domestic commodity market enjoys greater growth potential in terms of trading volume and position. With new categories and businesses coming into operation within this year, futures trading is estimated to maintain high-speed growth.

Outlook for Commodity Futures Market Policy

The State Council forwarded *Opinions of National Development and Reform Commission on Deepening the Reform of the Economic System in* 2013, wherein the construction of the bulk commodity futures market, including coal, iron ore and crude oil, and the treasury bond futures market is put on the agenda. In virtue of the favorable policy, the development and innovation of commodity futures categories is about to be pulled into the fast lane. Fit in easily with the realistic needs of the real economy, the commodity futures market will usher in an era of high-speed development.

Driven by the authority, the futures market is expected to present more innovations and breakthroughs in 2013, and the total number of futures categories is expected to increase from 31 in 2012 to more than 40. Charred coal, steam coal, iron ore, egg and potato are expected to come on stage one after another and further enrich the product variety of the domestic commodity futures market. Double effort will be made on the research of strategic categories such as commodity index and carbon credits and achievements will be made. The long-awaited treasury bond futures are ready to be launched. Following gestation and policy preparation for some time, now contract design, trading rules, technical system and risk control are all done for crude oil futures, a leading commodity. Both are expected to make their debut in 2013. The conditions are ripe for the launch of bulk commodity options, what marketers are the most looking forward to. All of the four futures exchanges are digging into simulated trading currently and are expected to launch it within 2013. By then, the picture of the futures market will be totally different. What deserves attention is that continuous trading of gold and silver futures is on the countdown and is expected to come into operation in mid-to-late June. This heralds a new opportunity for the commodity futures market.

Foreign Exchange and Gold Market Development Policy

Highlights of Foreign Exchange and Gold Market Development Policy in 2012

Table 5. 9   **Foreign Exchange and Gold Market Policy in 2012**

Date	Title of Policy	File No. or Issued by
6 January	Single bank platform was launched on the foreign currency pair market	China Foreign Exchange Trade System
6 February	*Notice on Issues Concerning RMB Settlement of Export of Goods by Domestic Enterprises*	PBC [2012] No. 23
12 March	*Notice on Foreign Exchange Management Issues Concerning Exchange Rate Exposure in Precious Metal Business of Banks*	SAFE [2012] No. 8
14 April	Expanded the Floating Band of the RMB Exchange Rate against the US Dollar in the Foreign Exchange Market	PBC Announcement [2012] No. 4
16 April	*Notice of SAFE on Issues Concerning the Improvement of Administration of Banks' Synthetic Positions in Foreign Exchange Settlement and Sale*	SAFE [2012] No. 26
24 April	*Administrative Measures for the Pilot Program of Domestic and Foreign Currency Exchange Franchise Business to Individuals*	SAFE [2012] No. 27
29 May	*Announcement on Starting Direct Trading between the RMB and the Japanese Yen*	SAFE Announcement
5 June	*Letter on the Focused-supervision List of Enterprises in RMB Settlement for Goods Export*	PBC [2012] No. 381
31 July	*Notice on Issues Concerning the Opening and Use of RMB Bank Settlement Accounts of Overseas Institutions*	PBC [2012] No. 183
29 November	*Interbank Gold Bilateral Transaction Rules* and *Interbank Gold Bilateral Transaction Product Guide of Shanghai Gold Exchange*	Shanghai Gold Exchange
December	*Notice on Issues Concerning Strengthening Gold Market Business Management of Banking Institutions*	PBC [2012] No. 238

Source: data collected by the research group.

Analysis of Foreign Exchange and Gold Market Development Policy in 2012

In September, 2012, the State Council endorsed *The 12th Five-Year Plan for the Development and Reform of the Financial Industry* (the *Plan*) jointly drafted by the PBC, CBRC, CSRC, CIRC and SAFE. As highlighted in the Plan, the fundamental role of the financial market in resource configuration will be cemented, the RMB exchange rate formation mechanism will be perfected, capital account convertibility of RMB will come true step by step, and a multi-level financial market system will be consummated during the 12th Five-Year. Moreover, it is required under the Plan to drive steady and proper development of the gold market, improve the gold market service system and perfect the gold market storage, transportation, delivery and gold account service system during the 12th Five-Year.

In 2012, along with progress in liberalization of RMB exchange rates, the foreign exchange market of China kept expanding in terms of depth and breath. In April, 2012, the PBC decided to expand the floating band of the RMB exchange rate against the US dollar in the foreign exchange market. In concert with this bold move, SAFE adopted the following measures. First, it fine-tuned the administration of banks' synthetic positions in foreign exchange settlement and sale, abolished the provisional lower limit to positions under cash basis of accounting for banks and facilitated flexible and preemptive foreign exchange trading and risk management by banks. Second, it widened the scope of the pilot program of domestic and foreign currency exchange franchise business to individuals. Third, it simplified market admission management for foreign exchange swap and currency swap businesses.

During 2012, the bilateral exchange rate of the RMB against the US dollar in the domestic foreign exchange market appeared quite stable, but the exchange rate of the RMB against a basket of currencies appreciated. At end-2012, the central parity of the RMB against the US dollar was 6. 2855 yuan per US dollar, up 0. 2 percent from end-2011, and it appreciated by a cumulative 31. 7 percent since the beginning of the exchange-rate reform in 2005. In 2012, the central parity of the RMB against the euro and the Japanese yen recorded a depreciation of 1. 9 percent and an appreciation of 11 percent on cumulative basis, respectively. According to BIS data, in 2012, the nominal effective RMB exchange rate against a basket of currencies appreciated 1. 7 percent and the real effective exchange rate excluding inflation factor appreciated 2. 2 percent. From the beginning of the RMB exchange rate reform in 2005, the nominal and real effective exchange rate of the RMB appreciated 23. 3 percent and 31. 9 percent on cumulative basis. On the domestic foreign exchange market, RMB exchange rate showed stronger resilience and marked two-way fluctuations in 2012. During the 243 trading days of 2012, overnight volatility of the central parity of the RMB against the US dollar averaged 44 basis points, almost flat with that of 2011. The central parity appreciated overnight on 122 out of the 243 trading days and depreciated on the remaining 121 trading days.

In 2012, the turnover of the domestic RMB foreign exchange market totaled 9. 18 trillion US dollars, up 6. 2 percent from the preceding year. Among this total, the turnover of the bank client market and the interbank foreign exchange market amounted to 3. 21 trillion US dollars and 5. 97 trillion US dollars, respectively. Foreign exchange spot trading declined slightly. In 2012, the turnover of foreign exchange spot transactions totaled 6. 14 trillion US dollars, down 1. 8 percent year on year. Its share of total turnover of the foreign exchange market tumbled to an all-time low of 66. 9 percent. Among this total, the turnover of spot foreign exchange settlement and sale by banks for their clients (excluding performance of forward contracts) was 2. 8 trillion US dollars, a year on year increase of 3. 2 percent; and the turnover of the interbank foreign exchange spot market amounted to 3. 4 trillion US dollars (average daily amount of 13. 8 billion US dollars), down 5. 5 percent from 2011. Foreign exchange spot trading shrank in 2012 for two reasons. First, sharp unilateral fluctuations occurred on the foreign exchange market on several occasions during 2012, and caused a tension on the market and led to inactive trade and weaker liquidity. Second, direct use of RMB in cross-border trade, investment and other economic activities reduced the demand for trading on the domestic foreign exchange market to some extent. Interbank foreign currency pair trading declined mildly. In 2012, the turnover of nine foreign currency pairs combined was equivalent to 85. 7 billion US dollars, a decrease of 9. 5 percent year on year. Among this total, spot transactions took up the biggest share, with a turnover equivalent to 62. 2 billion US dollars (average daily amount of 260 million US dollars), down 27. 4 percent from 2011. Broken down by currency, USD/HKD and euro/USD dominated spot transactions, and AUD/USD transactions kept growing for four consecutive years. This situation is in accord with international foreign exchange market landscape and the special economicties between mainland China and the Hong Kong SAR.

International gold price experienced wide shocks in 2012. Gold spot trading on Shanghai Gold Exchange shrank. The trading volume of gold on Shanghai Gold Exchange totaled 6, 350. 2 tons, a decrease of 14. 63 percent year on year, and its turnover posted 2, 150. 634 billion yuan, a decrease of 13. 18 percent year on year. Among this total, the trading volume during night session totaled 1, 273. 8 tons, a decrease of 516. 13 tons, or 28. 84 percent, year on year, and represented 20. 06 percent of total volume, down four percentage points year on year. The trading volume of all domestic OTC gold businesses of commercial banks as a whole edged up.

Main financial policies for the domestic foreign exchange market and gold market in 2012 are described as follows:

Liberalization reform of the interbank foreign exchange market was pushed forward and the floating band of the RMB exchange rate against the US dollar was expanded to 1 percent

As stated under Announcement [2012] No. 4 of the PBC, the floating band of RMB trading prices against the US dollar on the interbank spot foreign exchange market was expanded to 1 percent from 0. 5 percent, effective from April 16, 2012. That is to say, RMB trading prices against the US dollar on the interbank spot foreign exchange market may float up or down to a maximum of 1 percent around the central parity of the RMB against the US dollar quoted by China Foreign Exchange Trade System every day. The spread between the highest spot selling price and the lowest spot buying price of US dollar offered by designated exchange banks to clients must not exceed the central parity of the same day by 2 percent, compared with 1 percent before. As for other rules, *Notice of the People's Bank of China on the Administration of Trading Exchange Rates in the Interbank Foreign Exchange Market and Posted Exchange Rates of Designated Foreign Exchange Banks* (〔2010〕 No. 325) shall still apply. This marked further expansion of intraday floating band of the RMB exchange rate against the US dollar since 2007. It happened against the backdrop of improved balance of payments of China, movement of RMB exchange rate closer to its equilibrium level, and further development of the foreign exchange market, and can heighten the power of market supply and demand in exchange rate formation. As RMB exchange rate nearly comes to its equilibrium level, trade and current account surplus decreases and the funds outstanding for foreign exchange decelerate, the advancement in the RMB exchange rate reform can dampen the expectation for unilateral appreciation of RMB, heighten the role of the market in the RMB exchange rate formation mechanism and enhance resilience of RMB exchange rate.

Speaking of market response, average fluctuation range didn't change obviously before and after the floating band of the RMB spot exchange rate against the US dollar was expanded. As a result of the removal of the lower limit to positions under cash basis of accounting, forward and swap curves finally converged into one swap curve. The volatility of the RMB exchange rate against the US dollar showed a downtrend throughout the year. Implicit volatility was higher than realized volatility and gradually converged with realized volatility. One-year implicit volatility fell within the range of 2. 3 percent to 4. 5 percent and realized volatility within the range of 2. 1 percent to 2. 6 percent. After the floating band of RMB spot trading prices against the US dollar on the interbank foreign exchange market was expanded on April 16, daily maximum fluctuations of trading prices around the central parity averaged 0. 55 percent in the year, higher than 0. 18 percent in 2011. Trading prices continued fluctuating within the depreciation range around the central parity from late May to end-August, but moved to fluctuate within the appreciation range around the central parity after mid-September. Between late October and early December in particular, trading prices touched the 1 percent limit to floating below the central parity repeatedly.

Foreign exchange transaction management was more flexible and the administration of banks' synthetic positions in foreign exchange settlement and sale was perfected

To drive the development of the foreign exchange market, make foreign exchange trading and risk management by banks more flexible and preemptive and facilitate price discovery of RMB exchange rate, SAFE decided to fine-tune the administration of banks' synthetic positions in foreign exchange settlement and sale and abolish the provisional lower limit to positions under cash basis of accounting for banks that had been in force since November, 2010, based on balance of payments, and in accord with widened floating band of the RMB exchange rate against the US dollar on the foreign exchange market on April 16 and strengthened resilience of RMB exchange rate. Article 1 of *Notice of State Administration of Foreign Exchange on Relevant Issues Concerning Strengthening the Administration of Foreign Exchange Business* ([2010] No. 59) and Article 1 of *Notice of State Administration of Foreign Exchange on Relevant Issues Concerning Further Strengthening the Administration of Foreign Exchange Business* ([2011] No. 11) ceased to be in force. Moreover, a positive-negative interval was applied in the management of banks' synthetic positions in foreign exchange settlement and sale. The lower limit was lowered to below zero on the basis of the existing upper-lower limit to synthetic positions in foreign exchange settlement and sale. It marked the end of the compulsory foreign exchange settlement and sale system. After that, businesses and individuals are allowed to keep their foreign exchange receipts at their discretion, banks become more flexible and pre-emptive in foreign exchange trading and risk management and price discovery of RMB exchange rate is promoted.

Direct trading between the RMB and the Japanese yen was introduced

In order to promote bilateral trade between China and Japan, facilitate use of RMB and yen in trade settlement, and meet the needs of economic entities to lower currency conversion cost, authorized by the PBC, China Foreign Exchange Trade System (CFETS) started revamping the trading model of the RMB against the Japanese yen on the interbank foreign exchange market and developing direct trading between the RMB and the Japanese yen from June 1, 2012. According to the provisions, a market making system is adopted for direct trading between RMB and Japanese yen on the interbank foreign exchange market. The market makers shall undertake corresponding obligations, continuously provide the bid-offer price of RMB/JPY and make liquidity available for the market. The formation mechanism of the central parity of RMB against yen will be improved, whereby the central parity of RMB against the Japanese yen is calculated from the direct quotations offered by market markers instead of from the cross rates between the central parity of RMB against the US dollar and the exchange rate of the US dollar against the

Japanese yen. That is to say, CFETS enquires prices from market makers of RMB/JPY direct trading before the foreign exchange market opens on each trading day, and then announces the average of the quoted prices as the central parity of RMB against Yen for the day. CFETS is responsible for the management of direct trading between the RMB and the Japanese yen on the interbank foreign exchange market. The launch of direct trading between the RMB and the Japanese yen can help form direct exchange rate of RMB against the Japanese yen, lower the currency conversion cost of economic entities, promote use of RMB and Japanese yen in bilateral trade and investment, strengthen financial cooperation and support the growing economic and financial ties between China and Japan. The PBC gave a ringing endorsement of this. Since direct trading between the RMB and the Japanese yen was initiated on June 1, 2012, both trading volume and market liquidity improved immensely, with average monthly turnover exceeding 100 billion yuan. All of the ten market markers in direct trading quoted prices actively.

The scope of square-off of exchange rate exposure in precious metal business of banks was widened

In order to properly manage foreign exchange in precious metal business, SAFE widened the applicable scope of the existing policy for square-off of exchange rate exposure in gold business of banks to include silver, platinum and other precious metals, to make it easier for banks to offer precious metal investment products to clients and support keeping of precious metal among the public. Exchange rate exposure in precious metal business refers to a kind of exchange rate exposure to mismatch of domestic and foreign currency that arises from square-off of precious metal open positions on overseas markets after banks conclude precious metal spot transactions denominated in RMB on the domestic market (inclusive of but not limited to gold, silver and platinum). For exchange rate exposure in precious metal business for which record-filing is done, banks may square off the open positions in the same manner as settlement and sale of foreign exchange.

The pilot program of domestic and foreign currency exchange franchise business to individuals was rolled out

To deepen the pilot program of franchise business and drive sustainable and healthy development of domestic and foreign currency exchange franchise business to individuals in the pilot regions, SAFE revised *Administrative Measures for the Pilot Program of Domestic and Foreign Currency Exchange Franchise Business to Individuals*, and put it into force on May 1, 2012. Since roll-out of the pilot program of domestic and foreign currency exchange franchise business to individuals in November, 2009, the number of franchise holders has increased steadily, exchange service is better and the pilot work has led to positive results. *Administrative*

Measures for the Pilot Program of Domestic and Foreign Currency Exchange Franchise Business to Individuals is another impetus to the development of the RMB foreign exchange market. The implementation of *Administrative Measures for the Pilot Program of Domestic and Foreign Currency Exchange Franchise Business to Individuals* offers convenience to franchise holders in terms of market admission and everyday operation under the condition of controllable risks, and reserves room for their future development. Meanwhile, the Administrative Measures lay stress on post event data monitoring and regular on-site and off-site supervision to drive sustainable development of franchise holders.

Single bank platform went live on the foreign currency pair market

On January 6, 2012, China Foreign Exchange Trade System announced single bank platform of the foreign currency pair market going live officially, which stands for an attempt at optimizing the foreign currency pair market structure and trading mechanism. Under this model, one market marker may customize quoted prices for different member banks, and reflect pricing factors such as counterparty credit standing and transaction amount in the spread. Non-anonymous centralized clearing is adopted. As of December 31, 2012, 15 members were granted access to this platform. The trading system is running reliably and trade is active.

The management of gold business of banking institutions was reinforced

The PBC released *Notice on Issues Concerning Strengthening Gold Market Business Management of Banking Institutions* (〔2012〕No. 238) (the *Notice*) in December, 2012, and required banking institutions engaged in gold business to report business performance to the PBC regularly. The *Notice* is about creating a record-filing management system and improving the statistical and monitoring system for gold business, among other issues, and is of significance for regulating the gold business of commercial banks and promoting orderly development of both the floor and OTC gold market.

Interbank gold bilateral transaction was launched

After finishing record-filing with and obtaining the permission of the PBC, Shanghai Gold Exchange started trial run of interbank gold bilateral transaction on December 3, 2012. For this purpose, Shanghai Gold Exchange formulated *Interbank Gold Bilateral Transaction Rules* and *Interbank Gold Bilateral Transaction Product Guide*, in accordance with *Opinions on Promoting Development of the Gold Market* (〔2010〕No. 211), *Shanghai Gold Exchange Business Supervisory Rules* (〔2011〕No. 93), *Shanghai Gold Exchange Articles of Association*, and other rules and regulations, in order to assure the order of interbank gold bilateral transaction and protect the legitimate rights and interests of market participants. According to the rules, market participants approved by Shanghai Gold Exchange may conduct gold bilateral transactions through the foreign exchange trading system of China Foreign Exchange Trade System, and do clearing and delivery via Shanghai Gold Exchange. So far, 20 institutions were granted access to interbank gold bilateral transaction, including not only domestic commercial banks such as Industrial and Commercial Bank of China, China Construction Bank, Bank of China and Agricultural Bank of China, but also China limited corporations of HSBC, Standard Chartered Bank, ANZ Bank and United Overseas Bank. The launch of interbank gold bilateral transaction can help meet diversified investment needs of gold investors, enrich trading modes, deepen the function of the market and form a multi-level gold market trading system.

Gold ETF was proceeded to the examination and approval stage

Research and development of gold ETF started as early as three years ago. Since 2009, Hua An Fund Management Co., Ltd has been discussing the feasibility of gold ETF with Shanghai Stock Exchange and Shanghai Gold Exchange. Gold ETF is an important measure to support the construction of Shanghai as an international financial center and respond to the call of Shanghai municipal government for "innovation-driven transformation and development". The operation of gold ETF will involve interconnection between the ETF market and the gold market of China. It has been put on the agenda as one of the main tasks and strategies for the construction of Shanghai as an international financial center during the 12th Five-Year.

Illegal gold exchanges were shut down

Tempted by rapid increase in gold price and the zeal of investors, some regions and institutions opened unauthorized exchanges (gold trading platforms) in the last couple of years. These exchanges (gold trading platforms) were not well-managed, transgressed against the laws and regulations and exposed risks. To assure well-regulated development of the gold market, the PBC took a concerted action with relevant authorities to crack down on illegal exchanges dealing in gold and gold derivatives in the second half of 2011, and released *Notice on Strengthening Administration of Gold Exchange or Gold Trading Platform* (the *Notice*) at the end of the same year. As highlighted under the *Notice*, no locality, institution or individual, other than Shanghai Gold Exchange and Shanghai Futures Exchange, is allowed to open gold exchange, or to set up gold trading platform under other exchanges. Any work in progress must be stopped immediately. For those already in operation, new transaction must not be accepted. After the action was taken, the gold market went back to the right track. These administrative measures forcefully assure a well-regulated market, and lay the foundation for innovation and development of the financial market. The gold market of China is currently made up of the gold business of Shanghai Gold Exchange and the gold futures business of Shanghai Futures Exchange. These two markets grow together with the gold industry.

Policy Evaluation and Outlook

The 12th Five-Year Plan for the financial industry suggests sharpening up the ability to prevent and control risks in foreign exchange and balance of payments in the foreign exchange market. The Chinese government's *Annual Work Report* released on NPC and CPPCC in early 2013 clarified the goal to improve balance of payments. For this purpose, it is necessary to create a sound and sustainable balance of payments mechanism according to the policy of "expanding domestic demand, adjusting economic structure, narrowing external surplus and facilitating balanced growth". It is necessary to continue optimizing the RMB exchange rate formation mechanism, enhance exchange rate resilience, accelerate development of the foreign exchange market and give play to the role of the market in regulating balance of payments. In view of the progressive nature of the reform of foreign exchange administration, in foreign exchange policy-making in 2013, the present global economic and financial situation will be taken into full consideration and effort will continue to be focused on serving the real economy and sharpening up the ability to prevent and control risks in foreign exchange and balance of payments. Under the reform theme of changing the way of foreign exchange administration, foreign exchange administration will be optimized in all respects. In January, 2013, the SAFE held a National Foreign Exchange Administration Workshop. The priorities outlined on the meeting echoed with the above-mentioned expectations. To be more specific, the first task is to deepen the reform of the foreign exchange administration system in all respects, and to make trade and investment much more convenient; the second task is to strengthen macroscopic analysis and regional analysis of foreign exchange and to enhance foreign exchange monitoring and analytical ability and efficiency; the third one is to optimize cross-border fund flow monitoring system and to firmly maintain economic and financial safety of the country; the forth one is to press ahead with entity supervision, and to change old concepts and methods of foreign exchange administration; the fifth one is to manage and use foreign exchange reserves properly and to improve the operation and management system of large-scaled foreign exchange reserves.

As specified under the *12th Five-Year Plan for the Development and Reform of the Financial Industry*, it is important to drive a steady and proper development of the gold market, to improve the gold market service system and to improve the gold market storage, transportation, delivery and account service system during the the 12th Five-Year period. The Shanghai Gold Exchange wishes to grow bigger and stronger during the 12th Five-Year period, through innovations in products and services, for example, by launching innovative products like the palladium and gold ETF, developing gold lease, lengthening trading hours, and tapping into the OTC bilateral transactions on the interbank market. Regarding the gold market prospect in 2013, it is necessary to strengthen infrastructure construction, tighten administration of gold business by financial institutions, to set up efforts on innovations, to develop the gold lease market, to fine-tune interbank gold bilateral transactions and to heighten liquidity. Commercial banks are encouraged to develop gold impawn financing and gold derivatives. More institutional investors will be attracted to join in the gold market and to optimize the investor mix. The gold market of China is currently made up of the gold business by the Shanghai Gold Exchange and the gold futures business by the Shanghai Futures Exchange. These two exchanges grow together with the gold industry.

CHAPTER 6

Financial Regulatory Policy

Highlights of Regulatory Policy of the PBC

Highlights of Regulatory Policy of the PBC in 2012

Table 6. 1   Regulatory Policy of the PBC in 2012

Date	File Name and Issued by	File No.
6 February	*Notice on Issues Concerning RMB Settlement of Export of Goods by Domestic Enterprises* (the PBC, MOF, Ministry of Commerce, General Administration of Customs, State Administration of Taxation and CBRC)	PBC [2012] No. 23
16 February	The General Office of the PBC issued *Notice on Issues Concerning Differentiated Deposit Reserve Requirement Ratio to Be Adopted for the County-level Division for Rural Financial Services in the Pilot Reform of Agricultural Bank of China in 2012*	PBC [2012] No. 24
20 February	*Opinions on Financial Support for Accelerated Development of the Tourism Industry* (the PBC, NDRC, National Tourism Administration, CBRC, CSRC, CIRC and SAFE)	PBC [2012] No. 32
1 March	*Opinions on Improving Financial Services for the Reform and Development of Water Resources* (the PBC, NDRC, MOF, the Ministry of Water Resources, CBRC, CSRC and CIRC)	PBC [2012] No. 51
6 March	The PBC issued *Notice on Properly Managing and Using Re-lending in Support of Agriculture and Encouraging Expansion of Lending to Agriculture, Farmers and the Countryside*	PBC [2012] No. 58
31 March	The PBC issued *Notice on Putting into Practice Subsequent Monitoring and Performance Assessment Policies, Incentives and Constraints for the Use of a Portion of New Deposits at County Financial Corporations in Bill Payment for Special Projects under Local Loan Assessment Policy and the Reform of Rural Credit Cooperatives in 2011*	PBC [2012] No. 86

Continued

Date	File Name and Issued by	File No.
17 May	*Notice on Relevant Matters Concerning Further Expanding the Pilot Program of Credit Asset Securitization* (co-released by the PBC, CBRC and the MOF)	PBC [2012] No. 127
5 June	*Letter on the Focused-supervision List of Enterprises in RMB Settlement for Goods Export* (the PBC, MOF, the Ministry of Commerce, General Administration of Customs, State Administration of Taxation, and CBRC)	PBC [2012] No. 381
31 July	The PBC released *Notice on Issues Concerning the Opening and Use of RMB Bank Settlement Accounts of Overseas Institutions*	PBC [2012] No. 183
23 August	The PBC issued *Notice on Implementing the Pilot Program of Expanding Applicable Scope of Relending in Support of Agriculture*	PBC [2012] No. 207
27 September	*Circular of the PBC on Tightening Management of Prepaid Card Business*	PBC [2012] No. 234
27 September	*Administrative Measures for Prepaid Card Business of Payment Institutions*	PBC Announcement [2012] No. 12
18 December	Matters Related to NAFMII's Releasing *Master Agreement for Bond Repurchase Transactions on the Interbank Market of China*	PBC Announcement [2012] No. 17
31 December	The PBC and CSRC signed Memorandum on *Strengthening Cooperation in Supervision over Securities and Futures and Jointly Maintaining Financial Stability*	

Note: This announcement only has a reference number, no file name. For the convenience of readers, the research group summarized the file content herein.

Source: sorted by the research group.

Analysis of Regulatory Policy of the PBC in 2012

In 2012, the PBC attached more importance to a steady economic growth, strengthened and improved financial macro control, in line with the keystone of growth amidst stability. As for regulatory policy, the PBC pressed ahead with the reform and development of the financial industry in an earnest manner, maintained financial stability and improved financial services and management in all respects. In accordance with *the Act of the People's Bank of China*, the PBC is responsible for supervising and managing the interbank loan market, the interbank bond market, the interbank foreign exchange market, and the gold market; for keeping the clearing and settlement system run soundly; and for monitoring anti-money laundering capital. Main regulatory policies of the PBC in 2012 have been formulated around its legal responsibilities and the specific requirements of the State Council.

Credit Policy

In 2012, the PBC encouraged financial institutions to boost credit support to the agricultural sector, farmers and the countryside by making use of the agricultural re-lending policy. In March, the PBC issued *Notice on Properly Managing and Using Re-lending in Support of*

Agriculture and Encouraging Expansion of Lending to Agriculture, Farmers and the Countryside and required all branches to make the most of the re-lending policy to encourage financial institutions to make more agriculture-related loans and support sustainable and solid growth of the rural economy. In August, the PBC issued *Notice on Implementing the Pilot Program to Expand Applicable Scope of Relending in Support of Agriculture* and started pilot work in the provinces of both Shanxi and Heilongjiang. While the rule remained unchanged that agriculture-related loans account for no less than 70 percent of all loans, the applicable re-lending financial institutions in support of agriculture in the pilot regions were expanded from rural commercial banks, rural cooperative banks, rural credit cooperatives and village and township banks based in counties, towns and villages to these four types of savings financial institutions based in cities.

In 2012, the PBC allocated an additional re-lending quota of 68.1 billion yuan cumulatively in support of agriculture, which was mainly used in the western regions and major grain-producing provinces (regions) with a high percentage of agriculture-related loans. As of the end of 2012, the agriculture-related re-lending quota totaled 220.3 billion yuan and the outstanding balance was 137.5 billion yuan, an increase of 28.1 billion yuan from the beginning of the year. Agriculture-related re-lending capital in 2012 totaled 209 billion yuan, an increase of 38.2 billion yuan from last year. Broken down by region, the agriculture-related re-lending quota and outstanding balance for both the western regions and major grain producing provinces (regions) accounted for more than 90% of the national totals. The re-lending support to rural financial institutions had salient effect on expanding credit support to agriculture, farmers and the countryside. As of the end of 2012, outstanding agriculture-related loans of all rural financial institutions reached 5.3 trillion yuan, up 16 percent on an annual basis. Generally speaking, the re-lending policy in support of agriculture worked positively to have encouraged financial institutions to increase more agriculture-rated loans and improve rural financial services, and helped to realize grain production growth for nine consecutive years and propelled development and bettered the environment of the countryside.

Deepen financial reforms

In 2012, the PBC made its effort to deepen the reform of large commercial banks. Significant progress was made in the pilot reform at the Agricultural Bank of China to build a dedicated division for rural financial services. The reform proposal for China Export & Credit Insurance Corporation was put into practice. Regional pilot programs of the financial reform in the Pearl River Delta, both Wenzhou and Lishui cities of the Zhejiang province, and Quanzhou city of the Fujian province were pushed forward at a steady pace. The PBC, the NDRC, the National Tourism Administration, the CBRC, the CSRC, the CIRC and the SAFE co-released

Opinions on Financial Support for Accelerated Development of the Tourism Industry and required financial institutions to strengthen and improve credit management and service for the tourism industry, to improve and optimize clearing and settlement services for the tourism industry and to boost tourism consumer credit. The PBC, the NDRC, the MOF, the Ministry of Water Resources, the CBRC, the CSRC and the CIRC co-released *Opinions on Improving Financial Services for the Reform and Development of Water Resources* and required financial institutions to make double efforts and design innovative financial products and services well-suited to the attributes, models and financing features of water resource projects, to expand financial support to water resource construction, to explore risk diversification and policy guarantee mechanisms for financial support to the reform and development of water resources and to enable the financial sector to serve the real sector better.

Expand cross-border use of the RMB

The PBC, the MOF, the Ministry of Commerce, the General Administration of Customs, the State Administration of Taxation, and the CBRC issued *Letter on the Focused-supervision List of Enterprises in the RMB Settlement for Goods Export* on June 5. All Chinese enterprises qualified for imports and exports are allowed to use the RMB as the currency of denomination, settlement, payment and receipts. On July 31, the PBC released *Notice on Issues Concerning the Opening and Use of the RMB Bank's Settlement Accounts of Overseas Institutions*, and gave permission to overseas institutions to use the RMB bank's settlement accounts, bringing greater convenience in trade and investment from abroad. As a result, the RMB settlement of cross-border trade and foreign direct investment swelled. The RMB settlement of cross-border trade spread out and international monetary cooperation expanded further in 2012.

Supervise the financial market

Under the leadership of the PBC, an inter-ministry coordination mechanism for corporate bonds was built in 2012. On May 17, the PBC, the CBRC and the MOF issued *Notice on Relevant Matters Concerning Further Expanding the Pilot Program of Credit Asset Securitization*, to fine-tune the administration of credit asset securitization and promote well-regulated development of the interbank bond market. In 2012, the PBC also launched interbank gold bilateral transaction and cracked down on illegal trading of gold and gold derivatives effectively.

Monitor financial risks and maintain financial stability

In 2012, the PBC took effective precautions against systematic financial risks, and tightened monitoring and analysis of private borrowing, real estate and governmental financing platforms. From a global, systematic and forward-looking perspective, it properly addressed the relationship between reasonable growth of credit and the improvement in the quality of bank loans, with a view to prevent proliferation of financial risks and moral risks. On December 31, the PBC and the CSRC signed a *Memorandum on Strengthening Cooperation in Supervision over Securities and Futures business and Jointly Maintaining Financial Stability*, in an effort to fill up the manpower deficiency in municipal and county-level supervision over securities and futures business, to enhance the efficiency of financial supervision and jointly maintain financial stability, by making use of the widespread network of the PBC. In general, the PBC intensified monitoring of financial risks, undertook all sorts of financial stability stress tests and pressed ahead with robustness evaluation of financial institutions in 2012.

Credit Information Collection and other regulatory policies

At the end of 2012, *Regulation on the Administration of Credit Information Collection Industry (Draft)* drafted by the PBC was deliberated and adopted by the State Council.[①] The PBC also pushed forward the standardization of financial statistics and steady transformation of accounting practices. The second-generation payment system and the Accounting Data Centralized System (ACS) of the central bank were deployed on schedule. *Administrative Measures for Prepaid Card Business of Payment Institutions* were formulated to effectively regulate the conduct of prepaid card business by payment institutions and prevent payment risks. The "zero-tolerance" action against counterfeit money also made concrete achievements. Nation-wide roll-out of institution credit code was almost completed. Anti-money laundering supervision was deepened. China became the first developing country that complies with the standards of the Financial Action Task Force on Money Laundering (FATF). Two pieces of regulations, such as the *Provisional Procedures for Handling of Syndicated Loans*, and 22 pieces of specifications, such as the *Provisions on the Entrusted Loans Business of Financial Trust and Investment Companies*, were repealed.

Policy Evaluation and Outlook

The financial policies made by the PBC in 2012 will continue to work out in 2013. As the policies of the PBC were beginning to take effect in 2012, it is foreseeable that the PBC will continue to uphold these policies. It will hold fast to the keystone of growth amidst stability and give the utmost importance to the policies for promoting financial stability and developing market economy.

Main regulatory policies of the PBC in 2013 will comprise the following respects:

Credit Policy

The PBC will continue to improve the evaluation of the guiding effect of credit policies,

---

① *Regulation on the Administration of Credit Investigation Industry* (Decree No. 631 of the State Council, the PRC) was adopted on the 228th executive meeting of the State Council held on December 26, 2012, and came into force on March 15, 2013.

guide financial institutions to extend credit support to key projects in progress or continued constructions, in agriculture, related to farmers and in the countryside, related to small and micro-sized enterprises, modern service industry and emerging industries, to better financial services for the benefit of people's livelihood, endorse financial projects that involve people's livelihood, including employment, poverty relief, and student loans, and to implement a differentiated housing loan policy.

Financial Reforms

The PBC will continue to urge large commercial banks and other large-sized financial enterprises to optimize rules related to modern financial enterprises, deepen the reform of rural credit cooperatives, press ahead with the pilot reform at the Agricultural Bank of China to build a dedicated division for rural financial services, perfect the rural financial service system through unremitted reforms, propel and deepen the reform of policy financial institutions, press ahead with the reform of interest rate liberalization, fine-tune the RMB exchange rate formation mechanism, put into force the policies from the central government, support accelerated development of private financial institutions, deepen the reform of key financial fields, and endeavour for better-quality and higher-level financial services for the real economy.

Expansion of Cross-border Use of RMB

The PBC will simplify the RMB settlement formalities and approval process for cross-border trade, continue to support the development of the Hong Kong SAR and other offshore RMB markets, and encourage the use and circulation of RMBs abroad. The PBC will also initiate cross-border RMB business for individuals, press ahead with the pilot program of the RQFII steadily, and do well in preparations for the pilot work of the Qualified Domestic Institutional Investors (QDII2). In addition, the PBC will continue to drive bilateral currency swaps and put into force the bilateral currency settlement treaties.

Regulate Financial Markets

The PBC will continue to drive innovations in bond products and interest rate risk management instruments, press ahead with the pilot program of credit asset securitization, do well in market admission and regulation of the bond issuances in the Hong Kong SAR by domestic financial institutions and the investment by foreign institutions in the interbank bond market, reinforce information disclosure, credit rating and other constraint mechanisms and regulate the market marker system, clearing agent and money broker business.

Monitor and Screen Financial Risk Rigorously

The PBC will firmly defend against systematic and regional financial risks, consummate the monitoring, evaluation and alarm system for systematic and regional financial risks, refine risk prevention and response plan, monitor risks in non-financial institutions with financing capacity closely, explore on-site evaluation of financial institutions' robustness and the business at risk of the banking sector, and carry on all tasks relatede to creating a deposit insurance system.

Highlights of Regulatory Policy of CBRC

Highlights of Regulatory Policy of CBRC in 2012

Table 6. 2   **Regulatory Policy of CBRC in 2012**

Date	File Name	File No.
9 February	Notice of CBRC on Putting to Rights Malpractices of Banking Institutions	CBRC [2012] No. 3
24 February	Notice of CBRC on Issuing Green Credit Guidelines *Green Credit Guidelines*	CBRC [2012] No. 4
31 March	Notice of CBRC on Improving the Client Complaint Handling Mechanisms of Banking Institutions to Effectively Protect Financial Consumers	CBRC [2012] No. 13
14 May	Notice of the General Office of CBRC on Strengthening Financial Services to Disabled Clients by Banking Institutions	CBRC [2012] No. 144
26 May	Implementation Opinions of CBRC on Encouraging and Guiding Private Capital into the Banking Sector	CBRC [2012] No. 27
8 June	*Administrative Measures for the Capital of Commercial Banks (for Trial Implementation)*	CBRC No. 1 Decree, 2012
25 June	Guidelines of the General Office of CBRC on Small-/Medium-sized Rural Financial Institutions' Implementing Innovative Financial Projects for the Benefit of Farmers and the Agriculture	CBRC [2012] No. 189
25 June	Guidelines of the General Office of CBRC on Small-/Medium-sized Rural Financial Institutions' Implementing the Project of Financial Services to the Countryside and Communities	CBRC [2012] No. 190
25 June	Guidelines of the General Office of CBRC on Small-/Medium-sized Rural Financial Institutions' Implementing the Sunshine Credit Project	CBRC [2012] No. 191
4 September	Interim Provisions for Commercial Banks' Supervision over Capital Management with Advanced Methods	CBRC [2012] No. 254
19 September	Notice of CBRC on Issuing *Administrative Measures for Loans to Farmers* *Administrative Measures for Loans to Farmers*	CBRC [2012] No. 50
7 December	Guidelines of CBRC on Innovations in Capital Instruments of Commercial Banks	CBRC [2012] No. 56
7 December	Notice of CBRC on Issues Concerning Transitional Arrangements for the Implementation of *Administrative Measures for the Capital of Commercial Banks (for Trial Implementation)*	CBRC [2012] No. 57

Source: data collected by the research group.

Analysis of Regulatory Policy of CBRC in 2012

In 2012, CBRC boosted healthy development of the banking sector by "defending the bottom line, strengthening services, tightening internal control and driving transformation". The banking sector performed soundly in general, with accelerating growth of assets, reliable asset quality and return rate, and commercial banks improved their risk-handling and capital capability, as well as operational efficiency. As of the end of December, 2012, the outstanding NPLs of commercial banks totalled 492. 9 billion yuan, marking an increase of 64. 7 billion yuan on a year-on-year basis. The NPL ratio was 0. 95 percent, down 0. 01 percentage points on a year-on-year basis. The liquidity ratio increased by 2. 7 percentage points on a year-on-year basis to 45. 8 percent. The loan-deposit ratio was 65. 3 percent, up 0. 5 percentage points on a year-on-year basis. The RMB excess reserves rate was 3. 5 percent, up 0. 4 percentage points on a year-on-year basis. Commercial banks realized an accumulative net profit of 1. 24 trillion yuan in the year, up 18. 9 percentage points on a year-on-year basis. The average ROA was 1. 3 percent, flat with that of last year. The average ROE was 19. 8 percent, down 0. 6 percentage points on a year-on-year basis. The weighted average capital adequacy ratio was 13. 3 percent, with a year-on-year increase of 0. 5 percentage points. The weighted average core capital adequacy ratio was 10. 6 percent, up 0. 4 percentage points on a year-on-year basis. (For details, please see Major Supervisory Indicators of Commercial Banks (Corporations) below.)

Table 6. 3   Major Supervisory Indicators of Commercial Banks (Corporations)

Unit: RMB100 million, %

Time / Item	2012			
	Q1	Q2	Q3	Q4
1. Credit Risk Indicators				
NPLs	4, 382	4, 564	4, 788	4, 929
Of which: Substandard	1, 801	1, 960	2, 028	2, 176
Doubtful	1, 909	1, 934	2, 074	2, 122
Loss	672	670	685	630
NPL Ratio	0. 94	0. 94	0. 95	0. 95
Of which: Substandard	0. 39	0. 40	0. 40	0. 42
Doubtful	0. 41	0. 40	0. 41	0. 41
Loss	0. 14	0. 14	0. 14	0. 12
Provision	12, 594	13, 244	13, 884	14, 564

Continued

Time Item	2012			
	Q1	Q2	Q3	Q4
Provision Coverage Ratio	287. 40	290. 18	289. 97	295. 51
2. Liquidity Indicators				
Liquidity Ratio	45. 66	46. 69	45. 23	45. 83
Loan-Deposit Ratio	64. 53	64. 33	65. 28	65. 31
RMB Excess Reserves Rate	3. 03	2. 74	2. 66	3. 51
3. Performance Indicators				
Net Profit (Current Year Accumulative)	3, 260	6, 616	9, 810	12, 386 *
ROA	1. 43	1. 41	1. 39	1. 28
ROE	22. 34	22. 29	21. 54	19. 85
NIM	2. 76	2. 73	2. 77	2. 75
NOINAC	20. 55	20. 63	19. 47	19. 83
CIR	29. 46	29. 52	30. 46	33. 10
4. Capital Adequacy Indicators				
Core Capital	55, 980	58, 754	61, 726	64, 340
Subordinated Capital	14, 819	15, 746	15, 853	17, 585
Capital Deduction Item	3, 834	3, 919	3, 863	4, 057
On-balance-sheet Risk-weighted Capital	449, 785	467, 221	484, 589	506, 604
Off-balance-sheet Risk-weighted Capital	71, 843	75, 284	76, 563	76, 108
Market Risk Capital Charge	315	342	372	388
Capital Adequacy Ratio	12. 74	12. 91	13. 03	13. 25
Core Capital Adequacy Ratio	10. 31	10. 41	10. 58	10. 62
5. Market Risk Indicators				
Accumulative Foreign Exchange Exposure Position Ratio	4. 25	5. 18	4. 65	3. 92
6. NPLs by Institutions				

Continued

Time	2012							
	Q1		Q2		Q3		Q4	
Institution	NPLs	NPL Ratio	NPLs	NPL Ratio	NPLs	NPL Ratio	NPLs	NPL Ratio
Commercial banks	4,382	0.94	4,564	0.94	4,788	0.95	4,929	0.95
SOCBs	2,994	1.04	3,020	1.01	3,070	1.00	3,095	0.99
JSCBs **	608	0.63	657	0.65	743	0.70	797	0.72
City Commercial Banks **	359	0.78	403	0.82	424	0.85	419	0.81
Rural Commercial Banks	374	1.52	426	1.57	487	1.65	564	1.76
Foreign Banks	48	0.49	58	0.58	63	0.62	54	0.52

Note: * cumulative net profit from January to December.

** In September, 2012, Shenzhen Development Bank and Ping An Bank merged to form the new Ping An Bank. Figures in the preceding table were not adjusted on comparable basis.

Source: http://www.cbrc.gov.cn.

In summary, in 2012, the CBRC mainly adopted regulatory policies in the following aspects:

Reinforce control over capital of commercial banks and come into compliance with international regulatory standards

In June 2012, the CBRC issued the *Administrative Measures for the Capital of Commercial Banks* (*for Trial Implementation*) (hereinafter 'the *Capital Measures*') which provides for regulatory capital requirements, capital adequacy ratio calculation, capital definition, credit risk-weighted asset measurement, market risk-weighted asset measurement, operational risk-weighted asset measurement, internal capital adequacy assessment procedures, capital adequacy ratio inspection as well as information disclosure requirements. Overall, the new regulatory capital system is not only in compliance with uniform international standards, but also reflects the objective requirements of promoting prudent operation of the banking sector and increasing its ability to service the real economy. The adoption of new regulatory standards will play a positive role in the steady operation of the banking sector and for the stable and healthy development of national economy.

In September 2012, the CBRC issued the *Interim Provisions for Supervision over Commercial Banks' Capital Management with Advanced Methods*, which specify the standards of banks adopting senior approaches and provide for approving procedures, approving conditions and subsequent inspection on senior approaches. In December 2012, the CBRC issued the *Guiding Opinions on Capital Instrument Innovation of Commercial Banks*, which sets forth basic principles for capital instrument innovation by commercial banks, specifys determining standards of qualified capital instruments and puts forth requirements for proceeding with capital instrument innovation. In December 2012, the CBRC issued the *Notice on Transitional Arrangements in Respect of Adoption of the Capital Measures* which specifies regulatory requirements for capital adequacy ratios in different years in the transitional period. On 1 January 2013, commercial banks shall satisfy minimum capital requirements, and domestic banks of systemic importance shall also satisfy additional capital requirements. At the end of 2013, the reserve capital ratio shall be 0.5%, and shall increase by 0.4% each year in the following five years. By the end of 2013, domestic banks of systemic importance shall have their tier-1 core capital adequacy ratio, tier-1 capital adequacy ratio and capital adequacy ratio arrive at 6.5%, 7.5% and 9.5% respectively, and other banks shall have their tier-1 core capital adequacy ratio, tier-1 capital adequacy ratio and capital adequacy ratio arrive at 5.5%, 6.5% and 8.5% respectively.

Rigorously control systemic and regional financial risks

In order to prevent systemic and regional financial risks and maintain safe and steady operation of the banking sector, confronted with the up-bound risk potential in the banking sector, in 2012, the CBRC purposely reinforced control over and set guidance in the area of platforms, real estates, incidents, off-balance sheet business and IT risks. Meanwhile, on the basis of in-depth studies, the CBRC independently made judgements, prudently analyzed and properly curbed new credit risks in certain industries, clustering risks among certain enterprises as well as risks associated with private finance and corporate guarantees in certain regions. Basically, the CBRC identified, monitored and reported risks as early as possible, controlled and handled risks promptly, effectively prevented risks from wide spreading and eliminated symptoms of systemic and regional risks.

Maintain control over non-bank financial institutions

In 2012, the CBRC internally issued the *Guidelines for Onsite Inspection of Trust Companies* and *Procedures for Joint Onsite Inspection Conference of Trust Companies*, which specify responsibilities of local CBRC offices, regulate conferences of joint onsite inspection of trust companies, make offsite supervision of trust business more effective and ensures the quality of such inspections. The CBRC repeatedly emphasized risk control in the trusts sector, reinforced prevention of risks associated with real estate trusts, platform loans, bank-trusts cooperation as well as other trusts business, and urged trust companies to properly perform all the ground work. In order to prevent risks in the trust sector, in mid-January 2012, the CBRC called a halt to bill trusts and through "window guidance", temporarily stopped trust companies from engaging into inter-financial institution deposits business. Subsequently, the regulatory authority provided "window guidance" for real estate trusts and government-trusts cooperation, and called a halt to cash pool trust business in October 2012.

Based on business characteristics offinance companies, the CBRC closely monitored liquidity indicators of finance companies; urged them to pay close attention to current assets and liabilities of their group companies, and to track and study prosperity of the industries they are associated with, so as to project and prevent potential liquidity risks coming from the group. In addition, the CBRC also urged and guided finance companies to operate cash pool of the group steadily and maintain internal and external liabilities of the group at a reasonable size.

Futher to the special inspections on asset quality of financial lease companies conducted in 2011, in 2012, the CBRC urged financial lease companies to implement improvement measures, to establish and improve the asset classification system as well as a mechanism for dynamic adjustment to asset quality classification, and classify assets accurately and set aside adequate provisions, so as to ensure true and accurate asset classification. The CBRC also studied how to proceed with classification-based supervision of financial lease companies.

As for automobile finance companies, currency brokerage firms, and consumer finance companies which were relatively late-born, in 2012, the CBRC basically developed the *Measures for Risk Assessment and Classification-based Supervision of Auto Finance Companies* (Improved Version), revised the *Administrative Measures for Pilot Currency Brokerage Firm Program*, started revising the *Administrative Measures for Pilot Consumption Finance Company Program* and revised the *Measures for Implementation of Issues Subject to Administrative Permit of Non-bank Financial Institutions* and *the Requirements for Catalog and Format of Application for Issues Subject to Administrative Permit of Non-bank Financial Institutions*, creating regulation framework for legitimate development of these institutions.

Continue to educate and serve for financial consumers and establish professional financial consumer protection institutions

In 2012, the CBRC continued to educate and serve for financial consumers, and reinforced public awareness of policies for key business areas. Given that innovative business in the banking sector develops and changes rapidly and is complicated in structure and highly professional, the CBRC organized the China Banking Association and other financial institutions in the banking sector to continuously reinforce public awareness and help the public have proper understanding of such business as wealth management, bank cards, electronic banking, and derivatives. The CBRC helped the public form scientific and correct concepts and understanding of risks and regulatory requirements. Particularly, public awareness was raised for in the area of marketing, suitability assessment, information disclosure, complaint management and risk disclosure in respect of innovative business, so that the public can capitalize on policies and regulations to protect their legitimate interests.

In 2012, the CBRC set up a financial consumer protection bureau whose main functions include developing overall strategies, policies and regulations for protecting financial consumers in the banking sector, establishing and improving the mechanism for servicing, educating and protecting consumers of financial institutions in the banking sector, and establishing and improving the complaints handling mechanism; organizing inspection of consumer protections work of financial institutions in the banking sector, and correct misconduct and impose punishment in accordance with law; and making overall arrangements in publicity and education for financial consumers in the banking sector. In the future, the bureau will play a bigger role in protecting financial consumers.

Policy Evaluation and Outlook

Currently, China's financial industry is on a stage of rapid development. The socio-economic development shows a positive outlook in the long term. Domestic markets provide vast potential for business, and the socialist market economy keeps improving, and industrialization, urbanization, informationization, and agricultural modernization are all proceeding synchronously, which provide good opportunities and favorable conditions for the development of banks and non-bank financial institutions. These are evidenced by satisfactory profitability of financial institutions represented by commercial banks in 2012. However, regulatory authorities should also be clearly aware that amid external impact and pressing need for internal transformation, banks and other financial institutions are taking on more risk and difficulties, raising increasingly the issue of risk control and supervision.

In 2013, the CBRC should accurately set development keynotes, service directions, key reform areas, risk limits, innovation principles and supervision directions for banks and other financial institutions. It shall further improve the modern financial system promoting macroeconomic stability, and supporting development of the real economy; it shall further promote in-depth reforms and transformation of banks and other financial institutions, further improve measures for preventing systemic and regional risks, and promote the improvements in both quality and efficiency of economic and financial development. In 2013, supervision of banks and other financial institutions (mainly in the banking sector) will focus on the following aspects.

Practically prevent and curb financial risks

The primary task is to hold the bottom line of no occurrence of systemic and regional risks, particularly the following three kinds of risks. Firstly, the CBRC require financial institutions to absolutely guard against credit default risks. As for such risks associated with platform loans, the

CBRC will continue to adopt the policy of "total volume control, categorised management, differentiated treatment and gradual elimination", so as to control total debt volume, optimize structure, and support reasonable finance requirements of eligible financing platforms of local government and key projects of the State. As for risks associated with property loans, the CBRC require financial institutions to carefully implement real estate control policies, to meet differentiated requirements of mortgages, and to reinforce name list management and pressure tests. The CBRC will reinforce supervision of enterprises' domino risks and take measures to guard against risks by categories. For risks associated with industries' over-capacity, the CBRC shall stick to the policy of either support or supress to keep risks under control. Secondly, the CBRC shall strictly control risks associated with off-balance sheet business; strictly management design, sale and investment of wealth management products, prohibit unauthorized sales, PE fund sales by banks and misleading sales. Banks shall maintain separate accounting treatments for fixed-income products and floating-income products. Thirdly, the CBRC shall rigorously guard against infection by external risks. The CBRC shall focus on protecting the banking system from external risks associated with private finance and illegal finance. Financial institutions in the banking sector and their employees are prohibited from participating in private finance, and banks' customers are prohibited from re-lending loans. In 2013, close attention should be paid to preventing credit default risks associated with platforms, real estate, high-risk business clusters and over-capacity industries, risks associated with off-balance sheet business through bank-securities cooperations, bank-fund cooperations, bank-insurance cooperations and bank-trust cooperations, as well as preventing infection by external risks involving shadow banking, private finance and illegal finance.

Guide banks and other financial institutions to actively support development of the real economy

The CBRC shall correctly guide the investment direction of loans, reinforce credit support for key areas and weak areas, and regulate utilization of loan to ensure that credit loans are injected into the real economy. Banks shall satisfy reasonable financing requirements of key projects of the State, further improve financial services for small and micro businesses and agriculture, rural areas and farmers, and ensure these growths not slower than the average growth in loans for the current year. Banks shall actively support industry upgrade, environmental protection, consumption, foreign trade and other key areas, and provide financial services to support urbanization. Banks shall moderately shift financial resources to underdeveloped areas and old revolutionary bases, areas inhabited by minorities, frontier areas and poor areas. The CBRC shall urge the banking sector to set price level reasonably, regulate its charges, fully comply with the "seven prohibitions and four publications" rule, and promote reduction in financial costs.

Vigorously promote reform and transformation of the banking sector

Firstly, The CBRC shall actively promote institutional reform, improve lean operation and services of financial institutions in the banking sector. The CBRC shall conduct in-depth studies on the "going global" strategy for China's banking sector, and optimize overseas market exploration. The CBRC shall steadily promote transformation of the rural credit cooperatives, and encourage rural credit cooperatives and rural commercial banks to set up businesses in villages. On the principle of business continuity and "approaching the grass-root level, approaching community and approaching residents", the CBRC shall explore to establish handy service networks in various forms and reinforce financial services in communities. Secondly, The CBRC shall take the opportunity of adopting new capital management measures, steadily push financial institutions in the banking sector to improve corporate governance, reinforce internal control, improve the IT and performance evaluation, set operating targets and evaluation indicators in a scientific manner, and reinforce endogenous powers for transformation in the growth pattern. The CBRC shall guide the market-based reform of interest rates, optimize categories, structure and quality of deposit and loan products, reinforce spread management and cost management for banks' intermediary business, and prudently try out pilot comprehensive operation program. Thirdly, the CBRC shall urge financial institutions in the banking sector to comply with consumer protection requirements, and widely carry out financial consumer education activities and the "sending financial expertise to the countryside" program. Fourthly, the CBRC shall encourage prudent financial innovation, support the banking sector to innovate financial products useful to the real economy, and accelerate the process of capital instrument innovation. Fifthly, the CBRC shall explore and innovate the way for private capital to enter the banking sector, and encourage private capital to participate in establishment of new-type banking financial institutions and reorganization and transformation of existing institutions.

Further maintain orderly development of the trusts sector

As compared with other financial institutions, trust companies have the widest investment scope and the most flexible investment means. Against the backdrop of continuous control over banks' credit supply, trust companies met the financing requirements of businesses and achieved a rapid development in 2012, with assets under their management secondary only to those of banks. However, redemption of the investment under trusts plans will peak in the first half of 2013. It is foreseeable that the CBRC will pay more attention to the orderly development to the trusts sector.

Reinforce improvement in and study on regulatory policies

In 2013, the CBRC will comprehensively reinforce its team building, pay attention to the ideological state of staff, improve organizational structure and emphasize integrity and proper work style, foster positive regulatory culture, continuously improve the ability and expertise of its regulatory teams and improve a regulatory system which organically combines micro and macro prudence. In 2013, as domestic and overseas macro environment becomes more complicated, regulatory tasks will become more arduous. The CBRC will comply with requirements of continued and healthy development, strike a balance among steady growth, inflation control and risk prevention in a scientific manner, and make use of bottom-line thinking, counter-cycle supervision, anticipatory and fine-tuning adjustments to make its work more forward-looking and well-planned.

Highlights of Regulatory Policy of CSRC

Schedule of Major CSRC Regulatory Policies in 2012

Table 6. 4　　　　Major Regulatory Policies for the Securities Sector in 2012

Issued on	Policies	Issued by
2 January	Work Procedures of the Listed Company M&A Review Committee of the CSRC (Revised in 2011)	CSRC
12 January	Reply of the State Council on Approval of Establishing and Improving Inter-ministry Joint Meetings of Exchanges	State Council
3 February	Notice on Adjusting the Application Conditions for Securities Eligible Accounting Firms	MOF, CSRC
12 February	Guidelines for Effectiveness Assessment of Compliance Management of Securities Companies	SAC
23 February	Guiding Opinions of SPC on Providing Judicial Guarantee for Prevention and Elimination of Financial Risks and Promotion of Financial Reform and Development	SPC
7 March	Notice on Improving the System of Temporary Intra-day Suspension on the First Day of Listing of IPO Shares	SZSE
8 March	Notice on Strengthening Supervision over Early Dealings in Newly Listed Shares	SSE
13 March	Notice on Duly Performance by Securities Companies of the Duty to Prevent and Curb Speculation in New Shares	CSRC
19 March	Standards for Practices of Securities Rating Firms	SAC
28 April	Guidelines for Further Deepening the Reform of the New Share Offering System	CSRC
4 May	Notice on Further Implementing Issues Relating to Cash Dividends of Listed Companies	CSRC
22 May	Interpretation of Some Issues on Law Application to Criminal Cases Involving Insider Trading and Insider Information Disclosure	SPC, SPP
8 June	Provisional Regulations on Strengthening Supervision of Abnormal Stock Transactions Related to Material Asset Reorganization of Listed Companies	CSRC

Continued

Issued on	Policies	Issued by
19 June	*Standards for Practices of Securities Analysts*, *Practicing Rules for Securities Study Reports*	SAC
20 June	*Regulation concerning Some Issues on Implementing the Administrative Measures for Domestic Securities Investments of QFIIs*	CSRC
28 June	*Notice on Improving the Delisting System for SSE Listed Companies*	SSE
28 June	*Notice on Improving the Delisting System for Companies listed on Main Board and SME Board of SZSE*	SZSE
31 July	*Provisional Administrative Measures for Honesty Supervision in the Securities and Futures Market*	CSRC
27 September	*Measures for the Management of Information Security and Assurance in the Securities and Futures Industries*	CSRC
31 October	*Administrative Measures for Securities Investments Fund Management Companies*, *Interim Provisions on Administration of Subsidiaries of Securities Investment Fund Management Companies*, *Measures for Pilot Program of Asset Management for Specific Clients of Fund Management Companies*	CSRC
13 December	*Notice concerning Relevant Issues on Deepening the Reform of Fund Approval System*	CSRC
14 December	*Principles for Corporate Governance of Securities Companies*	CSRC
21 December	*Regulatory Requirements for Management and Utilization of Offering Proceeds of Listed Companies*, *Regulatory Guidelines on Document Submission and Review Procedure for Overseas Stock Issuance and Listing of Joint Stock Companies*	CSRC
28 December	Revised *Securities Investment Law* adopted at the 30th meeting of the Standing Committee of NPC	Standing Committee of the NPC

Source: data collected by the research group.

Analysis of Major CSRC Regulatory Policies in 2012

Ramp up efforts to regulatory reform and innovation

In October 2012, during the sixth regulation sorting and triming activities organized by and subject to administrative approval of the State Council, the CSRC cancelled and invalidated 32 items subject to administrative approval in total, representing 10.2% of total number of items removed by departments directly under the State Council. According to statistics, since 2001, the CSRC has cancelled a total of 136 items subject to administrative approval in six batches. Meanwhile, the CSRC ramped up efforts to combat insider trading, and worked closely with other ministries and committees to form a comprehensive crime prevention and control system. Regulatory innovations peaked at the Financial Innovation Conference held in May 2012, and the 11 key areas to be reformed in China's securities industry covered all aspects of securities companies, including business, management, products and operating patterns. In order to reinforce innovation awareness and enthusiasm of securities related companies, the CSRC removed, adjusted and delegated nearly 100 items previously subject to administrative approval in the first half of 2012, in order to give impetus to innovation by securities related companies. ①

Reform of new share offering and delisting system

In March 2012, the CSRC solicited opinions on plans to reform share offering system. On April 28th, the CSRC officially issued the *Guidelines for Further Deepening the Reform of the New Share Offering System*, which reiterates that reform of the new share offering system will be market oriented, and improvements in review of offering applications will focus on adequate, complete and accurate information disclosure, and puts forth six pieces of specific opinions. On May 18th, the CSRC revised the *Measures for the Administration of Securities Offering and Underwriting*. On May 23rd, both the Offering Supervision Department and the ChiNext Offering Supervision Department of the CSRC issued the *Circular of Problems Relating to Offering Price of New Shares* to specify relevant issues on pricing of new share offering. On June 28th, the SSE and the SZSE respectively issued the *Proposal for Optimizing the Delisting System of Listed Companies of Shanghai Stock Exchange*, and the *Proposal for Improving and Optimizing the Delisting System of Listed Companies of the Main Board and the SME Board of Shenzhen Stock Exchange*, and revised relevant *Stock Listing Rules* accordingly. Problems with new share offering have been long standing in China's capital market. For the first time, reform of the new share offering system mentioned secondary offering, attracting close attention from the market. As the delisting system is fundamental to the capital market, only the implementation of effective delisting system can practically promote reasonable and effective resource allocation in the securities market and promote structural adjustment and industry upgrade.

Ramp up efforts to combat illegal behaviors in the securities market

Combating insider trading became the focus of the CSRC's efforts to enforce law in 2012. On 23 February 2012, the SPC issued the *Guiding Opinions of SPC on Providing Judicial Safeguards for Prevention and Elimination of Financial Risks and Promotion of Financial Reform and Development*. On May 22nd, the SPC and the SPP jointly issued the *Interpretation of Some Issues on Law Application to Criminal Cases Involving Insider Trading and Insider Information Disclosure*. This is China's first legal document particularly for determination of and punishment on criminal cases involving insider trading, and specifically provides for definition of insiders,

---

① 2012 Top Ten News on China's Capital Market, Financial Times, 8 January 2013.

determination of insider trading and measurement of criminal circumstances and punishment standards. Against such background, investigations into insider trading cases were reinforced significantly. In the first half of 2012, the CSRC took combating insider trading as its focus of law enforcement, and 96 insider trading cases were investigated, accounting for 53.3% of all new cases. [1]

Increase investors' protection and education

The investors' protection bureau of the CSRC was officially established at the end of 2011 and put into operation at the beginning of 2012. Its main responsibilities include: drafting securities and futures investor protection policies and regulations; assessing development and implementation of securities and futures regulatory policies for their adequacy and effectiveness in investor protection; making overall plan for, organizing, inspecting and evaluating investor education and service in the stock and futures market; coordinating and promoting establishment of and improvement in the investors' service, education and protection mechanism; studying the investor complaint acceptance system, promoting improvements in treatment procedures and operation mechanism, and organizing relevant organs to provide investor consulting services; promoting establishment of and improvement in the remedy system for infringed investors; supervising management and utilization of investor protection fund in accordance with law; organizing and participating in exchange and cooperation in investor protection with regulatory authorities at both home and abroad. It is known that the China Securities Investors Protection Funds Corporation Limited will be put under the management of the investors' protection bureau. [2]

Adopt revision of the *Securities Investment Fund Law*

On 28 December 2012, the 30th meeting of the Standing Committee of the 11th NPC adopted the revised *Securities Investment Fund Law*, which shall come into force as of 1 June 2013. Firstly, the revised *Securities Investment Fund Law* extends its application to PE funds. The revised version defines both public offering and private offering and differentiates between mutual funds and PE funds by fund contract execution, offerees, promotion methods, fund registration, information disclosure and custody to effect moderate and proper supervision. Secondly, the CSRC promoted mutual funds to upgrade into wealth management institutions by reducing formalities for administrative approval, cancelling examination of qualification of fund

---

[1]　Statement of Audit and Law Enforcement on Securities and Futures in 1H12, http://www.csrc.gov.cn/pub/newsite/jcj/gzdt/201208/t20120803_213491.htm, visited on 4 April 2013.

[2]　CSRC Establishes the Investor Protection Bureau to Manage Investor Protection Funds, Oriental Morning Post, 11 January 2012.

custodians, cancelling formalities for approval for branch establishment by the fund manager and for any change in 5% (or less) shareholding and for alternation to the Articles of Association, lowering market access thresholds for fund mangers and permitting fund managers to improve incentive mechanisms through shareholding by professionals and other means. The revised version also provides adequate legal space for financial institutions including fund management partnerships and insurance asset management companies as well as other eligible PE fund managers to engage in mutual fund business and for financial institutions other than commercial banks to engage in fund custody business.[1] Thirdly, the revised version reinforces fund investors' protection, supplements measures for risk control and treatment, adds legal liability provisions, specifies rules on banning entry into the market, increases punishments, in order to make the fund sector develop in a more regulated and legal manner.

Continue to improve dividend distribution rules of listed companies

In May 2012, the CSRC issued the *Notice on Further Implementing Issues Relating to Cash Dividends of Listed Companies*, pursuant to which listed companies shall improve its cash dividend policy and specify their dividend decision procedures in the Articles of Association, and the board of directors shall provide a specific demonstration of return for shareholders, and adequately listen to opinions of independent directors and medium and small shareholders. Meanwhile, according to CSRC officials, the above requirements shall be observed in the IPO, refinance and the M&A, and companies not distributing dividends shall disclose detailed reasons thereof and describe a plan for utilization of undistributed dividends. Under existing legal framework, the CSRC will give adequate consideration on development stages and industry characteristics of relevant companies, further study and improve the mechanism by linking dividends to refinance qualifications of listed companies. These will work out the external constraint mechanism and improve the investment return mechanism.

Policy Evaluation and Outlook

In 2012, unprecedented efforts were made in the regulatory reform of China's securities market, and many new policies and rules were launched, which included revision to the *Securities Investment Fund Law*, reforms of the new share offering and delisting system, combating insider trading, improving exchanges, improving dividend distribution mechanism of listed companies and reinforcing investors' protection and education, which involved all aspects of reforms and development of the capital market and fully reflected CSRC's determination and persistence to make regulatory innovations. A healthy and sustainable development of the capital

---

[1] Adoption of Revision to Securities Investment Fund Law, Shanghai Securities News, 31 December 2012.

market in a long term hinges on reasonable regulations, fair play and protection of a number of medium and small investors. The comprehensive launch and gradual deepening of this round of regulatory innovations, are undoubtedly great good news for China's developing securities market. Increased regulatory efforts and improved regulatory measures have had and will continue to have significant effects on institutional development and legal environment of China's securities market. In 2013, the CSRC will take large steps to deepen reforms, particularly to further deepen reforms of the new share offering and delisting system, reinforce corporate governance of listed companies, increases efforts to investigate illegal behaviors on the securities market and improve investors' education and protection.

Highlights of Regulatory Policy of CIRC

Schedule of Major CIRC Regulatory Policies in 2012

Table 6.5   Major CIRC Regulatory Policies in 2012

Date	Document	Issued by
4 January	Notice Concerning Some Issues on the *Administrative Measures for Insurance Provisions and Premium Rates of Personal Insurance*	CIRC
12 January	Notice on Distributing and Printing the *Regulations on Management of Reinsurance of Property Insurance Companies*	CIRC
12 January	Notice on Distributing and Printing the *Regulations of Accounting and Financial Work of Insurance Companies*	CIRC
17 January	Notice on Duly Providing Insurance Consumer Protection	CIRC
17 January	CIRC Opinions on Strengthening and Improving Quality of Claim Settlement for Property Insurance	CIRC
12 January	Notice on Strengthening Management of Claim Settlement for Agricultural Insurances	CIRC
29 January	Notice on Relevant Issues Including Adjustments to Regulatory Fee Rates for Insurance Business	CIRC
6 February	Notice on Relevant Issues on Adjusting Some Items Subject to Administrative Approval for Foreign-funded Insurance Companies	General Office of CIRC
14 February	Notice on Comprehensive Treatment of Misleading Sales in the Personal Insurance Sector	CIRC
21 February	Notice on Printing and Distributing the *Guidelines for Management of Claim Settlement for Motor Vehicle Insurance*	CIRC
23 February	Notice on Reinforcing Management of Provisions and Premium Rates for Commercial Insurance for Motor Vehicles	CIRC
27 February	Notice on Printing and Distributing *Annual Total Risk Management Report Framework and Risk Monitoring Indicators of Personal Insurance Companies*	CIRC

Continued

Date	Document	Issued by
28 February	Notice on Furthering Regulating Incentives for Insurance Intermediary Institutions	CIRC
1 March	Notice on Printing and Distributing the *Regulations on Internal Control Basic Data, Assessment and Accounting on and of Provision of Non-life Insurance Business of Insurance Companies*	CIRC
26 March	Notice on Suspension in Granting Market Access to Regional Insurance Agencies and Some Institutions Concurrently Operating Insurance Agency Business	CIRC
29 March	Notice on Printing and Distributing the *Plan for Development of the 2nd Generation of Solvency Supervision System of China*	CIRC
28 April	Notice on Relevant Issues on Further Regulating Order in the Property Insurance Market	CIRC
28 April	Notice on Further Reinforcing Management of Investment-oriented Insurance Business of Insurance Companies	CIRC
15 May	Notice on Relevant Issues on Issuance by Listed Insurance Companies of Secondary Convertible Bonds	CIRC
17 May	Notice on Printing and Distributing the *Measures for Managing Retrospective Analysis of Provision for Non-life Insurance Business of Insurance Companies*	CIRC
30 May	Notice on Issues Relating to Preparing and Submitting Assessment Report for Provision for Non-life Insurance Business of Insurance Companies	CIRC
12 June	Notice on Printing and Distributing the *Plan for Roll-out of Petty Personal Insurance*	CIRC
12 June	Notice on Further Regulating Market Access to Insurance Agencies	CIRC
27 June	Notice on Issues Relating to Reinforcement of Solvency Management of Insurance Companies	CIRC
16 July	CIRC Notice on Printing and Distributing the *Interim Measures for the Investment of Insurance Funds in Bonds*	CIRC
16 July	CIRC Notice on Printing and Distributing the *Provisional Measures for Discretionary Investment Management of Insurance Funds*	CIRC
16 July	Notice on Issues Relating to Equity and Real Property Investment of Insurance Funds	CIRC
16 July	CIRC Notice on Printing and Distributing the *Provisional Measures for Management of Insurance Asset Allocation*	CIRC
16 July	Notice on Implementing the Principle of Legal Operational and Legal Supervision to Practically Protect Interests of Insurers and Insureds	CIRC
19 July	Notice on Printing and Distributing the *Guidelines for Compensation Management of Insurance Companies* (*Trial*)	CIRC
25 July	Measures for Management of Controlling Shareholders of Insurance Companies	CIRC
6 August	CIRC Notice on Printing and Distributing the *Guiding Opinions on Reinforcing Anti-Insurance Frauds*	CIRC

Continued

Date	Document	Issued by
18 August	Notice on Issues Relating to Health Management Service Provided by Health Insurance Products	CIRC
14 September	Notice on Supporting Specialized Operation of Insurance Agency Business by Automobile Companies	CIRC
29 September	CIRC Notice on Printing and Distributing the *Guideline for Determining Misleading Sales of Personal Insurance*	CIRC
12 October	Notice on Financial Product Investment of Insurance Funds	CIRC
12 October	Notice on Printing and Distributing the Provisional Regulations on Management of Infrastructure Debt Investment Plans	CIRC
12 October	Notice on Printing and Distributing the *Specific Rules for Implementing the Provisional Measures for Management of Overseas Investments of Insurance Funds*	CIRC
12 October	Notice on Printing and Distributing the *Interim Measures for the Participation of Insurance Funds in the Trading of Financial Derivatives*	CIRC
12 October	Notice on Printing and Distributing the *Regulations on Insurance Funds' Participation in Stock Index Futures Transactions*	CIRC
23 October	CIRC Notice on Printing and Distributing the *Guiding Opinions on Holding Personal Insurance Companies Liable for Misleading Sales*	CIRC
2 November	Notice on Issues Concerning Implementation of the *Guidelines for Compensation Management of Insurance Companies* (*Trial*)	CIRC
2 November	Notice on Issues Concerning Implementation of the *Administrative Measures for Audit on Directors and Senior Management of Insurance Companies*	CIRC
2 November	CIRC Notice on Submitting Annual Information Disclosure Report	General Office of CIRC
5 November	CIRC Notice on Canceling and Adjusting the Sixth Batch of Items Subject to Administrative Approval	CIRC
7 November	CIRC Notice on Printing and Distributing the *Measures for Assessment on Comprehensive Control of Misleading Sales in the Personal Insurance Sector* (*Trial*)	CIRC
21 November	CIRC Notice on Invalidating Some Regulative Documents	CIRC
11 December	Notice on Promptly Curbing Resident Disturbance Caused by Telephone Sales	CIRC
17 December	Decision of the State Council on Revision to the *Regulations on Compulsory Traffic Accident Liability Insurance for Motor Vehicles*	State Council
25 December	Notice on Printing and Distributing the *Provisional Measures of CIRC for Management of Electronic File Transmission System*	General Office of CIRC

Source: data collected by the research group.

Analysis of Major CIRC Regulatory Policies in 2012

New investment policies were launched in due time, while new achievements were made in

market-based reforms of utilization of insurance funds

The insurance regulatory authority launched 12 new regulatory policies for fund utilization including the *Provisional Measures for Management of Insurance Asset Allocation*. New regulatory policies for investments were market oriented. The CIRC made reforms in an all-round manner, reinforced top-level design and coordination for reformd, established and improved the insurance fund utilization innovation system to facilitate development, reform and innovation by means of opening-up. The CIRC focused on risk prevention and proportionately combined internal control with external supervision. Overall, new policies loosened control over, expanded the scope of and improved the risk control mechanism for utilization of insurance funds.

The CIRC expanded channels and added new offerings. New policies covered all investment instruments anticipated by the industry, and "permitted insurance institutions to loan cash and stock and invest in stock index futures business", "increased the offerings and scope of overseas investments by insurance funds", "opened the scope of domestic equity and real property investments", "added new unsecured bond products" and "expanded the scope of infrastructure debt investment scheme".

The CIRC streamlined the insurance companies' business channel with banks, securities firms and trust companies. Investment of insurance funds were released from existing restrictions and linked to banks, securities firms and trusts. Funds and securities firms were admitted to participate in insurance fund management, and insurance institutions were permitted to invest in collective asset management schemes sponsored and established by securities firms, collective trust schemes of trust companies, as well as credit assets-backed securities and income-guaranteed wealth management products of commercial banks. Insurance asset companies were permitted to participate in collective trust schemes, enterprise annuities, provident housing funds and other enterprises as asset managers. Based on client requirements, insurance fund management companies could develop investment strategies, develop asset management products and open relevant accounts in the name of the investment portfolios.

The CIRC updated concepts and reduced red tapes. The CIRC loosened control and reinforced supervision. It replaced approving formalities with mechanism, actively reduced administrative approvals, cancelled all approving formalities except for substantial investments and asset management products, and established venture capital constraint mechanism.

New policies for insurance fund investment made utilization of insurance funds more regulated, professional and flexible, which would have significant impacts on insurance companies. Firstly, asset allocation management would become more important for insurance investments. Insurance companies were urged to identify the nature of insurance funds, set relevant investment policies, support innovation to insurance products and improve profiting pattern from the very beginning. Secondly, insurance companies had large room for investment operation. Thirdly, insurance companies were pressed to improve their investment abilities. Lastly, as investment risk increased, risk management would become more important for insurance companies.

In summary, the string of new policies complied with macro economic policies of the State and satisfied realistic investment requirements of insurance institutions. Provided risks were controllable, adoption of these initiatives would enable the insurance sector to better serve projects concerning people's livelihood and the real economy, support the capital market reform, and promote business innovation of commercial banks, securities companies and fund management companies, having profound significance on the development of the insurance market and even the financial market.

The 2nd generation of solvency supervision system took shape, marking a stride towards regulatory modernization of the insurance industry

On 29 March 2012, the CIRC issued the *Plan for Development of the 2nd Generation of Solvency Supervision System of China* (the *Plan*), pursuant to which China shall endeavor to build a new generation of solvency supervision system oriented by considerations on risks, suitable for China's specific conditions and tailored for characteristics of the emerging insurance market in 3 to 5 years.

Solvency supervision was the core of insurance supervision and key to insurance consumer protection. From 2003 to the end of 2007, the CIRC had built up the first generation of solvency supervision system with Chinese characteristics, which promoted insurance companies to form the concept of capital management and improve operating management expertise, and played a very important role in preventing risk and promoting scientific development of China's insurance industry. Financial situation has changed violently both at home and abroad in recent years. Internationally, after the financial crisis, international financial reform has been advancing rapidly, and the pace of international synchronization of financial supervision has accelerated significantly. The banking sector issued the *Basel Accord III*, and international insurance regulatory rules are experiencing a dramatic reform. In October 2011, the IAIS issued 26 new core regulatory principles, and was developing a globally uniform framework for insurance group supervision, taking solvency supervision as its core components. EU was vigorously promoting Solvency II, scheduled to come into force in 2014. The Solvency Modernization Program launched by the NAIC was intended to adjust the solvency supervision system and was completed at the end of 2012. Therefore, the coming several years would be a key stage for rebuilding international insurance supervision landscape. Domestically, China's insurance market and capital market developed at faster paces, raising higher and higher requirements for risk prevention and supervision. Existing solvency supervision system could not satisfy regulatory requirements in new situation in some aspects. Against such backdrop, the CIRC decided to develop the 2nd generation of solvency supervision system and launched the development plan.

The *Plan* specified ideological guidance, organization, general goal, overall framework, basic principles, implementation steps and work mechanism for the 2nd generation of solvency supervision system. The *Plan* put forth three general goals. Firstly, it built a solvency supervision system in three to five years not only consistent with international standards but also suitable for the development stage of China's insurance industry. Secondly, in the course of institutional development, it continued to promote insurance companies to build and improve total risk management system and improve industry risk management and capital management level. Thirdly, through institutional development, it continued to improve international influence of China's solvency supervision system and improve international position of China's insurance industry. The *Plan* established three basic principles: taking China's specific conditions as the base, maintaining consistence with international standards and being oriented by considerations on risks. Accommodating the international wave of insurance regulatory reforms, the *Plan* required that the 2nd generation of solvency supervision system adopt the internationally universal "three-pole" framework. The first pole was about capital adequacy requirements, mainly quantitative regulatory requirements, which included assets and liabilities assessment standards, paid-in capital standards, minimum capital standards, capital adequacy ratio standards and regulatory measures. The second pole was about risk management requirements, mainly solvency related qualitative regulatory requirements, which included total risk management requirements, and inspection by regulatory authorities of capital measurement and risk management. The third pole was about information disclosure requirements, mainly solvency related transparency regulatory requirements, which included reporting to regulatory authorities and information disclosure to the public. The *Plan* also divided the development into five stages, summary and assessment, thematic study, system formation, testing and improvement, and launch and operation, and determined three work mechanisms to mobilize forces of the entire industry, improve transparency and reinforce international exchange.

Development of the 2nd generation of solvency supervision system was of great significance to protecting insurance consumers, promoting steady operation of the insurance market, improving risk identification and prevention ability of the industry, maintaining the economic and financial safety of the State, promoting changes in growth pattern of the industry, enhancing the insurance industry's ability to serve national economy, improving insurance supervision skills, making financial supervision more coordinated, improving China's international position in terms of insurance supervision, enhancing international competitiveness of China's financial industry and promoting scientific and healthy development of China's insurance industry.

Important issues in the four state-owned insurance companies were handed over to the Organization Department of the CPC Central Committee, and insurance regulatory system presented a new landscape

In March 2012, four SOEs (PICC, China Life, Sinosure and China Taiping) were handed over to the Organization Department of the CPC Central Committee organizationally. After this adjustment, the power of appointment in respect of the four SOEs would be transferred to the Organization Department of the CPC Central Committee, while the CIRC would be mainly responsible for supervision of insurance companies. Before the adjustment, the CIRC took charge of both human resource management and business development, and market regulation and consumer protection of the four SOEs. These two functions contradict with each other in their goals. The above adjustment represented a dramatic change in the regulatory pattern, and organizationally divided market supervision function from industry supervision function, making the position of insurance supervision clearer. According to some comments, except for the upgrade to vice-ministerial level, the four SOEs had not changed fundamentally, because their direct (on indirect) substantial shareholder remained the Ministry of Finance, lacking specific investors. Therefore, this adjustment was possibly preparation for establishing the financial state-owned assets supervision and administration commission.

The CIRC focused on consumer protection and thoroughly solved certain long-standing problems

Just after taking office, Mr. Xiang Junbo, CIRC's Chairman, made it clear that "insurance supervision should begin with and rest on consumer protection". At the beginning of 2012, the regulatory authority issued the *Notice on Duly Providing Insurance Consumer Protection* to make arrangements for consumer protection. Throughout 2012, beginning with the most outstanding problems reported by a number of consumers, the regulatory authority launched a special program to treat misleading sales and solve difficulties in claim settlements, and took this opportunity to set up and improve the consumer protection mechanism.

Firstly, the CIRC fully proceeded with treatment of misleading sales of life insurances. In February 2012, the CIRC issued the *Notice on Comprehensive Treatment of Misleading Sales in the Personal Insurance Sector*, in order to make overall arrangement for handling misleading sales of life insurances. Subsequently, the CIRC issued the *Guideline for Determining Misleading Sales of Personal Insurance*, the *Guiding Opinions on Holding Personal Insurance Companies*

Liable for Misleading Sales and the *Measures for Assessment on Comprehensive Control of Misleading Sales in the Personal Insurance Sector (Trial)*. Through these rules and measures, the CIRC further regulated the standards for determination of and enforcement against misleading sales, and reinforced principal responsibilities of insurance institutions. Life insurance companies checked themselves against the 158 items contained in 7 procedures of sale rules. Special inspection was made on telephone sales and insurance brokerage business of banks. Misleading sales were curbed to some extent and sales activities became more regulated.

Secondly, the CIRC conscientiously solved difficulties in claim settlements for vehicle insurances. Throughout the year, the regulatory authority reinforced regulation of provisions and premium rates of vehicle insurances, formulated guidelines for management of claim settlements for vehicle insurances, unified procedures for claim settlements and standardized claim settlement services. Difficulties in claim settlements were included in the scope of regulatory punishments, and inspection and supervision efforts were ramped up. Treatment of difficulties in claim settlement had yielded preliminary result, and with claim settlement period shortened by 9 days as compared with that in the previous year, case settlement rate reaching 109% and number of pending cases declining by 7% on a year-on-year basis. Meanwhile, pending claims for property insurances were handled.

Thirdly, the CIRC improved the consumer protection mechanism. The CIRC opened national hotline number 12,378 for insurance consumer complaints, and over 70,000 incoming calls were received by service representatives. The CIRC endeavored to fix the director reception day and established the social insurance inspector system. It set up and improved the insurance dispute mediation and resolution mechanism, established 219 mediation institutions across the country, successfully resolved 9,280 cases by mediation and recovered economic loss of RMB 320 million for consumers. It properly solved 15,268 consumer complaints. It increased positive media coverage and placed commercials on the CCTV, the CNR and other media.

The CIRC ramped up efforts to combat insurance frauds, creating a favorable environment for development of the industry

In recent years, as the insurance market developed rapidly, the risk of insurance frauds increased, greatly impairing consumers' interests, the financial market's order and the credit system's development. In July 2009, the CIRC launched the special program of combating fake insurers, fake policies and fake claims. 32 fake insurers, 200,000 fake policies and 16000 fake claims were identified in total; 149 cases were transferred to the police for investigation. From March to August in 2012, the insurance industry joined the police in a "war" against insurance frauds, during which nearly 2,500 insurance criminal cases were investigated and over 4,000 suspected criminals were seized, involving a value of RMB 1.4 billion and reducing economic loss of RMB 0.8 billion. This was the first time for the insurance industry to be fully engaged in a nationwide battle against economic crimes, yielding solid results. Some criminal gangs who had cheated insurance companies for a long time were seized, a number of criminals fraudulently living on insurance compensation were frightened, and made-up difficulties in claim settlement were eliminated, which created favorable conditions for insurers to improve quality of claim settlement service, improved environment for development of the insurance market and consolidated the result of reform and development of the insurance industry. On this basis, on 6 August 2012, the CIRC issued the *Guiding Opinions on Reinforcing Anti-Insurance Frauds* (*Guiding Opinions*), in order to further establish the anti-frauds system and build a long-term, effective mechanism for combating insurance frauds.

According to the *Guiding Opinions on Reinforcing Anti-Insurance Frauds*, the purpose of anti-insurance fraud efforts was to build up an anti-insurance fraud system embracing government guidance, joint enforcement, company dominance and industry coordination. A basically sound anti-fraud system could effectively curb the momentum of fraud crimes and significantly improve the ability to prevent and eliminate fraud risks. The *Guiding Opinions* also set forth eight key areas of current and future anti-fraud efforts: (1) to improve the anti-insurance fraud system; (2) to crack down all kinds of insurance frauds; (3) to improve the ability to control fraud risks; (4) to reinforce the ant-insurance fraud supervision system; (5) to build up the anti-fraud cooperation platform of the industry; (6) to improve the anti-insurance fraud coordination system; (7) to reinforce studies, exchange and education; and (8) to set up long-term effective anti-insurance fraud mechanism.

Policy Evaluation and Outlook

2013 is a year crucial to the realization of the 12th Five Year Plan. At the national insurance supervision conference on 24 January 2013, Mr. Xiang Junbo, the CIRC's Chairman specified that insurance supervision efforts in 2013 should mainly focus on the following aspects.

The CIRC shall firmly hold the bottom line of non-occurrence of systemic and regional risks

Risk prevention is an urgent task of current insurance supervision efforts and a key issue relating to the long-term development of the insurance industry. Reinforcing risk prevention should be the number one focus of insurance supervision. Particularly, close attention should be paid to maturing payment and surrender risk, fund utilization risk and solvency risks of life insurances, business risk of investment-oriented non-life insurance, case risk, as well as risk transmission in comprehensive operation, so as to firmly hold the bottom line of risk tolerance. (1) Reinforce dynamic risk surveillance and early warning. (2) Study and reinforce macroprudential supervision. (3) Reinforce emergency tacking ability. (4) Reinforce regulatory cooperation.

The CIRC shall ramp up efforts in consumer protection

(1) Continue to handle misleading sales and solve difficulties in claim settlement. (2) Improve the insurance dispute mediation and resolution mechanism. (3) Promote insurance companies to improve service quality and levels. (4) Spread insurance knowledge in various forms.

The CIRC shall continue to proceed with reform and innovation

Taking a pragmatic attitude, from a perspective of protecting consumers' interests and promoting scientific development of the industry, it shall try to solve common and urgent problems that can be resolved through efforts. This is the key of reform in this year and solid results should be seen. (1) Develop specific plan for top-level design of regulatory system. (2) Establish the insurance operation and insurance institution service evaluation system. (3) Establish the classification-based management system for practitioners. (4) Proceed with development of the information sharing platform of the industry.

The CIRC shall endeavor to make achievements in restoring order to the market

(1) It will identify the sharpest problems, and mainly investigate fake service charges, fake receivables, fake approval of surrender charge, fake claim settlement, provisions and premium rates for which approval formalities are not duly fulfilled, untruthful provisions as well as other offences against laws and regulations. It will continue to comprehensively handle misleading sales of life insurances and tackle unreasonable competition activities including promising high returns in violation of regulations. It will regulate the market of concurrent operation of insurance brokerage business, particularly by vehicle merchants. It will strengthen comprehensive inspection, and in particular, focus on shareholder behaviors, capital safety, solvency, and reasonableness of provisions. It will practically crack down insurance frauds and money laundry to further optimize the environment for development of the insurance industry. (2) It will focus on key areas and key companies, reinforce overall planning for onsite inspection to avoid repeated inspections. It will focus on supervision of commercial vehicle insurances, compulsory traffic insurance, agricultural insurance and crucial disease insurance, and reinforce supervision on banks and post offices, which carry out insurance brokerage business. It will closely watch problematic large companies, conduct internal control and compliance inspection on two or three life insurance companies. It wil thoroughly handle commercial briberies in the insurance sector, carefully implement the CIRC *Notice on Cracking down Commercial Briberies through Insurance Business* forwarded by the CPC Central Disciplinary

Committee, and absolutely rectify unfair transactions. (3) It will promptly impose punishments in respect of offences against law and regulation. It will develop the measures for punishments on offences against laws and regulations in the insurance industry, and gradually unify investigation and punishment standards across the country. All suspected crimes should be transferred to the judicial organs. (4) It will reinforce accountability of senior officers and the controlling entities. It will both investigate relevant entities and punish liable personnel, and reinforce the accountability system to link offences to legal liabilities and qualification of senior officers and to organizational and product approvals, so as to make market supervision more specific and effective.

The CIRC shall reinforce supervision over insurance corporations

Currently, offences and risks in the insurance market arise at the bottom level but have their roots in the headquarters. Whether a company can operate legitimately and steadily depends directly on ideological guidelines and control abilities of the headquarters, and legal awareness and executive power of senior officers. By reinforcing supervision over corporations, twice as much can be achieved with half the effort. (1) It will reinforce solvency supervision. Companies with inadequate solvency and insufficient capital must be imposed upon regulatory measures including capital increase and restrictions on business, organization, compensation package and expenses. It will proceed with development of the 2nd generation of solvency supervision system, and start developing various regulatory standards. (2) it will reinforce supervision over corporate governance. It will vigorously implement relevant regulations and practically promote corporate governance to shift from "compliance in form" to "effective governance". It will conduct special inspections on internal audit of insurance companies for its compliance, completeness and effectiveness, and push insurance companies to improve their internal control. It will try to establish the independent directors' intervention system, reinforce inspection and supervision of ultimate shareholders of insurance companies, and inspect on equity transactions and connected transactions. It will improve the information disclosure system, make insurance operation more transparent and reinforce public supervision. It will stick to the practice that regulatory authorities attend at board meetings of insurance companies, improve the information transmission system between regulatory authorities and the insurance companies. (3) It will reinforce supervision over fund utilization. It will determine major contents and vulnerabilities of new policies for fund utilization and make improvements based on feedbacks from the industry. It will steadily proceed with market-based reform of offering system of products including infrastructure and real property debt schemes. It will guide and support the industry to make innovation to products and mechanisms. It will set up the assets and liabilities matching supervision committee of the CIRC to reinforce hard restrictions on assets and liabilities management and weaken supervision through percentage restrictions. It will urge companies to reinforce liabilities management, and improve assets and liabilities matching levels. By reference to prevailing international standards, it will study and develop the internal control standards and risk owner system for insurance asset management. It will study and establish the solvency restraint system through the entire process of insurance fund utilization. (4) it will proceed with development of the market access and exit mechanism. It will improve the transparency of market access and exit, and establish the review committee system. It will promptly issue and adopt the system of grade and classification-based regulation of business scope of insurance companies and the system of market access for branches of insurance companies. It will introduce new investors, and study regulatory measures for new capital investment including the PE investment funds. It will reinforce study on market-based M&As and reorganization, and improve the risk tackling mechanism.

References

[1] International Monetary Fund. Annual Report 2012, Working Together to Support Global Recovery [M]. Washington, 2012.

[2] Bank for International Settlements. BIS Annual Report 2012/2013 [M]. Basel, 2013

[3] The World Bank. Global Financial Development Report 2013: Rethink The Role of The State in Finance [M]. Washington, 2012.

[4] Wu Xiaoling, He Haifeng. China Financial Policy Report (2012) [M]. Beijing: China Financial Publishing House, 2012.

[5] Que Zikang. Theory and Experience of A Multi-level Capital Market [M]. Shanghai: Shanghai Jiao Tong University Press, 2007.

[6] Xu Hongcai. A Study of China's Multi-level Capital Market System and Regulation [M]. Beijing: Economy and Management Publishing House, 2009.

[7] Wang Guogang, Chief Editor. Researches on Creation of a Multi-level Capital Market, Beijing: People's Publishing House, 2006.

[8] Hu Haifeng. A Multi-level Capital Market: From Spontaneous Evolution to Government System Design [M]. Beijing: Beijing Normal University Press, 2010.

[9] Gao Luan, Chief Editor. Annual Report on China's OTC Market Development (2009 – 2010) [M]. Beijing: Social Sciences Academic Press (China), 2010.

[10] Gu Gongyun, Chief Editor. Legal System Construction for the OTC Market [M]. Beijing: Peking University Press, 2011.

[11] Gao Luan, Chief Editor. Annual Report on China's OTC Market Development (2010 – 2011) [M]. Beijing: Social Sciences Academic Press (China), 2011.

[12] Xia Bin, Chen Daofu. China's Financial Strategy 2020 [M]. Beijing: People's Publishing House, 2011.

[13] Balance of Payments Analysis Group, SAFE. China Balance of Payments Report 2012 [M]. Beijing: China Financial Publishing House, 2013.

[14] Monetary Policy Analysis Group of the PBC. China Monetary Policy Report (Quarter Four, 2012) [M]. Beijing: China Financial Publishing House, 2013.

[15] CBRC: China Banking Regulatory Commission Annual Report 2012 [M]. Beijing, 2013.

[16] CBRC: China Banking Industry Annual Operating Report (2012) [M]. Beijing, 2013.

[17] CIRC. 2011 – 2012 Annual Report of China Insurance Market [M]. Beijing: China Financial Publishing

House, 2012.

[18] Xiang Junbo. Speech on 2013 National Insurance Regulation Work Meeting, January, 2013.

[19] Li Fengyu. Status Quo, Problems and Countermeasures of Information Disclosure of China's Securities Market [J]. Journal of Financial Development Research, 2012, 10.

[20] Bai Bing, Lu Yunjiao. A Study of China's OTC Market Development-Based on Comparative Analysis of Domestic and Foreign OTC Markets [J]. Inquiry into Economic Issues, 2012, 4.